Anthony Luzzatto Gardner

Stars with Stripes

The Essential Partnership between the European
Union and the United States

Anthony Luzzatto Gardner
London, UK

ISBN 978-3-030-29965-1   ISBN 978-3-030-29966-8 (eBook)
https://doi.org/10.1007/978-3-030-29966-8

© The Editor(s) (if applicable) and The Author(s) 2020
This work is subject to copyright. All rights are solely and exclusively licensed by the Publisher, whether the whole or part of the material is concerned, specifically the rights of translation, reprinting, reuse of illustrations, recitation, broadcasting, reproduction on microfilms or in any other physical way, and transmission or information storage and retrieval, electronic adaptation, computer software, or by similar or dissimilar methodology now known or hereafter developed.
The use of general descriptive names, registered names, trademarks, service marks, etc. in this publication does not imply, even in the absence of a specific statement, that such names are exempt from the relevant protective laws and regulations and therefore free for general use.
The publisher, the authors and the editors are safe to assume that the advice and information in this book are believed to be true and accurate at the date of publication. Neither the publisher nor the authors or the editors give a warranty, expressed or implied, with respect to the material contained herein or for any errors or omissions that may have been made. The publisher remains neutral with regard to jurisdictional claims in published maps and institutional affiliations.

Cover credit: Isaac Ruiz Soler/eStudioCalamar

This Palgrave Macmillan imprint is published by the registered company Springer Nature Switzerland AG
The registered company address is: Gewerbestrasse 11, 6330 Cham, Switzerland

To my two Alejandras and Nicolas

Acknowledgements

Several weeks before the US presidential election in November 2016 I started to suspect that Hillary Clinton would lose and that I would therefore not be able to prolong my diplomatic mission as US ambassador to the European Union. Many people, including several very experienced pollsters, were telling me that I was worrying for no reason. Nonetheless, I started making plans about what to do in case the unthinkable did occur.

Soon after President Trump's victory, I called Jörg Monar, the Rector of the College of Europe in Bruges, Belgium, as well as Joe Weiler, President of the European Institute, and Brigid Laffan, the director of the Schuman Centre at the European Institute in the outskirts of Florence, Italy. These two institutions are among the leading centers of learning related to the European Union. I am thankful that both generously agreed to host me during my brief but productive stays.

Although I considered applying to the College of Europe for a one-year masters degree as I was finishing my studies at Harvard in 1985, I wound up doing a two-year program in international relations at Oxford instead. It was at Oxford that I became fascinated with the European Community, as it was then known, thanks to a seminar taught by a brilliant young Greek professor, Loukas Tsoukalis (now the head of Greece's leading think tank). My mini-sabbatical at the College of Europe more than thirty years later partly compensated for my missing that unique experience as a young graduate student.

On January 20, 2017, as Donald Trump was occupying the Oval Office, my wife and I drove out of our official residence for the last time and moved into a romantic apartment in downtown Bruges. Every day for three months I would walk along canals, over bridges and past palaces built with the wealth generated from trading with the world. The burghers of Bruges didn't think that trade is a zero-sum game in which one side loses if the other gains. I couldn't help feeling the irony that many centuries later some countries that had grown rich from trade were trying to make themselves "great" by closing themselves off from the world with walls and protectionism.

During my stay at the College I had the great pleasure of spending a lot of time with young, dynamic and optimistic students from all over the world, including several from the United States, who believed in European integration and the contributions of the EU institutions to European prosperity and security. I am very pleased that the College has partnered with the Fletcher School of Law and Diplomacy at Tufts University to offer a two-year joint Masters in Transatlantic Affairs. The program is off to a terrific start and I would like to see it thrive, including a growing contingent of US students who want to study EU affairs.

My stay at the European University Institute was equally memorable. The institute is housed in several historic Tuscan villas nestled in a haven of beauty and tranquility. For five months I was able to participate in a rich calendar of events and meet with brilliant post-graduate researchers and professors who are leaders in their fields. Every morning when I woke up with my wife and opened the shutters of our bedroom, I would see a gorgeous landscape of rolling hills and cypress trees bathed in sunlight. My commute to the institute, in my mother's thirty-year-old red convertible Alfa Romeo Spider, was a dream. At the end of every day my wife and I would say a little prayer: "Thank you, Donald, for having made this possible." The view from our terrace, on which most of this book was written, offered enough inspiration to ward off depression about the increasing damage to US-EU relations.

Many academic books have been written on each of the topics covered in this book; unlike those books, my aim is to address a wider audience and to offer a practitioner's perspective on US-EU relations. Several researchers at the German Marshall Fund and the Atlantic Council, as well as many individuals on both sides of the Atlantic, with direct knowledge of the topics in this book, read the text and suggested many valuable improvements.

I would also like to thank the following people who were kind enough to help in reviewing parts of the text, as well as contributing suggestions for improvement: Erik Barnett, Professor Anu Bradford, Frances Burwell, Peter Chase, David Cohen, Ambassador Daniel Costello, Dr. Emmanuel De Groof, Gilles de Kerchove, Jonathan Elkind, Karl Falkenberg, Dan Fried, Mike Froman, Ignacio Garcia Bercero, Danny Glaser, Professor Thomas Hale, Dan Hamilton, Doug Hengel, Amos Hochstein, Daniela Kietz, Christian Leffler, Cristina Lobillo, Stan McCoy, Giles Merritt, Maarten Meulenbelt, Ole Moehr, Dick Morningstar, Manuel Navarrete, Richard Nephew, Professor Sebastian Oberthur, Ana Palacio, Andreas Papaconstantinou, Jonathan Pershing, Ken Propp, Dominique Ristori, Artur Runge-Metzger, Astrid Schomaker, Sheherezade Semsar de Boisesson, Pedro Serrano, Thomas Skordas, Chris Smart, Claus Sorensen, Maria-Francesca Spatolisano, Susanna Sprague, Vladimir Sucha, Bart Szewczyk, Jim Townsend, Roberto Viola, Caroline Wefer and Jake Werksman.

Needless to say, all errors and omissions are my responsibility alone. The opinions expressed in this book are personal and should not be ascribed to any of the institutions with which I work or to their clients. Everything in this book is based on publicly available information.

I was privileged to follow in the footsteps of many highly qualified ambassadors to the EU, both Republican and Democratic. The US Mission to the EU is one of the most important diplomatic posts of the United States; it is critical that the post be led by professionals with significant relevant experience, not by ideological opportunists good at raising money. When that doesn't happen, the United States will inevitably pay a price. My predecessors and I were committed to deepening relations between the US and the EU and believed that the interests of the US are best served by promoting European integration. I was extremely fortunate to follow in the footsteps of Bill Kennard who left many admirers in Brussels because of his charm and deep knowledge. I frequently benefited from his wise counsel.

An ambassador should focus on advancing national foreign policy priorities, rather than promoting narrow party political objectives. This is in contrast to the US Ambassador to Germany, Richard Grenell, who has said that he wants to "empower" conservative movements in Europe. US Ambassador to the UK, Robert "Woody" Johnson has been a loud cheerleader for Brexit, even though at least half of the UK population opposes it, because it is in tune with the president's ideology. The fact that Brexit damages US national objectives is, apparently, unimportant.

It is inconceivable how any ambassador would consider it appropriate to solicit a foreign power to interfere in US politics. My successor was called to testify before Congress about his involvement in threats by the Trump administration to withhold military aid to Ukraine unless it provided information about former Vice President Biden's son. At first he alleged that there had been no "quid pro quo" before amending his testimony to acknowledge the exact opposite once his recollection had been "refreshed" by the clear testimony of others. President Trump subsequently fired him for that. During my diplomatic mission, I participated in many discussions with EU and US officials on substantive matters related to Ukraine, such as sanctions and energy security. But I never traveled to Ukraine because I didn't think such a trip was a justifiable use of US taxpayer money.

I was also fortunate to have EU ambassador David O'Sullivan, one of the EU's most accomplished diplomats and trade negotiators, as my counterpart in Washington D.C. We spoke frequently and openly on many matters, including during some tense moments involving transatlantic disagreements over trade and data privacy. I am grateful for his friendship, Irish wit and generosity in explaining the finer points of the EU machinery. Similarly, one of the highlights of my diplomatic mission was to work with the highly capable (and often under-appreciated) civil servants of the EU institutions.

I shall forever remain grateful to President Barack Obama for having appointed me to my diplomatic mission. He served with dignity and intelligence and, in my judgment, will go down in history as one of the country's finest presidents. I would not have been appointed without the support of two of my closest friends in the world: Tony Blinken, who served with great distinction as Deputy National Security Adviser and Deputy Secretary of State, and Mike Froman, who served with equal distinction as Deputy National Security Adviser for International Economic Affairs and as US Trade Representative. I will always feel great respect and gratitude for them both.

I would also like to express my admiration for the men and women of the US Foreign Service. I had the pleasure of knowing a few during my father's assignments as US ambassador to Italy and Spain and I would later work with many myself at the US Mission to the EU. They are a talented and dedicated group who often work under very challenging circumstances. They deserve the support of their country as they are the nation's first line of defense and ably promote its political and economic interests.

Finally, I am grateful to my family for putting up with my long absences during the writing of this book when I could have spent the time more enjoyably with them. Our family dog, a wire-haired dachshund, showed particular patience. Curled up at my feet, he would look up with quizzical eyes whenever I started venting out loud about the Trump administration's misguided efforts to undermine the European Union.

Praise for *Stars with Stripes*

"*Stars and Stripes* is eloquent evidence that President Barack Obama was right to make Tony Gardner America's representative to the European Union. From the Paris Climate accords to the crisis in Ukraine, from Brexit to the new digital economy, Gardner was not simply a witness to history—he helped to shape it, as this vivid account demonstrates. No American better understands the EU—its immense accomplishments, its shortcomings and the challenges it must address going forward. No American is a better advocate for the proposition that, especially in these disorienting and dangerous times, America and Europe must remain partners of first resort. Read this wonderful memoir because it illuminates the recent past but more importantly because it helps light the way to the future."

—Antony Blinken, *Deputy Secretary of State, 2015–2017*

"Ambassador Tony Gardner provides in this important book a first-hand account of his service as President Obama's Ambassador to the European Union. He makes a compelling argument against President Trump's acrimonious attitude towards the EU as a disservice to America's long-term interests with this vital global partner."

—Nicholas Burns, *Harvard University Professor and Under Secretary of State for Political Affairs 2005–2008*

"For anyone interested in transatlantic relations, this insider's account is indispensable reading. Tony Gardner's deeply personal story of his experience as President Obama's Ambassador to the European Union reflects both his keen understanding of the two sides of the Atlantic and his enduring belief in the power of transatlantic cooperation to meet the 21st century challenges we face from China to tech."
—Karen Donfried, *Senior Director for Europe, National Security Council, 2013–2014*

"It's hard to think of anyone on either side of the Atlantic who knows the Europe of today better than Tony Gardner. He has met, and often built close personal friendships with, most of the leading political players. He has learned its main languages. Going back to the dying days of the Cold War, Gardner has seen its history play out first-hand. And as a young trainee at the old European Commission and later as the US ambassador to the EU, he has gained an insider's deep understanding of how Brussels really works. In *Stars with Stripes* Gardner tells his and Europe's recent story with flair, feeling and great insight."
—Matthew Kaminski, *Editor-in-Chief, POLITICO, and Founding Editor of POLITICO Europe*

"The story Anthony Gardner tells is both informative and entertaining. The book is based on first-hand experiences and well-researched facts. It is a must-read for those interested in the transatlantic partnership and European politics written by a true advocate for multilateralism and the long-standing alliance between the United States and the European Union."
—David McAllister, *Member of the European Parliament and Chairman of its Foreign Affairs Committee*

"Tony Gardner's memoirs from his time as US Ambassador to Brussels may look like a souvenir from a bygone era. However, they are a powerful reminder of why the transatlantic bond is unbreakable and was able throughout times to overcome periods of tension. His testimony reads as an impassioned plea for a stronger transatlantic cooperation. It profusely

demonstrates that our interests are better served when we work together. More than a tale from the past it is a call for action for the future. Tony Gardner excelled as diplomat and is now shining as an author."
—Federica Mogherini, *High Representative of the Union for Foreign Affairs and Security Policy and Vice-President of the European Commission, 2014–2019*

"Ambassador Tony Gardner, who led US-EU relations through one of its busiest and strategically important periods, brings this relationship to life with real-world stories from the diplomatic front—from the Ukraine crisis to the Paris Climate accords. It is a must-read for anyone who questions the value of US-EU cooperation to keep 700 million people more prosperous, free, healthy, and safe."
—Ambassador Victoria Nuland, *Assistant Secretary of State for European Affairs, 2013–2017*

"At a time when transatlantic relations are under greater strain than at any time since the foundation of the EEC, Ambassador Tony Gardner's book comes as a refreshing blast of sanity and wisdom from an American with a deep knowledge of and sympathy for Europe.

Gardner brings profound understanding of the EU which comes only from critical but reliable friends, who understand that what has kept the West secure, democratic and prosperous for generations goes far beyond the NATO partnership. Well aware of the EU's shortcomings, but acutely conscious of its history and of the risks from the fraying of transatlantic ties, Gardner offers lessons from his vast personal diplomatic history which instruct us on how, whatever the current obstacles, we might build a transatlantic partnership which endures in the 21st century."
—Sir Ivan Rogers, *UK Permanent Representative to the European Union, 2013–2017*

"Few understand the importance of the transatlantic relationship as well as Ambassador Tony Gardner. He knows that it is vital for America and Europe to work together on the digital economy, trade, and data privacy in order to shape a prosperous shared future. His first-hand insights will be valuable to anyone who cares about this vital partnership."
—Ginni Rometty, *Executive Chairman and Former CEO, IBM Corporation*

"Tony Gardner writes with exceptional depth and precision on his experiences as United States Ambassador to the EU during historic years for the EU and the US-EU relationship. Tony's passion and expertise provide valuable insights on the transatlantic relationship and offer lessons on how we can build a stronger future together."
—Brad Smith, *President, Microsoft Corporation*

"There are few Americans—indeed, there are few Europeans—who understand the EU as well as Tony Gardner. This book is not only a welcome primer on US-European relations, but it provides behind-the-scenes accounts of the most important geopolitical events of the last decade, including Russia's invasion of Ukraine and Brexit, to make clear how important transatlantic economic and diplomatic ties remain—and what is at risk if they falter."
—Peter Spiegel, *US Managing Editor*, Financial Times

"Tony Gardner tells us in this book about his life experience in Brussels, from his time as a young trainee at the European Commission all the way to his time as a US Ambassador to the EU. His story reflects the changes and challenges he faced, as someone in a position of power, but also as a human being, at a time when peace and stability were threatened from many sides. His commitment was crucial for the Transatlantic relationship. As a bridge between Europe and the United States, he tells us that things are never as good or bad as they seem, but if there is cooperation, a strong alliance, and especially if you have passion in what you do, you can successfully tackle all the changes and challenges you will encounter."
—Antonio Tajani, *President of the European Parliament, 2017–2019*

"The structural break-up in American foreign policy and transatlantic relations has prompted Tony Gardner to write a memoir. How did it go in the 'past,' when people listened to each other, showed respect for their partners, and looked for solutions to problems? Tony Gardner tells his story like a gentleman, with knowledge of and respect for the facts, with a deep understanding of the EU and the USA, and with a passion for both. A diplomat and a lawyer, with a heart for what we once called the West."
—Herman Van Rompuy, *Former President of the European Council 2009–2014 and Former Prime Minister of Belgium 2008–2009*

Contents

1	Introduction	1
2	A Personal Mission	25
3	Brexit	57

Part I Economic Ties

4	Trade	105
5	Data Privacy	149
6	The Digital Economy	191

Part II Security Ties

7	Sanctions	241
8	Energy Security	279

9	Law Enforcement Cooperation	311
10	Military and Security Cooperation	351

Part III Saving the Planet Together

11	Climate Change and the Environment	379
12	Foreign Aid and Humanitarian Assistance	423
13	Conclusions	449

List of Figures

Fig. 1.1	"Putin, Obama & EU" (© Peter Schrank, 2015. *The Economist*. Reprinted with Permission)	5
Fig. 1.2	Ambassador Gardner with European Commission President Juncker, November 2015 (*Source* From author's own collection)	11
Fig. 1.3	"Millau Viaduct" (© Daniel Jamme/Eiffage. Reprinted with Permission from Foster + Partners)	22
Fig. 2.1	Cartoon of Ambassador Gardner as a gondolier rowing across the Grand Canal (© Marco Villard, POLITICO Sprl [previously *European Voice*], POLITICO.eu, May 22, 2014)	30
Fig. 2.2	Ambassador Gardner with European Commission President Barroso, March 2014 (*Source* "Presentation of the credentials of the Heads of Mission to José Manuel Barroso, President of the EC" © European Union, 2014. *Photographer* Georges Boulougouris. Reprinted with Permission)	34
Fig. 2.3	Ambassador Gardner with European Council President van Rompuy, 2014 (*Source* From author's own collection)	35
Fig. 2.4	Ambassador Gardner briefing President Clinton in the Oval Office, fall of 1994 (*Source* From author's own collection)	37
Fig. 2.5	From Left to Right: Alejandra Mac-Crohon Gardner, Ambassador Gardner, Ambassador Lute, Ambassador Bauer, and Vice President Biden, 2015 (*Source* From author's own collection)	41

Fig. 2.6	Ambassador Gardner and President Obama in Brussels in March 2014 (*Source* From author's own collection)	42
Fig. 2.7	EU–US Summit, March 26, 2014 (© European Union, 2014. EP—Audiovisual Service. *Photographer* Lieven Creemers. Reprinted with Permission)	53
Fig. 3.1	Ambassador Gardner and Boris Johnson, then UK foreign secretary, at their reunion in November 2016 (*Source* From author's own collection)	59
Fig. 3.2	Boris Johnson stuck on a zip line (© Kois Miah/Barcroft Media, 2012. Reprinted with Permission)	61
Fig. 3.3	The UK's negotiating position toward the EU (© Kevin Kal Kallaugher, 2019. *The Economist*, Kaltoons.com. Reprinted with Permission)	93
Fig. 7.1	Secretary Kerry and Ambassador Gardner meet European Commission President Juncker in Brussels, Belgium to discuss sanctions and other matters (© 506 collection/Alamy Image Bank, 25 March 2016)	244
Fig. 11.1	Ambassador Gardner, his father Richard Gardner, and Vice President Gore in the Vice President's office, spring of 1995 (*Source* From author's own collection)	380
Fig. 11.2	Cover of *Der Spiegel*, Issue 23 (2017) after President Trump's Decision to Withdraw the US From the Paris Agreement (© Edel Rodriguez. Reprinted with Permission from *Der Spiegel*)	416
Fig. 13.1	Ambassador Gardner and Secretary Kerry at Brussels airport in the Summer of 2016 (*Source* From author's own collection)	451

CHAPTER 1

Introduction

"Athens, Athens, conditions for Bruges please." Every evening on the way home from my office I would hear my embassy driver Alain Dupaix speak these words into a long-range walkie-talkie. "Athens" was the code word for the guardhouse outside the official residence in which I lived for three years as the Ambassador to the European Union. "Bruges" was the code word for the official vehicle when I was riding in it. And every night, except for one following the terrorist attacks in Brussels in March 2016, the guardhouse would radio back the message: "conditions green at all locations." That meant that it was safe to approach. But conditions were hardly "green" when I arrived at my diplomatic post in Brussels on March 3, 2014. They were amber and started flickering red a few months thereafter.

This was a stark contrast to the heady optimism I had experienced as a young intern in the European Commission, the executive arm of the European Union, in 1990–1991. The European Economic Community, as it was then known, had launched an ambitious program to break down national boundaries inhibiting a true single market in the flow of goods, services, workers, and capital (as largely exists in the United States). Brussels felt like a Washington, DC in the making—the capital of an increasingly unified (and expanding) area of nation states. The Berlin Wall had just fallen and the newly liberated countries of Central and Eastern Europe were waiting at the door for financial and technical assistance, as well as eventual membership in the club. I took the rather unusual decision in 1992 to start my legal career in Brussels, rather than in the

© The Author(s) 2020
A. L. Gardner, *Stars with Stripes*,
https://doi.org/10.1007/978-3-030-29966-8_1

1

United States, in the belief that Brussels would increasingly be at the heart of Europe.

The admission into the bloc of three new members in 1994, ten more in 2004, and a further two in 2007 boosted optimism about the future of the European integration project. Despite the deep slump that Europe experienced in the financial crisis shortly thereafter, continuing optimism seemed justified when the Norwegian Nobel Committee awarded its Peace Prize to the European Union in 2012 for its contribution "to the advancement of peace and reconciliation, democracy and human rights in Europe" for over six decades. Croatia joined the club in 2013 and other applicants from the Balkans had started the application process.

But by the time I arrived at post in March 2014, the mood had worsened dramatically. The future suddenly wasn't what it used to be, to paraphrase the adage of Yogi Berra, an American baseball player. Upon my arrival, I received two recently published books about the EU with identical titles: "Unhappy Union." The first was written by Professor Loukas Tsoukalis, who had sparked my interest in the EU during my studies at Oxford in the mid-1980s; the second was written by John Peet and Anton La Guardia, two journalists for *The Economist* whom I had met before my departure from my home in London. They argued that the Union is like a dysfunctional marriage that stays together, not out of love or idealism, but out of practical concerns: the high financial costs of breakup (especially the breakup of the Eurozone and a return to national currencies) and the fear of being alone and with less influence in an increasingly turbulent world. One might add that there are also fears of what would happen to the "children"—the recent arrivals from Central and Eastern Europe—if the marriage were to end in divorce: They might well slide back into bad habits of authoritarian rule or might be sucked back into the chilling embrace of Mother Russia.

Storm Clouds Over Crimea

There was no doubt that the Unhappy Union was already in difficulty by early 2014. Things were about to get significantly worse. Crimea, a territory gifted to Ukraine by the Soviet Union in 1954, provided one of the most serious crises that were to define my diplomatic mission. At the end of 2013, Ukrainian Prime Minister Viktor Yanukovych, under heavy pressure to accept cheaper gas and financial aid from Moscow, refused to sign a trade and political association agreement with the EU that would have led to closer integration into Western Europe. Anger about this refusal, as well as indignation about the widespread corruption of government officials, led to protests that culminated in mid-February with riot police and snipers killing dozens of peaceful demonstrators.

I was watching these dramatic events unfold in Frankfurt, Germany, where I was taking an intensive German language course as I waited for final Senate confirmation of my ambassadorial appointment. Over one weekend, as I was tucking into my Sunday brunch at a local restaurant, I practically gagged on my müesli when I saw that all the leading German newspapers were widely reporting a conversation, between my friends and future colleagues, US Assistant Secretary of State Victoria Nuland and Geoffrey Pyatt, US Ambassador to Ukraine. In that conversation, probably intercepted and leaked by the Russian secret services, Nuland dismissed EU concerns about the US desire to impose punitive sanctions and to have the United Nations play an intermediating role in the crisis. "Fuck the EU," she said. I thought to myself: "Well, my future assignment just got more interesting." Even the normally pro-American *Süddeusche Zeitung* published a scathing editorial arguing that the remark (though intended to remain private) displayed an emblematic lack of respect for Europe.

In the weeks before my arrival, a new technocratic and pro-Western government had been formed; Yanukovych and other high government officials had fled the country for Russia. Armed men without insignia (but acting on instructions of the Russian military) had taken over the Supreme Council of Crimea and strategic sites, such as the Sevastopol Airport and the port hosting the Russian Black Sea Fleet. In the subsequent days, the occupation of Crimea was completed, with a pro-Russian government installed and Crimean independence declared. Russia formally annexed the territory in mid-March.

As described in Chapter 7, I devoted a significant portion of my diplomatic mission to ensuring a coordinated US–EU response to these events, including the implementation and repeated renewal of strict sanctions against Russia.

My first official meeting on the first day of my arrival in Brussels on March 3, 2014, was with the Ukrainian Ambassador to the EU, Konstantyn Yeliseyev, later to become the National Security Adviser of Ukrainian President Petro Poroshenko. My last official meeting on my last day on January 20, 2017, was with his successor, Ambassador Mykola Tochytskyi. By contrast, I never had a formal meeting with my Russian counterpart, Ambassador Vladimir Chizhov, a long-time veteran of the Brussels diplomatic corps. When asked about the clear presence of Russian troops in Ukraine, he denied that there were any there: "Let me assure you that the Russian army is not an army of the future which can make its soldiers invisible."[1]

Without coordinated US–EU sanctions on Russia, Moscow might well have decided to press its advantage even further in Crimea and beyond. (The separate sanctions that the US and the EU imposed on Iran, also described in Chapter 7, were equally effective in bringing Teheran to the negotiating table to hammer out a comprehensive agreement that limited its nuclear ambitions.) I also participated in US efforts to assist the EU, described in Chapter 8, to enhance Ukraine's ability to withstand Russia's use of gas supplies as a political weapon and to improve the EU's energy security.

Although the Russian aggression in Ukraine was tragic, I was grateful to Vladimir Putin for helping to deflect attention from a transatlantic rift over data privacy caused by allegations of US government surveillance, including of European citizens. As *The Economist* astutely observed: "Unwittingly, perhaps, Vladimir Putin is playing Cupid to America's Mars and Europe's Venus: By seizing Crimea, he has rekindled the love lost between the transatlantic allies."[2] I hung the cartoon accompanying the article on the wall behind my office desk. It depicted Putin as cupid, bare-chested, and wearing army fatigues, just after firing his arrow at a tree where the US and EU have carved their initials in the shape of a heart. In the distance, President Obama and a woman dressed in the EU flag are walking arm in arm. As the article argued, "Russia is reminding both sides of the ties that bind." Without the Ukraine crisis, the "love lost" due to the rift over data privacy would have been much worse (Fig. 1.1).

Storm Clouds Over Data Privacy

Even with this helpful deflection of attention, Europe's loss of trust in the US because of perceived breaches of European citizens' privacy rights became the single greatest preoccupation during my diplomatic mission. As described in Chapter 5, I focused considerable energy on addressing

---

[1] Remarks before the European Parliament, January 28, 2015. https://push.tass.ru/en/russia/774264.

[2] "Putin's Arrow," *The Economist*, March 29, 2014.

1 INTRODUCTION 5

Fig. 1.1 "Putin, Obama & EU" (© Peter Schrank, 2015. *The Economist*. Reprinted with Permission)

this problem as it had the potential to poison the well of US–EU relations and frustrate progress toward numerous common objectives.

One important objective was the negotiation of a Transatlantic Trade and Investment Partnership Agreement (TTIP). As described in Chapter 4, I was actively involved in the public outreach and strategy of the negotiation. Other important objectives, described in Chapter 6, were to ensure that the EU's Digital Single Market Program would be consistent with US interests and to promote a transatlantic digital economy. The US and the EU made important progress in all these areas but our failure to conclude TTIP will remain my biggest regret.

The transatlantic rift was due in large part to the actions of Edward Snowden, an outside contractor at the National Security Agency. In 2013, he had fled to Hong Kong with highly classified documents about US intelligence programs (that he subsequently leaked to the press). Some of the leaks related to previously clandestine surveillance programs to collect user data from many leading US technology companies and to harvest significant information from Internet activity around the globe. Based on these leaks, German magazine *Der Spiegel* reported that the NSA had placed listening devices in EU diplomatic offices in Washington and New York, breached an EU computer network that provided access to internal e-mails and documents, and accessed phone lines in EU headquarters in Brussels.[3] Bill Kennard, my friend and predecessor in my post, valiantly coped with the fallout of these revelations prior to his departure in July 2013.

Many in Europe saw Snowden as a brave "whistle blower" who had done a great public service. In 2013, he had been shortlisted for the European Parliament's Sakharov Prize, Europe's top human rights award. I strongly disagreed with this view. He appeared to have joined the NSA (and stayed a mere six weeks) for the specific purpose of inflicting maximum damage on the United States; much of the leaked information revealed sources and methods of US intelligence, thereby putting lives at risk and compromising military readiness and defenses against terrorist threats. According to the House Permanent Select Committee on Intelligence, Snowden had regular contact, from the moment of his arrival in Moscow, with Russian intelligence services and shared information with them.[4]

Things got even worse in the fall when news reports in Germany revealed that the US intelligence services had been tapping the cell phone of German Chancellor Angela Merkel. News reports alleged that the eavesdropping was being conducted from equipment stationed on the roof of the US Embassy in Berlin, next to the Brandenburg Gate, the German Parliament and government offices. There were further allegations over the following months. For example, the NSA had allegedly exploited its cooperation agreement with the German intelligence services to spy on European politicians and companies. The US and the UK, moreover, had allegedly hacked into the internal computer network of Gemalto, a European company and the world's largest manufacturer of SIM cards for mobile phones, to steal encryption keys to monitor mobile communications.

Although President Obama and the Chancellor quietly patched up the serious breach in trust, the incident caused significant disruption in transatlantic relations. This was true above all in Germany where data

---

[3] Michael Birnbaum, "European Leaders Angry About Allegations of US Spying," *The Washington Post*, June 30, 2013.

[4] Edward Jay Epstein, "The Fable of Edward Snowden," *The Wall Street Journal*, December 30, 2016.

protection has been a highly sensitive issue since Hitler's dictatorship and Eastern Germany's authoritarian regime, both of which had collected masses of personal information in order to crush dissent. By contrast, the NSA revelations elicited a collective yawn in the United Kingdom, an established democracy where the government and intelligence services command widespread respect.

The Snowden disclosures were a black cloud that threatened to cast a shadow over the entire US–EU relationship. A few days after I arrived in Brussels, I strolled around my new neighborhood in Uccle, a leafy suburb, and came across a large outdoor advertisement of Carlsberg Beer: "Unhacked by the NSA Since 1847." I thought to myself: Houston, we have a problem. Lack of trust in the United States, due to data privacy concerns, had even entered popular culture.

In the fall of 2013, the European Commission, under pressure from the European Parliament (especially its Committee on Civil Liberties, Justice and Home Affairs), called for a reassessment of the US–EU Terrorist Financing Tracking Program (TFTP). This program, described in Chapter 9, has been a critically important tool for the US and its allies in combating serious crime and terrorism worldwide. It enables the US government, under strict controls, to obtain financial transaction information related to serious crime and terrorism from the Society for Worldwide Interbank Financial Telecommunications (SWIFT), a Brussels-based global provider of financial services, including a nearly universal routing code for bank transfers.

The agreement had been painstakingly negotiated and approved in 2009, before being at first rejected by the European Parliament in 2010, revised and then finally ratified four months later after intensive lobbying and a high-profile visit of Vice President Biden to Brussels. The Snowden disclosures had prompted concerns that the US had been collecting SWIFT data in a manner not explicitly authorized by the agreement: by direct intercepts of private companies' IT systems rather than by means of serving subpoenas on SWIFT itself. These concerns were put to rest during intensive discussions between Under Secretary of the Treasury David Cohen and EU Commissioner Cecilia Malmström in the final months of 2013.

The Snowden disclosures raised broader difficulties about the data privacy protections afforded to EU citizens' personal data in the US, especially at the hands of US intelligence services. The European Commission, the European Parliament, and the Article 29 Data Protection Working Party, an independent European advisory body on data privacy, had all expressed grave concerns that the Safe Harbor Agreement, concluded in July 2000, was not working as intended. As part of this agreement, the European Commission found that companies complying with certain privacy principles and registering their certification met EU requirements and could therefore transmit European citizens' personal data to the United States as part of their commercial activities.

The Snowden disclosures not only put in jeopardy the SWIFT and the Safe Harbor arrangements, thereby undermining US–EU cooperation across the board. They also posed massive commercial risks for our leading IT companies. In the fall of 2013, Germany's biggest telecommunications firm, Deutsche Telekom, announced plans for a German "Internetz"—a national routing system which would send data packets via German pathways when the sender and recipient were both in Germany. Atos, a French leader in digital services, was lobbying the French government to impose a requirement that French companies store their data locally. Other European companies were talking about a "Schengen data zone" allowing the 26 countries belonging to the area of free travel to exchange data securely among themselves.

When I arrived at my post, I quickly realized that protecting TFTP, enhancing and saving Safe Harbor, and restoring trust in the US would be Job Number One. As described in Chapter 5, I played a role in the negotiation of Privacy Shield, the successor agreement to Safe Harbor, that the US and EU scrambled to negotiate after the European Court of Justice invalidated Safe Harbor in October 2015. As described in Chapter 9, I also contributed to the conclusion of a so-called Umbrella Agreement for the transfer of data between law enforcement authorities after four years of intensive negotiations. I focused significant energy on promoting legislation in the US that grants EU citizens the same rights as US citizens under the 1974 Privacy Act with regard to personal data transferred under the Umbrella Agreement. Without this legislation, that corrected years of discrimination against EU citizens, the Umbrella Agreement would never have seen the light of day.

During my Senate confirmation hearings, Senators Chris Murphy and Ron Johnson, the co-chairs of the European sub-committee of the Foreign Affairs Committee, pointedly told me that my job was not to go abroad and apologize for the important work of US intelligence services. Many US allies, they argued forcefully, were benefiting from these activities to bolster their domestic security. During my diplomatic mission, I repeatedly observed that Congress, the Administration, and the US private sector harbored significant bitterness at European hypocrisy. Europe was not only free riding on US intelligence; some national intelligence services, especially those in the UK and France, were operating with significantly fewer checks and balances than in the US. European companies were also fueling criticism of the US to steal business away from their US rivals. European citizens' data was routinely transferred to other countries (including Russia, China, and Iran) that clearly don't respect European privacy protections.

A Toxic Brew: Economic Fragility, Mass Migration, Brexit, and Terrorism

Conditions in this Unhappy Union that I found upon my arrival were also flickering amber, rather than green, because of a stubbornly persistent economic slump, lasting seven years after the financial crisis hit in the summer of 2007. That crisis had painfully exposed the precarious foundations of the currency union: While financial union (including banking union and capital markets union) had progressed, fiscal and political union had not.

Martin Feldstein, a well-known economist and Harvard professor, had famously argued that the euro would inevitably fail as a result of imposing a single currency on a heterogeneous group of countries. In 1997 and again in 2002, he predicted that Europe's economic and monetary union would lead to international conflict among European countries and between Europe and the United States. While that had proven overly gloomy, it was true that the euro had accentuated, rather than diminished, economic differences among members of the Eurozone.[5]

Growth was anemic in many of the 28 members of the EU, with unemployment higher than in the United States; youth unemployment was especially alarming, reaching over 20% in Italy and higher still in Spain and Greece. Italy was already suffering from a decade of stagnation and Greece was struggling to avoid defaulting on its loans. A short while after

---

[5] Martin Feldstein, "EMU and International Conflict," *Foreign Affairs*, November–December 1997. In 2002, he concluded: "The euro has thus caused tensions and conflicts within Europe that would not otherwise have existed. Further steps toward a permanent fiscal union would only exacerbate these tensions." "The Failure of the Euro: The Little Currency That Couldn't," *Foreign Affairs*, January–February 2002.

my arrival, the European Commission, along with the European Central Bank, the Eurogroup (of Eurozone finance ministers), and the International Monetary Fund (IMF) were locked in a frantic effort to keep Greece on a path of economic reform that would allow it to stay inside the Eurozone. I was astonished that the EU would allow a debt crisis in a small economy on the periphery of Europe to metastasize into a threat to European, and even international, financial stability.

The US Treasury played an important role mediating between these institutions and Greece. At key points of the negotiations, when it seemed Greece might choose (or be forced) to leave the Eurozone, the US Treasury urged compromise and rationality on both sides. Goodwill was often in very short supply between the EU institutions and the IMF, on the one hand, and Greece, on the other. Many thought the main culprit was Yannis Varoufakis, the Greek Finance Minister during the first half of 2015, who repeatedly alienated EU and member state officials. Athens considered Washington to be an honest broker and US interventions, especially by President Obama with Greek Prime Minister Tsipras, proved crucial.

Not everyone was happy with US involvement. My German counterpart, Ambassador Reinhard Silberberg, pointedly observed during one of our meetings that the EU wasn't lecturing the US about how to solve the Puerto Rican debt crisis. The comparison, however, was not apposite as the Puerto Rican crisis did not, unlike the Grexit crisis, carry the risk of international contagion.

Conditions were flickering red in the fall of 2015 when over 1 million refugees poured into Europe, largely from Syria through Greece and the Balkans into the heartland of Europe before many settled in Germany, Sweden, and the Netherlands. This was a crisis of a wholly different dimension from other crises because it was far more tangible to local populations. The very visible presence of refugees in at least several EU member states added cultural and ethnic insecurities to economic anxieties. National leaders who took anti-immigrant stances were rewarded at the polls, whereas those who followed more liberal policies faced a popular backlash. The events appeared chaotic, with frontline states ill-equipped and sometimes unwilling to fulfill their obligations to receive and process asylum requests.

With the EU institutions often lacking the power to act, and member states increasingly pursuing independent and inconsistent national actions, border fences sprouted across the bloc and the Schengen area of free movement appeared to be at risk. Many were declaring Schengen "dead" as one member state after another imposed "temporary" border controls. Nine days after Hungary's move to seal its southern border drove refugees into Slovenia, the Prime Minister of Slovenia Miro Cerar called on his fellow Central and Eastern European leaders for emergency talks. "If we don't find a solution…then it is the end of the European Union." European Commission President Juncker stated that the end of Schengen could cause the collapse of the euro and even of the single market (Fig. 1.2).

Largely as a result of economic weakness and the refugee crisis, euroskepticism grew significantly throughout the EU, not only in Hungary, the Czech Republic, and Slovakia, but also in traditional bastions of pro-EU sentiment such as Italy and Spain. Extreme populist movements were threatening to win national elections in Austria, the Netherlands, and France. While this did not happen, the United Kingdom voted in a national referendum to leave the EU; this was the first time that a member (let alone a major one) had decided to do so in the history of the

Fig. 1.2 Ambassador Gardner with European Commission President Juncker, November 2015 (*Source* From author's own collection)

bloc, and it triggered a crisis of confidence in the future of the Union. As ambassador to the EU, I was involved in assessing the consequences of a UK vote to leave and I helped clarify the US position before the referendum.

Brexit is perhaps one of the greatest acts of self-harm committed by any country in living memory. As described in Chapter 3, I and many other officials in the Obama administration were flabbergasted by the decision to call an In/Out referendum, as well as by the hugely misleading campaign led by the Leavers. We predicted, accurately I believe, that Brexit would have negative consequences for the EU and especially the UK and, furthermore, that it would weaken the US–EU partnership in some areas where the UK has played an important role (such as sanctions). Nonetheless, as I argue in this book, the EU will continue to offer key capabilities that will make it an essential partner of the US.

On top of all these crises, Europe faced a steady stream of terrorist attacks, many of them masterminded in the Brussels commune of Molenbeek, a stone's throw from US Mission to the EU. Two months after I arrived, a Frenchman of Algerian origin living in that commune killed four people at a Jewish Museum in downtown Brussels, two blocks from where I had lived for five years in the early 1990s.

The weapons used in terrorist attacks in Paris in January 2015 were traced back to the Brussels train station Bruxelles Midi. In August 2015, a Moroccan national who had lived in Molenbeek opened fire with a Kalashnikov (acquired near the same station) on a high-speed train from Amsterdam to Paris, before being subdued by passengers. And, worst of all, two French terrorists living in Brussels traveled to Paris in November of that year to carry out a killing spree that took the lives of 130 people and injured hundreds.

The fear in Brussels, even among US diplomats who had served in hardship posts around the world, was palpable. One of the key objectives I had during my tenure was to promote closer cooperation between the United States and the European Union in combating serious crime and terrorism. These efforts are described in Chapter 9.

The End of Europe?

In late fall of 2015, the crescendo of lamentations in the press on both sides of the Atlantic and among Europe's political leaders about the proliferating challenges facing the EU reached its climax. Like many European media outlets, an article in *The New York Times* Sunday magazine, entitled "Has Europe Reached Breaking Point?" featured a long, gloomy article on the refugee crisis, the risk of Greece leaving the euro, Russian aggression, and terrorism.[6] Presidents, chancellors, and prime ministers competed with one another by issuing apocalyptic warnings of Europe's imminent demise. The EU was capable of dealing with one big crisis at a time, but was it capable of dealing with multiple, large, and interlocking crises all at once?

I recall watching the 2016 State of the Union address by European Commission President Jean-Claude Juncker from the public gallery in the European Parliament in Strasbourg. It was a down-beat admission that solidarity was fraying in the EU:

> There is not enough Europe in this Union. And there is not enough Union in this Union…The European Union is, at least in part, in existential crisis…never before have I seen such little common ground between our Member States….Never before have I seen so much fragmentation, and so little commonality in our Union.[7]

There was no doubt that the events of the prior two years had placed substantial strain on the European Union. Dramatic events had called for rapid, effective action; but, as in the past, the EU had continued its practice of muddling through. While that approach had proven to be sufficient in calmer times, it was clearly inadequate in more turbulent ones. As Wolfgang Munchau of the *Financial Times* had damningly put it: "The EU has an innate tendency towards foul compromises and fair-weather constructions."[8]

Hairline fissures had been spreading along the marble floor of the EU temple. Several had been there for some time: One dividing the prosperous North of creditor countries and the stagnating South of debtor nations, and another separating a euro-skeptic fringe from a Europhile core. Other fissures were more recent: between a socially liberal West and

---

[6] Jim Yardley, "Has Europe Reached Breaking Point?" *The New York Times*, December 15, 2015.

[7] State of the Union Address 2016: Towards a Better Europe—A Europe that Protects, Empowers and Defends, Strasbourg, September 14, 2016.

[8] Wolfgang Münchau, "Europe's Multiplicity of Crises Is Not Accidental," *Financial Times*, January 3, 2016.

an increasingly autocratic East; between those favoring tougher sanctions on Russia and those favoring a policy of accommodation; and between those willing to take in immigrants and those who refused to allow any. The fact that enlargement, one of the EU's signature accomplishments that had anchored Spain, Portugal, and Greece in liberal democratic systems, had failed to prevent democratic backsliding in recently admitted member states (such as Hungary and Poland) was sapping the EU's confidence in its mission.

Increasingly harsh criticism of Germany was one example of fraying solidarity. In the highly charged atmosphere in Greece, some of the Greek media and politicians regularly invoked Germany's Nazi past when rejecting the program of economic austerity promoted by the EU, the European Central Bank, and the IMF. It was even more disconcerting to witness leading members of the Polish government do the same in their regular barbs about German power. The collegiality of EU heads of state meeting in the European Council had certainly declined, with Chancellor Angela Merkel repeatedly the target of harsh criticism.

The Greeks and Poles were not alone. Italian Prime Minister Matteo Renzi vociferously blamed Berlin for acting as if solidarity is a one-way street. He claimed that Berlin demanded austerity and alignment with EU sanctions on Russia that caused economic pain in Italy, while doing nothing to help Italy cope with significant refugee flows. Moreover, Berlin helped defeat the South Stream pipeline project that would have brought Russian gas into Europe through Italy while supporting the North Stream pipeline project that will bring Russian gas into Europe through Germany. At critical moments Berlin appeared to be taking unilateral decisions that had major implications for all of Europe. At one critical European Council meeting in March 2016, called to discuss proposals on how to deal with the Syrian refugee crisis, many participants objected when they were presented, as a *fait accompli*, a deal negotiated in secret the night before by the Chancellor, Turkish Foreign Minister Ahmet Davutoğlu and Dutch Prime Minister Mark Rutte (holding the rotating EU presidency).

Criticisms of Germany were increasingly met with impatience and hostility in Germany itself. The German public largely believed the prevailing narrative of the popular press (rarely challenged by the government) that the imbalances in the Eurozone are solely due to the sloth of debtor countries and the virtue of Germany and fellow surplus countries. Rather than acknowledging that Germany is the single largest beneficiary of the Eurozone and single market, by enabling German exports to be competitively priced and widely sold thanks to free access to its neighbors' markets, a large part of the German electorate was demanding an end to a "transfer union" in which Germany would underwrite bailouts.

Under the weight of proliferating and deepening crises, the EU's governance was visibly creaking. Many of the crises touched the raw nerves of national sovereignty and therefore had to be dealt with through intergovernmental decision-making among heads of state, rather than through the so-called community method of supranational decision-making in which the European Commission plays a critical role. Crisis mode was becoming the norm, with heads of state traveling to Brussels every three to four weeks in all night marathon summits, rather than four to six times per year as in the past. Often the communiqués were rushed and unclear, with ministers left to figure out what had actually been decided. Many other important, but not critically urgent, issues were not getting the attention they deserved.

In the dark days of 2016, I was repeatedly fielding inquiries from Washington about when the wheels were going to fall off the EU bus. I never thought that they would and I said so in repeated cables, paraphrasing Mark Twain by concluding that "reports of the EU's death are much exaggerated." It would be a mistake, I argued, to underestimate the political will of EU leaders to defend the integration project. The international media was overly focused on the problems, without giving due credit to what was being achieved.

I did not think that Schengen would collapse because the member states knew that the costs of such a collapse would be prohibitive: One study by the Bertelsmann Foundation estimated that the permanent introduction of border controls in the EU would cause a decline in economic output of between nearly €500 billion and approximately €1.4 trillion over a ten-year period due to the interruption of supply chains, inventory and storage costs, and harm to tourism and cross-border labor mobility.[9]

I was influenced by a wise observation that Herman van Rompuy, then EU President of the European Council, made over lunch together in

---

[9] Bertelsmann Foundation, "Departure from the Schengen Agreement," 2016. https://www.bertelsmann-stiftung.de/fileadmin/files/BSt/Publikationen/GrauePublikationen/NW_Departure_from_Schengen.pdf.

2016. While acknowledging the proliferation of the fissures, he noted that no San Andreas Fault had yet emerged. The fact that the fissures were running in multiple directions depending on the issue, rather than running along one axis dividing one group from another, meant that the member states still appreciated the value of trade-offs and the need to compromise. It is true, former European Commission Spokesman (and current Commissioner) Margaritis Schinas once confided in me, that few member states consider themselves as shareholders in a common project and therefore fail to see that investments made today will produce dividends in the future. But I also believed that the glue of solidarity would probably hold the project together.

The member states of the EU had walked to the edge of the cliff and had looked into the abyss, before stepping back. The frequently repeated aphorism of Jean Monnet, the EU's most famous founding father, had proven to be correct: "Europe will be forged in crises, and will be the sum of the solutions adopted for those crises." As a result of the perfect storm that washed over the EU's deck, the crew adjusted the rigging, added more ballast, solidified the hull, and improved the navigation.

Today, the EU is better equipped to cope with another financial crisis thanks to supervisory powers granted to the European Central Bank to monitor the financial stability of the Eurozone's largest banks; a permanent bailout fund to provide financial assistance to Eurozone countries or banks in difficulty; and rules to ensure the orderly winding up of failing banks with minimal costs for taxpayers and the real economy. Moreover, member states have agreed to pool sovereignty to enhance the ability of the Union to protect its external borders, combat terrorism, and enhance its energy security.

The Brussels Bubble

For three years, I had a privileged position from which to witness both the challenges facing the EU and the many areas in which the US and EU have worked together to confront regional and global crises. When I mentioned during a family dinner that I might want to describe these in a book one day, my then 14-year-old daughter Alejandra immediately replied: "Don't do that, Daddy: no one will read your boring book; and besides, when you return to London you need to focus on making enough money to pay for my school fees."

I had to admit that she had a point given the stratospheric UK boarding school fees that no book royalties would cover. Bookshelves already groaned with many scholarly, detailed tomes on US–EU relations. One of my predecessors had already written a book about the EU as an emerging superpower. Most readers in the United States ignore the existence of the European Union and even in Europe many find it difficult to understand. As American columnist Tom Friedman put it, including the words "European Union" in the lead of a column in the United States was akin to putting up a "Do Not Read" sign.[10]

This book focuses on the EU, specifically its main institutions, rather than its member states. Unlike some observers, I find the former just as interesting as the latter. Explaining the EU to a non-expert audience requires stepping out of the "Brussels bubble" and viewing things with proper perspective. Brussels, like Washington, is an extremely self-referential microcosm where it is easy to believe that one is living at the epicenter of events.

Armies of lawyers, lobbyists, and consultants all feed from the same trough of minutiae about legislation, policy information, personnel changes, and gossip. Since 2015, Brussels has had its own version of the *Politico* "Playbook," an early morning update on key EU-related information; thousands now start their days scrolling through these e-mails on their way to work. The degree to which Brussels is a bubble really hit home when my wife and I were invited to see Mozart's opera *Mitridate, Re di Ponta* performed at Brussels's famous La Monnaie Theatre. This opera, written in 1770 and describing events in 63 BC during the conflict between Rome and Pontus, was staged as a crisis summit of the European Council, replete with press conferences and bilateral meetings.

The EU's slow and elaborate procedures can be rather more frustrating than operatic. Some officials from EU member states treat their visits to Brussels like visits to a proctologist: something disagreeable, even painful, but rather necessary. Sometimes the EU is like the *Echternachter Springprozession*, an annual dancing procession in Echternach, Luxembourg, in which dancers take three steps forward and two steps backward—thus taking five steps to advance one. It is no wonder that it takes the dancers several hours to jig their way one and a half kilometers.

Meetings of the EU institutions can be rather painful because of the number of member states represented around the table. Soon after my arrival, I had the opportunity to accompany US Secretary of Agriculture

---

[10] Tom Friedman, "Friends and Refugees in Need," *The New York Times*, January 27, 2016.

Tom Vilsack to meet his 28 counterparts—ministers of agriculture from each EU member state—in Luxembourg. As Greece was then holding the six-month rotating presidency of the Council, the Greek Minister of Agriculture, Giorgios Karasmanis, had the privilege of speaking first in Greek. The EU Commissioner for Agriculture, Dacian Cioloș, delicately nudged him and whispered a suggestion that he speak in English as no one at the table spoke Greek. But the minister continued for ten minutes, followed by ten minutes of translation delivered by an assistant seated next to him.

The topic of the entire twenty-minute intervention focused on the glory of feta cheese and the necessity that cheese can only be called feta if it is made in Greece. I was tempted to respond that, by that logic, all countries except for Bermuda, Denmark, and France should be banned from selling Bermuda shorts, Danish pastries, and French salad dressing, respectively. (The topic of "geographical indications," a form of intellectual property protection that the EU extends to a long list of European food and drink names, emerged as a major stumbling block in the Transatlantic Trade and Investment Partnership negotiations. From an American perspective, the list contains a number of generic names.) After the Greek minister had finished, each of the other 28 ministers spoke for about five minutes on each of their favorite topics. Near the end of this marathon, Secretary Vilsack leaned over to me and asked: "Is this the way you spend all your time in Brussels?" Fortunately, it was not.

There were plenty of moments of levity to punctuate the bureaucratic meetings. During my tenure, the annual "press reviews," a vaudeville show organized by the British press corps, compared Martin Selmayr, the powerful Chief of Staff to President Juncker, to Darth Vader. In the opening to one skit, a deep voice intoned:

> The empire is now in the grip of one man who rules with absolute power, whose word is final. He can kill his enemies with a thought, a gesture, or a directive...or worse, reassign them to a job in the farthest reaches of the galaxy....such as Luxembourg. His name, which many dare not speak, is....Darth Selmayr.

Fortunately, I found my regular meetings and lunches with Darth Selmayr to be productive and enjoyable. On the eve of the Juncker Commission taking office in 2014, we had a brief skirmish with our light sabers about trade negotiations (fortunately the Force was with me). Quickly thereafter, we quickly developed an honest channel of communication in which I always found him charming, razor smart, and open to find solutions.

The Brussels bubble can sometimes appear like an episode of Star Wars. I recall one article published in *Politico* in particular that asked its readers to guess whether certain sentences had been uttered by a character in Star Wars or by an EU official.

> Trade disputes, endless plenary sessions with speeches in many languages, the breaking apart of longstanding alliances and coalitions – we must be talking about the European Union, right? Wrong! We're talking about the 'Star Wars' galaxy which may be far, far away but when it comes to political dialogue sounds an awful lot like Brussels.[11]

This was not the first time that the comparison had been made. Some seasoned observers of the EU scene told me that the Members' Bar of the European Parliament in Strasbourg reminded them of the Star Wars bar scene because one could find some rather interesting extra-terrestrials there—some humanoid but others not. I spent many hours in that Bar lobbying parliamentarians on data privacy, the TTIP transatlantic trade negotiations, and digital economy issues.

The EU can sometimes appear to be a surreal cartoon strip. After all, Brussels is home to a museum to René Magritte, the renowned Belgian surrealist painter, and to a major cartoon-strip museum. One of the leading tourist attractions is the Mannequin Pis, a statue near the Grand Place of a small and unremarkable boy urinating. The massive and blackening hulk of the Brussels Palace of Justice has become emblematic of Belgium's occasionally dysfunctional government. Since 2003, it has been shrouded in scaffolding erected to repair its cracked stonework and collapsing ceilings. In 2010, the scaffolding needed repairs and required its own scaffolding. And in 2017, police forensic experts had to don hazmat suits to enter its evidence storage area.

A few kilometers away, in Park Leopold outside the Brussels headquarters of the European Parliament, there are sculptures of ostriches, several of them with their heads in the sand. The UK tabloid press had a field day when it discovered them:

---

[11] Craig Winneker, "Who Said It: 'Star Wars' or the European Union?" *Politico*, December 14, 2015.

The birds, surrounded by a wasteland of overgrown weeds, perhaps are also meant to represent Europe's response to Islamist terrorism, the migrant crisis, or the cultural destruction caused by financial stagnation and youth unemployment.[12]

The truth behind the ostriches was that they were paid for by Brussels, not the EU, and were meant to be a reminder that the park used to be a zoo. Not far away from the park, however, lies a more relevant and truthful symbol: The massive building housing the Representation of the Free State of Bavaria. Dwarfing most national embassies, the building reflects its outsized influence.

The EU institutions are also littered with amusing symbols. The European Parliament building in Strasbourg has such a complicated numbering system for its offices—arrayed in concentric broken circles—that even parliamentarians and seasoned visitors have a hard time finding them. The EU's foreign ministry and foreign minister are inelegantly named the European External Action Service and the High Representative for Foreign and Security Policy—titles that have "the ring of Gilbert and Sullivan to it"[13]—because some member states believe that the simpler names would imbue the EU with trappings of statehood.

The Reason for This Book

Despite my daughter's warning and the difficulties of writing about the EU, my experience in Brussels convinced me of the need for a first-hand non-academic account addressed to informed but non-expert readers about how the United States and the European Union work together, how their foreign policy tools are complementary, and, finally, why regional and global stability depends on their continued joint leadership. Although there are certainly areas of friction, also detailed in this book, their interests are aligned on most issues.

I saw plenty of evidence for that, including in the areas of law enforcement, counterterrorism, sanctions policy, and energy security. It was also clear in how the US and the EU worked closely in the areas of climate change and the environment (as described in Chapter 11), foreign aid

---

[12] Nick Gutteridge, "Symbolic! Brussels Wastes Cash on Sculpture Garden—With Ostriches Burying Heads in Sand," *Express*, August 31, 2016.

[13] John Peet, "The Future of the European Union," *The Economist*, March 25, 2017.

and humanitarian assistance (as described in Chapter 12), and even in the area of military and security cooperation (as described in Chapter 10).

Given my family and professional ties on both sides of the Atlantic, I naturally arrived at my post in the hope of deepening and broadening the US–EU relationship. I wanted to build more bridges. Walls are rarely the solution. The Trump administration came to office with the opposite view. Monica Crowley, Assistant Secretary for Public Affairs at the US Treasury, posed in front of the Berlin Wall, a symbol of oppression for millions of people, and tweeted that "Walls Work."

My preference for bridges influenced my choice of how to decorate the official residence. The State Department had offered me the chance to pick some artwork from their large storage facilities, but my wife and I declined as we thought the choice rather uninspiring. I therefore chose art depicting bridges as a symbol of what the US–EU Mission was seeking to accomplish. After contacting a number of leading architectural firms of the world, including those of Norman Foster and Santiago Calatrava, we covered the walls of the residence with pictures of spectacular bridges that are both architectural and artistic marvels. They served as a good launchpad for conversations at the embassy about the need for more bridges and fewer fences in trade, data privacy, and the digital economy (Fig. 1.3).

When I left my post on January 20, 2017, with the arrival of the new Trump administration, I was very concerned that transatlantic fences would replace bridges and that President Obama's promotion of the transatlantic partnership, building on the work of his predecessors, would unravel. President Trump had given an extraordinary interview in which he had claimed "indifference" to whether the EU succeeds or fails and in which he described the EU as a vehicle of German power, as a "consortium" set up to beat the United States in trade and as a dysfunctional, largely irrelevant institution on the verge of breaking up.[14] His only apparent experience of the EU was with the difficulty in obtaining planning permits for his golf course in Scotland. A columnist suggested a plausible reason for his hostility:

> To a former New York property developer, the EU is the equivalent of a zoning commission objecting to a garish neon façade, or the bulldozing of a playground. The simple act of it saying no enrages him.[15]

---

[14] *The Times*, January 16, 2017.

[15] Shawn Donnan, "Why a Trump Trade War Is More Likely with the EU Than China," *Financial Times*, May 29, 2018.

Fig. 1.3 "Millau Viaduct" (© Daniel Jamme/Eiffage. Reprinted with Permission from Foster + Partners)

When President Trump called European Council President Donald Tusk shortly after the election, he had only question: What EU nation would follow the UK out the door of the bloc? To my horror, the President appeared to be receiving counsel from Nigel Farage, a rabid euro-skeptic and purveyor of cartoon-strip caricatures of the EU.

It was against this backdrop that I took the unusual decision of calling a parting press conference—described the next day on the front page of the *Financial Times* as "pugnacious"—to denounce the "lunacy" of backing populist movements and the breakup of the EU.[16] I warned against any effort to sideline the EU in favor of a purely bilateral and transactional relationship with a number of member states, especially the United Kingdom, because the EU is a critical partner with important assets and because most member states would insist on dealing with the US through the EU on many issues. I noted that ever since President John F. Kennedy

---

[16] Alex Barker, "Trump Team Rang EU and Asked 'What Country Is Leaving Next'?" *Financial Times*, January 13, 2017.

administrations of both political parties have supported European integration because it has been beneficial to US economic, political, and security goals. The US business community has been a cheerleader of European integration because it has promoted prosperity and stability and, in turn, a favorable environment in which to trade with and invest in Europe. "To think that by supporting fragmentation of Europe we would be advancing our own interests is sheer folly."

I have always believed that Europe, including specifically the EU institutions, and the United States are each other's natural partners. When I read the extraordinary statements of the incoming president and his administration about the EU, the North Atlantic Treaty Organization, and key European allies, I found myself humming the theme song to the hit movie Ghostbusters. "Who you gonna call" when you find something strange or weird that doesn't look good in the neighbourhood? Europe and the United States had busted quite a few ghosts over the past decades. Undermining that relationship is just an invitation to let some pretty spooky ghosts into the house. Vladimir Putin is just one of them.

At the post-mortem election breakfast I co-hosted on November 9, 2016 with my friends and colleagues, Doug Lute and Denise Bauer, ambassadors to NATO and Belgium, respectively, I could not hold back my true feelings. I quoted from one of my favorite poems, "The Second Coming" by William Butler Yeats:

> Things fall apart; the centre cannot hold...
> The ceremony of innocence is drowned;
> The best lack all conviction, while the worst
> Are full of passionate intensity.

I was not the only one to worry about a potential Bonfire of the Sanities. Donald Tusk, then President of the European Council, wrote a letter to EU heads of government on the eve of their summit in Malta in February 2017, noting that "worrying declarations by the new American administration all make our future highly unpredictable." The letter went so far to list the United States as a geopolitical risk for the bloc, in addition to Russia, China, terrorism and uncontrolled migration. "Particularly the change in Washington puts the European Union in a difficult situation, with the new administration seeming to put into question the last 70 years of American foreign policy."[17]

---

[17] Press Office, General Secretariat of the Council, January 31, 2017.

At the end of December 2016, the incoming administration had asked me, along with all other non-career ambassadors appointed by President Obama, to step down from my post no later than January 20, 2017, at noon. It was a breach of decades of precedent whereby ambassadors were given several months to arrange for good-byes and to plan for an orderly return to private life. Fortunately, my transition seemed predestined: Having listened to the radio call of "Athens, Athens, conditions for Bruges, please" for three years, it seemed logical to head to the College of Europe in Bruges for a period of reflection. As we sped away from the official residence on our last day, I couldn't help thinking to myself that, while a book would not pay my daughter's school fees, the story of the essential partnership between the US and the EU might one day help to repair the damage to the relationship that was bound to occur.

CHAPTER 2

A Personal Mission

When I announced to my then 12-year-old son Nicolas that President Obama had named me Ambassador to the European Union, his eyes opened wide with disbelief and he pointed a finger at me: "You?" It was not a morale-boosting moment. But it forced me to articulate why I believed I was suited to be the representative of the United States to the European Union. I believe in the power of the EU to do good in this world and I believe in the power of the relationship between the EU and the United States to advance our common objectives on a wide range of regional and even global issues. We are, in short, indispensable partners in an increasingly turbulent world.

I had eagerly accepted the president's offer because my personal and professional life has been intimately connected with Europe and specifically with the EU institutions. Steve Jobs observed in his famous graduation address at Stanford University in 2005 that "You can't connect the dots looking forward; you can only connect them looking backwards." That observation resonates with me. Looking backward, one of the few threads that connect all the dots is my interest in the EU. Following my father's death in 2019, I conducted an archeological dig through decades of my papers in our Connecticut country house. I found an issue of the *Harvard International Review* that I edited in 1984 on the future of the European Community, an issue of the *Columbia Journal of Transnational Law* that I also edited in 1990 on the significance of the EU's Maastricht Treaty, and a book I wrote in 1996 on US–EU relations.

© The Author(s) 2020
A. L. Gardner, *Stars with Stripes*,
https://doi.org/10.1007/978-3-030-29966-8_2

Europe in My Blood

From the moment of my arrival in Brussels, I refused to wear a "friendship" lapel pin (with the flags of the United States and the EU), unlike nearly all my fellow US ambassadors who sported pins featuring their host countries, because I felt my commitment to the relationship should speak for itself. It was in my heart; it didn't need to be on my lapel.

My personal attachment to Europe became rather painfully clear when I had to undergo vetting by the FBI after my nomination. The disclosure form asked every candidate to a Senate-confirmed post to provide 15 years of travel records. As I had been based in London for the past 14 years and had been traveling several times per week to continental Europe and further afield, this was a monumental task. An even more challenging question on the form asked me whether I had "close and/or continuing contact with a foreign national within the last 7 years" with whom I or my wife was "bound by affection, influence, common interests and/or obligation." I considered asking the FBI whether I should list every physical contact I have had with my Spanish wife, but I feared that the FBI would not be amused. In the end, we decided to list my wife's thirty Spanish cousins and my Italian relatives, along with their e-mails, addresses, phone numbers, and professional histories. The completed form was 281 pages and had taken three intensive months of work to complete.

My attachment to Europe is deeply rooted in Italy. In addition to my US citizenship, I have been proud to have Italian citizenship through my Italian mother. I adopted my mother's maiden name, Luzzatto, as my middle name after her death in 2008 to honor the family's remarkable history. My maternal grandparents, Bruno and Resy Luzzatto, had to flee Italy and Benito Mussolini, a bombastic narcissist who wanted to Make Italy Great Again but who wound up destroying his country. Mussolini's granddaughter Alessandra, a former member of Italy's fascist party, served as a Member of the European Parliament. I was delighted when she took to her Twitter account a few years ago to say that I "speak nonsense."

Bruno Luzzatto was an engineer and manager of an aluminum plant near Venice. One of my prized possessions is a photograph of Bruno in that plant during an official visit of Fascist officials; he stands to one side, dressed in khaki, while the visitors in the black uniforms of the Fascist party stride down the center. Bruno never joined the party, following in the footsteps of his father Giuseppe, who had resigned from his position of CEO of the largest Italian insurance company rather than collaborate. Other members of his family, including Bruno's uncle, decided to collaborate to advance their careers (although they naturally justified themselves by saying that they were looking out for the good of the country).

Following the introduction of the anti-Jewish Racial Laws by the Fascist regime in October 1938, my grandparents, along with my six-year-old mother and 4-year-old uncle Francis, fled through Switzerland to Normandy and then to Tarrascon, a small mountain town in southern France. This was a painful decision because the Luzzattos—who had produced eminent rabbis, economists, and intellectuals—had resided in Venice since the early 1500s.

Although Bruno was fortunate to find a job at an aluminum factory in Tarrascon, he and his family had to move on to Marseilles shortly thereafter when the Vichy government shut the factory down and shipped the aluminum production to Germany for the war effort. Bruno's work permit was due to expire within weeks, along with the family's ration card. He called upon the military attaché in the Italian consulate to see what could be done. As my uncle Francis later described in *The Washington Post*: "To the officer the circumstances were clear: if your name is Luzzatto, you are Jewish. If you left Italy and do not want to return, you are anti-Fascist. If you want to remain in Marseilles, you are trying to escape from Europe."

Despite these evident facts, the officer wrote an official letter of support to the Vichy authorities allowing my grandfather's family to stay. And as a result, my grandfather applied for admission to Australia, Argentina, Brazil, and the United States. For months, he paid daily desperate calls on the US consulate. When Bruno died in 1988, my uncle found in his papers a copy of a letter addressed to the Vichy Autorité Compétente Française informing him that a visa to the United States had been granted to Bruno and his family. The letter, dated December 5, 1940, is signed by Myles Standish, Vice Consul of the United States.[1] It is the same name as the leader of the Pilgrims who invited the local Indian tribe to the first Thanksgiving in 1621. Thanksgiving always retained a special significance for my mother's family.

My mother saw the Statue of Liberty for the first time on April 1, 1941. She, my uncle, and my grandparents were in New York Bay aboard

---

[1] Francis Luzzatto, "Escape from the Nazis," *The Washington Post*, July 26, 1987.

the Serpa Pinto, a Portuguese ship that they had boarded in Lisbon. She read the words written at the base of the Statue: "Give me your tired, your poor, your huddled masses yearning to breathe free..." Writing in an Italian newspaper in 1986, the centenary of the Statue, my mother described her emotions:

> "When we passed in front of the Statue in the grey dawn of that morning," she wrote, "we were all on deck with our eyes directed at Her...Everyone around me was crying; they were embracing each other...However, Lady Liberty gave me hope and I made a pact with Her... I wanted at all cost to succeed. I wanted to become a real American. I wanted her to be proud of me."[2]

In the wall above my office desk hangs a framed telegram from Bruno to his relatives in Venice announcing the family's safe arrival in the United States and bearing the stamp of the Fascist regime's censor.

After his arrival in Washington, my grandfather joined other Italian Jewish engineers in the State Department's unit responsible for providing the US military with information on Italy's industrial infrastructure. He then worked in Paris on the Marshall Plan to help Europe recover from the war's devastation, before serving with NATO in Brussels and retiring in Rome. As a child, I would spend every summer in Venice and in Rome where my grandmother patiently taught me Italian on her geranium-filled terrace. These were happy memories and more than made up for the occasional teasing I was subjected to in New York primary school for being half-Italian. "Why does the Italian Second Navy have glass-bottom boats?" one boy asked me during lunch break. "To look at the First Italian Navy."

The family link with Italy was further strengthened when President Carter appointed my father, Richard Gardner, US ambassador to Italy in 1977.[3] I recall one dinner from that period at which my mother announced that the Italian government was likely to fall the next day. My father responded that the morning senior staff meeting at the embassy had discussed the matter and had concluded that the government was stable. When the government did fall the next day, my father asked my

---

[2] Danielle Luzzatto, "La Guardai, Ero Salva," *Il Progresso*, [ ] 1986.

[3] His memoires of those years is captured in his book, *Mission Italy*, published by Rowman & Littlefield in 2005.

mother over dinner what had been her source. "I was at the hairdresser," she said, "and the woman next to me, who is the mistress of Minister [X], told me in great detail of his plans to introduce a motion of no confidence for which he had enough votes." She then paused for dramatic effect, as she had trained to be an actress: "You know, dear, you really should spend more time at the hairdresser, and less time with your senior staff. You might get better information." That episode always reminded me of the importance of unofficial relationships. When I recounted that episode to my senior staff, I don't think they found it very amusing.

Memories of my life in Rome include the turbulent political events, including the assassination of Italian Prime Minister Aldo Moro and the terrorist campaign of the Red Brigades, but the most memorable moments were my frequent visits to my grandparents' house two blocks away from the embassy residence. My sister Nina later went on to marry an Italian diplomat, Ambassador Francesco Olivieri, and to live in Rome for several years where she became friendly with Federica Mogherini, the EU's High Representative for Foreign Affairs and Security Policy during my diplomatic mission. My family's connections to Italy, and to Venice in particular, were highlighted upon my arrival in Brussels when *The European Voice* published a cartoon of me as a gondolier rowing across the Grand Canal. At one of the lunches that Mogherini hosted for Secretary John Kerry, she pointed at me and joked: "John, you should know that you have a great Italian ambassador to the EU!" (Fig. 2.1).

My family history repeatedly reminded me of the importance of the transatlantic bond and the necessity to stand firm against Russian aggression and to uphold the principles of democracy, human rights, and the rule of law that the United States and the European Union share. The crisis triggered by the Russian invasion of Ukraine was a personal, not just a professional, matter for me. At the age of fourteen, and during my father's service as US ambassador to Italy, I had torn down Communist party banners that had been defacing the beautiful clock tower in St. Mark's square in Venice. Even though I had taken the precaution of waiting until the square was empty at 3 a.m., I could have triggered a minor diplomatic incident had I been apprehended.

Fig. 2.1 Cartoon of Ambassador Gardner as a gondolier rowing across the Grand Canal (© Marco Villard, POLITICO Sprl [previously *European Voice*], POLITICO.eu, May 22, 2014)

The Importance of Transatlantic Values

After the annexation of Crimea, the Baltic Republics rightly worried that they could be the next targets of Russian aggression. When I sat in the Latvian Parliament with parliamentarians from the United States, the European Union, and Latvia during the semi-annual Transatlantic Legislators Dialogue in June 2016, I recalled how Latvians from all walks of life manned the barricades around the same building in January 1991, braving freezing temperatures and potential death at the hands of the Soviet Army, to prevent a Communist coup. I had seen the evil of the Soviet Union with my own eyes, as a student at Leningrad State University, an intern in the Institute of US–Canada Studies of the Soviet Academy of Sciences and as an intern in the US Embassy in Moscow. These experiences led me to take my family to Riga's Museum of National Occupation so that they could see how Latvia had been traded like a piece of real estate between the totalitarian regimes of Hitler and Stalin.

While the coordinated US–EU response to the Russian invasion of Ukraine was one of the (largely) unsung successes of the relationship, I was occasionally frustrated at the hesitation of the White House to move faster with tougher sanctions, and I was disappointed that several EU member states preferred to negotiate endlessly with Moscow at any cost, while leaving the Ukrainians dangerously exposed. I had grown up believing that values matter and that it is an obligation to support those who fight for freedom.

In 1987, I had traveled to Prague to smuggle reading materials to some of the signatories of the Charter of 77, a human rights manifesto. In 1983, I had studied Polish at Krakow's Jagiellonian University as a pretext to meet members of the Solidarity resistance movement. I had the memorable opportunity to interview Lech Wałęsa, then under house arrest in Gdansk, and to smuggle the tape out of Poland, despite being stopped by the ZOMO, the Polish paramilitary police. Shortly after my arrival in Brussels as ambassador, I presented a copy of the interview to his son, Jarosław Wałęsa, a Member of the European Parliament. The fact that in one generation, a country like Poland could make a peaceful transition from military law to democracy was a reminder of the EU's hugely significant contribution to European and, indeed, world peace and stability.

The EU doesn't necessarily guarantee that positive evolution, however. When I arrived in Brussels, I was reunited with a Hungarian Member of the European Parliament, József Szájer, whom I had gotten to know when he was a Soros Fellow at Oxford. I had been full of admiration for his courageous struggle in the early 1990s for Hungarian independence, along with his old friend Viktor Orban, now Prime Minister of Hungary. Szájer has been a steadfast apologist for the many measures that EU democratic watchdogs have concluded amount to a serious weakening of Hungarian media and judicial independence. Prior to the Trump administration, the United States shared EU concerns about the erosion of Hungarian democracy, increasing corruption and anti-semitism.

During my diplomatic mission in Brussels, I observed several moving historical commemorations that reminded me of the importance of democracy, human rights, and the rule of law. On November 11, 2014, many towns across Europe, especially in Belgium, observed the centenary of the outbreak of World War I. I took my family to visit the Passchendaele Memorial Museum, including the recreation of the trenches, and the Commonwealth graves at Tyne Cot, to remind my children of the horrific cost that past generations paid for our freedom. At a nearby American cemetery, my family came across a white gravestone of a Private named William Fossum from Minnesota; barely an adult and far from home, he died on November 11, 1918, the very day that Armistice was declared. The famous poem "In Flanders Fields"[4] came to my mind:

> To you from failing hands we throw
> The torch; be yours to hold it high.
> If ye break faith with us who die
> We shall not sleep, though poppies grow
> In Flanders fields.

November 2014 was the 25th anniversary of the fall of the Berlin Wall and the escape of millions from their Soviet prison to become free Europeans. The East Germans had called that wall the "Anti-Fascist Protection Rampart"—exhibiting the same cynical disdain for the truth as Vladimir Putin. I had first seen the wall during a visit in 1987 and then in the fall of 1991 when I worked in the German Privatisation Ministry housed in the former Luftwaffe Headquarters in East Berlin.

In early December 2014, my wife and I went to Bastogne to commemorate the 70th anniversary of the great battle that took place there and the heroism of American troops who held back a German offensive as part of the larger Battle of the Bulge in the Ardennes. It was freezing cold and snowing, like the conditions back then, but we were warmed by the amazing spirit of the veterans from that battle who were present.

I have never forgotten the role that the United States played in saving my mother's family, to give my grandfather and his children the opportunity to start anew, and to rebuild the country of their birth. These things have always been engraved in my mind and heart. I recall vividly that my maternal grandparents never permitted me to criticize the United States in their presence, even during the troubled days of the Watergate Crisis that the family discussed passionately during our Italian holidays. I have always believed that the United States is, in the words of my Harvard Professor Joe Nye, "bound to lead"; it alone among nations has the power and the values to lead the world. Despite mistakes, the world has benefited enormously from US leadership.

---

[4] Written by Major John McRae, May 1915, during the Second Battle of Ypres.

"Going Native"?

When I was in the State Department preparing for my mission, I heard an anecdote about how former US Secretary of State George Schultz used to call new ambassadors into his office. He would ask them to point to "their country" on a big globe in a corner of his office. Almost invariably the ambassador would point to the country to which he or she had been named. Schultz would explode: "That's not your country!" Pointing to the United States, he would shout: "This is your country, and don't you ever forget it."

I never needed a reminder of that, but it was a salutary warning that US-based government officials would always suspect an ambassador of having gone "native" by taking the side of the government to which he or she was accredited. Given my background, this was a constant concern of mine. During many occasions in which I sought to explain the rationale behind the policies of the EU or the member states, I feared that my opponents would deploy the "gone native" argument against me, especially during the hotly contested negotiations on data privacy and the Transatlantic Trade and Investment Partnership Agreement (TTIP).

Although I never went "native," I did feel like a local upon my arrival in Brussels to take up my post. When I presented my credentials to José Manuel Barroso, the President of the European Commission, and Herman van Rompuy, the President of the European Council, I was met by the jovial head of the European Commission's protocol office, Nicolas de la Grandville. "We really must do something about our internship program," he joked, "because people like you see the insides of what we do and then return years later to sit on the other side of the table!" (Figs. 2.2 and 2.3).

I had been fortunate to be an intern in the Directorate-General for Competition Policy of the European Commission in the early 1990s. During that period, I was exposed to the way in which the EU handles antitrust matters such as abuse of copyright, cartels, and restrictions on retailers' distribution practices. My friend Mike Froman, whom I had gotten to know earlier during our graduate studies at Oxford and with whom I worked intensively on TTIP when he served as US Trade Representative, also worked as an intern in the Forward Studies Unit that provided policy planning for the Commission's leadership.

It was my experience at the European Commission that convinced me to stay to work on antitrust matters in an international law firm, rather

Fig. 2.2 Ambassador Gardner with European Commission President Barroso, March 2014 (*Source* "Presentation of the credentials of the Heads of Mission to José Manuel Barroso, President of the EC" © European Union, 2014. *Photographer* Georges Boulougouris. Reprinted with Permission)

than return to Wall Street and a more traditional career path. I formed close friendships with many Commission officials, such as Daniel Calleja, a brilliant Spanish lawyer who rose to become director-general for the internal market and then for the environment.

I was fortunate to have found my first apartment on the third floor of a building owned by Wittamer, well known for the chocolates and pastries it still sells from its ground floor shop. Every day on my return from work, I would find a tray outside my door with the latest Wittamer confections and a handwritten note from its owner. Perhaps it was this sweet experience that made me a fervent believer in the European Union.

Living in Brussels during the early 1990s also had its share of frustrations. *The Washington Post* had published an article on my tribulations living in the capital, including the long waiting time to get heating and a telephone line for my apartment. The article had described the bureaucracy as a "bilingual frankenstein's monster run amok" and quoted me

Fig. 2.3 Ambassador Gardner with European Council President van Rompuy, 2014 (*Source* From author's own collection)

as saying that the 19 communes were like "little Ghaddaffis" exploiting their high degree of autonomy.[5] Services, such as telephone lines and heating, are cheaper and of better quality today. The capital continues to suffer from being a territory that is politically and linguistically disputed among the French-speaking Walloons and the Dutch-speaking Flemish.

---

[5] Sharon Waxman, "Brussels: Capital of Confusion," *The Washington Post*, June 9, 1993.

The communes operate on occasion like fiefdoms that often don't cooperate with one another or federal or regional authorities. Six different police forces operate in Brussels, a city of only 1.2 million people, complicating efforts to have an integrated approach to countering terrorism.

Crafting a Transatlantic Agenda

My belief in the power of the US–EU relationship was solidified during my experience as the official handling matters relating to the EU and key member states such as Germany, France, Italy, and Spain, on the National Security Council staff. I found US relations with the EU to be fascinating because it was like two-dimensional chess played on one supranational board and another member state board. Any approach toward the EU that ignored its rich complexity, or sought to import US ways of doing business, would be doomed to fail. I had already seen many US businesses in Brussels flounder in this regard.

When I arrived on the first day of my job as Director for European Affairs in October 1994, my colleagues were delighted that I wanted to focus on the EU because "no one around here cares about that stuff." They were all engaged in the rather more glamorous high diplomacy of conflict resolution in the Balkan War (Fig. 2.4).

The EU's continued efforts at political integration, including through the creation of a common currency, were largely ignored. A week after arriving in Washington I called the Treasury Department to ask what the Clinton administration's policy was toward EU plans to create a single currency. I was told to my astonishment that the administration didn't need to have a policy because the single currency would never come about. This error was rooted in the belief that the single currency was only an economic project, with apparent flaws, and not equally a political project. And it was a classic case of the United States underestimating the EU's political will.

Even as a 32-year-old, I was fortunate to be given wide discretion to work closely with our US Mission to the European Union and my mentor, Ambassador Stuart Eizenstat, on all matters affecting the US–EU relationship. I saw the promise of the partnership to promote joint interests on a transatlantic, European, and even global basis. But I also understood why many of my colleagues did not share my enthusiasm. For example, I witnessed the rather uninspiring content of US–EU Summit meetings and the EU's penchant for issuing communiqués and seeking to be a

Tony —
When you talked,
we all listened!
Thank you for your
outstanding service at the NSC.
Sandy Berger 5/28/03

Fig. 2.4 Ambassador Gardner briefing President Clinton in the Oval Office, fall of 1994 (*Source* From author's own collection)

player on every global issue, regardless of whether it had relevant assets or ideas to contribute. And I observed how member state embassies in Washington routinely undercut the profile of their own EU Delegation to the United States; during the French Presidency of the Council (that rotates every six months), for example, a delegation from Paris sought to exclude the EU Delegation from a meeting with my boss, National Security Adviser Tony Lake, even though the meeting was on European affairs.

My last, and most memorable, experience as a White House official was accompanying President Clinton on Air Force One to Madrid in December 1995 to attend a US–EU Summit and the signing of the New Transatlantic Agenda. That document, in which I had been intimately involved, called for the US–EU relationship to evolve from joint consultation to joint action in a number of areas by specific target dates.

It proposed a "New Transatlantic Marketplace," essentially a transatlantic free trade agreement, to reduce or progressively eliminate tariff and non-tariff barriers that hinder the flow of goods, services, and capital between Europe and the United States. The US and the EU convened a Transatlantic Business Dialogue in 1995 to serve as an official business sector advisory group on trade and investment issues. The "New Transatlantic Marketplace" laid the intellectual groundwork for the Transatlantic Trade and Investment Partnership Agreement launched one year before my arrival in Brussels.

The core purpose of the Agenda was to enhance structured foreign policy cooperation—specifically the promotion of peace, democracy, and prosperity around the world. While we obviously failed to achieve that goal in the cases of Russia and the Middle East, there have been some notable successes.[6]

We certainly achieved the goal of promoting peace, democracy, and prosperity, through the transition to a market economy, in Central and Eastern Europe. Although the weakening of the judiciary, media, and civil society in Hungary and Poland is a worry, and although Romania and Bulgaria are still struggling to root out corruption, Central and Eastern European countries have made a remarkable and nearly bloodless transition to peaceful, democratic, and stable market democracies. The enlargement of the EU to the area, including the application of EU law, played a key role in this remarkable achievement. But US–EU coordination in providing technical and financial assistance was also important.

The states of the former Soviet Union have had a more difficult time, due to intensive Russian political, economic, and military efforts to keep them within Moscow's sphere of influence. Ukraine remains a work in progress, with significant (albeit slow) achievements in transparency and the rule of law. Its trajectory has been miraculous in light of the human and economic costs of fighting Russian aggression.

The Agenda also sought to "assist recovery of the war-ravaged regions of the former Yugoslavia, and to support economic and political reform and new democratic institutions." The Dayton Accords ended

---

[6] Anthony Gardner, "The Long-Term Significance of the New Transatlantic Agenda," *European Voice*, November 13, 1996. https://www.politico.eu/article/long-term-significance-of-new-transatlantic-agenda/.

the Yugoslav War and established peace in Bosnia Herzegovina. Slovenia and Croatia joined the EU. Although Serbia has been careful not to antagonize Russia and remains reliant on Russian energy and military equipment, it has steadily pursued its aim of EU membership. Albania is a NATO member and in 2016 became a candidate member for EU accession. The US and the EU have promoted political and economic reforms in Montenegro and Bosnia Herzegovina, in the face of persistent Russian efforts to undermine their transitions with disinformation campaigns and illicit funding of political parties. Under the leadership of the former High Representatives for Foreign and Security Policy, Catherine Ashton and Federica Mogherini, the EU has promoted the normalization of relations between Serbia and Kosovo. The US and the EU have worked together intensively to enable a special prosecutor to investigate and a specialized tribunal based in The Hague to try those accused of war crimes in Kosovo.

The Trump administration has unfortunately deprioritized the promotion of anti-corruption, transparency, and good governance around the world, especially in the Balkans, thereby complicating the EU's mission there and potentially leaving a vacuum that Russia, Turkey, and other states may fill.

In the Agenda, the US and the EU pledged "to coordinate, cooperate and act jointly in development and humanitarian assistance." Representing 80% of all official development assistance worldwide, the parties have coordinated at both a country and program level to eliminate wasteful overlap and improve a division of labor that reflects each side's strengths, thereby improving the quality and impact of international aid and relief.

In the Agenda, the US and the EU also pledged to "cooperate on the fight against illegal drug trafficking, money laundering, terrorism, organized crime and illicit trade in nuclear materials." Here again, the parties have achieved a great deal, not just on a bilateral level between the US and individual member states of the EU, but also with Europol, the EU's law enforcement agency, and the European Commission.

Other areas of collaboration mentioned in the Agenda include climate change and data protection. The digital economy, in its infancy at the time of the Agenda, was barely mentioned, as was military cooperation in light of the EU's modest capabilities. But in the past few years, the parties have collaborated closely in these areas as well.

Supporting the EU in the Obama Administration

I have strongly believed during my service at the White House and thereafter that the European Union is an essential partner of the United States on these and many other regional and global issues. That view was shared widely in the Obama administration. Vice President Biden repeatedly engaged with the EU institutions at critical moments to advance key objectives in our trade and data privacy agenda (Fig. 2.5). In his Address to the People of Europe in April 2016,[7] to which I contributed, President Obama told his audience:

> your accomplishment – more than 500 million people speaking 24 languages in 28 countries, 19 with a common currency, in one European Union – remains one of the greatest political and economic achievements of modern times.

And he added that he considered it a necessity because European and US security and prosperity are indivisible. He went even further, asserting that the EU is of global importance (Fig. 2.6):

> A strong, united Europe is a necessity for the world because an integrated Europe remains vital to our international order. Europe helps to uphold the norms and rules that can maintain peace and promote prosperity around the world.

These speeches followed very much in the footsteps of over 60 years of *bipartisan* support for European integration. On July 4, 1962, President John F. Kennedy had issued a ringing endorsement of the common market:

> We believe that a united Europe will be capable of playing a greater role in the common defense, of responding more generously to the needs of poorer nations, of joining with the United States and others in lowering trade barriers, resolving problems of commerce, commodities, and currency, and developing coordinated policies in all economic, political, and diplomatic areas. We see in such a Europe a partner with whom we can deal on a basis of full equality in all the great and burdensome tasks of building and defending a community of free nations.[8]

---

[7] Remarks to the People of Europe, Hannover Messe Fairgrounds, April 25, 2016.

[8] Address at Independence Hall, Philadelphia, July 4, 1962.

Fig. 2.5 From Left to Right: Alejandra Mac-Crohon Gardner, Ambassador Gardner, Ambassador Lute, Ambassador Bauer, and Vice President Biden, 2015 (*Source* From author's own collection)

This view has been shared by every president, of both parties, since Kennedy up until President Trump. In his historic address to the European Parliament in 1985, President Ronald Reagan had reaffirmed that "America remains…dedicated to the unity of Europe." President George H. W. Bush had also repeatedly spoken in favor of an integrated Europe and of the EU's emerging global leadership role.[9] On the 60th anniversary of the Treaty of Rome in 2017, the Senate issued a bipartisan resolution paying tribute to the contributions of the EU and the US–EU partnership.

These views stand in sharp contrast to the Trump administration's cartoon-strip caricatures of the EU. According to the president, the EU

---

[9] In an address to Boston University on May 21, 1989, for example, he had said: "This Administration is of one mind. We believe a strong, united Europe means a strong America…The United States welcomes the emergence of Europe as a partner in world leadership."

Fig. 2.6 Ambassador Gardner and President Obama in Brussels in March 2014 (*Source* From author's own collection)

"was put there to take advantage of the United States"[10] and its principal purpose has been to beat the United States in trade; he has accused it of being a strongly protectionist bloc (while pretending that the US market is entirely open) and merely a vehicle for German power. He has expressed his indifference as to whether the EU succeeds or fails, but in practice his administration has actively sought to divide and undermine the EU.

[10] Shawn Donnan, "Trump Plays Game of Chicken with Brussels," *Financial Times*, May 2, 2018.

The six decades of US support prior to the Trump administration for European integration were not born of starry-eyed idealism, but rather stemmed from an appreciation of its benefits for US trade with and investment into Europe. The support has been rooted in a realistic analysis that many regional and global problems are simply not capable of being resolved by the United States acting alone. Europe, acting in a coordinated manner, can be an effective partner in promoting shared values and objectives. Naturally, the United States is occasionally inconvenienced by a strong, more united, and independent voice on foreign policy that differs from its own, but this is more than offset by the fact that on the big issues the views of the US and the EU converge far more often than they diverge.

The European project and institutions have contributed significantly to the creation of a zone of democracy, stability, and prosperity that is the envy of the world. The ultimate proof of this is that millions of people from all over the world risk their lives every year on hazardous land and sea journeys to reach Europe's shores—not just for economic reasons, but because Europe is an attractive model of freedom and tolerance that offers people enormous opportunities to fulfill their dreams.

The EU certainly has struggled to communicate what it does, even within its own borders, however. That is because it is often noticed—like a windowpane—only when it is dirty or broken. When it is clean and transparent, it remains invisible. The challenge has always been to remind people that, even though it is usually invisible, it plays a key role by letting the light in and keeping the cold air out.

Observing Some EU Flaws

That doesn't mean to say that there aren't legitimate reasons to be critical of some aspects of the EU. I too have had moments of doubt about whether the EU has become too unwieldy, bureaucratic, and slow. Due to small member states' insistence that they each appoint a commissioner, the College of Commissioners has consisted of 28 members (before the departure of the UK), more than the number of substantial portfolios. The need to maintain geographic balance in top positions within the European Commission has hindered the ability to make appointments on merit. Top positions within the EU institutions, such as the presidencies of the Commission, European Council, and Parliament, are sometimes allocated on the basis of national and political affiliation, rather than solely on competence. Occasionally, national governments appoint their commissioners as a pre-retirement gift or to keep them out of national politics.

The EU seems capable of taking big decisions, including significant reforms, only when its leaders are at the cliff edge, facing the abyss and with a knife to their throats. That was certainly the case during the 2008–2010 financial crisis, the negotiations with Greece about its threatened departure from the euro (and possibly even the EU) in 2015, and the migration crisis of 2015–2016. Decision-making by all-night crisis meetings between national leaders became almost routine. Once national leaders had taken the tough decisions and the immediate urgency of the crises lifted, they returned to old habits of postponing further reforms.

Sometimes there is a dangerous chasm between short-term rhetoric and long-term reality that can have serious negative consequences. For example, the EU occasionally pays lip service to the need for a "European Army"—a plan that is totally detached from reality because there won't be the means or political will to carry it out for several decades. The result of this rhetoric is to awaken deep-seated (and misguided) US concerns about any useful actions the EU takes to achieve greater autonomy in military and security matters because they purportedly will undermine NATO.

Although the EU excels at making laws, it has fallen short in enforcing them—largely because of the uneven rigor with which member states implement EU legislation into national laws. It often appears that there is one set of laws for the big member states and another set for the smaller ones. That certainly has been the bitter conclusion of the latter when France, Italy, and even Germany have breached the EU's fiscal rules that are supposed to be backed by penalties.

The EU has also had great difficulty ensuring that all member states live up to basic standards of human rights, including the independence of the media and judiciary. The EU's tolerance for sinners among its flock reminds me of an anecdote I once heard about how Italian Prime Minister Aldo Moro sought to convince Swedish Prime Minister Olof Palme about Sweden's ability to live by all the bloc's rules if it joined. Moro explained that the European Community is like joining the Church: You must have faith and know your catechism in order to be admitted, but you can sin and be forgiven once you're in.

During my mandate in Brussels, I was repeatedly lectured, especially by left-wing members of the European Parliament, that the US market is "the wild west" with hardly any rules, while Europe imposes high standards that permit a civilized way of life. The facts show that this is a gross caricature.

For example, it was the US Environmental Protection Agency that broke the story about Volkswagen's illegal installation of "defeat devices" to cheat emissions tests. The Joint Research Centre, the Commission's in-house research arm, had warned five years before the scandal broke in 2015 about the presence of such devices, but no action had been taken.

It was the US Treasury that went public in 2018 with its claims that ABLV, Latvia's third largest lender, had engaged in "institutionalized money laundering"—including violations of North Korean sanctions. Europe's top financial regulator, Daniele Nouy admitted: "…it's very embarrassing to depend on the US authorities to do the job."[11] Another major money laundering scheme was uncovered in Estonia in 2018. Denmark's Danske Bank revealed that about €200 billion in questionable money had flowed through its Estonian branch between 2007 and 2015.

Many US and EU businesses fairly complain that EU decision-making remains opaque, despite improvements over the past years. The main reason is that most legislation goes through a process called "trilogue"— informal meetings in which the European Parliament and the Council, assisted by the European Commission, try to agree on a common text based on their initial positions before the combined text is voted according to the formal legislative procedure. Although the process has proven to be efficient, the EU's own Ombudsman acknowledges that it is opaque as few details are revealed about meetings' timing or content. Once a combined text is agreed on, often an early stage of the legislative process, it is rare that outside parties have effective opportunities to amend it.

Another legitimate complaint is that the EU does not enshrine best scientific evidence as part of its legislative program; under pressure from certain member states, the opinions of the EU's own food safety bodies have been routinely ignored and key exports of the United States, including agricultural products containing genetically modified organisms, hormone-treated beef, and poultry and beef carcasses that have been treated with certain antimicrobial washes, have been barred entry under specious consumer safety grounds. The elimination of the role of Chief

---

[11] Richard Milne, "Latvia Banks Scandal Leaves European Regulators Red-Faced," *Financial Times*, April 5, 2016.

Scientific Adviser at the European Commission in 2014 was not a good sign about the commitment to enshrine scientific evidence in EU policymaking.

The €58 billion that the EU spends per year on its Common Agricultural Policy, accounting for 40% of total expenditures, is frequently criticized as being opaque, inefficient, harmful to the bloc's environmental goals and a source of patronage and corruption, especially in Central and Eastern Europe.[12]

In my view, businesses also have some legitimate concerns about how the EU's antitrust policies operate. I have been a staunch defender of this core part of the EU's mission, perhaps because I served as an intern in the Directorate-General for Competition Policy and later worked on EU antitrust matters in a Brussels-based law firm. I have also defended Margrethe Vestager, Executive Vice President of the European Commission responsible for competition and digital policies, against unfair attacks, including by writing in the *Financial Times* to criticize President Trump's inaccurate depiction of her as "anti-American."[13]

However, it is legitimate to point out that EU antitrust procedures are flawed because the European Commission is judge, jury, and executioner all rolled into one. The fact that the European Commission does not have to prove its initial case before a judge—as is the case in the United States—has very practical effects. The case teams are frequently staffed by smart young, professionals who have usually never worked in the private sector; they frequently form an early view on their cases, based on academic theories rather than real-world market effects; they enjoy an extraordinary amount of discretion and are rarely challenged by their bureaucracy. The introduction of procedural reforms, such as a hearing officer (essentially an independent arbiter of procedural fairness), and the greater emphasis on sound economic analysis, have had a positive, but

---

[12] See, for example, Selam Gebrekian, Matt Apuzzo, and Benjamin Novak, "The Money Farmers: How Oligarchs and Populists Milk the E.U. for Millions," *The New York Times*, November 3, 2019. https://www.nytimes.com/2019/11/03/world/europe/eu-farm-subsidy-hungary.html.

[13] Anthony Luzzatto Gardner, "Vestager Is Certainly Not Anti-American," *Financial Times*, July 2, 2019. https://www.ft.com/content/0a78c864-9bfb-11e9-9c06-a4640c9feebb.

limited, impact. The rest of the European Commission will almost never challenge the views of the Directorate-General for Competition. While appeals are of course possible, they are lengthy and usually of little use to parties who restructure or abandon their transactions.

As successful as the EU's foreign policy has been in numerous instances, it is also not immune from some criticism. Rather than focus its limited human and financial resources on the EU's neighborhood, the European External Action Service seeks to be relevant in nearly every part of the world and on a vast array of issues, even where it has limited influence. Sometimes it drops the ball in areas where it has the experience and the competence. Senior EU diplomats admitted to me that the Syrian refugee problem in Turkey was certainly foreseeable well before it exploded into a crisis. Much more could have been done earlier to address the problem.

EU foreign policy procedures can be very slow and bureaucratic. Meetings of the Political and Security Committee of the Council, responsible for the EU's common foreign and security policy, are lengthy exercises in finding lowest common denominator positions among the member state ambassadors to the EU and often result in anodyne communiqués.

Some of the EU's consultative institutions, like the Committee of Regions and the Economic and Social Committee, moreover, are extremely expensive to run and have limited impact, despite the numerous opinions that they produce. And the European Parliament, with which I interacted intensively as ambassador, is not a fully fledged parliament in the sense that, unlike perhaps any other parliament in the world, it does not have the power to raise revenues, impose taxes, and initiate legislation. It can only modify or block legislation proposed by the European Commission.

Is the EU Too Diverse?

On many occasions during my mandate, I found myself in the public gallery of the European Parliament in Strasbourg looking down on the hemicycle with 751 parliamentarians seated in front of an enormous EU flag. I couldn't help wondering whether this vision was in fact a mirage. Is the glorious diversity in Europe's economies, cultures, histories, and languages an insurmountable challenge to the project of integration? Are the divergences too great to forge a common sense of identity and purpose?

Gideon Rachman of the *Financial Times* has gloomily compared the EU to the League of Nations, a body set up after World War I to solidify international cooperation and the rule of law but swept away by turbulent international events that it couldn't control.[14] While I think that this is far too gloomy, there is no doubt that solidarity is still shallow, varying considerably by country and by the year in which Europeans are polled. Perhaps, this is because many Europeans identify with Europe for intellectual reasons, rather than emotional ones. As Bono, lead vocalist for the rock band U2, has aptly observed, Europe is a thought that needs to become a feeling.

Only positive feelings—a sense of attachment to a purpose—can overcome deep divergences. There aren't many similarities between Estonia and Cyprus, Ireland and Bulgaria, Sweden and Greece. Many of the member states are at very different stages in their economic development: Luxembourg's GDP per capita is over five times that of Romania. Some of them are minnows, with populations a fraction of mid-size cities and GDPs smaller than the cash balance of Apple. Their different histories, cultures, and political traditions complicate dialogue.

Some of the member states face serious challenges with corruption, while others uphold admirably high standards of transparency and ethics. Some snub their noses at EU fundamental rights by pursuing a brand of "illiberal" democracy, including attacking the independence of the judiciary and the media, as well as undermining civil society; others feature a healthy system of checks and balance on executive power.

Some member states have a rather spotty record at enforcing EU rules, and their citizens appear to consider laws as almost optional or at least relevant only for the weak and those without connections. My Italian friends remind me of the wonderful dictum: "*Fatta la legge, trovato l'inganno*" (people will always find a way around the law).

In many areas of Europe, citizens feel primary allegiance to their town or region rather than to their country or to Europe. That has complicated efforts to forge a European identity. The wonderful Italian word

---

[14] Gideon Rachman, "The Crises That Threaten to Unravel the EU," *Financial Times*, September 14, 2015. https://www.ft.com/content/7e9a64a0-5ac3-11e5-9846-de406ccb37f2.

"*campanilismo*," roughly translated as a person's strong attachment to his city's bell tower, expresses the strength of local feeling. My Venetian friends liked repeating an old saying that captured how the inhabitants of the lagoon turn up their noses at their neighbors: "*Vicentini mangia gatti, Veronesi tutti matti*" (people from Vicenza eat cats, those from Verona are all nuts). The Florentines have their own version: "*Meglio un morto in casa che un Pisano all'uscio*" (better to have a corpse at home than someone from Pisa on the doorstep).

Differences in national identity can be managed when there are a limited number of countries sitting around the decision-making table. Every visit to the thirteenth floor of the Berlaymont building in Brussels, the sanctum of the President of the Commission and his team of 28 commissioners, reminds me of this point. In a corner of one of the rooms stands the original conference table of the Commission from the 1960s, when there were just six members. While it is true that the group was not entirely homogeneous even then, especially when one compares Italy with the other members, meetings must have had the feeling of a family sitting around a kitchen table. Today that feeling is lost as commissioners strain to see the faces of their partners on the other side of the massive table.

Critics charge that the European Parliament is prone to grandstanding and self-serving attempts to increase its power. Other observers have claimed that the European Parliament is a graveyard of failed national parliamentarians interested in a well-paid sinecure. While these judgments are too harsh, many did seem underworked and bored due to the limited amount of legislative activity. That led the European Parliament to issue lengthy non-binding declarations, often on topics over which the European Parliament has no influence.

Some parliamentarians seemed rather eager to improve their MEP ranking as determined by the website mepranking.eu, partly based on how many written questions they ask the European Commission. The inevitable result of this absurd ranking system has been a steep increase in the number of pointless questions such as: "Does Water Hydrate?" and "Does the Commission attribute the death of culture in France to its absorption in the EU?"[15]

---

[15] Maia de la Baume, "Do MEPs Ask Too Many Questions? Do They?" *Politico*, September 9, 2015.

Despite my reservations, I felt that the hemicycle in front of me was a noble vision. Legislators from 28 large and small member states and representing a broad array of political persuasions from extreme right to extreme left were assembled in one place to debate peacefully in 24 "official" languages. I found it irritating that the press corps, especially the British one, focused mostly on the parliament's more colorful, and less important features, rather than on the substantial amount of hard work put in by many dedicated parliamentarians.

I loved my regular visits to the European Parliament and always found my interactions with the parliamentarians to be worthwhile. On one of these visits, I was told that the Chinese ambassador to the EU had recently addressed the same group and had tartly observed when heckled: "You are here to listen to me, I am not here to listen to you." I made a point of starting my opening remarks by saying the reverse: "You are not here to listen to me, I am here to listen to you."

I found the European Parliament to be a temple of free speech, even accommodating the schoolyard antics of the far-right UK Independence Party and the French National Liberation Front, whose representatives regularly interrupted debates with insulting anti-EU tirades. Gianluca Buonanno, one of the MEPs from Italy's Northern League, showed up for a debate on anti-terrorism measures in full camouflage gear and sporting a black beret; on another occasion, he wore a shirt combining the faces of German Chancellor Angela Merkel and Adolf Hitler.

I found the Euro-parliamentarians to be a wonderfully diverse group, representing states that had provided the world with the greatest achievements in culture, science, and political thought. Many of these states, including long-standing and more recent members, had recently made the transition from authoritarian to democratic rule. In order to maintain a sense of solidarity, the most populous states (especially Germany) had agreed to be underrepresented so that the least populous states could be overrepresented—similar to the United States Senate. Malta and Luxembourg, for example, each have six parliamentarians for their populations of 450,000 and 600,000 respectively (one parliamentarian for every 80,000–100,000 people), whereas Germany has 96 parliamentarians for its population of 83 million (one parliamentarian for every 860,000 people).

That, of course, does not prevent Germany from playing a highly influential, if not dominant role, in European parliamentary politics; Germans have frequently occupied the posts of president and heads of the European People's Party and the Socialists and Democrats, the two main political groups, as well as senior positions in the European Parliament's civil service and in the key positions of committee chairs and rapporteurs who do the heavy lifting on legislative work.

"And Yet It Moves"

During the thirty years that I have followed EU affairs, I have always been more impressed by the bloc's promise than by its shortcomings. Influenced by my family history and by my time behind the Iron Curtain, I have never failed to appreciate the EU's role as an invisible and often underappreciated windowpane that lets the light in and keeps the cold air out.

My cautious optimism, even during the period of my diplomatic mission, proved justified: The euro did not fail; Greece did not leave the euro or the EU; even though Britain did decide to leave, this decision led to an unprecedented unity among the 27 remaining members; Schengen did not collapse; EU unity was maintained during the implementation and repeated renewal of sanctions on Russia; the refugee crisis was brought under control; economic growth (though still anemic in most countries) did return throughout the bloc and even outpaced US growth in 2016; populists were beaten back in key elections (although scoring strong results in Germany, Austria, Poland, and the Czech Republic); euro-skepticism receded in nearly every country; and following the election of President Emmanuel Macron in 2017, France started to implement sensible economic reforms and exert intellectual leadership that may revive the traditional Franco-German motor of European integration.

When some of my colleagues in the Obama administration complained to me that the European Union was hopelessly slow, I would quote a phrase uttered by Galileo Galilei after being forced by the Inquisition to recant his view that the earth revolves around the sun: "*Eppur si muove*" (And yet it moves). Similarly, the European Union does move, while appearing immobile. It has made significant progress on key legislation to improve banking union, a digital single market, energy union, the protection of external borders and internal security, and many other areas.

One of the toughest challenges of my diplomatic mission was to translate the European Union to the Washington bureaucracy. I often felt that some of my colleagues committed the fundamental error of seeing the EU as a static snapshot, rather than as a dynamic film. They were like people walking into a cinema in the middle of a film, observing a few frames of chaos, before concluding that the story would end in disaster. The problem was that few had much historical perspective on the European Union and they had little patience to understand its complicated institutional framework and occasionally impenetrable jargon. Few remembered how long it took the United States to achieve its union: It was not until 1863 that uniform national banknotes were introduced and not until 1913 that a Federal Reserve was created.

When colleagues in the administration asked me about the "President of Europe," I would have to explain that there are Presidents of the European Commission (the executive of the EU), the European Council (the body that organizes and sets strategy for the EU heads of government), the European Parliament (the directly elected assembly of parliamentarians), the Council (the body consisting of national ministers whose president in most configurations changes every six months), and finally the Eurogroup (the informal body that brings together ministers from the euro area to discuss matters relating to the euro). If anyone was still awake after that explanation, I would try to put her to sleep by explaining the difference between "implementing" and "delegated" legislative acts or the "comitology procedure" by which member states control how the European Commission implements EU law. I admit that this was cruel and unusual punishment.

The question about the "President of Europe" reminded me of the oft repeated, and almost certainly apocryphal, story that Secretary of State Henry Kissinger would ask "Whom do I call if I want to speak to Europe?" There has never been a single number and never will be in Europe, not even in Berlin, just as there is rarely a single number to dial in the United States, as most issues are handled in competing power centers in the administration and Congress. During the US–EU Summit meetings that were held during my diplomatic mission, I observed with some amusement the perplexity of our delegation about the officials sitting on the other side of the table: "Who *are* all these people and what exactly is it that they do?" (Fig. 2.7).

A Unique Superpower

My former colleagues in the National Security Council, who were happy to delegate all EU issues to me because they didn't care about them,

Fig. 2.7 EU–US Summit, March 26, 2014 (© European Union, 2014. EP—Audiovisual Service. *Photographer* Lieven Creemers. Reprinted with Permission)

made the mistake of judging the EU by the metric of hard power. In the mid-1990s, of course, the EU was unimpressive when judged this way. In 1991, Mark Eyskens, then Belgium's foreign minister, acknowledged that the EU was an "economic giant, a political dwarf and military worm." The woefully inadequate response of the EU to the breakup of Yugoslavia, despite the grandiloquent promise of Luxembourg's then foreign minister Jacques Poos that "this is the hour of Europe…not the hour of the Americans," would bear this out.

Since the early 1990s, the EU has matured dramatically. The EU has significantly improved its ability to speak with one voice and project influence in the world, thanks in large part to the institutional changes brought about in the Lisbon Treaty passed in 2009 after nearly a decade of acrimonious debate.

Although the EU remains *principally* a "soft power," it has a wide array of very effective tools—including the expansion of democracy and good governance through its enlargement process, technical assistance, and financial aid—that have made Europe, the region, and even the world a safer place. In many areas, including competition policy, trade, data privacy, and the digital economy, it is a superpower that sets global standards that affect millions of people's lives. I was repeatedly struck during my diplomatic mission that the top brass of the US military appreciates the importance of "soft power" very well, sometimes more so than our civilian leaders.

As part of the "Embassy training" that I received before arriving at my post, I and other ambassadorial appointees were flown down to MacDill Air Force Base in Tampa, Florida, where we received a briefing by Admiral William McCraven, the head of Special Operations Command (SOCOM). As the Admiral had led the raid on Osama Bin Laden and managed an elite fighting force destined for the most challenging military operations, I was expected a briefing focused on "hard power." But almost the entire briefing focused on how his command engaged in civilian missions such as the construction of schools, water treatment facilities, and other infrastructure in volatile parts of the world. The message was clear: The military was investing in "upstream" activities to stabilize unstable areas and minimize the danger of military intervention "downstream" when conflict might break out.

When I pointed out that SOCOM's mission overlaps with activities undertaken by the Department of State and US AID, the foreign aid department of the US government, McCraven gave a memorable reply:

> If I could take $1 billion out of my $7 billion budget and give it to the State Department and US AID, I would because these things are their main area of expertise. But I can't because Congress trusts people in uniform like me more than it trusts people in suits like you.

As I discovered subsequently, this was such a true statement: US diplomats are all too often wrongly considered by their own government as weak, too sympathetic to foreign countries and ineffective.

The European Union remains, therefore, an effective partner of the United States. Although I believed this already before my arrival in Brussels, I was impressed at the breadth and depth of the relationship that is far more important than any other relationship either side has elsewhere. That has been reflected in the fact that administrations on both sides of the aisle have, with rare exceptions, treated the EU as a serious diplomatic assignment. When I looked at the photographs of my predecessors in the lobby of the Mission, dating all the way back to 1961, I felt privileged to be in the same group.

While I knew that the US–EU relationship extended far beyond economic issues to encompass, for example, sanctions policy, foreign aid and humanitarian assistance, human rights, the fight against infectious diseases, climate change, and the promotion of anti-corruption and democratic institutions, it came as a surprise to me just how much we were doing together in areas such as law enforcement and military and security affairs.

I grasped the enormous breadth of our partnership with the EU when I looked at the organizational chart of the US–EU Mission in Brussels. I noticed that only half of the 180 staff members come from the State Department. The other half comes from nearly every US government department, including the Departments of Agriculture, Commerce, Treasury, Homeland Security, and Defense, as well as many agencies such as the Federal Aviation Agency and the Food and Drug Administration, and the Patent and Trademark Office. It has been one of the few embassies to be growing rather than shrinking under the pressure of budget cuts.

When I arrived in Brussels, I knew I would immediately meet all the people at the top of the EU hierarchy. But I knew from my prior government experience that it was just as important, if not more important, to know those within the bureaucracy who, regardless of title, get things done. I immediately contacted an old friend, Ana Palacio, former Spanish foreign minister and EU commissioner, to ask whether she could provide me with a list of such people. I called them "dentists" and told her a story to explain why.

When my Spanish wife and I wanted to get married in Toledo in 1997, we chose Santa Maria La Blanca, a former church and former synagogue, as the place where we wanted to celebrate the ceremony with a priest and a rabbi. Doing this proved to be extremely challenging because the place, a museum administered by the Archbishop of Toledo, did not permit religious ceremonies. When the Archbishop turned down our request, we asked my father, then serving as US ambassador to Spain, to inquire with the Spanish government's department of religious affairs, but without success. I asked the Prince of Asturias (now King of Spain), whom I had gotten to know in Washington during my government service, whether he could make inquiries. He was generous enough to do so but was unable to change the result.

Soon after receiving this bad news, my mother had lunch with a Spanish employee of the US Embassy to Spain. Upon hearing the tale, he replied that he might be able to lend a hand. Having solicited so many important people, my mother was rather skeptical and asked him to explain. "I know a dentist," he said. This was not terribly promising. But he explained further that the following week he was scheduled to see his dentist who was also the dentist of the Archbishop. The following week the employee reported that he had explained the situation to the dentist and that the dentist, by coincidence, was scheduled to see the Archbishop for a sensitive tooth extraction in a few days. I don't want to know what influence the dentist brought to bear; all I know is that the Archbishop agreed to the wedding. There have no other weddings celebrated since in Santa Maria La Blanca. The lesson has stayed with me: Sometimes in life it is not by scaling the hierarchy that you get things done, but rather by knowing the right people.

Upon my arrival in Brussels, I received a copy of a book by Peter Baldwin entitled *The Narcissism of Minor Differences: How America and Europe Are Alike*. Sigmund Freud had coined the phrase "the narcissism of minor differences" to account for the "intense energy invested in parsing divergences that, to an impartial observer, might seem trivial and inconsequential." Baldwin conducted an exhaustive statistical comparison of the United States and Europe on the economy, crime, health care, education, culture, religion, the environment, and many other areas. He concluded that, though there are some differences in views between Europe and America, in almost all cases these differences are not greater than the differences among European nations. The debate about purported ideological differences has "degenerated into ideological posturing, motivated by local politics and tactics... Vast cauldrons of rhetorical soup have been boiled from meagre scraps of evidence."[16]

While the election of Donald Trump has widened the Atlantic, I still believe that it is far smaller than widely believed. And it isn't too wide for broad, beautiful bridges.

---

[16] Peter Baldwin, *The Narcissism of Minor Differences* (Oxford University Press, 2010).

CHAPTER 3

Brexit

"It will be bloody brilliant," gushed Boris Johnson as we met again in the residence of the permanent representative (ambassador) of the UK to the European Union in mid-November 2016. When he noticed my quizzical look, he added: "Trump's victory is a huge opportunity for Britain; like Brexit, it is all about taking back control."

I thought the comment rather amusing in light of his earlier statement, well before Trump had emerged as a serious presidential candidate, that Trump displayed "stupefying ignorance" that made him "unfit" to be president.[1] His critics might observe that it was all rather normal behavior for a weathervane politician, adept at pointing in the direction of the prevailing wind. When Boris achieved his lifelong ambition to become Prime Minister in July 2019, President Trump paid Boris the ultimate accolade by calling him "Britain Trump." He was not the only one who found the two of them strikingly similar: *The Economist* magazine featured them on its cover as "Twitterdum" and "Twaddledee" dressed as Lewis Carroll's Tweedledum and Tweedledee.

Soon after becoming foreign secretary in July 2016 Boris had sought to make light of his earlier descriptions of Hillary Clinton as Lady Macbeth

---

[1] Matt Dathan, "Boris Johnson Says Donald Trump 'Betrays a Stupefying Ignorance That Makes Him Unfit to Be US President,'" *The Independent*, December 10, 2015. https://www.independent.co.uk/news/uk/politics/boris-johnson-says-donald-trump-betrays-a-stupefying-ignorance-that-makes-him-unfit-to-be-us-a6766871.html.

© The Author(s) 2020
A. L. Gardner, *Stars with Stripes*,
https://doi.org/10.1007/978-3-030-29966-8_3

and as a "sadistic nurse in a mental hospital."[2] Boris had also ascribed President Obama's warnings about Brexit to his "part-Kenyan heritage" and hence his "ancestral dislike of the British Empire."[3] Even this was rather tame stuff compared to his description of black people as "piccaninnies" with "watermelon smiles"[4] and a bawdy limerick he had penned for *The Spectator* suggesting that Turkish President Erdoğan enjoyed copulating with goats.[5] These comments would have been more than enough to destroy any other mortal politician, but they appeared to enhance his appeal.

My friend and former colleague Sir Ivan Rogers, the UK's highly capable ambassador to the EU (before resigning in early 2017 in exasperation at his government's Brexit policy), had organized my reunion with Boris as part of a series of meetings in Brussels aimed at educating the newly minted foreign minister about the challenges of Brexit. A few days before our reunion, Boris had prophesied that Britain would make a "titanic success" out of Brexit. Perhaps he was unaware that the Titanic sank, with more than 1500 lives lost due to criminal irresponsibility[6] (Fig. 3.1).

I explained to Boris why the Obama administration had serious concerns about the impact of Brexit on the United States and the European Union; why I thought Her Majesty's Government appeared to be misreading the mood in the EU; and why the likely trajectory of the exit negotiations would be more challenging than he thought. He would have none of it. "We've broken free into a wide world of possibilities. If the EU thinks it can lock the UK in a dungeon and give us a good kicking on our way out, they are deeply misguided."

I objected to that description, stating that the EU was not out to punish the UK. For nearly three decades, I have negotiated deals in the private and public sectors. I suggested to Boris that in any negotiation it

---

[2] Boris Johnson, "I Want Hillary Clinton to Be President," *Telegraph*, November 1, 2007.

[3] Boris Johnson, "UK and America Can Be Better Friends Than Ever—If We LEAVE the EU," *The Sun*, April 22, 2016.

[4] Stephanie Busari, "'Watermelon smiles' and 'piccaninnies': What Boris Johnson has said previously about people in Africa," *CNN*, July 24, 2019. https://www.cnn.com/2019/07/23/africa/boris-johnson-africa-intl/index.html.

[5] Douglas Murray, "Boris Johnson wins The Spectator's President Erdogan Offensive Poetry competition," *The Spectator*, May 18, 2016. https://blogs.spectator.co.uk/2016/05/boris-johnson-wins-the-spectators-president-erdogan-offensive-poetry-competition/.

[6] Jessica Elgo, "Brexit will be titanic success, says Boris Johnson," *The Guardian*, November 3, 2016. https://www.theguardian.com/politics/2016/nov/03/brexit-will-be-titanic-success-says-boris-johnson.

Fig. 3.1 Ambassador Gardner and Boris Johnson, then UK foreign secretary, at their reunion in November 2016 (*Source* From author's own collection)

is important to be aware of the red lines of the party sitting across the table and to have a realistic understanding of one's own leverage. Ignoring these would be a pathway to disaster. Negotiating with the EU would require serious preparation and strategic thinking, not the improvisation and glib self-confidence that often sufficed in student debates at Oxford University. I could hear Sir Ivan chuckling in the background. He would later deplore the UK government's "tutorial-level plausible bullshit" and "supreme self-confidence that we understand others' real interests better than they do."[7]

There was no way, I argued, that the EU would treat the UK better as a departing member than it would treat the remaining 27 members; even the smallest EU members, especially Ireland with the only land border of the EU with the UK, would matter more than the UK. The EU would

[7] Simon Kuper, "How Oxford University Shaped Brexit—And Britain's Next Prime Minister," *Financial Times*, June 21, 2019. https://www.ft.com/content/85fc694c-9222-11e9-b7ea-60e35ef678d2.

always have a "hierarchy of interests" in which self-preservation and the continued existence and development of the union, anchored in the indivisibility of the rights and obligations of the single market, would always take precedence.

There was no way the UK could "cherry pick" its rights and obligations. Allowing the UK to get a custom-made deal, with all the benefits and few of the burdens of EU membership, was pure fantasy as this would encourage other EU member states to get their own custom-made deals. The UK could not transition from membership with significant opt-outs from EU obligations to non-membership with significant opt-ins to EU rights. Sir Ivan agreed:

> Once you leave the EU, you cannot from just outside the fence achieve all the benefits you got just inside it…That is unavoidable. It is not vindictive…it is just ineluctable reality.[8]

Berlin and Rome would not ride to London's rescue to protect their exports of motor vehicles and prosecco, as Boris had quipped. Believing that Germany and Italy consider the EU as merely a trading bloc and would let their industries set Brexit policy was a basic misreading of the facts. Moreover, the process of withdrawal set forth in the EU treaties had been purposefully slanted to favor the EU, and it would be wise to recall that the EU's economic and political weight was vastly greater than that of the UK.

BORIS TURNS THE TIDE OF THE BREXIT REFERENDUM

Boris had recently penned a biography of Winston Churchill, presumably in the hope of inviting comparisons of himself with the great statesman.[9] Some of his critics might argue that he is the most un-Churchillian character imaginable: self-serving, undisciplined, and with no discernible moral compass. These critics might point out that Churchill would not have misled the Queen and prorogued parliament on false pretenses, as the Supreme Court suggested he had done in a historic judgment in September 2019.

---

[8] Speech at the University of Liverpool, "Brexit: Nine Lessons to Learn," December 13, 2018. http://www.astrid-online.it/static/upload/roge/rogers_brexit-speech_13_12_18.pdf.

[9] Boris Johnson, *The Churchill Factor: How One Man Made History* (Riverhead Books, 2014).

Fig. 3.2 Boris Johnson stuck on a zip line (© Kois Miah/Barcroft Media, 2012. Reprinted with Permission)

Several years ago, I attended a performance of Donizetti's opera *The Elixir of Love* in which Dulcamara, a traveling quack doctor, convinces the hapless character Nemorino to withdraw his life's savings to buy a bottle of a magical potion (in reality a bottle of cheap wine). My companion at the opera reminded me that during the Brexit referendum campaign Boris had traveled the length and breadth of the UK in a red bus to convince voters to leave the EU. Emblazoned on the sides of the bus was the claim that Brexit would save the UK £350 million per week (£18 billion per year), money that could be invested in the National Health Service (Fig. 3.2).

The claim was like cheap wine labeled as an elixir: The UK was sending £13 billion gross per year to the EU, but received £4.5 billion in regional and agricultural subsidies, and the private sector received a further £1.4 billion directly from the EU budget. The net £7 billion figure was not much more than what Norway, a non-EU member, was paying into the EU budget per year for the privilege of frictionless access to the single market. Membership of the European Union costs citizens, including British ones, less than a cup of coffee per day.[10]

I did not hide my disagreement with everything that Boris said. I subscribed entirely with the judgment of Martin Wolf, columnist for the *Financial Times*, that the Brexit referendum was "the most irresponsible act by a British government in my lifetime."[11] Donald Tusk, President of the European Council, had gone much further, stating that there is a "special place in hell" for those who had pushed Brexit without a plan. I had been struck, both during and after the referendum, that a significant constituency in the UK—a country well-known for its cool pragmatism and rationality—was acting rather like the emotional Greeks had done earlier when the Syriza government had refused to cooperate with the EU on its proposed bailout.

Greece had shown nationalistic defiance of the EU's demands, before ultimately accepting the bailout under far worse terms after the Greek economy had collapsed. The Syriza government had radically overestimated its negotiating leverage and underestimated the unity of the EU 27; it had wrongly assumed that it could gain more favorable bailout terms because a Greek exit from the euro would be more damaging for the EU 27 than for Greece. In a twist worthy of a Greek tragedy, Prime Minister Tsipras warned Brexiteers to learn from Greece's mistakes and understand that chauvinist nationalism does not solve a country's problems.[12]

Some Brexiteers overestimated the UK's negotiating leverage and assumed that a divided EU would splinter and give the UK what it wanted in order to keep running a healthy trade surplus. Justice Minister Michael Gove chirpily predicted that the UK would "hold all the cards" the day after it voted to leave. David Davis, secretary in charge of Brexit at the time, declared that "There will be no downside to Brexit, only a considerable upside." Whatever one's views of Brexit, those comments were manifestly false.

The Brexiteers were happy to stoke a national mood of defiance, talking up the attractions of "no deal." But by making almost no concrete preparations for such an outcome they rendered the threat

---

[10] Ryan Heath and Hanne Cokelaere, "The Cappuccino Index," *Politico*, January 16, 2018.

[11] Martin Wolf, "The Self-Inflicted Dangers of the EU Referendum," *Financial Times*, May 26, 2016.

[12] Tony Barber and Kerin Hope, "Brexit Shows Flaws of 'Nationalistic' Politics, Says Greek PM," *Financial Times*, April 23, 2019. https://www.ft.com/content/cca5ee6c-6429-11e9-a79d-04f350474d62.

completely unconvincing. While EU unity held, the UK government was in an embarrassing state of internal division. As a result, they were ultimately doomed to accept harsh realities under far worse conditions for a divorce than those that could have prevailed earlier. Under both the Grexit and Brexit scenarios, it would inevitably be the more economically vulnerable members of society who would bear the greatest economic brunt of demagogic populism.

Boris was arguably one of the critical reasons why the Leave campaign had galvanized into an effective force. Although the US Embassy in London had consistently predicted that the UK would vote to remain, Sir Ivan had been right to warn me that Boris's surprise decision to back Leave had seriously increased the risks of a different outcome. News in late May 2016 that net immigration in 2015 had hit 330,000, the second highest figure on record and far higher than the "tens of thousands" that Prime Minister Cameron had repeatedly promised, had also strengthened the hand of those who claimed (falsely) that EU membership was responsible for the EU's inability to control its external borders and maintain sound health and social services. Sir Ivan reminded me that unlike the prior UK referendum on EU membership in 1975, when Britain's economy was performing far worse than that of Europe, the situation had now reversed and Europe was therefore looking less attractive.

Many of us in the Obama administration were worried that a referendum had been called in the first place: History was full of examples of referenda being determined by factors totally unrelated to the question posed. It was completely predictable that the real question—are British citizens willing to pay an economic price of losing privileged access to the UK's most valuable market in their desire to repatriate notional "sovereignty"?—would never be debated properly. Other issues, above all immigration and nationalist sentiment, would inevitably dominate. In the case of the In/Out referendum on Europe, not only was the UK's membership in the EU at stake, but also potentially Scotland's place in the UK. Scotland favored continued membership in the EU and had repeatedly threatened to hold another referendum on independence if the UK chose to leave. Why take that monumental risk?

We were also perplexed at the manner in which Cameron had called the referendum. Perhaps the decision was not just about uniting the Tory Party by throwing more red meat to the influential euro-skeptics; the Prime Minister clearly felt that the party had to protect itself against the risk that the UK Independence Party could win seats in conservative districts in the upcoming election. And he genuinely did seem to feel that the

British people were owed a clear vote on the EU because it had evolved significantly since the last UK referendum 40 years ago.

But we were scratching our heads at why on earth he had agreed that the outcome of a referendum would be determined by a straight majority rather than a super-majority. Why decide that the referendum would be binding on the government when it was purely advisory? Why deprive 16- and 17-year-olds the right to vote when they had been able to do so in the Scottish referendum on independence and when this age group had so much at stake in the outcome? Why deprive British expats the right to vote if they had lived more than 15 years outside the UK? And why on earth allow sitting cabinet members to openly oppose the government's pro-Remain position without sanction? To top it all off, the Prime Minister was attempting a rather uncomfortable ideological conversion that the public greeted with predictable skepticism: While he had long sniped at the EU as an ineffective power-hungry bureaucratic machine run amok, he was suddenly professing his conclusion that membership provided important economic and security benefits. Turning lead into gold overnight would have been as likely as alchemy.

Briefing the Secretary

Boris was in a good mood that mid-November afternoon, despite our differences. I had introduced him a few months earlier to Secretary John Kerry when both had attended a breakfast meeting in Brussels for the foreign ministers of the EU 28. When he and Boris appeared before journalists in London later that day, the secretary stated that I had "regaled" him over dinner the night before with stories about my experiences with Boris at Oxford University and during our early careers in Brussels and later in London. "[Our ambassador to the EU] told me that this man is a very smart and capable man," he said, pointing at Boris. "That's the Boris Johnson I intend to work with…" That line provided Boris with some sorely needed air cover after some serious journalistic bombardment about his past. Johnson looked relieved: "Phew, I can live with that." Kerry laughed, approached Boris and told him with a wry smile: "It's called diplomacy."[13]

---

[13] Carol Morello, "Kerry Meets with Boris Johnson, and It's a Friendly but at Times Awkward Affair," *The Washington Post*, July 19, 2016.

I had indeed regaled the secretary with stories about Boris during our dinner the evening before the breakfast meeting in June. I had recounted how I had met Boris at Balliol College, Oxford, in 1986. Even in those early years, Boris had exhibited many of the traits that would define his behavior as foreign minister (and subsequently Prime Minister). I later sent my observations in a confidential cable to a restricted group at the White House and State Department. President Obama apparently enjoyed it.

I first met Boris soon after his appointment as president of the prestigious Oxford Union debating society, a traditional launchpad for aspiring British politicians. It was a few days after President Ronald Reagan had ordered missile strikes against Tripoli in April 1986. Boris appeared on my doorstep late one evening and asked whether I would consider opposing the motion in an upcoming Oxford Union debate: "This House Condemns American Imperialism and Aggression in Libya." Although I disliked President Reagan's politics, I agreed out of conviction that the strike was justified. At my maiden speech at the Oxford Union, I complimented Boris on his appointment as president. As I knew that Boris was studying classics, I teased him that his appointment was the finest since the Roman Emperor Caligula had named his horse a consul.

As Secretary Kerry and I enjoyed some of Belgium's fabled cuisine, I described how Boris had pretended not to really want to be president of the Union, while desperately campaigning for it. Even in those early days, he was intensely competitive and clearly interested in politics. In order to be elected in the anti-elitist left-wing atmosphere of those years, he needed to gloss over his ambition, education at Eton, upper-class friendships and privileged upbringing. He clearly aimed for the highest office but couldn't show it. In one of his typical, self-deprecating dissimulations, he said in a 2012 appearance on the Late Show with David Letterman: "My chances of being PM are about as good as finding Elvis on Mars, or my being reincarnated as an olive." It appears that one can indeed find Elvis on Mars or be reincarnated as an olive.

Boris was an accomplished performer in the Oxford Union where I thought that a premium was placed on rapier wit rather than any fidelity to the facts. It was a perfect training ground for those planning to be professional amateurs. I recall how many poor American students were skewered during debates when they rather ploddingly read out statistics; albeit accurate and often relevant in their argumentation, they would be jeered by the crowds with cries of "boring" or "facts"! This was the environment in which Boris thrived: The crowd yearned for politics as entertainment.

Boris and I overlapped in Brussels in the early 1990s when I was an intern in the antitrust division of the European Commission and then a lawyer with an international law firm, while he was a correspondent for the *Daily Telegraph*.[14] According to multiple press reports, he had just been fired from his first reporting job at *The Times* of London for inventing a quote. A decade later he was removed from his posts as Conservative Party Vice-Chairman and shadow arts minister based on allegations that he had dismissed as "an inverted pyramid of piffle." This Houdini-like escape from failure may have convinced him that the laws of gravity only apply to others and that he could charm his way to the top during his entire life. Boris's father, Stanley Johnson, a former European Commission official, wrote a thinly fictionalized account of Brexit in which one of the characters, an "ebullient, blond-haired former Mayor of London," could be serious "if it was absolutely necessary."[15] But was it ever really necessary?

In a lengthy article for the *Daily Telegraph* in mid-March 2016 announcing his decision to back the Leave campaign, he claimed to have "informed" his readers in the early 1990s about the dangers of one-size-fits-all "euro-condoms" and the "great war against the British prawn cocktail flavour crisp." He had indeed reported on these stories, but they were almost entirely fictitious. I always suspected that he knew the truth: He had partly grown up in Brussels, had attended the European School, and was the son of an accomplished Eurocrat.

Old habits die hard. In the final weeks of Boris's successful campaign to become Prime Minister in July 2019 he argued that if Britain were to leave the EU without a deal, it would be able to negotiate a free trade agreement with the EU during the "implementation period." But there was a bit of a snag, as Deputy Prime Minister David Lidington pointed out: That period was part of the Withdrawal Agreement that Prime Minister May had negotiated with the EU. In the event of no deal, there would

---

[14] His boss at the time, Max Hastings, has written: "There is room for debate about whether he is a scoundrel or mere rogue, but not much about his moral bankruptcy, rooted in a contempt for truth." Max Hastings, "I Was Boris Johnson's Boss: He Is Utterly Unfit to Be Prime Minister," *The Guardian*, June 24, 2019.

[15] Stanley Johnson, *Kompromat* (Oneworld Publications, 2017).

be no Withdrawal Agreement and hence no "implementation period." Boris did not see any reason to retract the statement.

Boris later went on to claim that the UK could negotiate a standstill arrangement with the EU, continuing their zero tariff and zero quota arrangements, even after leaving the EU with no deal because of an obscure article of the World Trade Organization rules. But there was a bit of a snag, as anyone with a basic understanding of WTO rules realized: The article only applies to goods and not to services (40% of the UK's exports to the EU) and only if there is an agreement between the parties to move toward a free trade agreement. The EU would have no incentive, quite obviously, to offer the UK frictionless access to its market if the UK left without a deal and without paying its bills. Boris saw no reason to retract the statement.

In a speech delivered in the Isle of Man shortly thereafter, he dramatically brandished a plastic-wrapped kipper and attacked outrageous EU red tape for regulating the smoking of kippers and requiring them to be transported in "ice pillows." The crowd loved it. But there was a bit of a snag, as 60 seconds of fact-checking on the Internet would have revealed: The Isle of Man is not in the EU and the EU does not make rules on the packaging of smoked fish. The rules, it turns out, were made in the UK. Why bother with the facts when making stuff up is so much more fun?

Decades earlier his steady stream of euro-myths had launched an industry that continues to this day in the British tabloid press. In 1994, *The Sun* also reported that the EU was mandating smaller condom sizes, refusing to accommodate for what they believed were "larger British assets."[16] The EU helpfully explained that the standardization work on condoms carried about by the European Committee on Standardization (not an EU body) was voluntary and related to "quality and not to length."

I told Secretary Kerry that I had a folder on my desk in Brussels that bulged with similarly amusing non-stories, including the purported efforts of the European Commission to ban barmaids' cleavages[17] (apparently more spectacular in Britain), prohibit the sale of traditional British sausages and the recycling of tea bags and prevent children under eight years old from blowing up balloons. My personal favorites, however, were the story in *The Sun* (under the headline "Hair Hitlers") that devilish

---

[16] *The Sun*, October 19, 1994.
[17] "Hands Off Our Barmaids' Boobs," *The Sun*, August 4, 2005.

eurocrats were scheming to ban hairdressers from wearing high heels[18] and the story in *The Sunday Express* that the same eurocrats were plotting to "carve up Britain" by merging southern England and northern France into a territory called "Arc Manche."[19]

While it was tempting to laugh all of this off as merely good, harmless fun by tabloids hoping to boost sales, the steady drip-feeding of denigrating stories about the EU had seeped into the wider British consciousness. Boris had created the monster of euro-skepticism and many in the Conservative Party had caressed and fed the monster for years. It was possible to ignore it until it put on serious weight and started thrashing about.

When the Leave campaigners released a film featuring a standard "EU regulated man" waking up from sleeping on an "EU regulated pillow" (five EU laws about pillowcases, 109 about the pillow inside) to turn off his "EU regulated" alarm clock (11 laws) and enter his "EU regulated" bathroom (65 laws) to use his "EU regulated" toothbrush (31 laws), it was widely believed. Never mind that the references to EU laws were in fact simply the result of hits following a simple search on the EU's legal database. Fiction had become fact.

While we were tucking into our dessert, I told Secretary Kerry that Boris's experience in Brussels had been formative. He knew that his writing in Brussels was having an impact, even though he was only 26. In a later interview, he admitted:

> I was just chucking those rocks over the garden wall and listening to this amazing crash from the greenhouse next door over in England...Everything I wrote from Brussels was having this amazing explosive effect on the Tory Party, and it really gave me this, I suppose, rather weird sense of power.[20]

In my opinion, he had understood that covering European Community affairs in a factual way was altogether too taxing and would be a career dead end; so he simply decided to make it entertaining, thereby gaining

---

[18] Tom Newton Dunn, "Hair Hitlers: EU Rules to Ban Hairdressers from Wearing Rings and Heels," *The Sun*, April 9, 2012.

[19] Macer Hall, "EU Wants to Merge UK with France," *The Sunday Express*, May 2, 2011.

[20] Interview on BBC Radio, as reported by Estelle Shirbon and William Schonberg, "From Brussels Bashing to Brexit, Boris Bets Against EU," *Reuters*, March 1, 2016.

notoriety and a wide readership. Those early years as a correspondent shaped his subsequent relationship with the media and with the facts. He brilliantly sensed the power of "alternative facts" decades before the Trump administration did so. As he subsequently noted with candor:

> It is possible to have a pretty good life and career being a leech and parasite in the media world, gadding about from TV studio to TV studio writing inconsequential pieces and having a good time.[21]

I told Secretary Kerry that, according to some critics, Boris believes in three main things. First, he believes in himself and his self-advancement. According to news reports, he had as foreign secretary penned a draft Remain-backing article for the *Daily Telegraph* before deciding to publish an article with exactly contrary views in favor of Brexit.[22] In his memoirs released in September 2019, David Cameron claimed that Boris "didn't believe in Brexit" but decided to back it in order to bolster his popularity among party activists. Perish the thought.

Second, I told the secretary that Boris believes that the normal rules don't apply to him, meaning that he can have the best of any two worlds. He had himself said that "My policy on cake is pro having it and pro eating it."[23] Lesser mortals must choose. The UK will eventually discover the consequences of "cakeist" policies. Unfortunately for Marie-Antoinette, her quip about letting people eat cake didn't work out too well for her.

Boris had succeeded brilliantly by creating an entertaining and instantly recognizable Brand as a disheveled and charming performer, with P. G. Wodehousian turns of phrase and self-deprecating humor. He understood earlier than most that in a world of sensory overload, Brands play a critical role in capturing attention. In some ways, I explained, he has tried to be the Oscar Wilde of his generation: outrageous, witty and always the subject of conversation. As Wilde had once remarked: "There is only one

---

[21] Alice Audley, "Boris Johnson's top 50 quotes," *The Telegraph*, June 18, 2014. https://www.telegraph.co.uk/news/politics/london-mayor-election/mayor-of-london/10909094/Boris-Johnsons-top-50-quotes.html.

[22] Jessica Elgot, "Secret Boris Johnson Column Favoured UK Remaining in EU," *The Guardian*, October 16, 2016. https://www.theguardian.com/politics/2016/oct/16/secret-boris-johnson-column-favoured-uk-remaining-in-eu.

[23] Steven Poole, "'Cake': Europe's new codeword for Britain's impossible Brexit demands," *The Guardian*, July 5, 2018. https://www.theguardian.com/books/2018/jul/05/word-of-the-week-cake.

thing in life worse than being talked about, and that is not being talked about."

When Secretary Kerry asked me how he should deal with his British counterpart, I advised that he could offer Boris guidance and international credibility in the hope of encouraging his statesmanship. Perhaps Boris would see his high-profile job as an opportunity to break free from the chains of his Brand to become what he may have been secretly craving to become for years: a respected figure on the world stage. Perhaps behind the Brand there lurks someone who desperately wants recognition as a serious intellectual. Perhaps the secretary could encourage the hidden Boris Johnson—the intelligent, creative, articulate one—to emerge. In Shakespeare's *Henry IV* Part II, Prince Hal stops making merry in the pub with Falstaff to emerge as a leader to help his country in times of crisis. Optimists believe that Boris can do the same.

DICTATORSHIP AND VASSALAGE

I never expected Boris to change his tune on the EU, however. On the widely watched Andrew Marr television show, Boris had described the EU as a "jail where the jailor has accidentally left the door open." This was tame compared to his statement that the EU's ambitions were similar to those of Adolf Hitler. When facts prove stubbornly uncooperative, it is always useful to invoke World War II. Not to be outdone, Michael Gove had compared the economists who had warned against Brexit to Nazi propagandists against Albert Einstein. This was well-calibrated to appeal to the millions of Britons who consume an endless amount of television documentaries about the war.

World War II was not the only historical reference point in the Brexiteers' arsenal. In the spring of 2016, I was called to testify before the UK House of Commons Select Committee on Brexit to give the Obama administration's view on how Brexit would impact UK–US and EU–US relations. After I had finished describing why the US considered the EU a significant and effective partner, and that Brexit would negatively impact both, one of the committee's members, MP Andrew Rosindell, shook his head and said that I was woefully misinformed: "Mr. Ambassador, the EU is a totalitarian super state and it is time for the UK to break free, just as you Americans broke free from the British Empire." All Britain needed was a Paul Revere to lead a British rebellion against the EU's red coats and King Jean-Claude Juncker.

But Biblical references sound so much more authoritative than mere comparisons to the American Revolutionary War. In March 2019, Boris declared that it was time to "channel the spirit of Moses in Exodus and say to Pharaoh in Brussels – Let my people go."[24] Presumably he didn't mean to suggest that Brexiteers would spend forty years wandering in the desert before reaching the Promised Land of milk and honey—or perhaps, more appropriately, fish and chips.

One of my more deliciously bizarre moments occurred in 2015 when I was attending an oral hearing at the European Court of Justice in Luxembourg. A case had been lodged by two UK members of parliament against the UK's surveillance law called the Data Retention and Investigatory Powers Act. I was astonished to see one of the complainants, none other than the arch-Brexiteer David Davis. He had railed against the outrage of the EU imposing its writ on the UK; and yet there he was, having brought a case that invoked the EU Charter of Fundamental Rights to strike down legislation of his own government. Like Alice in Wonderland, I muttered: "Curiouser and curiouser."

I didn't think things could get any more Monty Pythonesque until I saw Anne Widdecombe, newly elected MEP for Nigel Farage's Brexit Party, compare Brexit in her maiden speech at the European Parliament in July 2019 to prior uprisings of "slaves against their owners, the peasantry against the feudal barons, colonies…against their empires…" She seemed unaware that in the hemicycle of the European Parliament there were many representatives of countries that considered the EU to be a liberator and a guarantor of democracy. The Brexit MEPs were, of course, perfectly free not to attend the European Parliament or pick up their generous paychecks. The reason Britain was still a member of the EU more than two years after serving notice to leave was not because the EU had locked the doors but because the British political system had been hopelessly deadlocked.

The UK tabloids regularly railed against "dictatorial Brussels" and the "ever-expanding super-state" employing armies of bureaucrats at huge expense. The Open Europe think tank had continued to perpetrate the myth that 170,000 people work for the EU institutions, twice as many as for the British Army. In reality, 33,000 people are employed by the European Commission; in the European Parliament around 7500 people work in the general secretariat and in the political groups (on top of the 751

---

[24] *Daily Telegraph*, March 25, 2019.

members elected officials and their small staffs); and about 3500 people work in the general secretariat of the Council. By contrast, the UK employs 409,000 civil servants (excluding security personnel), nearly ten times the number of civil servants employed by the EU.

While there was doubtless significant waste, this has been largely due to member states and not the EU itself. By a three to one majority, members of the European Parliament voted to establish a single seat in Brussels, thereby ending the monthly shuttling of people and documents between Brussels and Strasbourg that costs roughly £100 million per year. The vast European Parliament buildings in Strasbourg, which I visited seven times over my three years, lie vacant about 320 days per year when the four-day monthly sessions are not being held. But under pressure from Strasbourg, which gets a £20 million annual economic boost per year from the traveling circus, France has exercised its right under the EU treaties to veto plans for a single seat.

Member states, and not the EU, are also responsible for the stratospheric costs of translation. The right to speak in one's own language generates 380 language permutations and an annual translation and interpretation bill of 1 billion euros; it has also resulted in Gaelic and Maltese being recognized, although no more than five MEPs have the fluency to speak in Gaelic and nearly every one of the 450,000 Maltese (0.07% of the EU total) speaks English.

The rabid Brexiteers often liked to pretend that their hero, Prime Minister Margaret Thatcher, would have similarly rebelled against a tyrannical union. But that was not at all clear. She had agreed to a vast increase in qualified majority voting and, with Lord Cockfield, played a role in the EU's vast regulatory exercise of creating the single market. Her famous speech at the College of Europe in Bruges, often invoked as the first rallying cry of euro-skeptics, actually contained a rather interesting passage:

> Britain does not dream of some cosy, isolated existence on the fringes of the European Community. Our destiny is in Europe, as part of the community.

When I heard the Brexiteers' cartoon-strip caricatures of the EU, I was often reminded of a wonderful scene in Monty Python's *Life of Brian* in which the members of the Judean People's Front are meeting secretly. The leader asks: "What have the Romans ever done for us? They've bled us white, the bastards. They've taken everything we had, and not just from us, from our fathers, and from our fathers' fathers." One activist tentatively suggests that the Romans did, after all, give them the aqueduct. A second adds: sanitation. A third adds: roads. Others chime in: irrigation, medicine, education, health, wine, and public baths. The EU can't take credit for roads, sanitation and so on, of course. But it can certainly take credit for a great number of good things. The trouble was that successive Conservative governments never challenged the anti-EU caricatures in order to ensure that the wider public was aware of the benefits of EU membership.

Mark Twain once said that "It's not what people don't know that causes all the trouble; it's what they know for sure that just ain't so." Nigel Farage, the head of the UK Independence Party, famously declared that "we are not governed from Westminster, we are governed from Brussels." At the House of Commons Select Committee that I attended, MPs Andrew Rosindell and Daniel Kawczynski declared that over half of the UK's laws were imposed on London by Brussels. With the same flair for factual accuracy, Kawczynski later tweeted that the UK never received any of the aid disbursed by the Marshall Plan as it all went to Germany. In fact, the UK was the primary beneficiary, receiving 26% of the funds while West Germany got 11%.

David Campbell Bannerman, British Member of the European Parliament, repeatedly claimed that between *50* and *80%* of the UK's laws come from the EU. These laws represent "bureaucratic diktats from Eurocrats" and "huge transfers of sovereignty to the EU" that sideline the "Mother of all Parliaments" at Westminster.[25] Campbell Bannerman later called for anyone guilty of "EU loyalty" to be tried under the Treason Act. I had images of myself being escorted by a Beefeater to the gallows at the Tower of London.

Boris himself had warned about the "slow and invisible process of legal colonisation."[26] In his resignation letter in July 2018, he claimed that the Prime Minister's Brexit plan of maintaining regulatory alignment with the EU in goods and agriculture (not services) in order to maintain some key advantages of the single market meant that Britain was "truly headed for the status of a colony."

---

[25] David Campbell Bannerman, *Time to Jump: A Positive Vision of Britain Out of the EU* (Bretwalda Books, 2013).

[26] Boris Johnson, "There Is Only One Way to Get the Change We Want—Vote to Leave the EU," *Daily Telegraph*, March 16, 2016.

Charges of colonization succeeded in grabbing media attention. Alas, they were fiction. In 2010, a House of Commons Research Paper concluded that from 1997 to 2009 6.8% of primary legislation (statutes) and 14.1% of secondary legislation (statutory instruments) had a role in implementing EU obligations "although the degree of involvement varied from passing reference to explicit implementation."[27] Even if one were to take into account EU obligations that are not usually transposed into legislation at national level, the percentage would probably fall well short of 50%.

Along with many others in the Obama administration, I simply could not understand the repeated argument that Britain had become a vassal state and that it was necessary to "take back control" over borders, money, and laws. Even Prime Minister May, who had backed Remain as a minister, apparently felt obliged to repeat the mantra that Britain needed to become a "fully independent, sovereign country" and that leaving the EU was the only way to achieve this.

One of the more bizarre aspects to this argument is that many of its proponents pointed to Norway as a model of how one could be a sovereign state and still benefit from the EU single market. One supposedly authoritative commentator, Roger Bootle, has claimed that Norway only adopts a small percentage of EU legislation.[28] The reality is that, according to an independent study commissioned by the Norwegian government, the country has had to incorporate approximately three-quarters of all EU laws into its domestic legislation (without having any vote in EU affairs) as a price of continued frictionless access to the EU single market. And that is on top of being a major contributor to the EU budget.

The "take back control" argument was part of an effort to sell the British public a halcyon past in which Britain stood tall, carried weight in the world, and had far fewer foreigners living within its borders. Unlike most politicians who win elections by selling visions of the future, the Brexit leaders were actually selling visions of the past—one seen through seriously rose-tinted glasses. The Brexiteers understood very well that, as Philip Stephens of the *Financial Times* put it, "People who have lost

---

[27] House of Commons Research Paper 10/62, "How Much Legislation Comes from Europe?" October 13, 2010.

[28] Roger Bootle, *The Trouble with Europe* (Nicholas Brealey Publishing, 2014), p. 157.

faith in the future are seeking solace in old, imagined, certainties."[29] It is no wonder that the highest percentage of support for Brexit was to be found in the older generation, some of whom may have yearned for an imagined England—Anglo-Saxon and dotted with pristine cricket fields. When I heard the speeches of some Brexiteers, I was repeatedly reminded of Miss Havisham, the character in Charles Dickens's *Great Expectations*, who tried to defy time by stopping the clocks and living alone in her dark crumbling mansion.

Taking Back Control

The "take back control" argument has suckered not only many voters in the UK, but apparently also key members of the Trump administration. The president himself has referred to the EU as an "anchor" around the UK's ankle. National Security Adviser John Bolton argued that the EU elites treat citizens like "peasants" and that a post-Brexit "newly independent Britain" should be welcomed as if Britain had been anything other than independent as a member of the EU. It is rather unlikely, to say the least, that the other 27 EU member states consider the EU to be a millstone (otherwise they would have left) or are deluded in thinking that they are anything but independent.

Robin Niblett, director of Britain's leading foreign policy think tank, the Royal Institute for International Affairs (Chatham House), demolished the "take back control" argument in a well-researched study:

> Apart from EU immigration, the British government still determines the vast majority of policy over every issue of greatest concern to British voters – including health, education, pensions, welfare, monetary policy, defence and border security. The arguments for leaving also ignore the fact that the UK controls more than 98% of its public expenditure.[30]

Moreover, the overwhelming majority of the EU legislation "inflicted" on Britain has actually been passed frequently with the UK's consent, if not with its encouragement.

---

[29] Philip Stephens, "Nostalgia Has Stolen the Future," *Financial Times*, July 25, 2018.

[30] Robin Niblett, "Britain, the EU and the Sovereignty Myth," Chatham House, May 2016. https://www.chathamhouse.org/sites/default/files/publications/research/2016-05-09-britain-eu-sovereignty-myth-niblett.pdf.

The story of the European directive setting maximum noise levels for garden lawnmowers is instructive. When euro-skeptic Tory MPs learned about this piece of legislation, they were appalled and cited it as evidence of overreach by Brussels. How dare those nameless, faceless, and overpaid eurocrats interfere with the God-given rights of the British to mow their lawns noisily? The trouble with the story is that Her Majesty's Government had not opposed the legislation, but rather voted in favor of it in order to protect a level playing field within the single market. The legislation prevented Germany from setting low maximum decibel limits that would have excluded noisier British imported lawnmowers. What the euro-skeptics failed to understand, moreover, is that the European Commission did not inflict the legislation on the hapless British; it had been approved by national governments. A paradox of the EU is that in order to liberalize the circulation of goods and services throughout the EU it is necessary to regulate and therefore interfere in the affairs of the member states.[31]

As I watched the campaigning leading up to the Brexit referendum, I thought that the "take back control" argument could be easily rebutted. I was puzzled why Cameron and the Remain campaign were not being more assertive on this point. After all, the government's own "EU Balance of Competences" review concluded—in 32 voluminous and detailed reports published in 2013 and 2014—that nearly all the powers exercised by the EU were broadly beneficial to Britain. Rather wonkishly, I had read a fair number of the reports and asked our Mission to the EU to report to Washington on them. Even in the sacred area of financial services, the reports had concluded that the EU had not usurped powers that belonged by right to the UK. Instead of shouting the results of this monumental effort from the rooftops, the government bizarrely chose to bury it. One possible reason is that Cameron did not want to annoy the euro-skeptics in his party and cabinet.

The argument that the EU had undermined British parliamentary democracy was also bizarre because successive British governments had rightly decided to pool certain aspects of Britain's sovereign powers in the EU in order to achieve national objectives that were not achievable when Britain acted alone. These objectives include fighting against climate change, constraining Iran's nuclear program, combating terrorism,

---

[31] Philip Stephens, "Why Europe Needs Cross-Border Lawnmower Regulations," *Financial Times*, October 15, 2013.

and promoting energy security, the single market, international free trade and an open digital economy. The UK has signed roughly 700 international treaties that could be (incorrectly) attacked as impinging on its sovereignty.

When the UK had joined NATO, the International Monetary Fund, and many other multilateral institutions, it had agreed to follow regulations jointly set by foreigners, in exchange for influence. In some instances, such as the International Criminal Court, it had agreed to subject itself to the judgments of a foreign court. Geoffrey Howe, Solicitor General under the Conservative government of Prime Minister Edward Heath, introduced the European Communities Bill in 1972 by stating that "the purpose of the application to join the Community is a fundamental and deliberate use of sovereignty to engage in sharing sovereignty to the greater advantage of us all." The absolutism of the Brexiteers' view of sovereignty made no sense. As *The Economist* noted: "Many talk of being sovereign as if it were like being pregnant: one either is or is not. The truth is more complex. A country can be wholly sovereign yet have little influence."[32] Absolute sovereignty would be worthless if it undermined the ability of British governments to ensure the security and prosperity of its citizens.

The Brexiteers' vision of Britain swimming in the "global ocean" once it had unshackled itself from the EU corpse amounted to rhetorical flatulence. Brexiteers, like Roger Bootle, argue that "the only entity that it makes sense to belong to is the world" as if the UK would seriously consider giving up its other memberships in international organizations, such as the United Nations (including its place on the Security Council), and as if other EU countries are prevented from belonging to the world.

Exiting the EU in the belief that stronger relations with the Commonwealth, the United States, and China would strengthen Britain's hand was misguided. Every study produced inside Whitehall suggested that leaving the single market would leave Britain poorer and less able to promote its interests overseas. Free trade agreements with the Commonwealth would be insignificant compared to the size and growth of the EU market; agreements with emerging economies like China, India or Brazil, or with the United States would be difficult to achieve. It was therefore in the UK's interest to stay within both the EU single market and customs area.

---

[32] *The Economist*, "Dreaming of Sovereignty," March 19, 2016.

Any attempt to regain sovereignty with regard to regulations would come at a cost in terms of accessing the single market. The Leavers seemed to be unaware that the vast majority of British businesses want the UK to remain aligned with EU regulations (with a few exceptions) and to avoid a "bonfire" of European regulations.

The UK's Relationship with the EU

The supreme irony of the Brexit debate was that the UK had actually achieved most of its aims as a member of the EU. It had been, for example, the key proponent of enlargement of the EU to the East, including the entry of ten new members in 2004, a further two in 2007 and another one in 2013. It was this enlargement that had enabled a significant number of Poles and Romanians to enter the UK in order to work. I enjoyed reminding my colleagues in Washington of a seminal episode in the UK television series *Yes Minister*:

> *Minister*: Surely the Foreign Office is pro-Europe, isn't it?
>
> *Permanent Secretary*: Yes and no, if you'll forgive the expression. The Foreign Office is pro-Europe because it is really anti-Europe. The Civil Service was united in its desire to make sure the Common Market didn't work. That's why we went into it.
>
> *Minister*: What are you talking about?
>
> *Permanent Secretary*: Minister, Britain has had the same foreign policy objective for at least the last 500 years. To create a disunited Europe. In that cause we have fought with the Dutch against the Spanish, with the Germans against the French, with the French and Italians against the Germans, and with the French against the Germans and Italians. Divide and rule, you see. Why should we change now, when it's worked so well?
>
> *Minister*: That's all ancient history, surely.
>
> *Permanent Secretary*: Yes, and current policy. We had to break the whole thing up, so we had to get inside. We tried to break it up from the outside, but that wouldn't work. Now that we're inside, we can make a complete pig's breakfast of the whole thing. Set the Germans against the French, the French against the Italians, the Italians against the Dutch. The Foreign Office is terribly pleased. It's just like old times.
>
> *Minister*: Surely we're committed to the European ideal.
>
> *Permanent Secretary*: Really, Minister!
>
> *Minister*: We're not? Then why are we pressing for an increase in the membership?

Permanent Secretary: Well, for the same reason. It's just like the United Nations in fact. The more members it has, the more arguments it can stir up. The more futile and impotent it becomes.
Minister: What appalling cynicism.
Permanent Secretary: Yes, we call it diplomacy, Minister.

At the heart of this amusing exaggeration lies a kernel of truth: The UK has seen enlargement as a means of preventing the deepening of European integration. Moreover, the UK succeeded in keeping the full benefits of the EU internal market, while securing more opt-outs than any other EU member state on major policies such as the euro, the Schengen area of free movement without border controls, and justice and home affairs. It naturally kept full control over foreign and defense policies.

Moreover, the UK had provided critical intellectual and diplomatic support to the European Commission in the promotion of an integrated single market. Lord Cockfield had been a key architect of the single market as Vice President and Commissioner responsible for the internal market during 1984–1988. The UK had also successfully promoted free markets and free trade, competition, better regulation and "subsidiarity" (the principle that decisions should be taken as closely as possible to the citizen, rather than by the EU). It is rather odd that so many Britons believe the EU reflects the French antipathy for liberal economic policies. The French often complain about the opposite: That the EU is too bloody British because ever since the 1980s the European Commission has been opening markets and deregulating, driven by a philosophy of economic liberalism.

Along with other European experts in the Obama administration I understood, of course, that Britain has had a uniquely transactional relationship with the EU; its membership was always rooted in an accountant's analysis of costs and benefits, rather than in an emotional attachment or in geostrategic objectives. It was almost as if the UK had acted like a husband who marries for the tax benefits, before discovering that his spouse had actually expected a loving relationship. Many UK governments would claim over the years that the goalposts of the union it had joined had shifted—from the pure economic focus of a free trade area to an increasing political focus. But the reality is that the political focus had been there from the start; every other member that joined understood this.

The UK's transactional approach was so different from that of the other EU members. Italy, the European country closest to my heart, saw membership as a way of trading incompetent national governance with cleaner and more effective governance imposed from the outside. Spain, Portugal, Greece, and Central and Eastern European states saw membership as a way to be anchored in a democratic and prosperous Europe. The Benelux saw it as a way to magnify their influence and hence to counterbalance the weight of the big European states. France saw it as a way to counterbalance Germany and ensure export markets for its agricultural products. Germany saw it as a way to re-emerge as a power by healing the wounds of the war and ensuring export markets for its industries, both within the EU and with the rest of the world through free trade agreements negotiated by the European Commission. The EU was born just as much with a political agenda as an economic one. The Brexiteers who suggested otherwise had missed the plot.

I was frustrated by the Brexiteers' repeated assertions that the UK had been marginalized in EU decision-making and that it was shackled by a sea of red tape. This was not just tabloid mythology; it was presented as fact by supposedly authoritative commentators. Economist Roger Bootle, for example, stated that:

> the UK's share of the vote is now down to 8% and its ability to influence let alone block measures affecting its interests is decidedly limited...British people have to accept laws imposed on them as a result of byzantine intrigue between the unelected European Commission and the leaders of the other European member states.[33]

The reality is different. The UK share of the vote in the EU Council (representing the member states) is actually 12%, down from 17% when the UK joined. More importantly, most Council decisions are made by consensus after negotiation; it is rare for votes to be taken and even rarer for member states' objections on important issues to be overruled. In other words, the vote share doesn't express the UK's influence. According to the UK's Independent Fact-Checking Charity, the UK has been on the "losing side" about 2% of the time since 1999, although that figure has risen slightly over recent years. Many studies have concluded that the UK government's positions have been closer to final policy outcomes than in most other member states.[34] The "dilution" of the UK's influence,

---

[33] Roger Bootle, *The Trouble with Europe* (Nicholas Brealey Publishing, 2014), pp. 44, 46.

[34] For example, see Simon Hix, Professor of Political Science at the London School of Economics, "Is the UK Marginalised in the EU?" *The Guardian*, October 19, 2015.

if any, has been the result of the expansion of qualified majority voting (in the place of unanimity), accepted by none other than Prime Minister Margaret Thatcher.

Many Brexiteers bang on about how the European Commission consists of unelected bureaucrats. That is a caricature. Although the European Commission is not directly elected, it is certainly *democratically accountable*. For example, the College of Commissioners must be approved by the European Parliament that *is* directly elected. The European Commission regularly reports on its activities to other EU institutions and very often takes their views into account. More fundamentally, however, the European Commission *cannot* be directly elected because it should be relatively immune from political influence. It is the guardian of the EU treaties and is tasked with having a pan-European perspective.

Many Brexiteers seemed blind to the basic fact that the European Commission is the executive branch that proposes legislation, but that passage into law requires the consent of representatives of directly elected governments and the European Parliament. More importantly, it was clear to any informed observer, especially during the Eurozone and migration crises, that power was being increasingly exercised by member states' heads of government in the European Council and their representatives in the Council of Ministers, with the European Commission and the European Parliament playing subordinate roles.

While it is absurd to claim, as does Roger Bootle, that the EU has inflicted a "ludicrously intrusive flood of regulations"[35] on the UK, there have been instances in which the EU has passed legislation that the UK has found objectionable. Examples include the Working Time Directive (that lays down maximum daily and weekly working time, minimum daily rest, minimum breaks during the working day, minimum paid annual leave and extra protection for night workers), as well as the Agency Workers Directive (guaranteeing workers hired through employment agencies pay and conditions equal to employees in the same business who do the same work). Whenever I spoke to representatives of UK businesses about the impact of restrictive labor legislation, they would nearly always object to measures taken by their own government more than they would

---

[35] Roger Bootle, *The Trouble with Europe* (Nicholas Brealey Publishing, 2014), p. 171.

about those of the EU.[36] In fact, the UK is known for its habit of gold-plating EU regulations in many areas, including in financial services. On the whole, the UK remains one of the least regulated large high-income economies despite being a member of the EU.

Rather than being a "hostage, locked in the boot of a car…driven by others to a place and at a pace that we have no control over" in Michael Gove's memorable phrase,[37] the reality is that the UK has been in the front seat of the EU car, often with its hand on the steering wheel. As I had reported from Brussels, it was nonsense to argue that the EU had perverted the original direction of the bloc by embracing "ever closer union" as a binding goal to compel a march to a United States of Europe.

The treaties actually refer to "ever closer union of the *peoples*" of Europe, not governments. The phrase is of long-standing origin: It featured in the 1957 Treaty of Rome that established the European Economic Communities, and the UK signed up to it without issue at least six times, first when signing up as a member and then through subsequent treaty changes. Moreover, as the heads of government have repeatedly stated, it is a symbolic phrase rather than a strict legal provision determining paths of integration. The treaties oblige the EU to respect the histories, cultures, traditions, and political structures of the people of Europe.

Cameron's Opt-Outs

Despite these facts, appearances were more important than reality. It was clear that in order to defeat Brexit Prime Minister Cameron had to negotiate a clear opt-out from "ever closer union" in the New Settlement announced in February 2016. The text stated that Britain has a "specific situation" under the treaties and "is not committed to further political integration." The statement was significant in that it made clear that EU members are now moving not just at different speeds, but toward different ultimate destinations.

Cameron had also won a significant concession from the EU 27 by agreeing to a mechanism to limit the access of EU workers newly entering the UK's labor market to in-work benefits, such as tax credits and

---

[36] For example, the higher minimum wage for people aged 25 and over; the apprenticeship payroll tax for large companies; restrictions on skilled migrant workers; and the requirement for large companies to publish their gender pay gaps.

[37] "Michael Gove sets out post-exit UK-EU trade vision," *BBC News*, April 19, 2016. https://www.bbc.com/news/uk-politics-36074853.

housing benefits. The benefits would be slowly phased in during a period of four years from the beginning of employment (rather than banned, as originally proposed by the UK) if EU migrants were "putting an excessive pressure on the proper functioning of its public services." The final settlement with the EU included an acknowledgment that this was already in evidence in the UK and that the four-year break would be available to Britain for seven years.[38] Moreover, the UK won the point that it (and other EU member states) should be allowed to index child benefit payments to the standard of living in the member state where the child lives. Unfortunately, these points did not seem to sway the Brexiteers' view that the EU had been responsible for substantial net immigration.

The view was contrary to the facts. Over the past twenty years, about two-thirds of the immigration into the UK was from *outside* the EU. For a few years around the referendum that figure shifted to just over half (today it is around 70%). Successive UK governments had been free to reduce non-EU immigration, unfettered by the EU, but had not done so.

I and many of my colleagues in the Obama administration were amazed at the sheer brazenness of the Brexiteers' exploitation of fears about immigration. Many of the advertisements alleged (falsely) that the EU was intending to admit Turkey as a new member. Billboards masterminded by Nigel Farage showed hordes of Syrian refugees snaking across European roads. The Brexiteers conveniently forgot that the UK had repeatedly urged its fellow EU members to accelerate the pace of EU enlargement to new members. Becoming a member of the EU necessarily meant the right of free movement, thanks to the Schengen area, and the right to work in another EU state.

The UK had been a key proponent of the 2004 wave of accession, the single largest expansion in EU history, that brought in ten new members with standards of living below the EU median. (The UK had even been beating the drum about the need to accelerate Turkish membership, repeatedly ignoring the overwhelming consequences for employment and social stability of granting rights of free movement to 80 million people.) Whereas many EU countries chose to apply a lengthy transitional regime that imposed travel and work restrictions on citizens of the new EU members, the UK chose not to do so. And yet now the UK government seemed obsessed with EU immigrants, especially from Poland and Romania. Surely, it was foreseeable that workers from these and other new members of the EU would want to work in the UK.

---

[38] Daniel Korski, "Why We Lost the Brexit Vote," *Politico*, October 20, 2016.

Some of the Brexiteers oddly seemed to want to cut back on EU immigration in order to give preference to *increased* immigration from outside the EU. This was the view of Syed Kamall, for example, a member of the European Parliament of Indo-Guyanese descent from the European Conservatives and Reformists party. Over an Indian dinner in Brussels, he explained that the UK could finally stop discriminating against immigrants from the Indian subcontinent without pesky EU rules on free movement of labor. I found this view somewhat bizarre, as it suggested that net immigration into the UK post-Brexit would not in fact decline. Furthermore, I doubted very much that the average pro-Brexit elderly white voter would necessarily be pleased at swapping European (Christian) immigrants with non-European (Muslim and Hindu) immigrants.

Much of the EU immigration represented youth from Central and Eastern Europe and the Baltic states who were eager to price themselves into work. A booming economy at full employment, as well as a comparatively high minimum wage and a strong currency, had ensured that immigrants would come. Every economic study showed that they are net contributors to the UK economy because they pay more in taxes than they take out in benefits (probably quite different from the aging British pensioners in Spain). During the two decades I have lived in the UK, I have repeatedly marveled at how often coffee bars, hotels, and restaurants are staffed by young and cheerful EU immigrants. Apparently, British young people don't want these jobs.

President Obama Speaks Out

All of these reasons had colored my views as I reported back to Washington on Brexit and urged the White House to speak up. The president did so on several occasions; it was appropriate to do so in light of the significant equities the United States had at stake. Many of us believed, partly due to encouragement by Downing Street, that the president's hugely positive image among British youth might help make the case. I helped develop the themes of his pronouncements on Brexit. For example, "Having the United Kingdom in the European Union gives us much greater confidence about the strength of the transatlantic union." By being inside the EU, the UK had helped to make the world a safer and more prosperous place since World War II. "We want to make sure that the United Kingdom continues to have that influence. Because we believe that the values that we share are the right ones, not just for ourselves, but for Europe as a whole and the world as a whole."[39] In an editorial for the *Daily Telegraph*, the president presented some of the key arguments we thought should be convincing:

> As citizens of the United Kingdom take stock of their relationship with the EU, you should be proud that the EU has helped spread British values and practices – democracy, the rule of law, open markets – across the continent and to its periphery. The European Union doesn't moderate British influence – it magnifies it. A strong Europe is not a threat to Britain's global leadership; it enhances Britain's global leadership…the US and the world need your outsized influence to continue, including within Europe…in today's world, even as we all cherish our sovereignty, the nations who wield their influence most effectively are the nations that do it through the collective action that today's challenges demand.[40]

While it was perfectly appropriate to make these points, I was disappointed that the president chose to warn the UK that it would go "to the back of the queue" of countries with which the United States would seek to negotiate free trade agreements. As most Americans would never use the British word "queue," some commentators immediately assumed that a speechwriter had inserted a talking point from Downing Street. Rather predictably, the comment was interpreted as a threat and it backfired badly. He should have said that, while the United States has concluded many bilateral agreements (including recently with Colombia and South Korea), it would naturally give preference to regional trade agreements like the Transatlantic Trade and Investment Partnership Agreement with the EU because they would yield much greater economic impact. Our able chief trade negotiator, Mike Froman, also made the legitimate point that Britain has far greater leverage at the negotiating table when it is part of the EU.[41]

When President Trump visited the UK in July 2018, he also created a firestorm by stating that Prime Minister May's handling of the Brexit

---

[39] Full transcript of BBC Interview with President Barack Obama, July 24, 2015. http://www.bbc.co.uk/news/world-us-canada-33646542.

[40] Barack Obama, "As Your Friend, Let Me Say That the EU Makes Britain Even Greater," *Daily Telegraph*, April 23, 2016.

[41] Shawn Donnan, "Top US Trade Official Warns on Brexit," *Financial Times*, October 28, 2015.

talks was "unfortunate." Some observers concluded that he was doing the reverse of what Obama had already done. But the two interventions were not remotely similar. Obama had made his statement to support a sitting Prime Minister at his request. Trump made his statement to undermine a sitting Prime Minister during a State visit; he disrespectfully stated that the Prime Minister was botching the Brexit negotiations and working against the will of the British people as expressed in the referendum and he had, to boot, endorsed her rival, Boris Johnson, who had resigned just a few days before.

Some reactions to President Obama's statements were vitriolic. Boris Johnson accused the United States of "outrageous and exorbitant hypocrisy":

> To this day the Americans refuse to kneel to almost any kind of international jurisdiction…Would the Americans knuckle under to a NAFTA commission and parliament generating about half their domestic law? Would they submit to a NAFTA court of justice – supreme over all US institutions – and largely staffed by Mexicans and Canadians whom the people of the US could neither appoint nor remove? No way.[42]

Conservative MP John Redwood responded to President Obama by saying that "If letting foreign countries impose laws on you, levy taxes on you, and spend your money is such a good idea why doesn't he create an American Union so Mexico can have common borders with the US?"[43] I wish I had a euro for every time these arguments have been thrown at me. It is clear from this book that I believe that the EU has provided the UK important benefits, substantially exceeding the costs (even if one were to view the EU as merely a marriage of convenience). At a more fundamental level, moreover, the comparison with the United States is flawed because the UK is not a superpower. Unlike the US, the UK *needs* to belong to a regional organization like the EU to project influence.

While Brexiteers were unhappy with the Obama administration for its public statements on Brexit, they missed the fact that the concerns

---

[42] Boris Johnson, "Americans Would Never Accept EU Restrictions—So Why Should We?" *Telegraph*, March 16, 2016.

[43] John Redwood, "Obama gets Europe wrong again. Why doesn't he allow free immigration from Mexico and Cuba then?" *The Commentator*, July 24, 2015. http://www.thecommentator.com/article/59.

expressed represented settled wisdom among the vast majority of US foreign policy experts on both sides of the political aisle. For example, 13 former secretaries of defense and foreign affairs spanning four decades wrote letters in *The Times* to warn that Brexit would diminish Britain's place and influence in the world.[44] Moreover, eight former US Secretaries of the Treasury described Brexit as a "risky bet" that would jeopardize the City's role as a global financial center.[45]

Moreover, many reputable national economic research bodies, such as the National Institute for Economic and Social Research and the Institute for Fiscal Studies, as well as the UK Treasury, the Bank of England and the Confederation of British Industry, agreed that Brexit would over time lead to lower trade flows, less investment and slower growth. 280 economists wrote an open letter agreeing with the Treasury's analysis about the range of downside risks to the UK economy. The International Monetary Fund and the Organization for European Cooperation and Development also expressed concerns. The Commonwealth countries, Japan, India, and China did the same. Only Russia and Britain's other enemies had reason to cheer Brexit. But none of this seemed to matter in the increasingly dysfunctional public debate. Michael Gove summed up the environment when he announced that "this country has had enough of experts." Later, he cheerfully proclaimed that global warming isn't so bad after all because it enables British producers of sparkling wine to surpass French champagne.[46]

THE IMPACT OF BREXIT ON US–EU RELATIONS

President Obama's statements were rooted in considerable US government analysis on the impact of Brexit on US, European, and UK interests. The US Mission to the EU, including myself personally, participated during many months in an assessment of Brexit's impact on every area of US foreign, economic, and security policy. The conclusion was that, except in

---

[44] Francis Elliott and Matt Chorley, "Don't Vote For Brexit, US Defence Chiefs Warn," *The Times*, May 10, 2016. https://www.thetimes.co.uk/edition/news/dont-vote-for-brexit-us-defence-chiefs-warn-2nncnhplw.

[45] John Murray Brown, "Former US Treasury Secretaries Warn on Brexit," *Financial Times*, April 20, 2016. https://www.ft.com/content/7b6b1514-06d4-11e6-a70d-4e39ac32c284.

[46] Sarah Knapton, "'English sparkling wine will be better than Champagne as climate warms' says Michael Gove," *Daily Telegraph*. https://www.telegraph.co.uk/news/2018/08/02/english-sparkling-wine-will-better-champagne-climate-warms-says/.

a few and relatively minor areas, the impact would be substantially negative. While there were many detailed reasons for this conclusion, three stand out.

First, as suggested above, the United States has considered (at least until the arrival of President Trump) that the European Union is an effective partner, despite all of its defects. And given that the United States and the UK see eye to eye on nearly every foreign, economic, and security issue, it is natural that Washington would want the UK "inside the EU tent" influencing EU decision-making and making the EU more economically liberal, Atlanticist, and pro-NATO. There is no way, for example, that Washington could have implemented an effective sanctions regime against Russia after its invasion of Ukraine without the EU's involvement. The UK was a key part of this success because it had exercised crucial diplomatic and moral leadership within the EU institutions and had supplied the bulk of evidence needed to support designations of individuals on sanctions lists that would hold up to scrutiny in EU courts. While the UK could of course participate in international sanctions as a non-EU member, the backbone of the EU 27 to pursue sanctions might soften and transatlantic coordination would become more complicated.

Without the EU, the United States could not have finalized the Joint Comprehensive Plan of Action limiting Iran's nuclear ambitions. The EU's embargo on Iranian oil exports was critical in bringing Teheran to the negotiating table. Secretary Kerry had repeatedly expressed to me his admiration not only of UK, German, and French diplomatic involvement, but also that of Federica Mogherini, EU High Representative for Foreign Affairs and Security Policy. Moreover, the EU had played the leading role in combating piracy off the Horn of Africa and in brokering settlements between Serbia and Kosovo and with the Burmese military junta that paved the way to free elections. Without the EU, the climate change negotiations in Paris would not have been successful. Europe's development assistance and humanitarian aid programs would not be as effective and Washington would have a harder time coordinating its efforts with those of Europe.

While Washington enjoys strong bilateral law enforcement cooperation with many member state capitals, the United States has found Europol to be an effective partner in combating serious crime and terrorism. The EU's European Arrest Warrant, allowing criminals and terrorists to be swiftly extradited across European frontiers, and the EU Passenger Name Record directive, requiring air carriers to transfer to member states key passenger data to assist in law enforcement, were among the EU's important contributions.

Moreover, many of us in the Obama administration were concerned about what Brexit would mean in the military field. The UK has the biggest defense budget in Europe and arguably its most effective armed forces. The UK has contributed roughly 15% of the common costs of the EU's military operations. It has supplied ships and operational headquarters for important naval missions, including the one in Somalia and one to disrupt the business model of human smuggling and trafficking networks in the Southern Central Mediterranean. Its nationals have made up a significant portion of the EU's Crisis Management and Planning Division staff. The EU has relied on the UK to secure United Nations Security Council mandates approving EU military operations, as well as to deepen cooperation with NATO.

The second core reason why many of us in the Obama administration were concerned about Brexit was that the EU 27 would be at risk of being even further unbalanced. Ever since the UK's entry into the European Community, Germany, France, and the UK have been like the three legs of a stool; removing one of the legs would make the structure rather unstable. The traditional Franco-German tandem, that had propelled European integration, had long existed in name only because of persistent French economic weakness. For at least the first two decades of its existence, the culture of the European Commission had been thoroughly French: The institutions worked in French and the bureaucracy reflected French mentalities, procedures, and priorities. But since then, French influence had been slowly ceding ground to the growing influence of British and German bureaucrats. While Britain's semi-detached status within the EU, and increasingly acrimonious relationship with the EU in the decade prior to Brexit, undermined London's influence within the EU institutions, Britain still carried a great deal of weight because of the quality of its intellectual contribution and diplomatic skills.

Brexit would mean that the EU institutions would be even more under the control of Berlin. I witnessed repeatedly during my diplomatic mission how Germany appeared to be the predominant voice at the EU table. Although criticisms that the European Commission is a German-run institution are very wide of the mark (other countries hold more of the key posts), decisions in the Council (representing member state ministers) and the European Council (representing EU heads of government) certainly do reflect German priorities. On critical issues—including relations with Russia, especially after its invasion of Ukraine, the threat of a Greek departure from the euro (Grexit), and the refugee crisis—policies in Berlin carried the day. Everyone in the EU institutions seemed to be obsessed with the question: "What does Chancellor Merkel think?"

German predominant influence is quite natural as most policies have financial implications and Germany is Europe's economic powerhouse that writes the biggest cheques. And German inaction (for which Chancellor Merkel has often been accused) would be far worse than German influence. But German predominance isn't healthy over the long term. The more that EU citizens outside of Germany consider the European integration project to be in the interests of Germany alone, the less they will be prepared to sustain it.

The third core reason for our concern about Brexit was that the EU might shift toward a more protectionist, more interventionist, and less market-friendly approach. The influence of European forces promoting national champions, industrial policy and state planning, and the dilution of free competition rules and free market liberalism, might increase. We worried about the future of our cooperation with the EU on data privacy regulation and the digital economy, where we had done so much together. The UK had played an important role in enabling the US and the EU to negotiate the Privacy Shield agreement and to keep the Digital Single Market proposals relatively benign for US technology firms. These concerns seemed to be borne out when, soon after the Brexit referendum results, the French government immediately announced its intention to promote a less market-friendly approach. France and Germany are now urging the new Commission under German President Ursula von der Leyen to pursue an industrial policy.

Our fourth concern was that Brexit would injure the interests of many US firms, both in manufacturing and services (especially financial), that had chosen the UK in large part as a launchpad into the much larger EU single market. Moreover, we were concerned that it would be a body blow for the EU's self-confidence and that it would lead to a long period of introspection that would diminish its ability to engage with us on our wide external agenda. The UK, as well, would be potentially overwhelmed by a tsunami of legislative and bureaucratic efforts needed to create a host of new regulatory institutions, pass vast amounts of legislation and rush to negotiate new trading arrangements to replace those that it benefited from as an EU member.

We also worried that Brexit would provide a fillip to populist movements on the continent and increase the likelihood of copy-cat referenda, leading to a fracturing and potentially the dissolution of the EU. Although our initial fears were borne out, with populist parties in France, the Netherlands and Denmark calling for plebiscites, we were eventually proven to be too pessimistic. Those parties were defeated at the polls and public opinion rallied in favor of the European Union. The European elections in May 2019 resulted in a more fragmented European Parliament with weakened center-right and center-left parties but they were far from the result that populists had hoped for.

One of the few upsides of Brexit, we reasoned, is that it would discourage the EU 27 from adopting an overly regulatory and protectionist agenda. The logic behind that conclusion was that such an agenda would trigger an unacceptable loss of competitiveness if the UK, the world's sixth-largest economy parked a few kilometres off the European continent, were to choose less regulatory and more market friendly policies.

After the Brexit vote, some influential voices in the administration (egged on by our embassy in London) thought we should change tack entirely and clearly favor the UK in its negotiations with the EU, specifically with regard to minimizing the financial settlement and launching contemporaneous talks about the divorce and the new partnership. I thought that was counterproductive as it would not lead the EU to change its clearly defined positions, underpinned by legal obligations in the EU treaties. Our interests were not to plump for our traditional British friends, as wonderful and deep as the special relationship might be, because the EU would be a far more capable partner than the UK going forward.

The real problem, as I explained to Washington, was the sloganeering and the magical thinking taking hold in London. Delusions about the EU, of course, had deep roots in the UK. I recalled that Chancellor Rab Butler had dismissed the negotiations in Messina on the Treaty of Rome in 1957, the key foundation of the European Economic Community, as "archaeological diggings in an ancient Sicilian town."

The best way to help our friends in London, I thought, was to delicately remind them of their true relative position in the world. This was not a negotiation between equals. The EU took almost half of Britain's exports (12% of British GDP), whereas Britain took less than 10% of the EU's (3% of EU GDP). Britain's trade deficit was mostly with the Germans and the Spanish, not with the other 24 member states that would have to agree on a trade deal. The idea that Germany would ride to the UK's rescue in the negotiations on a new UK–EU partnership agreement would be disappointed, just as similar hopes had been during the negotiations for a settlement agreement before the referendum: Berlin's clear priority was to ensure the cohesion of the EU 27.

A Failure of Leadership

The Brexiteers were adept at sloganeering. They repeated the comforting mantras of "take back control" and "global Britain." They boldly predicted that the UK would have ready on Brexit day fully fledged trade deals with the EU and fast-growing countries. Of course, that was fiction. They asserted that it would be no problem for the UK to leave without a deal because the UK could happily live with WTO trade rules that would then apply. That ignored the facts that tariffs would come into force and a host of non-tariff barriers would add friction to UK–EU trade. Most important, WTO rules don't cover many of the service sectors that the UK cares about, including financial services.

As a cabinet minister, Theresa May had given a cogent speech in April 2016 explaining why, on balance, it was not in the UK national interest to leave the EU.[47] As Prime Minister, she assumed the responsibility of doing what she had opposed. She uttered a number of rather Sphinx-like pronouncements, such as that she was in favor of a "red, white and blue Brexit" and that "Brexit means Brexit." She asserted that "no deal is better than a bad deal," and affirmed that the UK would get a bespoke deal delivering everything it wanted. Like the title of Luigi Pirandello's play *Six Characters in Search of an Author*, these were slogans in search of a strategy. And they consumed most of the two-year period that the EU treaties had provided for exit negotiations. The prime minister had triggered the two-year withdrawal period in March 2017 without a clear roadmap of what the UK wanted to achieve. By the time she presented her first detailed proposals in July 2018, roughly two-thirds of the negotiating time had been used up (Fig. 3.3).

Voters in any democracy naturally have the right to express their views and every democratically elected government should respect them. It was

---

[47] Theresa May addresses audience at the Institute of Mechanical Engineers in central London, April 25, 2016. https://www.gov.uk/government/speeches/home-secretarys-speech-on-the-uk-eu-and-our-place-in-the-world.

Fig. 3.3 The UK's negotiating position toward the EU (© Kevin Kal Kallaugher, 2019. *The Economist*, Kaltoons.com. Reprinted with Permission)

rather odd, however, for the Leavers to claim that the people should only be asked their opinion once and never again. It was rather odd that those stridently defending the UK Parliament's "sovereignty" against Brussels *diktat* argued in the same breath that parliament should not interfere with the results of one referendum—decided by a razor-thin margin and on the basis of misinformation. (The fact that Boris had glorified British parliamentary sovereignty during the Leave campaign did not prevent him as Prime Minister from attacking parliament for thwarting his no-deal Brexit plans.)

The central problem, however, was that at no time did Prime Minister May analytically lay out for the British people the realistic choices facing them following the Brexit referendum and the consequences of each choice. Rather than manage Brexit as a national project of historic importance that required cross-party talks, she focused on managing her divided party and cabinet. The result was that the government spent more time negotiating with itself than it spent negotiating with Brussels.

May's approach was to agree reluctantly to the demands of the hardliners, including by drawing negotiating red lines that severely boxed her in.

The most extraordinary, and catastrophic, miscalculation was to state that the UK would leave the EU single market and customs union without fully appreciating that this would *by necessity* require a border between Northern Ireland and the Republic of Ireland (or require a border in the Irish Sea between Ireland and the UK if Northern Ireland stayed within the EU single market and customs union). It should have been patently clear that the EU 27 had to protect the integrity of its single market and union by carrying out border checks. Trying to achieve a Brexit on these terms while preventing a border was always going to be a hopeless exercise.

The EU initially proposed a solution to the border issue that would keep Northern Ireland in the EU customs union and parts of the single market. The solution would apply in the event that a future partnership with the UK (such as a comprehensive free trade agreement) did not find technological or other means of avoiding a hard border while ensuring the integrity of the EU single market and customs union. When this "backstop" proved unpalatable to the UK because it would allegedly undermine the unity of the UK, the EU and UK agreed on a different arrangement that would keep the whole of the UK in the customs union but only Northern Ireland in parts of the single market. That solution enraged Prime Minister May's coalition partner, the Democratic Unionist Party of Northern Ireland, because it would require checks on goods in the Irish Sea. There was simply no way to accommodate May's red lines and avoid a hard border somewhere. And it was foreseeable that the EU could not agree to a time-limited "backstop" as it had to protect its customs union and single market.

The UK government refused to listen to the many experts in EU affairs who would have pointed out why its approach was doomed to fail from the very start. In the spring of 2019, I was stunned to learn from a distinguished former UK permanent representative to the EU that the UK government had never asked his advice during the Brexit negotiations; to his knowledge, moreover, none of the other former permanent representatives had been asked their advice either. Several senior civil servant and business figures told me that Prime Minister May never asked any questions during their briefings with her. It seemed as if the government was not only misinformed, but simply didn't care.

When negotiations with Brussels predictably stalled, the sloganeering started reaching fever pitch. As Samuel Johnson once said, "Patriotism is the last refuge to which a scoundrel clings." The Brexiteers repeatedly invoked the "spirit of Dunkirk" as if the EU were an advancing Nazi Panzer corps. On the fringes of the Tory Party conference in early October 2017 Conservative MP Jacob Rees-Mogg invoked battles against the French in 1815, 1346, 1415 and 1805: "[Brexit]...is the Magna Carta...it's Waterloo, it's Agincourt, it's Crecy...and Trafalgar. We win all of these things."

Listening to this sloganeering was rather dispiriting, especially for an Anglophile like myself who had grown up admiring the great English virtues of pragmatism and the quality of UK government (especially its civil service). Having spent a lot of time in Southern Europe, regrettably prone to unstable and even chaotic governments, I thought the UK was different. I had never imagined that the fate of a country could be sacrificed on the altar of party or even personal ambitions.

The core "I can have my cake and eat it too" delusion was that the UK could move from being an EU member with nearly all the opt-outs it desired to being a third party with all of the opt-ins it desired, preserving all the benefits of membership without the burdens. This delusion could never escape the forces of gravity.

The failure of Prime Minister May to show leadership by explaining the consequences of Brexit merely emboldened the extremists. Sir Ivan, who had been warning of a "hard" no-deal Brexit for years, proved prescient when Boris became the new leader of the Conservative Party, largely on the basis of pledges to remove the Irish "backstop" and, if that failed, to take the UK out "come hell or high water." His victory in national elections in December 2019 was due in large part to a relentless focus on "getting Brexit done." Boris was also extremely fortunate to oppose Labor leader Jeremy Corbyn, widely viewed as a left wing extremist.

Remarkably, a poll of Conservative party members showed that a majority wanted to leave the EU even at the cost of economic hardship and at the risk of uniting Ireland and triggering a successful second Scottish referendum on independence. It is questionable whether the majority of Britons (especially the young and economically vulnerable) are prepared to pay that price.

From Great Britain to Little England?

Although some initial projections of a savage Brexit hit to the UK economy were quickly proven to be exaggerated, economic analysis two to three years after the 2016 referendum showed that the UK economy is already suffering. One detailed study conducted by Goldman Sachs in April 2019 estimated that Brexit was costing the UK around £600 million per week, equivalent to 2.4% of GDP, based on comparing the UK economy with a hypothetical "look alike" economy that did not withstand a Brexit shock.[48] Another study from the Centre For European Reform found in October 2019 that the UK economy was 2.9% smaller than it would have been if Britain had voted to remain in the EU.[49] Brexit is costing far more than the fictitious savings that Boris Johnson had put on his bus. A leaked confidential draft of the government's own EU exit analysis showed a significant hit to the economy under all Brexit scenarios.

The deal that Prime Minister Johnson has agreed with the EU is not very different from the offer proposed by the EU (and rejected by the UK) back in February 2018 for a "Northern Ireland-only backstop" that would have kept Northern Ireland in the EU customs union if other means of avoiding a hard border on the island of Ireland failed. The "backstop" is unnecessary because Northern Ireland will officially be part of the UK's customs territory (unlike in the EU's rejected proposal) in the sense that it will apply UK tariffs and participate in future UK free trade deals. However, Northern Ireland will de facto follow EU customs rules and therefore customs and other checks on goods trade will be required between Great Britain and Northern Ireland, i.e., within the United Kingdom, despite the Prime Minister's repeated assertions to the contrary. Northern Irish companies and farmers involved in trade south of the border will follow EU regulatory rules as well. In general terms, the dilemma facing the UK is unchanged: The greater the regulatory divergence, the less ambitious the UK–EU free trade agreement will be.

The Johnson deal does not guarantee that there will be no further delays to Brexit or indeed that the UK will not leave the EU without

---

[48] Adam Samson, "Brexit Costs UK £600 million per Week, Says Goldman Study," *Financial Times*, April 1, 2019. https://www.ft.com/content/fb6285a4-5460-11e9-a3db-1fe89bedc16e.

[49] John Springford, "The Cost of Brexit to September 2018," Centre for European Reform.

a deal. It is possible that a new UK government under Prime Minister Johnson might decide to leave with no deal rather than extend the transition period for another few years. Johnson himself has repeatedly argued that the trading relationship between the EU and Australia, governed by WTO rules, is a reasonable model for UK–EU relations when clearly it is not. It is rather bizarre to argue that WTO rules are sufficient when President Trump is busy ripping them apart.

It is unrealistic to expect that the UK and the EU can finalize a comprehensive free trade deal before the end of the transition period (that essentially extends the status quo until December 2020). A comprehensive free trade deal with the EU will not be quick or easy to negotiate. Irishman Phil Hogan, commissioner for agriculture under the Juncker Commission and currently trade commissioner under the von der Leyen Commission, will be particularly vigilant about tough agricultural issues and the Irish border. As the UK is a more important and geographically closer trading partner of the EU than Canada, the EU will be more concerned about the UK's ability to disrupt its economy without tough and binding provisions ensuring a level playing field.

Boris's great hope that the United States can serve as an enormous life raft after a post-Brexit economic slowdown is likely to be disappointed. Despite repeated promises of a big beautiful free trade deal between the US and the UK, it will be difficult to achieve. President Trump didn't exactly market the deal well during his state visit to the UK in 2019 when he claimed that the National Health Service, an institution that attracts very high support among the British, would be up for negotiation. He later rowed back from the comment, perhaps realizing that it was about as popular as proposing that Buckingham Palace should be turned into a Trump-branded luxury spa.

A free trade deal would be a fine thing. Some of the obstacles the US faced in its TTIP negotiations with the EU, as described in Chapter 4, will not be as problematic in US–UK negotiations. Although the UK has a few important geographical indications, they will probably not be a major stumbling block. Furthermore, the US is likely to ditch the idea of including investor-state dispute settlement on the ground that UK law and courts are entirely capable of dealing fairly with investors' complaints. It may also be the case that the Trump administration and Congress will show greater flexibility on public procurement with the UK than they did with the EU.

But many of the obstacles that plagued our TTIP efforts will be troublesome in US–UK negotiations as well. It is not at all clear, for example, that UK farmers will be keen on much more competition from US exports, especially so soon after losing EU subsidies. It is also doubtful that the UK will be keen on adopting US regulations, especially on food and product safety standards, when doing so would significantly impede UK exporters' access to the far bigger EU market. A UK digital services tax, if implemented, would impact large US technology firms and would trigger US retaliation, complicating efforts at concluding a trade deal. Moreover, it will be difficult for the US to negotiate a deal with the UK before it is clear what the UK's final trading arrangements with the EU will be.

During his state visit to the UK in 2018, President Trump warned that the UK's decision to remain aligned with EU regulations would "probably kill" a US-UK free trade deal. That was a wild exaggeration, albeit it did reflect the fact that the decision to align with the EU made such an agreement more complicated. And the statement ignored the reality that many US companies have invested in the UK in the expectation that the UK would continue to serve as a bridgehead into the larger EU market and therefore that UK regulations would remain aligned with those of the EU. While some US exports would increase if the UK abandoned EU regulations and adopted US ones, many US investors in the UK would not favor divergence with the EU. Moreover, the UK is highly unlikely to abandon EU regulatory obstacles to US agri-food exports (such as hormone-treated beef, poultry disinfected with chlorine, agricultural commodities containing GMOs, and pork from pigs fed with growth-promoting drugs) after Brexit in any event.

Due to its diminished negotiating leverage, it is highly unlikely that the UK could extract from the US as favorable terms as the EU would do in a US–EU free trade deal. And it may have to "pay" for the agreement by aligning itself with the United States on a host of issues unrelated to trade (at least under a second Trump administration). The UK wants to show it has an alternative to the EU, but it should also be realistic about the chances of the former real estate developer in the White House being sentimental about the special relationship. Moreover, the issue of the Irish border might be problematic. Nancy Pelosi, Speaker of the House of Representatives, has stated that no US–UK free trade deal will be ratified if the UK leaves the EU on terms that re-establish an intra-Irish border and undermines the Good Friday peace accords that brought peace and stability to Northern Ireland. A "hard" Brexit without an agreement with the EU is almost guaranteed to achieve that result.

Even if an ambitious US–UK free trade deal could be signed, it will not be nearly as significant as many people seem to believe. One exhaustive study about the impact of TTIP on the UK concluded in 2013 that it would increase UK national income between £4 and £10 billion pounds annually—equivalent to 0.14 and 0.35% increase in GDP.[50] Similarly, an internal UK government study in Whitehall concluded in 2018 that a free trade agreement would increase UK GDP by only 0.2% after 15 years. It will not come close to compensating for the loss of frictionless access to the EU market.

The UK wants to negotiate ambitious and favorable free trade agreements with both the US and the EU as soon as possible. But these objectives are contradictory, at least to some degree. It will not be possible to have one's cake and eat it too. The UK government under Prime Minister Johnson has made it clear that it wishes to be able to diverge from EU rules. Otherwise, it argues, what was the point of Brexit? But divergence means extra customs and regulatory checks on goods trade with the EU.

If economics were the only factor, the choice between the US and the EU would be pretty clear-cut as failing to align with EU rules would have a negative impact far outweighing the positive impact of a free trade agreement with the US. The choice between aligning with the EU and the US, however, is not purely based on economic factors of course. The desire to be "sovereign" appears to be driving policy choices. But that desire appears to be more theoretical than real.

The EU is pushing hard for the UK to respect its commitments to sign up to a "level playing field" with the EU that is intended to ensure that the UK does not engage in unfair competition. One area of particular concern for the EU is that the UK might dole out government subsidies once it is free from restrictive EU rules. The UK government insists that it rarely sought to grant such subsidies while it was an EU member and that it has no desire to do so when it leaves. There are many other examples

---

[50] Centre for Economic Policy Research, "Estimating the Economic Impact on the UK of a Transatlantic Trade and Investment Partnership (TTIP) Agreement Between the European Union and the United States," March 2013. https://assets.publishing.service.gov.uk/government/uploads/system/uploads/attachment_data/file/198115/bis-13-869-economic-impact-on-uk-of-tranatlantic-trade-and-investment-partnership-between-eu-and-us.pdf.

of where the UK insists on its right to diverge while saying that it doesn't intend to do so in practice. It is a message that many EU member states find contradictory and somewhat troubling. They are not willing simply to take the UK at its word. A level playing field with the UK matters much more than with Canada as the EU imports nine times more from the former than it does from the latter.

In sum, the UK appears to be willing to take an economic hit to the critical trading relationship with its largest and geographically closest partner, out of philosophical attachment to sovereignty, while giving preference to a less important trading relationship with a distant, albeit special, partner.

The UK's place in the world after Brexit will perhaps never recover. Years of mismanagement and division over Brexit have already tarnished its valuable reputation of being a stable, well-managed country. Out of economic necessity it will wind up being a rule-taker, most likely of EU rules over which it will have no influence. It will lose the benefit of many dozens of significant EU free trade agreements and hundreds of other international agreements regulating a vast array of economic activities; while it can naturally seek to replace these agreements with bilateral agreements of its own, it will almost certainly find that it will achieve worse terms because of its diminished leverage. Unable to harness the EU's influence in the many areas that are discussed in this book, the UK will find it harder to influence events in Europe and beyond. The world will look like a more forbidding place. As a convinced Anglophile who has been fortunate to have lived 22 years in the UK, that saddens me. The UK has been an enormously positive force for good in the world.

As much as I regret the UK's decision to leave the EU, it is a better outcome than a second referendum yielding a small margin in favor of Remain. Such a result would have deepened the wounds in a divided country. According to one poll, nearly three-quarters of Leave voters and slightly more than half of Remain voters believed that violence toward lawmakers was a "price worth paying" to get their preferred Brexit result.[51]

The only way to heal the deep Brexit wound will be for the UK to be outside of the EU for a significant time and for voters to understand

---

[51] Cristina Gallardo, "Poll: Violence Against MPs 'Price Worth Paying' to Get Brexit Result," *Politico*, October 24, 2019. https://www.politico.eu/article/poll-violence-against-mps-price-worth-paying-to-get-brexit-result/.

the consequences of that choice. Brexit has shocked millions of Britons into realizing, for the first time ever, that the EU is a force for good. Perhaps something positive will eventually emerge from that realization. It is also time for the UK to focus on non-Brexit problems. The key issues facing the UK, including education, infrastructure, productivity, and its health and welfare system, are far more important than Brexit. None has anything to do with the EU.

Some observers also harbor hopes that a future government might soon wish to take the UK back into the EU. They are likely to be disappointed as the EU is likely to evolve in a direction that the UK will find increasingly hard to accept. The five year plan of the new European Commission includes programs focusing on the EU's foreign policy coherence and assertiveness, including a European Defence Union and a bureaucracy dedicated to defense and space policy. Even more important, the EU intends to use majority voting more often in common foreign and security policy. These will be anathema to many British voters. And even if it weren't, it is likely that the majority of the EU 27 would not want to risk further integration progress by bringing a problematic member back into the fold. Brexit has already been a major unwelcome distraction for the EU from many other pressing issues.

As I listened to the chipper delusions of the Brexiteers while the UK tore itself apart in a seemingly endless psychodrama, I was reminded of Voltaire's satiric work *Candide* in which Professor Pangloss, the mentor of the protagonist Candide, repeats that "all is for the best" in the "best of all possible worlds." Optimism is not a substitute for serious leadership and it can lead to serious disappointment. "What is this optimism?" asks another character. Candide responds: "Alas, it is the madness of maintaining that everything is right when it is wrong."

Part I

Economic Ties

CHAPTER 4

Trade

On October 19, 2015, I found myself in one of the lecture halls of the College of Europe in Bruges to speak about the negotiations to conclude a Transatlantic Trade and Investment Partnership (TTIP) agreement. At the same event earlier that day, EU Commissioner for Trade Cecilia Malmström had to interrupt her presentation after several minutes when a dozen people stood up to sing multiple verses from the hit musical *Les Misérables*: "Do you hear the people sing?/Singing a song of angry men?"

The Commissioner remained, as always, smiling and composed. The audience had to regroup in an adjacent lecture hall before the event could proceed. My speech regrettably did not feature such a performance, but on the way out of the lecture hall I picked up a copy of the flyer: "Sing Away the TTIP." Similar singing protests interrupted many other TTIP events, including one hosted by the Transatlantic Business Council in February 2016 featuring a speech by our unflappable chief negotiator Dan Mullaney. Belgian Foreign Minister Didier Reynders and German Minister of the Economy Sigmar Gabriel also enjoyed separate free concerts.

This was merely one of the varied and inventive techniques deployed by the anti-TTIP activists. Brussels and many other capitals were plastered with "Stop TTIP" stickers and graffiti. In July 2016, dozens of activists from the heretofore unknown *Ensemble Zoologique pour la Libération de la Nature* disguised themselves as animals armed with vegetables, flowers, leaves, and branches, blocked entry to the negotiation center and pelted the negotiators with trash. On several occasions during the negotiations, I had the pleasure of seeing demonstrators dressed as giant chlorinated chickens and Trojan horses. Rallies usually featured banners about "frankenfoods" such as hormone-treated beef and genetically modified corn.

I always knew that TTIP would be a big challenge. But I thought then, as I still do now, that it was one of the most significant opportunities ever to deepen the US-EU economic, and especially political, relationship. It was a rare opportunity to boost transatlantic growth, set a gold standard for global trade deals that would enshrine our high standards in many areas, and promote regional and multilateral trade liberalization.

When TTIP was launched, the US and the EU together represented 60% of global GDP, 33% of world trade in goods, and 42% of world trade in services. TTIP was one of the main reasons that I had so enthusiastically accepted the appointment as US envoy to the EU and I had put it at the top of my agenda, including in my Senate confirmation hearings. However, the conditions for TTIP in Europe were already difficult upon my arrival in 2014 and became tougher in 2015. Organizers of the "Stop TTIP" campaign collected over 3.2 million signatures from 23 member states in the space of one year. That was triple the number required for a European Citizens' Initiative, a mechanism introduced by the Lisbon Treaty to enable citizens to call directly on the European Commission to take legal action.

The widespread resistance to TTIP in Europe surprised many Obama administration officials. In contrast, the negotiations were greeted positively in Congress and with a collective yawn by the US public, partly due to the focus on the trans-pacific free trade agreement, but principally because the idea of negotiating an agreement with a partner that shares our high standards (and does not pose a risk of low-wage competition) was largely uncontroversial.

Early Clashes over Dispute Settlement

One of the early flash points was over investor-state dispute settlement (ISDS). In a nutshell, ISDS refers to treaty-based protections granted to foreign investors by countries that want them to invest. The protections include the right to sue the host state before an international arbitration tribunal if it engages in an illegal and highly damaging action that prejudices the foreign investor, such as expropriation. This rather arcane issue attracted widespread (negative) attention, even in the popular media.

I found the controversy over ISDS deeply frustrating because many of the criticisms were simply misinformed. The whole point of the measures was to depoliticize disputes (that had all too often been subject to gunboat diplomacy in the past) and therefore to create a predictable environment for investors to invest and create jobs. Some critics falsely warned about a tsunami of investor claims, ignoring the fact that there have been fewer than 35 such claims on average per year for the past decade. The number was growing, but in line with global cross-border investment.

It was hypocritical for Europeans to claim that the US was inflicting ISDS on them when European states had negotiated as many bilateral investment treaties (BITs) incorporating ISDS provisions as the rest of the world combined. The opposition to ISDS in Germany was particularly bizarre because Germany had concluded 136 BITs, more than any other country in the world, over the past 60 years. As of 2015, investors from the EU were responsible for more than half of all known ISDS cases.

It was wrong to argue that ISDS favors investors; to the contrary, most cases are won by states. And in those cases where investors have won, they typically have recovered 10% on average of the damages they have claimed. Many of the cases regularly invoked by ISDS critics involved cases that have been *filed* and not yet decided or represented highly unusual and extreme outcomes. There was no evidence to suggest that ISDS interfered with a state's sovereign right to regulate by preventing it from changing legislation and offering investors an avenue to sue whenever their expectation of making a profit had been undermined. It was wrong to assert that ISDS only served the interests of multinationals, as many small and medium-sized enterprises (SMEs) also benefited from investment protection; they were arguably more needy of such protection because they typically have fewer political connections and resources to sue in national courts.

Above all, it was absurd to claim that ISDS is a "post-colonial" tool to protect investments in developing countries and unjustifiable in the case of investments in developed countries with advanced legal systems. EU member states have signed roughly 200 intra-EU BITs; Germany has signed 14 with other EU member states and five with non-EU members of the Organization of Economic Cooperation and Development (consisting of highly developed economies). In three-quarters of the 117 known cases where an EU member state has been sued under ISDS provisions, another EU member state was the complainant.

Ireland has thrived thanks to huge foreign investment without ever having to agree to ISDS because of a well-respected legal system (and low tax regime). Nonetheless, even European investors believe that investment protections are necessary when investing in some member states with weak legal systems. Some of the "newer" EU member states had decided, soon after their liberation from the Soviet empire, to offer very favorable investor protection to attract investments, and they had gotten the benefit of that bargain.

The critics were right to point out, however, that some of the older BITs containing ISDS had been poorly drafted and subject to abusive behavior by investors. The answer, of course, was to improve the drafting, improve the transparency of proceedings, enable greater public participation, and shut down the possibility of abuse. We felt that the 2012 United States Model Bilateral Investment Treaty, the fruit of a multiple-year review with a wide range of stakeholders, did precisely that. One of the ironies of the opposition to ISDS in TTIP is that without TTIP those older European agreements would remain in place, including nine with the United States.

THE GERMAN PUZZLE

Ground zero of the opposition to TTIP, and specifically to ISDS, was in Germany, Austria, and Luxembourg. That was rather counterintuitive. Germany, Europe's export powerhouse that had become rich through trade and could become richer yet from increased transatlantic commerce, should have been the main cheerleader for the deal. German unemployment was very low—less than 5%—and its current account surplus a staggeringly high 8% of GDP. As a result of TTIP, German exports and corporate profits, including in the rich web of SMEs, would surely rise in the aggregate. Nearly every serious economic projection showed that the gross domestic products of member states in Europe, and especially Germany, would rise materially thanks to an ambitious trade agreement.

And yet support for TTIP in Germany sank like a stone—from 55% in 2014 to 17% by the fall of 2016.[1] By that time, roughly 70% of Germans

---

[1] "Attitudes Toward Global Trade and TTIP in Germany and the United States," Bertelsmann Foundation, August 2016, p. 7.

had a negative view of TTIP, double the average in most other European countries. This counterintuitive situation might be due in part to the fact that many Germans were so content with the status quo that they viewed any significant trade initiative as purely downside risk.

Moreover, an overwhelming part of the German public had been misled to believe that the agreement would only enrich the multinationals at the expense of consumers, lower workers' wages, compromise data and environmental protection, and weaken citizens' rights. It was also widely accepted that the agreement would substitute the EU's sacred "precautionary principle"—under which products must be proved 100% safe before they can be sold—with the US science-based approach that allows products to be sold unless there is proof that they are harmful.[2] That touched the raw nerve of fear that TTIP would undermine product safety and food quality by forcing discerning European consumers to eat foods stuffed with hormones and treated with chemicals.

According to one report released in the spring of 2014, only 4% and 2% of Germans trusted American auto safety and food standards, respectively (as opposed to 91% and 94% trust in German standards).[3] Despite this very low trust, German tourists in the United States were not being massacred on American roads and in restaurants due to jerry-built cars and infected foods. The reality, as confirmed by multiple studies by respected European and American researchers, was that neither side can claim to enforce stricter precautions against health, safety, and environmental risks than the other.

Even more troubling, and surprising, was that support for free trade itself was plummeting in Germany. According to the German newspaper *Die Welt*, less than half of the German population had a positive view of free trade in April 2016, down from 88% two years earlier. "Anti-free trade views have become respectable."[4] Anti-TTIP protests brought hundreds of thousands of protestors to the streets of Germany, including

---

[2] In reality, this dichotomy is wildly overstated by the critics of the US approach. In the United States, precaution is built into our risk assessment and risk management activities. It is reflected in our practice of adapting regulations based on the experience gained in implementing them and on new evidence that becomes available.

[3] "Support in Principle for US-EU Trade Pact," Pew Research Center (in association with the Bertelsmann Foundation), April 9, 2014, p. 14.

[4] Martin Greive and Marc Nelle, "Der Deutsche Aufstand Gegen den Vertrag Mit Amerika," *Die Welt*, April 25, 2016.

250,000 in Berlin in October 2015, something not seen since the peace protests of the 1980s. Who ever thought trade could be as exciting as the Cold War and the threat of nuclear war?

The growing negativity toward TTIP was not limited to Germany, Austria, and Luxembourg. Opposition to TTIP was also growing in the United Kingdom. In February 2016, UK Labour leader Jeremy Corbyn described TTIP in the House of Commons as a threat to national sovereignty, workers, consumers, health, and the environment.[5] Labour Shadow Chancellor of the Exchequer John McDonnell said the deal would bring about a form of "modern-day slavery."[6] UK unions were obsessed with the notion that TTIP would undermine the National Health Service and force the privatization of public services. One of the Scottish Members of the European Parliament explained to me that grannies were showing up in her constituency in remote towns with anti-ISDS buttons on their blouses.

Belgium proved to be a particularly difficult country due to its highly decentralized political system. In addition to the Belgian national parliament, there are five sub-federal parliaments—for the southern Walloon region, the northern Flemish region, the Brussels region, the French-speaking community, and the German-speaking community (representing 70,000 people). Each of these has the power to block the federal government's approval of free trade agreements in certain circumstances. In mid-2015, all the sub-federal parliaments, except those representing the economically successful Flanders region and the Flemish-speaking community, issued solemn resolutions against the EU-Canada Comprehensive Economic and Trade Agreement (CETA) that was nearing completion.

The Walloon parliament persisted with its objections to CETA until the very last moment, nearly killing the deal in the spring of 2016 against the wishes of the remaining 99% of the EU population. While its objections were ostensibly grounded in concerns about ISDS and social, health, and environmental standards, the real reason was purely domestic: A majority of the Walloon parliament consisted of fringe parties that delighted

---

[5] Hazel Sheffield, "TTIP 'Must Include Human Rights,' Jeremy Corbyn Tells Cameron," *The Independent*, February 22, 2016.

[6] Anti-TTIP event at Conway Hall in London, October 8, 2015.

in destabilizing the federal government led by centrist Prime Minister Charles Michel.

The extraordinary situation in Belgium was not unique. Almost 1900 cities and municipalities declared themselves to be "TTIP-free zones." Many of the 19 city councils in Brussels, each representing roughly 50,000 people, went to extraordinary lengths to criticize the negotiation. When I heard during a dinner organized for me in Amsterdam that the city council had also declared itself to be "TTIP-free," I nearly fell off my chair. The city's entire history was linked to free trade; it was a monument to the entrepreneurial genius and free-trading spirit of the Dutch people.

The spreading opposition to TTIP (and CETA) was also striking because the EU had been negotiating free trade agreements for many years (including a recent significant deal with South Korea) without popular resistance. The EU free trade deal with Japan, concluded in 2018, and covering a market of 600 million people and 30% of global GDP, was negotiated and finalized with barely a ripple of dissent. Anti-American sentiment was clearly one reason for the starkly different public reaction to TTIP.

While the US and the EU had clashed during prior decades on trade issues, especially over agriculture, they had collaborated intensively on international trade liberalization. In December 2015, for example, the two had been instrumental in expanding the product coverage of the 1996 Information Technology Agreement that eliminated tariffs on $1 trillion worth of trade of IT products. The expansion, covering 9–13% of world trade, would increase global GDP by $190 billion per year, according to experts.

In July 2014, the US and the EU played a key role in launching negotiations on an Environmental Goods Agreement (EGA) to eliminate tariffs on many "green" goods crucial for environmental protection and climate change mitigation, such as solar panels, wind turbines, and water treatment equipment. The negotiations were put on hold at the end of 2016, due to Chinese demands and the change of US administration. And since the spring of 2013, the US and the EU spearheaded the Trade in Services Agreement (TISA), covering about 70% of the world's services economy in such areas as financial services, telecoms, e-commerce, health care, transport, and mobility of professionals. These negotiations are also on hold due to the change of US administration.

The US and the EU have also cooperated on a variety of unfair Chinese trade practices, including steel oversupply, industrial subsidies, and intellectual property theft. This is one of the few areas in trade where the US and the EU continue to cooperate intensively (together with Japan) under the Trump administration.

So why was TTIP immediately engulfed in European controversy? Part of the reason is that the objectives of the negotiation were so ambitious. Vice President Joe Biden liked to say that "If you're going to be crucified, you might as well do it on a big cross." That also applied to trade deals. Well, we collapsed early in our walk along the Via Dolorosa, long before we ever made it to the cross.

Hoping to Be Crucified on a Big Cross

As set forth in the Final Report of the High Level Working Group on Jobs and Growth that launched the negotiations in February 2013, the negotiations aimed at making substantial progress in three areas:

1. Market access, specifically the removal of customs duties on goods and restrictions on the provision of services, gaining better access to government procurement, and facilitating investment;
2. Improving alignment of the US and EU regulatory systems, enhancing cooperation on setting new regulations and eliminating unnecessary divergences in existing regulations (without lowering consumer or environmental protections); and cooperating on setting rules that address emerging challenges to the global trading system, such as ensuring high-level protection for intellectual property, the environment, and workers; and
3. Cracking down on new forms of anti-competitive behavior, including subsidies, privileges granted to state-owned enterprises, export restrictions on raw materials, and so-called "localization barriers" designed to protect domestic industries, services, and intellectual property.

Mike Froman, my dear friend and very able US Trade Representative, made clear on many occasions that TTIP had global significance: "...[it] not only enhances our mutual commitment to rules-based trade, but ... enhances our ability to strengthen the rules-based system around the world."[7] It would, moreover, strengthen the US-EU global partnership and help to revive the stalled WTO talks.

In its early efforts to trumpet the ambition of the negotiation, the Obama administration repeatedly referred to TTIP as "revolutionary." That backfired for a simple reason: It's not what you say, it's what people hear that counts. We thought we were describing the deal as big and exciting. But after six years of financial crisis and growing economic insecurity, later compounded by terrorism and unprecedented migration flows, much of the European public was in a "protective crouch" and in no mood for anything as scary as a revolution. I convinced Washington to describe the deal as "evolutionary"—one that would build on an already deep and beneficial economic partnership.

The $5.5 trillion transatlantic economy is the largest and wealthiest in the world, accounting for over one-third of the world's GDP in terms of purchasing power. The US and the EU are each other's largest trading partners: US-EU merchandise trade totaled roughly $807 billion during 2018, double the level at the start of the new century. 45 of 50 US states export more to Europe than to China, in many cases by a wide margin. 55% of total US global investment outflows goes to Europe, and Europe accounts for 54% of global investment inflows into the US. Affiliates of US companies in Europe generate sales over $3.1 trillion and employ 4.8 million workers, while affiliates of European companies in the United States generate sales of $2.5 trillion and employ 4.6 million workers.[8]

In many of the roughly 90 speeches I delivered on TTIP in 18 of the 28 EU member states, I described an ambitious transatlantic free trade deal as debt-free stimulus for jobs and growth in a Europe starved of both. Every serious study showed that TTIP would increase exports and investments, as well as create jobs. I argued that the deal was about providing consumers with more choice and better products at lower cost. It was about ensuring access to cheaper parts and raw material inputs, especially important for transatlantic trade between members of the same or related firms. Cheaper parts and other inputs could help reduce the

---

[7] Remarks by US Trade Representative Michael Froman on the United States, the European Union, and the Transatlantic Trade and Investment Partnership, September 30, 2013.

[8] AmCham EU, *The Transatlantic Economy 2019*. See also Daniel Hamilton, *Creating a North Atlantic Marketplace for Jobs and Growth*, Center for Transatlantic Studies, 2018.

cost of manufacturing in Europe, inflated by high energy and labor costs. By boosting growth, the deal could help fund pensions for retirees and health, safety, and environmental protections.

Much of what TTIP was seeking to achieve, I argued, was in fact a geographical extension of what the EU had already successfully achieved in creating a single market without tariff walls in which goods and services could flow freely. Original fears that the single market would sacrifice health and safety standards in order to achieve higher growth had proved to be unfounded.

Improving reciprocal market access was an important objective in the TTIP negotiations. The High Level Working Group report had made clear that the parties would seek to "eliminate all duties on bilateral trade, with a substantial elimination of tariffs upon entry into force, and a phasing out of all but the most sensitive tariffs in a short time frame." Tariff reductions were appropriately a key focus: Although trade-weighted transatlantic tariffs on goods average between 2 and 3%, the EU applies substantially higher tariffs, especially in agriculture, but also in industrial products, such as trucks, footwear, audiovisual products, and clothing; and the US also applies substantially higher tariffs on industrial products such as footwear, textiles, and clothing.[9] Even in the sectors where tariffs are low, they can be economically significant when profit margins are slim. According to one study, a transatlantic zero-tariff agreement could boost US and EU exports to each other by 17%.[10]

Market access was much more than tariff elimination, however. The High Level Working Group report expressed the parties' ambition to extend to each other the highest level of market access in services that either had granted to third parties in trade negotiations to date and to address remaining barriers while "recognizing the sensitive nature of certain sectors." The High Level Working Group report expressed the parties' aspiration to build on the highest levels of liberalization of investment flows and the highest standards of protection of investors against abusive state behavior that either side had negotiated with third parties to date. The report also included a pledge to offer substantially improved access to

---

[9] Commission Staff Working Document, Impact Assessment Report on the future of EU-US trade relations, March 12, 2013.

[10] Fredrik Erixon and Matthias Bauer, "A Transatlantic Zero Agreement: Estimating the Gains from Transatlantic Free Trade in Goods," European Centre for International Political Economy, Occasion Paper 4/2010.

government procurement at all levels of government (federal and subfederal) on the basis that US and EU firms would receive no worse treatment than the other in their respective home markets.

The real promise of TTIP lay in the second category of negotiating objectives: The non-tariff barriers that constitute "behind the border" obstacles to trade, including provisions that impose unnecessary costs and administrative delays stemming from divergent regulations. These barriers were a major reason why the US was running a goods and services trade deficit with the EU of $91 billion. Nearly every study on the impact of TTIP concluded that between one-half and three-quarters of the benefits would result from the removal of these barriers.

The problem was that their removal would be exceedingly difficult to achieve: they were highly technical and touched the raw nerve of regulatory sovereignty and stirred strong emotions about health and safety standards, food, culture, and way of life. The effort at eliminating non-tariff barriers was frequently mischaracterized as a free pass for companies to dilute health, consumer, and environmental protections. The reality was rather different.

From the start of the negotiations, the parties sought to improve "regulatory coherence"—essentially the alignment of their regulatory systems—through a mutual commitment to transparency, stakeholder input, and good regulatory practices such as the use of impact assessments and the periodic review of existing regulatory measures. The reason for this focus is that US and EU regulations will continue to diverge for as long as both sides write regulations based on analysis developed from different evidence.

They also agreed to pursue opportunities to improve regulatory compatibility in specific sectors of economic importance—especially auto safety, pharmaceuticals, and chemicals. In some (rare) instances, the parties might be able to harmonize their divergent regulations if they could agree on which regulations were best. When that was unachievable, they still might be able to grant mutual recognition of their regulations where they provided identical levels of protection. While that might sound straightforward, it is in fact very hard. For decades, the US and the EU have sought to strike mutual recognition agreements in economically significant areas but ended up with rather modest agreements in such areas as marine equipment. Finally, the US and the EU might be able to agree to find that each other's regulations provided equivalent degrees of protection, thereby eliminating the need for duplicative testing and certification costs. The parties also agreed to establish a framework to help identify opportunities for future regulatory cooperation, especially in emerging technologies.

Non-tariff barriers also include two important trade irritants. The first consists of sanitary and phytosanitary (SPS) measures to protect humans, animals, and plants from diseases, pests, or contaminants. A separate SPS chapter in TTIP would build on the key principles of the WTO, including requirements that each side's measures would be based on science and on international standards or scientific risk assessments, applied only to the extent necessary, and developed in a transparent manner without undue delay. The second consists of technical barriers to trade (TBT)—technical regulations and standards, and procedures for the assessment of conformity with them.

SPS issues have inflamed US-EU agricultural trade relations for decades. This is a shame because the US and the EU have remarkably complementary agricultural sectors: While the former has a competitive advantage in large-scale production of commodities, the latter focuses on intensive agriculture and value-added processed food production.

During one of my early consultations in Washington, I paid a call on the US Department of Agriculture (USDA) to review the outstanding disputes. I was handed detailed lists of SPS barriers to imports that the US and the EU had recently removed for one another and additional lists of barriers that remained. The first list of successes was rather short, and it was clear that each removal of a barrier by one side had been traded against the removal of a barrier by the other side. When I remarked that this looked like a "hostage exchange exercise," the team nodded in agreement. That has proven to be a slow, painful, and ultimately doomed approach. Discussions between US and EU negotiators on SPS issues almost always deteriorated into utterly sterile "talking point ping pong" with each side reading from prepared texts. The list of SPS obstacles contained some infuriating examples.

Although the EU and the US agreed for many years that their different approaches to testing molluscan shellfish (clams, scallops, oysters, and mussels) protected public health in a broadly equivalent manner, it took a decade to finalize a mutual recognition agreement in 2018 ending restrictions on bilateral trade. Bilateral trade in fresh fruits and vegetables is much lower than it should be. The US sells very low quantities to the EU, largely because the EU blocks imports of fruits and vegetables containing more than minute traces of pesticides, despite the fact that its limits are more restrictive than the standards accepted internationally and by the European Food Safety Agency. The US Animal and Plant Health Inspection Service, in turn, dragged its feet on approving imports of apples and pears from the EU—including from Poland even after its industry was decimated by Russian countersanctions related to its annexation of Crimea.

Whereas the EU lifted its restrictions on British beef imports in 2006 following the outbreak of "mad cow" disease in the early 1990s, the USDA published new rules on EU beef exports only in 2013, and it took over two years to inspect and approve slaughterhouses in just three EU member states to start shipping beef to the United States. At that rate, it would take 20 years before the whole of the EU is approved. To my amusement, moreover, the US has banned the sale of real French brie cheese made from raw unpasteurized cow's milk. The Food and Drug Administration declared in 2004 that all cheeses that are not aged for at least 60 days must use pasteurized milk. To my knowledge, the French are not dropping like flies from *E. coli* and listeria in their brie.

But the EU was certainly no saint in the area of SPS restrictions, either. Although the European Commission had agreed to allow the use of lactic acid to remove pathogens on beef carcasses just before my arrival, it had yet to agree to the use of similar "pathogen reduction treatments," such as the use of peroxyacetic acid (chlorine), for poultry. EU law prohibits the use of anything except water—that well-known disinfectant—as a sanitary wash for meat products, unless specifically authorized. And that was despite a clear opinion from the European Food Safety Agency that antimicrobial washes (including chlorine) for meat carcasses are effective and safe, especially against *E. coli* and campylobacter.

Sometimes the EU member states play the most inventive games as well. After 30 American lobsters had been found living in the wild off Sweden's coast in March 2016, the Swedish environment ministry asked the EU to reclassify them as an invasive species, which would have resulted in a live import ban (and the loss of $140 million of US exports). They seemed few and harmless enough, with their claws still banded, which is the way US lobsters are sold. Had they been "liberated" by animal rights activists? Or had the European lobby for inferior lobsters detected a way to avoid competition? According to the ministry, their mating habits were aggressive and could threaten Europe's lobster population through diseases and inbreeding. After my insistent prodding, the European Commission took a different view.[11]

A separate TBT chapter in TTIP would seek to promote greater openness, transparency, and convergence in regulatory approaches and related standards development processes. Objectives of the chapter included the adoption of relevant international standards, fewer redundant and burdensome testing and certification requirements, enhanced confidence in the parties' conformity assessment bodies, and improved cooperation on conformity assessment and standardization issues globally.

How much progress did we make toward these objectives in three and a half years of negotiations? While there was progress in some areas, the sad reality is that we fell far short of our ambitions. Reading the conclusions of the 15 negotiating rounds is like watching water boil: Much of the language is repetitive, with only discrete signs of movement. The most concrete achievement is that the parties exchanged offers to eliminate duties on 97% of tariff lines, a large majority of which would be phased out immediately upon entry into force of the agreement or phased out quickly.

The Progress Achieved

The US-EU Joint Report on TTIP Progress to Date, issued on January 17, 2017, summarizes other, more technical, areas of progress. For example, the parties built on prior progress toward defining principles of regulatory coherence and regulatory cooperation. The parties identified ways to reduce unnecessary burdens in transatlantic trade arising from redundant or duplicative product testing and certification requirements, especially in the manufacture of pharmaceutical products.

As a result of this work, the FDA and the European Medicines Agency signed in early March 2017, and fully implemented in 2019, a mutual recognition agreement on good manufacturing practices for active pharmaceutical products. This important agreement enables US and EU regulators to use inspection reports and other related information obtained during inspections of manufacturing facilities, conducted by either side, to determine whether a facility is manufacturing high-quality drugs. That, in turn, enables the parties to reallocate resources toward inspection of drug

---

[11] Shawn Donnan, "Maine Lobster Claws Itself Back from EU Ban," *Financial Times*, October 14, 2016.

manufacturing facilities with potentially higher public health risks across the globe, especially in developing countries. This makes it faster and less costly for both sides to bring medicines to market. Work continues to expand the scope of the agreement to veterinary medicines, human vaccines, and plasma-derived medicinal products.

The parties made modest progress toward the goal of recognizing each other's auto safety tests as providing an equivalent degree of protection to their own. And they developed a framework for regulatory cooperation to facilitate greater compatibility in future regulations. The US and EU agreed on measures to reduce red tape and delays at their borders, such as electronic filing of customs declarations. They also agreed on a dedicated chapter on SMEs that contained tools enabling them to exploit the opportunities of transatlantic trade.

But there were many more disappointments than achievements. From the US perspective, it was particularly disappointing that the EU did not table an offer to eliminate nearly all tariff lines, contrary to the clear objective of the High Level Working Group report and to the Council's negotiating mandate to the Commission.[12] The remaining 3% of tariff lines are of considerable importance to US farmers and ranchers, without whose support there is zero chance of getting a deal approved in Congress. Although non-tariff barriers (especially those impacting poultry, beef, and grain exports) were more important than tariff barriers in explaining the $12 billion and growing US agricultural trade deficit with the EU, the elimination of tariffs was nonetheless a significant negotiating objective. The EU could have pushed further on tariff line elimination while making clear that there would be no deal without agreement on all issues. Instead, it argued, to our irritation, that progress on the sensitive agricultural tariff lines would be tied to a host of other issues that were politically difficult for the United States.

The US was also irritated with the EU offer on the liberalization of services. While the US services offer was as ambitious as any it had ever proposed, the EU's offer fell short of what it had offered in its free trade agreement with Korea, or in its negotiations on the TISA or in its free trade agreement with Canada. The US had tabled a "negative

---

[12] The EU later claimed that it had always made clear that full duty elimination would not be possible for the most sensitive agricultural tariff lines, especially those relating to beef, poultry and pork. But the report states that "the goal of the agreement should be to eliminate all duties on bilateral trade...".

list" approach that liberalized all services sectors except those specifically scheduled, but the EU refused to do so (unlike in its agreement with Canada).

The EU argued that it would only contemplate adopting a "negative list" approach if the US provided a comprehensive list of all restrictions on services maintained by states and local entities. Not only was this unnecessary as European companies surely could inform the European Commission of any obstacles that they faced; it was also complex and costly to conduct an exhaustive audit. In the Korea-US free trade agreement, the South Koreans have been content to accept an illustrative list of such restrictions, rather than an audit.

US exceptions from the commitment to liberalize were far fewer than those tabled by the EU, both in terms of number and economic significance.[13] The EU had insisted from the beginning of the negotiations on a complete carve-out of audiovisual services from the agreement. And it refused to table any offer on financial services market liberalization (on the grounds that the US side didn't want to discuss intensifying financial market regulatory cooperation). While the US had offered to permanently guarantee EU service providers their current broad access to the US market, including at sub-federal level, the EU had reserved the ability to introduce new discriminatory measures in virtually all existing economic sectors, as well as in "new services"—defined as any service not identified by a UN classification scheme dating all the way back to 1991, before the Internet and a host of digital services.

The EU refused, moreover, even after the conclusion of the Privacy Shield Agreement in February 2016, to table text on electronic commerce, an important and growing component of transatlantic trade. And the EU slowed progress on core TBT issues, such as the ones that currently prevent US laboratories from testing products for the EU market, deny US stakeholders from participating in European standards development, and provide that European products are presumed to conform with European laws only if they meet standards developed by European standardization bodies (even if US standards are technically equivalent and globally relevant).

---

[13] The US list contained maritime transportation; gambling and betting; social services; and minority affairs. The EU list contained over 200 exceptions. The EU disputed the US characterization by arguing that many of the exceptions were maintained by individual member states (not across the EU) and were economically insignificant.

From the EU perspective, it was disappointing that the US refused to discuss how to make the Jones Act less restrictive. This federal statute from 1920 requires that all goods transported by water between US ports be carried on US-flagged ships, constructed in the United States, owned by US citizens, and crewed by US citizens and US permanent residents. Although international shipping from and to US ports (roughly three-quarters of the US maritime market) remains open to foreign competition, the domestic coastal market remains shut.

The US also refused to lift its equity caps on foreign ownership in the telecoms and aviation sectors. Moreover, the US tabled an offer on government procurement that barely loosened federal restrictions on foreign competitors and did nothing to increase state-level market access, and the US refused to entertain EU concerns about the protection of geographical indications on food and wine.

Progress on mutual recognition in the automotive sector proved to be much harder than anticipated. There had been high hopes that the 2011 Agreement between the US and the European Community on Cooperation in the Regulation of Civil Aviation Safety could have served as a model. It is thanks to this agreement, and its reciprocal acceptance of repair and maintenance standards for civil aircraft, that one can fly on an airplane and be confident of its safety, regardless of whether it has been serviced in the US or in Europe. If the Federal Aviation Administration and the European Aviation Safety Agency can agree to recognize each other's certifications, why can't the US and EU do so in the case of motor vehicles?

The economic case for the US and EU to recognize each other's auto safety rules as providing equivalent outcomes is compelling. Bilateral automotive trade accounts for one-tenth of total US-EU trade. If the parties would recognize each other's crash tests and related standards, auto manufacturers on both sides of the Atlantic could save up to 7% on the cost of producing each car and truck. But one of the core obstacles is that the National Highway Traffic Safety Administration (NHTSA) is restricted by its statutory authority from Congress to recognize foreign rules as equivalent only if there is supporting data. Short-cutting that authority would expose NHTSA to lawsuits from consumers. Several joint transatlantic studies found that no EU-wide database on crashworthiness—how well a car protects its occupants from injury in a crash—is as detailed as the one maintained by NHTSA. Regulators in some wealthier EU member states do, however, maintain richer data sets. Adjusting for the absence of EU-wide data, as well as radically different driving conditions, road conditions, per capita income, and vehicle types in Europe, proved to be difficult.

Crash tests weren't the only area of auto safety where mutual recognition proved difficult. Intensive discussions between the US and the EU in TTIP only managed to identify at most 15 relatively minor areas where each side could recognize the other's automotive safety regulations as fully or partially equivalent. Even that would have required additional evidence and lengthy rule-making procedures. Focusing on the harmonization of new regulations or standards and avoiding duplication of certification costs would have been a much more productive approach.

Some Lessons Learned

There are many lessons that can be gleaned from our failure to make more progress on TTIP. Two key lessons stand out. The first is that both sides must realize that TTIP is unlike any prior trade negotiation either has undertaken because the parties are of equal size and negotiating leverage.

The second key lesson is that such a significant enterprise will not occur without more political will. President Clinton had realized that NAFTA would only be approved if his administration was fully invested in that outcome. While President Obama and many members of his administration frequently endorsed TTIP, the president did not appear willing to invest sufficient political capital to get TTIP over the line. There were many things that the White House could have done but did not. It could have worked with Congress on US offers relating to public procurement or maritime services; it could have considered overruling the objections of the US Treasury to negotiating financial services regulatory cooperation; and it could have mandated agencies of the federal government (including the NHTSA and the FDA) to enhance regulatory cooperation with the EU.

Perhaps the president thought that it was not worth investing too much in TTIP because the Trans-Pacific Partnership (TPP) deal was bigger, further advanced in negotiations and more likely to conclude. I privately wondered whether the priorities should have been inverted. Concluding a trade agreement with a wealthy region that shares US values should be easier than concluding one with a region that includes developing countries with a weaker commitment to those values.

President Obama appeared to be convinced that the US had significant leverage with the EU. On three separate meetings with Jean-Claude Juncker, president of the European Commission, and Donald Tusk, president of the European Council, I heard President Obama point out that the EU needed the deal more than the US because the US economy was performing far better than the European economies (especially in terms of employment and growth). He also reminded the EU that it had originally approached the US with the proposal of a transatlantic free trade deal rather than the other way around. Not only was this indelicate, but it also had the predictable result of stiffening the EU's back. And it was overtaken by events rather dramatically, as Congress failed to approve TPP before the end of President Obama's term. When President Trump withdrew the US from the negotiations, the remaining members proceeded to conclude it successfully. European economies recovered, moreover, and the EU signed significant free trade deals with Canada, Japan, Vietnam, and the South American trade bloc Mercosur.

There was a slightly different dynamic on the European side. The European Commission and the European Council (representing EU leaders) repeatedly endorsed the negotiations in a series of solemn communiqués. To our and the European Commission's great irritation, however, many heads of state simply couldn't resist the pleasures of domestic politicking: Once back in their national capitals, they would be ambivalent about, or even criticize, the negotiations. Some leading members of national governments—especially Sigmar Gabriel, German Minister of the Economy, and Matthias Fekl, French Minister for Foreign Trade—were especially negative. As the European public naturally pays more attention to national news than to European communiqués, the inevitable result was that support for TTIP continued to disintegrate. If TTIP is to stand a chance of being revived, member states need to stop this Janus-faced behavior.

Politics will be even more important than usual because trust in institutions, particularly governments, is at an all-time low. Mistrust in the European Commission still runs deep in many member states, partly because some national leaders have cynically chosen to blame Brussels for all national ills rather than shoulder their responsibilities. The European Commission has also invited some of this mistrust in the past (before the adoption of greater transparency under Trade Commissioner Malmström) by treating member states, as a former commissioner told me, like mushrooms that are fed manure and left alone in the dark.

During my public appearances in Europe on TTIP, I felt that many of my messages were discounted because I was a spokesman of the US government. It reminded me of the old Zulu proverb: "I cannot hear what you say for the thunder of what you are." The Snowden allegations certainly clouded the prospects for TTIP under the Obama administration. And that was on top of the usual caricatures that European critics of the United States have been making for decades.

Mistrust in the United States has only increased as a result of the Trump administration's withdrawal from international agreements in which the EU has played a significant role (such as the agreement to curb Iran's nuclear ambitions and the Paris Agreement on climate change) and its attack on the multilateral rules-based order and institutions (such as the World Trade Organization). Trust has also suffered because of the administration's clear promotion of Brexit and its desire that the European Union should break up. The prospects of an ambitious US-EU trade deal under President Trump are low. While the EU Council approved a mandate to the Commission to negotiate such a deal, France (and several other member states) voiced serious reservations and the European Parliament's international trade committee expressed a negative view.

The challenge is greater than distrust of governments and anti-Americanism. I discovered soon after my arrival in Brussels that the debate about TTIP was just as much about the merits of free trade and globalization as it was about a free trade agreement. Many of TTIP's critics in Europe appeared to think that TTIP and free trade agreements in general were a way to deepen and accelerate globalization, a source of additional instability after years of economic hardship and feelings of physical and cultural insecurity stemming from migration and terrorism.

While the negative reactions to TTIP in Europe, especially in Germany, Austria, and Luxembourg, appeared counterintuitive at first blush, they actually reflected a normal human urge to slow down and seek greater control in times of change. Many TTIP critics appeared to believe that one can hit the pause button on globalization to allow companies more time to adapt. It reminded me of the hit musical in London's West End and Broadway called *Stop the World – I Want to Get Off.* I tried to explain, with mixed success, that globalization is a reality, whether we like it or not; that free trade agreements are actually a tool to shape globalization, especially when they are concluded between parties committed to high standards of consumer, health, labor, and environmental protections; and that many of the ills ascribed to globalization, including job losses and the decline of manufacturing, are largely the results of technology and automation. The choice is not between accepting or rejecting globalization; it is between whether we will shape it or be shaped by it.

FAILURES TO COMMUNICATE

One of the core problems afflicting the negotiations was that neither side really understood the drivers of public emotions. Both sides were so engrossed in the negotiations as a technocratic exercise that they failed to understand the need to engage in a professional political campaign. Such a campaign should have started with focus groups, targeted messaging and, above all, emphasis on narratives propagated through social media. It would have been far less timid, especially in attacking myths propagated by non-governmental organizations that saw opposition to TTIP as a great business model to attract financing. Moreover, a professional campaign would have emphasized emotions more than dry statistics.

I repeatedly saw that when our facts collided with the passion of many critics, the latter almost always won. Similarly, complex truths will nearly always be trumped by simple falsehoods. While it was, of course, unacceptable to engage in passionate falsehoods, it was possible to focus on narratives. To be fair, the European Commission and the Office of the US Trade Representative did ramp up their efforts to produce real-life stories, targeted to specific countries and sectors, especially about how the deal would benefit SMEs; but the efforts were late and under-resourced. Finally, such a campaign would have featured far more energetic and earlier efforts by all businesses to communicate the advantages of the deal for their employees.

In my judgment, it was a communications error to over-hype the deal. Both sides over-sold the potential of regulatory cooperation when it should have been clear that this would be extremely challenging. Each side allowed rhetoric to run way too far in front of reality.

The United States repeated the mantra that the deal could be concluded on "one tank of gas" by January 2017, less than four years after its launch. That jarred with the reality that the US and EU had been discussing a transatlantic free trade area on and off for over a decade; efforts by businesses to propose specific measures eliminating barriers to trade, such as the Transatlantic Business Dialogue formed in 1995, had yielded little progress; and the Transatlantic Economic Council, a cabinet-level body formed in 2007 to promote US-EU economic cooperation, had also been of marginal utility.

The European Commission also over-hyped the deal: It frequently repeated, for example, that it would increase EU GDP by 0.5% and put €565 of disposable income in the pockets of every European family.[14] The claim, based on optimistic assumptions at an early stage of the negotiations when we had no idea of the deal's final contours, simply invited skepticism. Many critics thought that the benefits were not only more modest, but also uncertain and remote, and would in any event be appropriated by multinationals and the professional classes that already benefit from globalization. By allowing the rhetoric to outstrip the reality of slow progress in the negotiations, we undermined our own credibility. And, perhaps most dangerously, we presented TTIP as the most important determinant of the US-EU relationship, when in reality the relationship is far deeper and broader. Many joint projects—including cooperation on the digital economy and the Internet of Things—are economically far more significant.

Rather than sell uncertain projections, it would have been wiser to focus on the jobs and revenues that regions, cities, and local communities derive from transatlantic trade, as well as to describe how prior trade deals had demonstrably led to export growth and job creation (at a higher income level). Since NAFTA was implemented 22 years ago, the United States has signed 17 other bilateral free trade agreements. Exports to those countries are growing twice as fast as the average. Moreover, exporting firms in the US pay a wage premium of between 13 and 18% compared with non-exporters.[15]

Our trade balance in goods with 14 of those countries improved following the agreements. While the trade deficit with South Korea has worsened following the Korea-US free trade agreement, there are numerous reasons for this that are unrelated to the deal. One recent study has concluded that "Modern deals and old NAFTA-style deals are as night and day. And so are the results."[16] The Korea-EU free trade deal has also proven beneficial to the EU, with exports of goods and services up by

---

[14] The European Commission, *Transatlantic Trade and Investment Partnership: The Economic Analysis Explained*, September 2013.

[15] "Coming and Going," *The Economist*, October 1, 2016.

[16] Jim Kessler and Jay Chittooran, "Night and Day: Post-NAFTA Trade Deals Yield Steady Surpluses," *Third Way*, April 2016.

77% and 82%, respectively from 2010 to 2018. During that period, the EU's trade in goods went from a deficit of €10.5 billion in 2010 to being broadly balanced.

In order to address the cynicism, it would have been wise to acknowledge that free trade agreements also produce losers, not just winners. It is meaningless to talk of "aggregate" gains to society according to economic theory; to those who lose out, it is of cold comfort that society benefits on average. Critics of free trade are right to point out that the benefits have too often been privatized, while the losses have been socialized.

Another major reason why the TTIP negotiations had difficulty achieving traction is that many critics considered them to be secretive and, therefore, suspect. Some of the most vocal criticism of TTIP's opacity came from those who attacked the substance of the negotiations. This was obviously a contradiction: How could one hate a deal that one allegedly knew nothing about? I was also irritated by those NGOs who demanded transparency from the US and EU on TTIP but whose own financing remained totally opaque. I suspected that some of them were receiving money from Russia; the Kremlin had made its hostility to the negotiations very clear and had shamelessly propagated disinformation about them through *Russia Today*, *Sputnik* and troll farms.

The proponents of the deal correctly argued that TTIP was the most transparent trade negotiation in history: There was an enormous amount of publicly available information, contained in government websites, briefings, and speeches, as well as consultations that each side was conducting with its legislatures, businesses, and civil society through many advisory committees. The US felt that its system of domestic consultations during trade negotiations worked well. More than 600 individuals, representing a broad array of interest groups, had security clearances allowing them to see and comment on all textual proposals before they are tabled. It was difficult to grant the wider public more transparency about our proposals than we were already granting to this group.

The proponents of the deal also correctly argued that the ratification process would ensure democratic accountability and that negotiators need to be able to discuss proposals in confidence in order to explore trade-offs, just as in any business negotiation. Criticism that proposals to enhance US-EU regulatory cooperation would give multinationals the opportunity to lobby in secret and subvert parliamentary democracy were wide of the mark; to the contrary, these proposals were aimed at enhancing the quality of legislation by promoting greater transparency, public participation, and accountability.

Nonetheless, the United States was on the back foot on the transparency debate, especially once the EU started publishing its textual proposals on its website, as well as explanatory documents regarding its negotiating objectives and summaries after each negotiating round. At first, we only permitted a few select parliamentarians and officials from the European Parliament to gain access to TTIP "consolidated texts" (combining the parties' textual proposals for each chapter) in a reading room housed in the European Commission. We agreed in December 2014 to provide EU member state officials access to these texts on a "need to know basis," but only under extremely restrictive conditions. For example, the officials had to visit US embassies, during two days each week by appointment only and for only two hours per visit; only two officials would be allowed to review documents at a time and they would be monitored by US embassy personnel.

Any possible security reasons for these procedures were significantly outweighed by the considerable ill will that they generated, especially among senior officials. In December 2015, the US agreed to allow these approved member state officials, as well as all national parliamentarians, to have access to the consolidated texts in reading rooms housed in approved ministries. Moreover, all members of the European Parliament would have access. But all these measures were discounted because they had come late and only under pressure.

While we were losing the transparency debate in Europe, we were failing to exploit some key tools in our arsenal to convince the European public about TTIP's attractions: We should have put even greater emphasis on the deal's geopolitical aspects and on the advantages for SMEs.

Public communication about the benefits of TTIP focused too heavily on the Trade and Investment components and too little on the Partnership component. That was a pity because one of the very few arguments that gained widespread traction, both geographically and across the political spectrum, was that properly negotiated free trade agreements are a tool to shape globalization as we—in the advanced economies and democracies—want: at a high level of protection for consumers, health, and the environment. Regional agreements often encourage other countries to embrace the same high standards and principles; history has shown that they stimulate multilateral trade liberalization, as demonstrated by the role of NAFTA in resuscitating the Uruguay Round.

The rules-based open trading system is increasingly competing with state-directed mercantilist models. If we don't set the rules of global trade together during the next five to ten years, then other countries whose weight in the global trading system is rising fast will do it themselves—and those rules will be at a lower standard than ours. The share of global trade accounted for by the US and the EU has dropped as emerging markets have risen; China will soon overtake both to become the most important global trading power. As President Obama stated in the State of the Union address in January 2015:

> ...China wants to write the rules for the world's fastest growing region. That would put our workers and our businesses at a disadvantage. Why would we let that happen? We should write those rules. We should level the playing field.

We could have silenced some of our critics with a cruder version of this argument: You may not like the United States, but surely you'd rather do a deal with us to lock in the high level of protections that define both sides of the Atlantic, rather than do a deal with countries that don't share them. United States Trade Representative Mike Froman frequently made this point:

> The United States can launch a race to the top, rather than be subject to a race to the bottom that we cannot win and should not run...In the Asia Pacific region, for example, over 200 trade deals have been struck in recent years and more are currently under negotiation. Unlike TPP and TTIP, the vast majority of these agreements make no commitment to protecting labor rights and environmental standards, creating disciplines on state-owned enterprises and promoting the digital economy.[17]

The Regional Comprehensive Economic Partnership Agreement promoted by China among ten South East Asian countries (including three of the top four economies in the world) does not feature these protections. Once the US withdrew from TPP, the remaining members signed an agreement without significant provisions on intellectual property and investment protections.

TTIP's geopolitical utility was particularly well understood in the Baltics and Central and Eastern Europe, naturally concerned about the Russian bear next door. By tying the EU more closely to the US in

---

[17] Michael Froman, "The Geopolitical Stakes of America's Trade Policy," *Foreign Policy*, February 17, 2015.

a deeper partnership, TTIP complicated Russia's eternal aim to divide Europe from America and thereby project greater influence to its West, especially over the countries that had recently escaped its chilly embrace.

In addition to focusing on the geopolitical component of TTIP, we should have emphasized even more the benefits of the deal for SMEs. The vast majority of SMEs in the US and the EU had not seized the opportunities of transatlantic trade. The agreement would have enabled more SMEs to sell across the Atlantic by reducing tariff and non-tariff barriers; even those who would not do so directly would have benefited from increased sales to customers who would.

The many SMEs in the automotive supply chain were a good example. The negotiations had made significant progress on "trade facilitation"—including the reduction of customs paperwork and clearance procedures, as well as special treatment (including the elimination of customs duties) for low-value shipments. The reduction of non-tariff barriers, such as the administrative costs of dealing with divergent and duplicative regulatory environments, would have a particularly beneficial impact for SMEs given their limited budgets, staff, and expertise relative to multinationals.

My experience from explaining TTIP in Europe taught me that the single most effective pedagogical technique was to invite the local press to accompany me on visits to SMEs. These resulted in human interest stories that were far more engaging than the mumbo-jumbo of trade talk.

It was on one such trip to Pfeilring in Solingen, Germany, that I sat down with the Pfeilring CEO, Torsten Korb, and a journalist from the *Rheinische Post* to discuss what TTIP might mean for his business. Korb was justifiably proud of his company's quality tableware and manicure products. He explained to me that his revenues were 20 million euro, only one million of which from sales to the US. He wanted to grow, but faced obstacles such as the significant cost of duplicative certification requirements on either side of the Atlantic (with US certification costing 5000–10,000 euros per product), unclear customs treatments for his products and often bewildering regulatory hurdles, both nationally and on the state level.[18]

On another trip to Worlée and Co. outside Hamburg, I sat down with the CEO, Reinhold von Eben-Worlée, the fifth-generation family owner. He proudly showed me around the plant that makes cosmetics, cleans

---

[18] Fred Lothar Melchior, "US-Botschafter am Schleifblock," *Rheinische Post*, March 8, 2016.

mushrooms, and packages dried fruits and vegetables that go into soups and seasonings. He described how this was a good business because customers wanted to avoid product recalls and were willing to pay good money to a company like Worlée that mastered the technologically complex art of eliminating nearly all bacteria and foreign particles in these products. Eben-Worlée explained that his revenues were 290 million euro, of which 10 million came from sales to the US. We sat down, together with a journalist from *Die Welt*, to calculate the potential cost savings that TTIP would bring his company. Just the elimination of the 6% tariffs applicable to his imports and exports would save 600,000 euros per year. That meant more profits, more investment in plant and equipment, and more jobs.[19]

It would have helped the cause of TTIP enormously, especially in its early days, had we been able to announce some concrete and significant "wins." Nothing succeeds like success. Achievements would have demonstrated forward momentum and would have been easier to sell than good intentions. And, crucially, businesses would have started investing real time and resources into supporting the deal, rather than waiting on the sidelines to see if the negotiations were getting traction.

One good way of showing success would have been to show early and significant ambition on tariff cuts. Regrettably, this did not occur. The US and EU exchanged offers in early spring 2014: While Washington offered to eliminate 88% of all tariff lines, with immediate duty elimination for only 69%, Brussels offered to eliminate 96% of all tariff lines, with immediate duty elimination for roughly 85%.[20] We explained that our negotiating style was to start low and build it up over time with the ultimate objective of eliminating all tariff lines; we argued that the initial offer was better than what we had traditionally tabled at the initial phase of trade talks with important trading partners; and we pointed out that the EU offer was not as good as it appeared because it was contingent on several conditions and contained exceptions to ultimate tariff elimination (essentially shielding sensitive agricultural items). Those exceptions included tariff rate quotas that set a quantitative limit for a given item

---

[19] Olaf Preuss, "Warum der Mittelstand auf das umstrittene TTIP setzt," *Die Welt*, June 16, 2016.

[20] "Under Pressure to Show TTIP Progress, US, EU Focus on Market Access," *Inside US Trade*, April 17, 2014.

under which it can be sold duty-free or with a low tariff, with high tariffs kicking in above that quantitative limit.

But the damage was done: Having convinced some skeptical member states to come forward with an ambitious first offer, the European Commission ended up with egg all over its face and was thereafter branded by those states as a boy scout negotiator. Irishman Phil Hogan, EU Commissioner for Agriculture (currently Commissioner for Trade), claimed vindication in his steadfast refusal to discuss tariff cuts in key agricultural areas. We remained on the back foot for more than a year until the US and the EU exchanged symmetrical offers in the fall of 2015 to eliminate 97% of all tariffs. The EU continued to tie further progress on tariff elimination on US movement in unrelated fields, including government procurement and geographical indications.

Changes Required in the US Approach

I left my post convinced that we could have made much more progress on TTIP, even though it was unlikely that we would actually finalize an agreement in three years. I remain convinced that this agreement is of great importance to deepen the partnership between the US and the EU. While the Trump administration never withdrew from TTIP, its protectionist policies have made significant progress toward an agreement highly unlikely. When the time is ripe, we need to take into account the lessons behind TTIP's failure in order to achieve an ambitious, but more tailored, agreement.

First, the United States should not seek to backload too many priority EU issues to the end game of the negotiations in the hope of exerting maximum political pressure on the EU to make concessions. I believe that we deployed that tactic in TTIP and it predictably failed. Whereas the US executive branch is capable of making big moves at the last minute, the EU decision-making apparatus is simply not suited to do that. Lengthy consultations are needed among the EU institutions and especially with the member states, among whom there are often very different perspectives. TTIP negotiations have a greater chance of success if they feature steady progress with only a few politically difficult issues reserved for the "end game."

Second, the United States needs to take a different approach on ISDS. During TTIP, we had allowed this issue to fester like a gangrenous limb, endangering the future of the entire agreement. In the future, the US and the EU could place provisions on investor-state dispute settlement in an agreement separate from the body of a free trade agreement. That would avoid the toothache of subjecting a free trade agreement to ratification by the European Parliament and 38 national and sub-federal parliaments.[21] Another option would be for the US and EU to drop ISDS altogether. It would not be the first time that the US would sign an FTA without ISDS: The one it signed with Australia left it out on the ground that each side trusts the other's laws and national courts.

Third, the United States should reconsider its refusal to include within TTIP provisions deepening cooperation on financial services regulation. That refusal led the European Commission to stop negotiating reciprocal access to financial services, an issue of enormous interest to the highly competitive US financial services industry that sees significant opportunities to expand its service offer in Europe. The US Treasury justified its position on the grounds that including financial services regulatory cooperation in a trade agreement would risk undermining the 2010 Dodd-Frank legislation that tightened US rules introduced after the 2008 financial crisis; that the EU was further behind the US in regulatory reforms; and that the US and EU already cooperate in multiple fora, both bilaterally in the Financial Markets Regulatory Dialogue and multilaterally in the G-20, the Financial Stability Board and the Basel Committee for Banking Supervision.

I was kept on an exceptionally tight leash in terms of what I could say on this issue during my public appearances on TTIP, but I thought that the European Commission's proposal deserved serious consideration. So did the Transatlantic Financial Regulatory Coherence Coalition, representing a large portion of the transatlantic financial services community, including the Securities Industry and Financial Markets Association (the US trade body representing the country's biggest banks and institutional investors) and the Association for Financial Markets in Europe.

While it was accurate in 2013–2015 to argue that the EU was lagging behind the US in its response to the financial crisis, it was less so following important banking sector reforms in the EU. Concerns that the EU secretly desired to harmonize at the lowest common denominator and to

---

[21] A European Court of Justice ruling in 2017 found that international agreements addressing investment disputes are of "mixed competence" among the European Commission and the Member States and therefore can only be approved by the European Parliament and 38 national and sub-federal parliaments.

oblige the US to endorse different EU priorities were misguided. The European Commission argued (correctly, in my view) that while existing fora for cooperation were useful, more could be done to reduce divergent implementation by US and EU regulators of internationally agreed principles. Moreover, meetings of US and EU regulators were too infrequent, ad hoc, backward looking, and often occurred at the last minute under market pressure.

While making clear that nothing would undermine the ability of regulators to regulate in the public interest, a framework for regulatory cooperation in TTIP would diminish regulatory fragmentation and enhance financial stability by enabling consistent implementation of internationally agreed standards, mutual consultations in advance of significant new financial measures (without unduly affecting the jurisdiction of either party), and joint examination of existing rules to examine whether they create unnecessary barriers to trade.

Fourth, the United States should prioritize the inclusion of an energy chapter in a future US-EU free trade agreement. As described in detail in Chapter 8, many EU member states, especially in the Baltic region and Central and Eastern Europe, have been extremely concerned about the reliance on imports of Russian gas. They are absolutely justified in their concern because of Russia's habit of treating gas exports as a political weapon and Gazprom as an arm of the Russian state. Moreover, the United States has worked hard with Europe to diversify European sources of imported energy and to create the necessary infrastructure to help ensure that gas and electricity flow more freely in Europe, thereby eliminating "energy islands."

Although the US negotiators drafted such an energy chapter and proposed it to the EU during TTIP, it was rather modest. We should have given more careful consideration, working together with Congress, to facilitating approval of US facilities to export LNG to Europe. This would have added more volume, lowered prices, and, most importantly, strengthened the negotiating hand of vulnerable EU states when dealing with Gazprom. And it would have provided a dramatic symbol of solidarity with Europe. The Trump administration has facilitated LNG exports with very positive effects: As Europe's third largest supplier of LNG, the US can provide significant diversification benefits and limit Russia's ability to use energy as a political weapon. This is one of the rare areas of the Trump administration's policies toward the EU that I applaud.

Fifth, the US needs to be pragmatic in a number of troublesome areas. We had already shown such pragmatism regarding audiovisual services that the EU had carved out of the negotiations. Although existing EU restrictions are protectionist, we were not negotiating to remove them because we recognized that they are a fact of life. Much of the US content industry has learned to live with EU and member state quotas and local production requirements for television, radio, and film. We were right, therefore, to focus on preventing further extensions of the restrictions, especially in digitally delivered services through the internet.

Similarly, the US should recognize that nothing is likely to change widespread European hostility toward the use of ractopamine, a drug used in pig feed in order to accelerate weight gain and promote lean meat. The drug is banned in every country except the US (where it is considered safe). The only way to address the ten-to-one imbalance of bilateral trade in pork in favor of the EU is for US pork producers to expand their ractopamine-free production lines.

The US should also recognize that EU public opinion is also hostile toward the use of growth hormones in cattle feed, even though they are considered safe in the US. Rather than allowing this issue to poison the negotiations, it would be advisable for the negotiators to state and for a final agreement to confirm (as in CETA) that nothing in the agreement would affect EU legislation on hormone-treated beef. The only way for US beef exporters to tap into the vast demand in Europe for high-quality US beef is to have separate hormone-free production lines.

Following US agreement in 2009 to lift retaliatory duties against the EU as authorized by the WTO, the US negotiated a memorandum of understanding with the EU allowing 48,200 metric tons of "high quality" non-hormone beef into the EU duty-free per year. But the US has been filling only half of that quota because it has been available to Australia, New Zealand, Uruguay, and Argentina under a first-come, first-served system and because US grain-fed beef costs more. During the Obama administration, USTR placed increasing pressure on the EU to increase the overall quota, carve out a larger amount of it just for US beef and/or define "high quality" in such a way that only grain-fed cattle would qualify. This was a major objective of TTIP especially after Canada benefited from a 50,000 metric ton hormone-free beef quota all for itself as a result of CETA. In 2019, the Trump administration concluded negotiations with the EU to allocate 35,000 metric tons of the total quota to the US.

The US should also recognize that it will not change widespread European hostility against genetically engineered (GE) food, even though this is a major economic issue for the United States. Whereas the EU allows the importation of food containing genetically modified organisms (GMOs) under strict labeling requirements, it does not allow the importation of GE crops. That is a real problem because more than half of US farmland is used to grow GE crops, including nearly all soybeans and maize and roughly three-quarters of the corn. Due to the zero tolerance of even infinitesimal traces of GMOs in crop shipments to the EU, shipments are denied entry and many producers simply prefer not to incur the risk of shipping at all. All this has resulted in a significant decline in US exports to the EU of soybeans. Moreover, major US agri-food and chemical companies have been injured by the significant backlog of applications to approve new GE agricultural products in the EU (due to an average processing time of 47 months, compared to the legally prescribed time of twelve months).

Nonetheless, this issue should not be allowed to infect and potentially kill a transatlantic free trade agreement. The US should agree with the EU on a clear statement that nothing in a final agreement would compel the member states or the EU to change their existing policies or procedures with regard to biotechnology. However, the US should continue to press the EU to respect its existing obligations (including listening to scientific advice) and timetables laid down under the EU legislative framework for approving GMOs. The US should also continue reminding the EU of its obligations under the WTO agreement on the application of SPS measures, including to base trade restrictions taken on public health grounds on sound science and limited to the extent strictly necessary. A WTO dispute settlement panel in 2006 found that the EU's de facto ban on GMO products violated that agreement.

The European Commission has been understandably frustrated that member states have repeatedly failed to approve or reject EU decisions on new biotech applications, thereby saddling the European Commission with the unpopular task of doing so. But it was troublesome that the Juncker Commission decided that the European Commission, the traditional apolitical "guardian" of the EU treaties should "give the majority view of democratically elected governments at least the same weight as scientific advice."[22]

---

[22] Jean-Claude Juncker, "A New Start for Europe: My Agenda for Jobs, Growth, Fairness and Democratic Change," Opening Statement in the European Parliament Plenary Session, July 15, 2014.

The US could launch a complaint against the EU's biotech approval process, but that would unleash significant anti-US and anti-trade reactions. One potential compromise would be for the US and EU to agree that GMO food exports from the US will be freely imported into the EU if they are labeled as such. Let consumers, rather than the nanny state, decide what they want to eat.[23]

Finally, the US needs to be pragmatic about the extent to which it can force the EU to adopt a rule-making system that looks like its own. According to the US "notice and comment" procedure applicable to executive agencies of the federal government under the Administrative Procedures Act, proposed rules are published well in advance; any stakeholder, including those in Europe, can comment on the rules and the comments must be published and responded to by the agency in adopting its final rule. While the European Commission has been making important strides (even pre-dating the commencement of TTIP negotiations) to improve the openness, transparency, and accountability of its rule-making system, it is unlikely to start publishing draft legislative proposals for comment prior to their adoption because this would undermine its prized power to initiate legislation.

As noted in my Personal Mission chapter, there is plenty of criticism, not only from the US but also within Europe, of the European Commission's limited consultations on draft legislation and the EU's basic method of passing legislation whereby detailed rules fleshing out general laws are drafted in an opaque process involving national experts. Sound science is sometimes overlooked, and the ability of private parties to challenge the rules is limited. The aim of minimizing transatlantic regulatory divergence through increasing alignment of regulatory processes is laudable. But it is open to question, however, whether a trade agreement is really the best vehicle to achieve this in light of the complexity, time, and sensitivities involved.

Changes Required in the EU Approach

The EU also needs to change its approach in order to promote the successful conclusion of a US-EU free trade agreement. It should withstand

---

[23] Several US states had introduced laws requiring labeling until they were preempted by the 2016 federal National Bioengineered Food Disclosure Law, establishing a nationwide standard for disclosing the presence of foods and ingredients from GE crops.

the temptation of drawing red lines and tying progress in each area to progress in many other areas. A more productive approach would be to seek progress in all possible areas, while naturally reserving the right not to agree to a final deal if the balance of benefits and costs are not right.

Moreover, the EU needs to be pragmatic about its ambitions with regard to geographical indications, maritime services, and government procurement.

With regard to geographical indications, the EU should focus on requesting clarifications of existing US law, especially regarding protections of consumers against misleading claims of geographical provenance. There is very little prospect of the US changing its trademark-based laws protecting food and wine names. The US is justified in pushing back against the EU's efforts to significantly expand protections under US law for European food and wine. It is rightly aggrieved that the European market remains closed to key US agricultural exports and that EU free trade agreements impose protections for geographical indications that restrict US agricultural exports to third countries. But the US frontal attack on EU geographical indications in TTIP proved to be pointless and counterproductive.

From the beginning of the negotiations, I had considered GIs to be an issue of extreme importance. The issue should have been treated as one to be resolved in the "mid-game" and not the "end-game." It was not as difficult to resolve as the bigger and thornier issue of government procurement, and it was the key to reaching agreement on an agriculture chapter, without which there would be no TTIP. The United States had more at stake than the EU in concluding such a chapter in order to reverse a growing bilateral trade deficit in agricultural products with the EU. According to one study, tariff elimination and a 25% reduction in non-tariff barriers in transatlantic trade would boost EU exports to the US by about 60%, while increasing US exports to the EU by about 120% by 2025.[24]

In one negotiating round after another, US negotiators argued that food and wines covered by GIs account for 0.1% of EU GDP, less than 0.3% of GDP in any EU member states and a 0% share in 13 member

---

[24] European Parliament, "Risks and Opportunities for the EU Agri-Food Sector in a Possible EU-US Trade Agreement," 2014, p. 11. http://www.europarl.europa.eu/RegData/etudes/STUD/2014/514007/AGRI_IPOL_STU%282014%29514007_EN.pdf.

states. They account for 2% of agricultural food exports, 0.0008% of all EU exports, and 0.2% of total EU employment. Why, they asked, are EU negotiators kicking up such a fuss and why are they imperiling progress on tariff elimination and services liberalization for the sake of GIs? The economic argument was interesting, but rather beside the point. In several key member states, including Italy, France, and Spain, GIs certainly do play a major economic role: EU food and wine exports protected by GIs are worth €15 billion euro. GIs accounts for 25–30% of EU trade in processed food exports; 80% of EU wine exports and nearly all exports of spirits are protected by GIs. The real importance of GIs, however, does not lie in the economic statistics: It is the widespread perception that they are critical to promoting European food quality, identity, and culture. There is no point in attacking a faith-based system on the grounds that it is not based on rational argument.

The EU has complained that the US trademark-based system for protecting food and wines involves high costs of registration and enforcement through the courts; that some EU GIs cannot be registered because of prior trademarks or because certain names granted protection in Europe are considered generic in the United States; and that the level of protection afforded by trademarks is lower than under geographical indications. US negotiators countered that in reality the costs are low and that there is no prospect of ensuring EU rights holders recourse to administrative action as an alternative to litigation.[25]

They also argued persuasively that it would be unfair to prevent the use of many European origin names used by European immigrants to the United States; indeed, it is quite likely that these immigrants have promoted EU exports of food and wine by adopting European names. The significant value, growth rates, and market share of exports to the US from key GI-rich exporters, such as Italy, suggest that US obstacles have not been as great as suggested. The upper and middle classes in the United States are increasingly showing greater sophistication in food consumption and

---

[25] The EU's FTA with Canada states that "Each Party shall provide for enforcement by administrative action…to prohibit a person from manufacturing, preparing, packaging, labelling, selling or importing or advertising a food commodity in a manner that is false, misleading or deceptive or is likely to create an erroneous impression regarding its origin." Article 20.19(4).

clearly value not only quality, but also the history and tradition, that European food and wine exports supply.

The real debate is around whether certain names deserve protection as true geographical indications or whether they are commonly used names to describe methods of production. In TTIP, the EU tabled a list of roughly 200 food, wine, and spirits names it wanted the US to protect, thereby preventing producers from using those names domestically or for export. Some names have a stronger claim to protection because they are compound names specifically linked to a place[26] or because they are known under their original national language. Other names, such as feta and parmesan, are widely used generic names considered unworthy of protection in the United States.[27]

The key test should be whether there is a real risk of consumer confusion about geographical provenance. In some cases, the EU has applied excessive rules that don't meet this test. The case of parmesan is one example. The EU courts have found that parmesan can be protected under EU law as an "evocation" of the geographical indication "Parmigiano Reggiano." As a result, Kraft can only sell its grated parmesan cheese in the EU under the name "Pamesello Italiano" even though there is likely to be no risk of consumer confusion with the Italian original. I doubt very much that many European consumers would confuse Kraft's tall green container containing grated cheese with the real thing. But the EU isn't satisfied with trying to block Kraft from the EU market; it wants to prevent Kraft from calling its cheese parmesan *even in the United States*. This sort of overreach irritated US government officials. But it was rather tame compared to the effort by some senior members of the Italian government to protect all "Italian-sounding" names. The idea that spaghetti, pizza, or even prosciutto "belong" to Italy was excessive and merely served to undermine the EU's more important argument about consumer deception.

There are already many statutes on the books in the United States that regulate the use of labels and packaging so that they do not mislead consumers about geographical provenance. All signatories to the WTO's Trade Related Aspects of Intellectual Property Rights Agreement must

---

[26] In the EU FTA with Canada, the names Brie de Meaux, Gouda Holland, Edam Holland, and Mortadella Bologna are protected, but not brie, gouda, edam, or mortadella on their own.

[27] Other cheese names include asiago, fontina, gorgonzola, and munster.

also provide interested parties with the legal means to prevent the geographically misleading use of labels and packaging. And self-regulation through the National Advertising Division of the Council of Better Business Bureaus aims to combat deceptive or unfair practices in advertising. Nonetheless, the US should be open to entertaining whether existing statutes or implementing rules need to be tightened further.

In some instances, it may be worth exploring whether some names may only be used if the labeling and/or packaging states in visible lettering "Made in the USA." But if the US goes down that road, it should gain the right to sell products it considers generic in Europe. After all, it is the consumer who should be free to decide on the basis of clear information. Secretary of Agriculture Vilsack argued that technology could help address the need for more, and clearer, consumer information about food. For example, consumers could use their smart phones to scan special bar codes or other symbols on food packages in grocery stores—not only to determine ingredients (and the presence of GMO), but also provenance.

The EU also needs to be pragmatic with regard to its negotiating objectives regarding maritime services. The EU should realize that the chances of Congress repealing the Jones Act are nil. But there is surely scope to explore flexibility in that legislation with regard to services that do not constitute shipping of goods between US ports. These services might include the shipment of empty containers, dredging, the refitting of ships (i.e., to become more energy efficient), and sea to shore services such as the maintenance of oil and wind turbine facilities. There is also scope for the Customs and Border Protection Agency to interpret more flexibly certain key provisions of the Jones Act through ruling letters.

The EU also needs to be pragmatic with regard to government procurement. It is not clear that the US needs to offer more than the EU to level the playing field, as the EU argues. The US and the EU can continue to debate the relative degrees of openness in their government procurement markets, but there will never be agreement on this point because there are so many ways of measuring openness, both legally and in practice. We have disagreed about the accuracy of our respective submissions on market access to the WTO under the Government Procurement Agreement. The US estimates that it guarantees EU suppliers roughly $320 billion worth of government procurement opportunities ($200 billion of which at the federal level); but the EU claims that the true figure is less than half that amount because of US "set asides" for US companies at the federal level and because the estimate of access to state-level procurement is inflated guesswork. The EU estimates that it guarantees US suppliers roughly $330 billion of government procurement opportunities; but the US claims that the true figure is at best half that amount because of restrictions.

During TTIP, US negotiators insisted that the situation in the EU "on the ground" is in fact far worse than what is reflected in EU law: Based on statistics in a 2011 study conducted by the EU, US suppliers competing for direct cross-border procurement secured only 0.016% of total EU government procurements. The EU claims that more recent statistics, following changes in EU government procurement rules, show far better results. US negotiators claimed that several academic studies agree with the US position that the EU government procurement market is not nearly as open as the EU claims. But the EU can point to its own studies demonstrating that these studies are analytically flawed.

US negotiators repeatedly sought to evidence US market openness by pointing to the many examples of large EU companies wining big ticket US federal and state infrastructure contracts (including highway, subway, airport and rail); but EU negotiators countered that these examples ignore the difficulties smaller EU companies face, as well as the burdensome requirements on all foreign companies to source US materials and establish a local business and manufacturing/assembly facilities in the US. The EU contrasts its fully functioning internal market for public procurement and the centralization of information about procurement contracts with the lack of an internal market or of a central information portal in the United States. The US complains about lack of transparency, language barriers, and the use of technical specifications designed to favor local suppliers.

It is hard to see how the US and EU can agree on their relative degree of market openness in government procurement when the available data is limited and subject to such conflicting interpretations. It would be more fruitful for both sides to make greater efforts to open their markets further, as specifically called for under the High Level Working Group report. The EU's negotiating mandate elevated the issue to a major negotiating objective. The reality, however, is that the political support in the US for greater openness is slender at the federal and state levels.

Nonetheless, the US should invest greater energy to loosen federal restrictions on government procurement, both in the form of the Buy American Act, that creates a national preference for the federal government's procurement of domestic construction materials, and the Buy

America Act, that imposes domestic content restrictions on grants by various federal government agencies to state and local governments. State governments could be more tightly involved in USTR's negotiation of government procurement in TTIP; the fact that Canada's provinces were tightly involved in Ottawa's negotiation of the Canada-EU free trade agreement shows that this is possible.

TTIP also suffered from the EU's lack of pragmatism regarding electronic commerce, services, and agricultural tariffs.

The EU refused to discuss a chapter on electronic commerce despite its enormous importance until the US and EU successfully concluded the Privacy Shield Agreement in early 2016. That agreement formalized EU recognition that US privacy laws are essentially equivalent to its own and ensure a legal basis for continued transfers of data from Europe to the US. This refusal was supposed to put pressure on the US to conclude Privacy Shield but it also had the regrettable result of undermining progress on TTIP.

The EU and the US are each other's largest markets for US digital services, over half of which are used to create products for export.[28] The EU clearly recognizes the importance of such a chapter in a free trade agreement. CETA contains one. In early 2018, the European Commission introduced rules on electronic commerce—including the prohibition of protectionist barriers to cross-border data flows, while ensuring the protection of personal data—that it would seek in future trade accords with Mexico, Chile, New Zealand, and Australia. A US-EU FTA is inconceivable without high-standard provisions on the digital economy, including the prevention of localization measures (requiring companies to build infrastructure and house data in countries they seek to serve); the promotion of free and open Internet; the prohibition of digital customs duties and discrimination of digitally delivered goods and services compared to

---

[28] Daniel Hamilton, "Creating a North Atlantic Marketplace for Growth and Jobs," Center for Transatlantic Relations, 2018. In 2011, the United States exported $357.4 billion in digitally deliverable services. This represented over 60% of US services exports and about 17% of total US goods and services exports. The United States had a digitally deliverable services trade surplus of $135.5 billion. Jessica Nicholson and Ryan Noonan, "Digital Economy and Cross-Border Trade: The Value of Digitally Deliverable Services," US Department of Commerce, January 27, 2014.

their physical counterparts; and the protection of critical source code or proprietary algorithms.[29]

In order for a US-EU FTA to succeed, the EU must significantly improve the services offer it tabled in TTIP, including by adopting a "negative list" approach, guaranteeing current levels of access, and eliminating the open-ended ability to discriminate against "new services."

Most important, the EU needs to make a much bigger effort to eliminate tariff and non-tariff barriers to US agriculture exports. Even if the US cannot substantially increase its GMO exports, there are many other barriers that can be addressed. When I arrived in Brussels, I learned that US agricultural exports totaled $155 billion, but only $13 billion went to the EU. The EU's agricultural exports to the US were double that amount and had been growing 8% per year since 1995. US agricultural exports, on the other hand, had been booming (especially to China and Southeast Asia), but in inflation-adjusted terms exports to the EU were one-third of their level in 1980 and our market share had been falling. We were facing EU tariffs two to three times as high as our own, as well as non-tariff barriers in every single major commodity group: meat, poultry, grains, horticulture, and dairy.

All Together Now

Both the US and the EU can take several steps to address some of the most pervasive concerns about a free trade agreement, including diminished sovereignty and lower quality of life. After destroying any likelihood of ISDS being in an agreement, sceptics of TTIP focused on regulatory cooperation as the next source of evil. They worried that institutionalized cooperation would lead to secret trade-offs between the US and EU at the expense of consumers, undermine checks and balances in their domestic regulatory processes, and discourage either side from entering into new regulatory initiatives.

The US and EU could take a page out of CETA and commit to inserting into a final text an interpretative statement reaffirming the right of governments to continue providing or expanding the range of certain public services (such as water, public health, and education) and to bring

---

[29] The key US negotiating objectives on electronic commerce under the Obama administration were well summarized by Deputy USTR Richard Holleyman in his "Digital Two Dozen" principles reflected in the Trans-Pacific Agreement.

back under public control such services that they had previously privatized. The statement should confirm the intention not to lower environmental, health, safety, or labor rights, including in order to promote trade and investment, and the right of governments to regulate in the public interest.

A transatlantic FTA should explicitly state that the aim of regulatory cooperation is to promote the effectiveness of each side's regulators, while respecting their autonomy. It should emphasize that the main purpose of such cooperation is to enhance regulators' ability to redirect resources to monitor imports from riskier jurisdictions, rather than the elimination of barriers for the sake of eliminating costs and boosting trade across the Atlantic. The US and the EU need to be pragmatic, however, about what they can achieve on regulatory cooperation in a trade agreement.

Neither side should use an FTA to impose its model of rule-making on the other. It has been nearly two decades since the parties concluded the 2002 Guidelines on Regulatory Cooperation and Transparency; an FTA can't operate on this kind of timescale. The Regulatory Cooperation Council between Canada and the US has been of some utility but that was built on decades of shared experience and trust-building through NAFTA.

Sectoral regulatory cooperation is also a long-term project. Regulators will always be reluctant to transfer authority to a foreign body or to admit that their way of doing things is not optimal. Greater high-level political pressure on regulators to cooperate is useful (and is often lacking), but it only goes so far. In the United States, it is important that Congress create the right incentives and provide the proper funding for US regulatory bodies to get serious about regulatory cooperation with advanced economies, including the EU.

US-EU regulator-to-regulator discussions on automotive standards should of course continue to focus on setting common standards that can then be adopted as global standards. But they are lengthy and complex. Perhaps it would make sense to detach these discussions from TTIP and focus instead on mutual recognition of each other's existing regulations. It might be easier to achieve mutual recognition in areas unrelated to crashworthiness, such as lighting and vision standards, seat belt anchorages, seat belt-ignition interlocks and automatic emergency braking, as well as to cooperate on future regulations (including those relating to autonomous and electric vehicles).

One of the key longer-term lessons about the failure of TTIP is that many people are turning against free trade and globalization because they feel that the gains flowing from them have been privatized by those at the top of the pyramid, while the costs have been socialized. Many populist leaders on both sides of the Atlantic have won power over the past few years by tapping into the feelings of frustration from those who felt left behind or ignored. While one can criticize the policies of the populists as being counterproductive, especially for their constituents, there is little doubt that the social contract—market liberalization in return for high standards of social protection—has broken down.

There are many domestic and transatlantic policy choices that help rebuild the case for trade. As argued in the conclusions to this book, there should be a concerted effort to ensure that trade adjustment assistance mechanisms—consisting of retraining and/or monetary compensation for those who lose their jobs from globalization—are better funded and more effective.

The failure of TTIP has cost the US-EU relationship dearly, as was made sadly clear in March 2018 when President Trump unleashed serious transatlantic trade tensions by imposing high tariffs on steel and aluminum imports, including from the EU, on the grounds of "national security." The EU naturally reciprocated with its own tariffs aimed at hurting key US exports, including from Congressional districts that supported the president. Throughout 2018 and 2019, the president threatened to impose tariffs on imports of cars from the EU on the same grounds. Auto tariffs would seriously inflame transatlantic tensions because EU automotive exports to the US are about ten times greater in value than EU steel and aluminum exports combined. Germany accounts for about 60% of Europe's $45 billion in annual exports of cars and car parts to the US. The idea that imports from close allies, such as Germany, at a time of peace could be considered a national security threat is disgraceful.

Under the Trump administration, the United States joined Russia and Saudi Arabia in their efforts to invoke the national security exception in WTO rules as a free pass to justify trade restrictive measures. A WTO panel logically found in the Russian case that while Russia's actions could be justified under the exception, there is no such free pass. The WTO may review trade restrictive measures to determine whether they have a plausible connection to national security. If this were not the case, every country could obviously invoke national security to do whatever it wants. That would be the law of the jungle. In a jungle fight, nobody comes out a winner, not even the big gorillas.

While a truce from US-EU trade hostilities held during 2018–2019, it was based on weak foundations. After a meeting with European Commission President Juncker in the White House in July 2018, the president announced a "big beautiful deal" whereby the EU would start buying more soybeans and LNG from the United States. Although EU member states make those decisions, not the EU itself, the president and his administration appeared not to notice. The European Commission understandably hyped the increasing export volumes (already well under way before the agreement) to placate the president and avoid the car import tariffs that would have serious consequences in Europe. The leaders announced the launch of discussions to liberalize trade between them, including the elimination of subsidies and non-tariff barriers, both of which are laughably unrealistic. Fundamental disagreements, including about whether agriculture would be part of the agreement, plagued negotiations from the start.

Although President Trump's repeated threats of imposing car import tariffs on the EU may result in some form of mini-deal with the EU that features lower tariffs on some goods and enhances regulatory cooperation, an ambitious trade deal seems unlikely. There is plenty of potential for an eruption of transatlantic trade disputes in the short term, including over EU member states' digital services tax laws and perhaps an EU challenge before the WTO regarding the trade diversionary effects of the US "phase one" trade deal with China.

As this book was going to press, the US and the EU were waiting for the culmination of a bitter 14-year dispute over aircraft subsidies granted to Boeing and Airbus. In September 2019, the WTO allowed Washington to hit the EU with billions of euros in punitive tariffs because of subsidies granted to Airbus contrary to WTO rules. In 2020, the WTO is scheduled to determine Airbus's appropriate retaliation against Boeing. It is welcome that the Trump administration is, at least in this dispute, prepared to work within the terms of the WTO dispute settlement process. But the president may exploit the case as another *casus belli* against the EU, undermining the fragile transatlantic trade truce. It would be far better to settle this bitter battle than to engage in another round of mutual retaliation.

Just as damaging as its threat of unilateral sanctions against the EU, the Trump administration has attacked some of the foundations of the multilateral rules-based trading system, including the WTO. By blocking appointments to the WTO dispute settlement body, the US has forced the EU and a group of 16 nations (including China and Brazil) to establish an alternative appeals system whereby members would voluntarily submit their disputes to arbitration. Despite pledging in July 2018 to work with the EU on WTO reform, the Trump administration has refused to engage on the EU's long list of concrete proposals to do just that despite agreeing (most probably) with the vast majority of them.

The EU's proposals focus largely on pressuring China to rectify its unfair trading practices, including massive subsidies, intellectual property theft, significant obstacles to market access, and the role of state-owned enterprises, to name a few. Perhaps the Trump administration has not engaged with the EU on these proposals because it doesn't believe that it needs the EU as an ally to deal with China. Or perhaps it actually prefers to tear the rules-based trading system apart. Turning world trade into a free for all brawl might bring short-term advantages as the US can focus its leverage in a series of bilateral, transactional agreements with weaker countries. But it will have serious long-term consequences for global prosperity and US influence.

The EU, unfortunately, appears particularly vulnerable to the Trump administration's objective of repatriating global supply chains. Major European exporting countries, above all Germany and Italy, rely on inputs from other countries for their exports. If globalization goes into reverse and supply chains are broken, countries with the largest trade surpluses, small domestic markets, and a reliance on export-driven growth will be most affected. The EU therefore has much at stake in the question of whether the US changes its trade policies.

CHAPTER 5

Data Privacy

On October 6, 2015, Joseph Daul, the influential head of the center-right pan-European People's Party, was proudly showing me around his farm near Strasbourg. As we were inspecting his livestock and chatting about ways to increase European support for transatlantic agricultural trade, my mobile phone rang with an urgent message. The legal adviser of the US Mission to the EU was calling from Luxembourg's European Court of Justice, the supreme court on matters of EU law. The court had just handed down a judgment effectively invalidating a critically important transatlantic data exchange agreement called "Safe Harbor." That agreement, concluded in 2000 between the United States and the EU, enabled companies in Europe to transfer EU citizens' personal data to the United States in a manner consistent with EU data privacy law.

Shortly after that call, I had to cut short my visit and an Alsatian meal of sausages, cabbages, and white wine in order to join a call with the White House Situation Room. This was the first in a long series of video conference calls that confined myself and senior members of my staff to a windowless, airless conference room in the embassy. An army of officials from the State Department, the Commerce Department, the Office of the Director of National Intelligence, the Treasury Department and the White House staff also participated. The impact of the court judgment on transatlantic data flows was so important that President Obama received regular briefings. By January 2016, the United States and the European Union had concluded a new data exchange agreement called "Privacy Shield."

© The Author(s) 2020
A. L. Gardner, *Stars with Stripes*,
https://doi.org/10.1007/978-3-030-29966-8_5

The case that triggered all of this frenetic activity, *Schrems* v. *Facebook*, involved an Irish lawsuit brought in 2013 against Facebook by Maximilian Schrems, a 23-year-old Austrian law student. Based on recent newspaper accounts of documents leaked by Edward Snowden, Schrems alleged that Facebook had been improperly allowing the National Security Agency to access data of its customers in the EU and, moreover, that the NSA *might* have accessed personal information in his Facebook account. Why the NSA would have been interested in him remained unclear. Rather than shut his Facebook account because of these unsubstantiated fears, he complained and then sued.

Schrems had originally brought a complaint to the Irish Data Protection Commissioner (DPC), the national regulator in charge of protecting data privacy, but it had rejected the complaint as "frivolous and vexatious" on the basis that Facebook had self-certified its adherence to the Safe Harbor program. Thanks to the European Commission's determination in 2000 that the program offered an adequate degree of data privacy protection consistent with EU law, more than 5000 companies had self-certified their adherence to numerous principles regarding the proper treatment of EU citizens' data. The Irish DPC ruled that it was bound by the Commission's "adequacy" finding and could not investigate further. Schrems appealed that rejection to the Irish High Court, which in turn referred several questions of EU law to the European Court of Justice.

The Safe Harbor program was of critical importance to transatlantic data flows and hundreds of billions of dollars in commercial transactions. Participants in the program included not only Fortune 500 firms, but also many small- and medium-sized companies in a wide variety of sectors (except financial institutions, communications and insurance companies, and non-profit organizations). Many of the members were US subsidiaries of European companies. The data in question included data as diverse as human resources data, hotel bookings, people's browsing histories, and a wide variety of business records. Not only did the program provide a much-need "safe harbour" giving certainty about the legality of transatlantic data flows, it also provided a "one-stop shop" establishing EU-wide standards of adequacy, thereby preventing national (and, in the case of Germany, regional) data protection authorities (DPAs) from imposing their own widely divergent standards.

As dramatic as the Court's judgment was, it had been expected for some time. Oral arguments at the Court in late March had clearly indicated the direction of travel. My legal adviser had reported from Luxembourg that the European Commission's advocate had wilted under withering questioning from the judges. The most hostile questioning came from the German judge, Thomas von Danwitz, who had authored prior judgments striking down EU laws as incompatible with EU fundamental rights and who was tasked with writing the judgment in *Schrems*. The current Safe Harbor program was flawed, the European Commission's advocate had conceded in oral argument, and he couldn't confirm that it provided adequate protection for EU citizens' data. The US, moreover, was "excessively relying" on that national security exception in the Safe Harbor Privacy Principles. According to that exception, adherence to the Principles could be limited to the extent "necessary" to meet national security requirements. The advocate pleaded for more time to conclude the ongoing negotiations to improve Safe Harbor.

THE COURT'S FLAWED JUDGMENT

In late September, one of the Advocates General, the senior jurists whose opinions the Court typically follows in their final judgments, had found that the Safe Harbor Agreement contravened EU law. Although we had long anticipated a negative result, we were taken aback that the Court had ruled less than two weeks after the Advocate General's opinion; this was highly unusual, as the gap would normally be several months, and it suggested that the Court had perhaps written its judgment at the same time as the Advocate General. The latter's opinion, released on September 23, infuriated quite a few people in the US government.

Since the Irish DPC had dismissed the complaint on its own motion, Facebook never had the chance to appear before the court. Nor did the US government have an opportunity to appear as an interested party before the Irish High Court proceedings to set the record straight. As it had not done so, it had no right to appear in the Luxembourg proceedings. The government had understandably been reluctant to discuss its surveillance practice in public but now it was in the worse situation of dealing with a catastrophic judgment based on inaccurate allegations.

We knew that recent jurisprudence of the Court regarding data privacy and the EU's Charter of Fundamental Rights would make the case hard to win. However, the Advocate General made several damaging assertions that were as sweeping as they were unfounded.

He referred to recent "revelations" in the press according to which "the NSA established a programme called 'Prism' under which it obtained unrestricted access to mass data stored on servers in the United States owned or controlled by a range of companies active in the Internet and technology field, such as Facebook USA." The Advocate General accepted as fact that the PRISM program, under Section 702 of the Foreign Intelligence Surveillance Act (FISA), enabled the NSA to have access "in a generalised manner" with regard to "all persons and all means of electronic communication, and all the data transferred (including the content of the communications) [is used] without any differentiation, limitation or exception."[1]

The PRISM program is one of the several surveillance programs operated under FISA Section 702. (Another one called "Upstream" enables the NSA to copy and search streams of Internet traffic as data flows across the telecommunications backbone, such as the network of cables, switches and routers, over which telephone and Internet communications transit.) Section 702 governs the acquisition of "signals intelligence"[2] *within* the United States in relation to *non-US persons* reasonably believed to be located *outside* the US. Unlike the United States, other countries do not require court oversight of surveillance for foreign intelligence purposes of foreigners overseas.

There are several other legal authorities for surveillance programs (not at issue in Schrems and not directly relevant to the Safe Harbor discussions). The first is what are known as "traditional" FISA orders, whereby the government may obtain individual orders from a specially constituted FISA Court to conduct electronic surveillance or physical searches in the United States if it can show "probable cause" that, among other things, the target is a "foreign power or an agent of a foreign power." These

---

[1] Opinion of Advocate General Yves Bot, Maximilian Schrems v. Data Protection Commissioner, Case C-362/14, September 23, 2015. http://curia.europa.eu/juris/document/document.jsf?docid=168421&doclang=EN.

[2] The National Security Agency defines signals intelligence as the production of foreign intelligence through the collection, processing and analysis of communications or other data, passed or accessible by radio, wire, or other electromagnetic means. The National Security Agency: Missions, Authorities, Oversight and Partnerships, August 9, 2013. https://www.nsa.gov/news-features/press-room/statements/2013-08-09-the-nsa-story.shtml.

orders have never been a source of controversy with the EU because they have a high evidentiary threshold and require individualized court scrutiny.

A second legal authority is Section 215 of the Patriot Act that permits the FBI to apply to the FISA Court for an order requiring a business to produce "tangible things" (such as books and records). The application must include facts showing reasonable grounds to believe that the "tangible things" are relevant to an investigation into foreign intelligence not concerning a US person or to protect against international terrorism or clandestine intelligence activities. It requires the use of individualized "selectors" (such as e-mails and telephone numbers) developed pursuant to court-approved procedures.

A third legal authority, Executive Order 12333, is the primary authority under which the NSA collects communications of foreigners *outside* of the United States.

The "revelations" on which the Advocate General had based his opinion stemmed from an inaccurate *The Washington Post* story that asserted: "The National Security Agency and the FBI are tapping directly into the central servers of nine leading US Internet companies, extracting audio, video, photographs, e-mails, documents and connection logs that enable analysts to track a person's movements and contacts over time."[3] On this basis, the Advocate General concluded that the European Commission should have terminated the Safe Harbor program because the unrestricted access of US intelligence services to data transferred from Europe to the United States constitutes an "an interference with the right to respect for private life and the right to protection of personal data, which are guaranteed by the Charter."

The edifice of the Advocate General's reasoning was built on sand. The Advocate General had pointed out that he was required to accept the facts as stipulated by the Irish High Court and that his job was to draw legal conclusions from the case file. The problem was that the Irish High Court had concluded, on the basis of mere press clippings in the pleadings filed

---

[3] Barton Gellman and Laura Poitras, "US, British Intelligence Mining Data from Nine US Internet Companies in Broad Secret Program," *The Washington Post*, June 7, 2013. The authors won a Pulitzer Prize for the story which has since been updated. https://www.washingtonpost.com/investigations/us-intelligence-mining-data-from-nine-us-internet-companies-in-broad-secret-program/2013/06/06/3a0c0da8-cebf-11e2-8845-d970ccb04497_story.html?utm_term=.42796be20b78.

by Schrems, that the accuracy of his allegations regarding US intelligence surveillance was "not in dispute" and that "the evidence now available would admit of no other realistic conclusion." The opposite was true but there was little that we could do.

Since negotiations to update Safe Harbor had not concluded by the fall of 2015, neither the Advocate General nor the European Court of Justice could take into account the significant progress that the US and the EU had achieved over the past two years. I had pressed during the summer of 2015 for an agreement to be finalized and made public, in large part because it might have had a positive impact on the proceedings. But we lost momentum, partly because the European Commission thought that the EU court's looming judgment would maximize pressure on the US to make further concessions, especially with regard to government surveillance programs. The delay in finalizing an agreement may have been all for the best as it allowed the two sides to address the court's sweeping criticisms comprehensively.

The working group established by the US government to deal with the brewing crisis decided, against my counsel, to respond publicly to the Advocate General through an opinion piece in the *Financial Times*. While I shared the general frustration, I believed it would be counter-productive for us to criticize a senior official of a foreign court. I argued that we would not take kindly to a foreign government publicly criticizing our own judicial proceedings, especially while they were still underway. Any statement, even one limited to establishing the facts, would inevitably be seen as an example of high-handedness. It certainly would have no bearing on the court's final judgment; as it turned out, that judgment was handed down on the day following the publication of the *Financial Times* article.

The article, authored by the General Counsel of the Office of the Director of National Intelligence Robert Litt, was scathing. While noting that the United States "fully respect[s] the European Union's legal process" (a phrase I urged be inserted), the article stated that the evidence demonstrated the opposite of what the Advocate General had taken on faith:

> [The Prism programme] can be used only when authorised by law, in a manner that protects the privacy of all persons, and with extensive oversight from all three branches of our government. The US legal framework for intelligence collection includes robust protection for privacy under multiple

layers of scrutiny and a remarkable degree of transparency. The decisions of judicial bodies should be informed by accurate information. Prism is focused and reasonable. It does not involve "mass" and "unrestricted" collection of data...[4]

This was not just the view of the Obama administration. The Privacy and Civil Liberties Oversight Board (PCLOB), an independent and bipartisan executive branch agency with responsibilities that include overseeing the use of "signals intelligence," concluded in July 2014 after an exhaustive review of classified material that the PRISM program is not based on the "indiscriminate collection of information in bulk."[5] Even the EU's own Fundamental Rights Agency appeared to agree with many experts' conclusions to that effect.[6] US intelligence services do not engage in indiscriminate surveillance of anyone, including ordinary European citizens. They do not have the legal authority, the resources, the technical capability or the desire to intercept all the world's communications. And they are not reading the e-mails of everyone in the United States, or of everyone in the world.

Intelligence collection is governed by a system of substantive and structural standards and checks. These originate in protections for American citizens and people in the US in the federal constitution and include federal statutes, executive orders, and administrative procedures. In addition, there is extensive oversight to ensure that the intelligence community is complying with legal safeguards and processes. That oversight includes civil liberties and privacy officers, including within the Office of the Director of National Intelligence, who supervise procedures to ensure that the relevant agency is adequately considering privacy and civil liberties concerns. Each agency has its own Inspector General with responsibility to oversee foreign intelligence activities; although their recommendations for corrective action are non-binding, their reports are made public and sent to Congress. Oversight is also exercised by the PCLOB; the President's

---

[4] Robert Litt, "Europe's Court Should Know the Truth About US Intelligence," *Financial Times*, October 5, 2015.

[5] Privacy and Civil Liberties Oversight Board, "Report on the Surveillance Program Operated Pursuant to Section 702 of the Foreign Intelligence Surveillance Act," July 2, 2014. https://www.pclob.gov/library/702-Report.pdf.

[6] European Union Agency for Fundamental Rights, "Surveillance by Intelligence Services: Fundamental Rights Safeguards and Remedies in the EU," 2015, p. 17.

Intelligence Oversight Board, the House and Senate Intelligence and Judiciary Committees; and the judiciary itself.

The US government does not have direct access to the central servers of Internet companies. Pursuant to the Section 702 PRISM program, the government may only serve a request on companies in the United States to deliver information relating to communications linked to certain "selectors"—such as telephone numbers and e-mail addresses—that the Attorney General and the Director of National Intelligence have reason to believe are being used to communicate or receive foreign intelligence information. The request must be authorized by the FISA Court on the basis that collection is consistent with the statute. Furthermore, the communications requested must relate to one of specifically enumerated and approved foreign intelligence purposes, such as combating terrorism. Companies who receive such requests may challenge them, including by appealing to the FISA Court. Once collected, there are strict procedures limiting the retention and dissemination of the information. Declassified opinions of the FISA Court show that it does not hesitate to exercise its oversight.

The PRISM program affects a small proportion of Internet traffic. There were only 92,707 "targets" of surveillance under the PRISM program in 2014, a tiny proportion of the 3.2 billion people who use the Internet.[7] The total number of customer accounts accessed by the US government in six-month periods in 2014 is revealing: 17,000 for Google, out of approximately 1.17 billion active users, and 10,000 for Facebook, out of approximately 1.55 billion active users.[8] The Internet traffic that is collected is subject to targeted queries based on specifically enumerated intelligence requirements. Only those items believed to be of potential intelligence value are presented to analysts for examination; therefore, only a fraction of the information collected is ever seen by human eyes.

Commenting on the findings of the Signals Intelligence Review that he had requested, President Obama said in January 2014 that:

> nothing that I have learned...[indicates] that our intelligence community has sought to violate the law or is cavalier about the civil liberties of their

---

[7] There were 89,138 targets in 2013 and 94,368 in 2015.

[8] Peter Swire, "US Surveillance Law, Safe Harbor, and Reforms Since 2013," p. 29. https://peterswire.net/wp-content/uploads/Schrems-White-Paper-12-18-2015.pdf.

fellow citizens...They are not abusing authorities in order to listen to your private phone calls or read your emails.[9]

The PCLOB report subsequently confirmed that there was no evidence of intentional abuse. Both it and the administration concluded that the information collection under Section 702 is valuable and effective in protecting national security and produces useful foreign intelligence. In Europe, observers noted that the president seemed primarily focused on privacy protections for US citizens. In reality, however, the president had also specifically stated that certain protections would be extended to foreigners—perhaps an unprecedented step for any government to take.

The Advocate General's opinion infuriated many US government officials because it had stated that US surveillance activities needed to be judged "by reference to the current factual and legal context," while doing nothing of the sort. It had taken absolutely no account of the significant (and public) reforms in both law and practices relating to intelligence promoted by President Obama during the past two years. These reforms had included limits on collection and policies to ensure that all persons are treated with dignity and respect, regardless of their nationality or place of residence. The reforms showed how the United States is a constitutional democracy under the rule of law, with independent judicial oversight.

The President of the European Court of Justice Koen Lenaerts was at pains to point out that "We are not judging the US system here, we are judging the requirements of EU law in terms of the conditions to transfer data to third countries..."[10] That was true, at least formally. The Court focused on the failure of the European Commission to provide detailed reasons for its conclusion in 2000 that the Safe Harbor program provided an adequate degree of data privacy protections. But the problem lay in the fact that the judgment was based on incorrect assumptions about the US

---

[9] Remarks by the President on Review of Signals Intelligence, January 17, 2014. https://obamawhitehouse.archives.gov/the-press-office/2014/01/17/remarks-president-review-signals-intelligence.

[10] Valentina Pop, "ECJ President on EU Integration, Public Opinion, Safe Harbor, Antitrust," *The Wall Street Journal*, October 14, 2015. https://blogs.wsj.com/brussels/2015/10/14/ecj-president-on-eu-integration-public-opinion-safe-harbor-antitrust/.

system, based on the factual record gathered by the Irish High Court and taken as fact by the Advocate General. The judgment concluded:

> "[The Safe Harbor decision] lays down that 'national security, public interest or law enforcement requirements' have primacy over the safe harbour principles, primacy pursuant to which self-certified United States organisations receiving personal data from the European Union are bound to disregard those principles *without limitation* where they conflict with those requirements and therefore prove incompatible with them. In light of the general nature of the derogation [relating to national security, public interest requirements and law enforcement requirements] ... [the Safe Harbor] decision *enables interference...with the fundamental rights of the persons whose personal data is or could be transferred from the European Union to the United States*" which is "not limited to what is strictly necessary." (emphasis added)

That view necessarily led, not only to the view that the Safe Harbor adequacy decision was invalid, but also to the view that national DPAs must retain their independent authority to investigate claims that transfers of data to a third country do not comply with EU law.

The judgment was extraordinary for many reasons. The facts before the Court did not show any evidence whatsoever of actual infringements by Facebook, or other US companies, of their Safe Harbor commitments. Yet it found that the Safe Harbor Agreement was invalid *since its inception* in 2000, thereby putting every company that had signed up to Safe Harbor at risk of lawsuits for data transfers conducted since that date. Moreover, it provided no grace period, either to give the US and EU time to conclude their agreement or to companies to find other methods of legally transferring data. (European DPAs declared shortly after the ruling that they would hold off taking enforcement action until January 31, 2016, but that they would in the meantime initiate investigations into complaints.) The massive uncertainty and economic dislocation that this caused seemed not to carry much weight in the Court's thinking. One of the ironies of the decision was that invalidation of Safe Harbor actually left EU citizens worse off because the Federal Trade Commission would no longer have authority to police commitments made under the program. Finally, the judgment had not seemed at all sympathetic to the reality that surveillance is fundamentally different from law enforcement: Whereas law enforcement focuses on finding the perpetrator of a particular past crime and can therefore be targeted, surveillance seeks to uncover potential threats or adversaries in the future and therefore needs to collect a broader range of information.[11]

In reacting to the Court's judgment, the European Commission was at pains to point out that other legal means of transferring data across the Atlantic in conformity with European privacy law continued to be available. These means included "binding corporate rules" (text approved by the competent national data protection agency for insertion into contracts governing the export of personal data *to another member of the same corporate group* in a non-EU country that does not provide an adequate degree of data privacy protection). They also included "standard contractual clauses" (text approved by the Commission for insertion into contracts governing the export of personal data *to third parties* in a non-EU country that does not provide an adequate degree of data privacy protection). But they are hardly suitable alternatives for everyone. They are expensive and time-consuming to put into place; moreover, standard contractual clauses require approval by national DPAs in some instances. A few days after the *Schrems* decision, the German DPAs highlighted the legal jeopardy resulting from the decision by reserving their right to challenge any data transfers occurring under either mechanism.

The European Commission also pointed out that there are other legal justifications for transferring data, including when necessary to perform a contract (the transfer of personal data to the US to conclude a hotel booking), important "public interest" grounds (including data transfers between law enforcement authorities), "vital interest" (including the transfer of medical records to save a person's life), and the free and informed consent of an individual (for each data transfer). But these alternative justifications were very limited in scope and not available on a systematic basis.

Anger at European Double Standards

Many of us in the administration found it truly absurd that the United States' data privacy protection regime was found wanting when data flows about EU citizens were occurring regularly to many autocratic states with

---

[11] The reaction in the US media was damning. For example, Richard Epstein, "Europe's Top Court Goes Off the Rails," *The New York Times*, October 8, 2015.

unfettered intelligence services. Who seriously believes that binding corporate rules and standard contractual clauses provide any protection from the intelligence services of Russia and Iran, for example?

President Obama had voiced frustrations about the Janus-faced attitude of our allies about US intelligence:

> ...a number of countries, including some who have loudly criticized the NSA, privately acknowledge that America has special responsibilities as the world's only superpower; that our intelligence capabilities are critical to meeting these responsibilities; and that they themselves have relied on the information we obtain to protect their own people.[12]

The Court's judgment deepened anger in the administration about European hypocrisy. The French government, for example, is no stranger to eavesdropping, including on its close allies. According to European Commission President Jean-Claude Juncker, French President Jacques Chirac once called him minutes after a confidential call Juncker had with President Bill Clinton. Without any pretense, Chirac asked Juncker why he had said something to Clinton. "Thanks for listening in, *mon ami*. Turns out, it's not always the US listening in on your phone calls."[13]

The governments of four member states including Belgium (which would benefit significantly from US intelligence support a few months later during the terrorist attacks in Brussels) and the European Parliament had supported Schrems during the proceedings. None of the member states spoke out publicly to acknowledge the importance of US intelligence cooperation to keep Europe safe. As *The Economist* put it:

> European countries' spy agencies benefit hugely from intelligence-sharing with America about terrorism, organised crime and the activities of countries such as Russia and China. That politicians fail to acknowledge this to their own voters smacks of timidity and ingratitude.[14]

---

[12] Remarks at the Department of Justice, January 17, 2014. https://obamawhitehouse.archives.gov/blog/2014/01/17/president-obama-discusses-us-intelligence-programs-department-justice.

[13] Jean-Claude Juncker, "Politico Brussels Playbook," November 29, 2019. https://www.politico.eu/newsletter/brusselsplaybook/special-playbook-edition-by-jean-claude-juncker/.

[14] Charlemagne, "Swords and Shields," *The Economist*, February 6, 2016.

Moreover, many academic studies have confirmed that the laws governing intelligence gathering in many other member states give greater freedom of action to government actions than in the United States.[15] One exhaustive report concluded that:

> Given the greater level of independent judicial involvement in approving surveillance orders, the range of transparency obligations imposed by law upon the intelligence agencies, and the extensive array of oversight mechanisms in place in the US, safeguards in the US legal order are in general more protective than those in effect in the EU...[16]

Following the terrorist attacks in France and the UK, those countries adopted far-reaching legislation that, in the words of Michael Hayden, former director of the NSA and the CIA, "would never have seen the light of day in the American political system."[17] France's anti-terrorism and surveillance laws make the Patriot Act look tame by comparison. These laws allow its intelligence services to capture communications to and from France by attaching "black box" filters to undersea cables. They allow the services to collect intelligence, even for French citizens on French territory, without any showing of "particularized suspicion," or prior independent approval or judicial oversight. Moreover, the laws allow the collection of information for a wide range of purposes, including for commercial advantage in large international tenders.[18] The Human Rights Commissioner of the Council of Europe, an international organization

---

[15] Winston Maxwell and Christopher Wolf, "A Global Reality: Governmental Access to Data in the Cloud," Hogan Lovells White Paper, July 18, 2012. Winston Maxwell and Christopher Wolf, "A Sober Look at National Security Access to Data in the Cloud," Hogan Lovells White Paper, May 22, 2013. The French Surveillance Law passed after the attacks in Paris enable intelligence agencies to tap phones and e-mails without seeking permission from a judge. It forces Internet service providers and phone companies to give up data upon request. It allows intelligence services to undertake bulk collection of "metadata" (information about communications) and retain it for five years.

[16] Sidley Austin, "Essentially Equivalent: A Legal Comparison of the Legal Orders for Privacy and Data Protection in the European Union and United States," January 2016. https://www.sidley.com/-/media/publications/essentially-equivalent---final.pdf.

[17] Michael Holden and Kate Holten, "UK Unveils Power to Spy on Web Use, Raising Privacy Fears," *Reuters*, November 5, 2015.

[18] Stephen Schulhofer, "A Transatlantic Privacy Pact?" in *Surveillance, Privacy and Trans-Atlantic Relations*, ed. David Cole, Federico Fabbrini, and Stephen Schulhofer

established to promote human rights, democracy and the rule of law in Europe, declared that many of the recently passed measures would fall foul of EU law because they "would be applied without any prior judicial review establishing their legality, proportionality or necessity."[19] The EU's Fundamental Rights Agency also found that some member state laws fall short of EU requirements.[20]

While some member state laws clearly fall short of EU standards, the United States was de facto the sole defendant in the court (without even having representation). While member states must verify the level of protection in a third country before permitting data transfers to that destination, EU law provides that no such verification is required for transfers within the EU. During one of our interagency conference calls, I suggested that we should carry out a "reverse Schrems" operation by finding an American client of a French Internet service provider willing to file suit before the French data protection authority to allege interference with his EU data protection rights because of the powers of the French intelligence services to access Internet traffic. If that case were referred to the European Court of Justice, the cat would really be set among the pigeons. A "reverse Schrems" would have forced national intelligence services to defend their surveillance programs before EU courts and prove that they were compatible with EU law.[21]

Will the EU courts apply the same scrutiny about the compatibility with EU law of member states' intelligence gathering as they did regarding US intelligence gathering? EU treaties provide that "the Union shall respect [member states']...essential State functions, including...-maintaining law and order and safeguarding national security. In particular, national security remains the sole responsibility of each member State." The 1995 Data Protection Directive provided that it did not apply to data processing operations "concerning public security, defence, State security..." The EU Charter of Fundamental Rights, moreover, makes clear that it does not extend the application of EU law, including the

---

(Bloomsbury, 2017), p. 180. Vincent Jauvert, "Comment La France (Aussi) Ecoute le Monde," *Le Nouvel Observateur*, July 2, 2015.

[19] Nils Muiznieks, "Europe Is Spying on You," *The New York Times*, October 27, 2015.

[20] EU Agency for Fundamental Rights, "Surveillance by Intelligence Services: Fundamental Rights Safeguards and Remedies in the EU," 2015. http://fra.europa.eu/en/publication/2015/surveillance-intelligence-services.

[21] A key judgment in 2016 held that Swedish and UK legislation permitting the general and indiscriminate retention of all traffic and location data is incompatible with EU law.

rights contained in the Charter, to areas beyond the powers of the Union (including State security).

Nevertheless, the EU's General Data Protection Regulation (GDPR) enables the Court to check, if asked to do so, whether member state restrictions on data privacy based on national security and defense justifications are "necessary and proportionate." In January 2020, an Advocate General of the Court delivered a non-binding advisory opinion that the bulk acquisition and use of communications data by the UK's security and intelligence agencies constituted "general and indiscriminate retention" of citizens' personal data and were incompatible with EU law. This suggests that the United Kingdom, once it leaves the EU, may struggle to negotiate an agreement with the European Commission ensuring the free flow of personal data from the EU to the UK. The Advocate General made similar findings about the data retention schemes of the security and intelligence agencies in France and Belgium. The judgment of the Court is expected in the fall. It will be interesting to see whether the sauce for the US goose is not sauce for the EU gander. That would be a perverse result.

THE ECONOMIC CONSEQUENCES OF THE COURT'S DECISION

The restrictions to data flows that appeared likely in the wake of the Snowden leaks and the *Schrems* judgment would have had significant economic consequences. Data is the lifeblood of transatlantic (and global) commerce. Nearly every company is a digital company in the sense that it relies on a secure and open flow of data. As two experts put it:

> Data is how a modern company understands and services its customers better. Data is what gives managers their understanding into what is happening around the world. And, increasingly, data is the product itself, serving as the raw material for new insights...Put simply, data and the consumption of data are not just a new natural resource – they are the key commodity in today's knowledge-based economy...The way we use data, the speed and effectiveness with which we collect it, analyse it – and ultimately share it – will set the winners from the losers in this modern world of cheap computing power...[22]

---

[22] Paul Hofheinz and Michael Mandel, "Uncovering the Hidden Value of Digital Trade," The Lisbon Council, Issue 19/2015.

The amount of data crossing the Atlantic daily is rising much faster than the exchange of goods and services: One indication of this is the 38% estimated compound annual growth rate in data-carrying capacity of transatlantic submarine cables until 2025. Digital trade is the fastest-growing segment of the global economy, representing nearly $10 trillion a year. Mobile data traffic alone grew 18 times between 2011 and 2016.[23] By contrast, global trade in goods and services, adjusted for inflation, rose at an average rate of just 2.4% during the same period.[24]

In 2017, the US exported $204 billion of digitally deliverable services to the EU, while importing $124 billion of such services from the EU. That was only part of the picture, because much of the cross-border data flows were not picked up in international trade statistics. For instance, businesses rely on cross-border data flows to communicate internally and with customers, vendors, and suppliers, to manage global supply chains, to access software in the "cloud" (in data centers across the globe rather than on local devices) and to collaborate globally on research and development. According to one estimate, products and services relying on the transatlantic transfer of data are expected to add $1 trillion in value to the US–EU economic relationship within the 2016–2026 period.[25] According to one European think tank, a serious disruption in transatlantic data flows would knock between 0.8% and 1.3% off EU GDP.[26]

Data storage needs have been exploding, as all this data—including pictures, documents, transaction records, and credit card details—have to be stored somewhere. Since the Internet and especially the provision of cloud-based services are dominated by US companies, many of the data servers are located in the United States. Transferring data across the Atlantic (in large part through the mechanism of Safe Harbor) has been a cheaper option than building data servers to host the data in Europe.

---

[23] Daniel Hamilton and Joseph Quinlan, The Transatlantic Economy 2019, Johns Hopkins University SAIS 2019. https://transatlanticrelations.org/wp-content/uploads/2019/03/TE2019_FullStudy.pdf, p. 35.

[24] Paul Hofheinz and Michael Mandel, "Uncovering the Hidden Value of Digital Trade," The Lisbon Council, Issue 19/2015.

[25] Garrett Workman, "TTIP: Underlining the Importance of Digital Trade," US Chamber of Commerce, May 5, 2016. https://www.uschamber.com/article/ttip-underlining-the-importance-digital-trade.

[26] "The Economic Importance of Getting Data Protection Right: Protecting Privacy, Transmitting Data, Moving Commerce," European Centre for International Political Economy, March 2014.

The lack of trust in US data privacy, triggered by the Snowden leaks, threatened to deliver a serious blow to many firms, especially in the cloud computing industry. A growing number of policy-makers around the world were mistakenly concluding that the security of data depends on where it is stored (when in fact the measures used to store it securely are far more relevant). In the decade prior to 2016, the number of significant data localization measures in the world's large economies nearly tripled from 31 to 84.[27] That included far-reaching legislation in Russia in 2015 and China in 2016.

Estimates in 2013 of the damage to the cloud computing industry ranged from $21.5 to $30 billion, according to one report, to as high as $180 billion, according to another report.[28] Many European firms identified a terrific opportunity to win business from their American competitors and to encourage their governments to adopt protectionist IT policies. In August 2013, 30 European CEOs proposed the creation of a "Schengen zone for data" (named after the EU area of passport-free movement of people); such a zone would enable the data of EU citizens to be hosted and processed only on EU territory. In February 2014, French President François Hollande and German Chancellor Angela Merkel voiced support for the development of communications networks that would avoid overseas data transfers. In June, the French government endorsed roadmaps for cloud computing and cybersecurity that included the use of a "secure cloud label" and a preference for working with companies certified by France's IT security agency (unsurprisingly difficult for non-French firms to obtain).

Creating walls around data threatened to kill off the global Internet and cause significant damage to growth and innovation. People now hold more information on a device in their pocket than they used to keep in

---

[27] Matthias Bauer, Hosuk Lee-Makiyama, Erik van der Marel, and Bert Verschelde, "The Cost of Data Localization: Friendly Fire on Economic Recovery," ECIPE Occasional Paper 3/2014. China enacted a law in 2016 that requires companies to store all their data within Chinese borders. A similar law took effect in Russia in 2015.

[28] Daniel Castro, "How Much Will PRISM Cost the US Cloud Computing Industry?" Information Technology and Innovation Foundation, August 2013. James Staten, "The Cost of PRISM Will Be Larger Than ITIF Projects," Forrester blog post, August 14, 2013.

their entire house. Data usage and global data transfer rates are exploding[29]; data is increasingly being held in the cloud. Free data flows are vital to the analysis of large pools of personal data and the extraction of insights from them to improve the services we enjoy and the quality of our lives. Restricting data flows also risked causing significant practical nuisances for consumers. In countless ways, consumers require their information to flow seamlessly across borders. Imagine how frustrating it would be if you could not complete a purchase online because your credit card information needs to be processed somewhere else; imagine having your airline reservation rejected because your passport information cannot be transmitted by the airline to the country to which you want to fly.

Nonetheless, US firms had to respond to the perceived benefits of data localization after the Snowden leaks. They were losing contracts with customers who preferred to store their information in Europe on the misguided assumption that it would be safer there than in the United States. As a result, they scrambled to keep those customers happy by building data centers in Europe: Google already had data centers in Finland and Ireland, but chose to expand its center in Belgium and build one in the Netherlands; Salesforce announced plans to open centers in the UK, France, and Germany; Apple chose to build data centers in Denmark and Ireland; Amazon did so in Frankfurt, in part to show understanding for German privacy preferences; and Microsoft committed to building new centers in the UK and expanding others in Ireland and the Netherlands.

Microsoft was also advertising a new "trustee" relationship with Deutsche Telekom, according to which the former would store data in Germany in data centers run by the latter under German law and therefore beyond the reach of US authorities. While the company explained that it was simply responding to customer demand and the reality that the global cloud was dead, some observers saw the decision as promoting the "Balkanization" of the Internet, by tacitly accepting that regions and even countries had a legitimate interest in building separate infrastructure and walling off data.

---

[29] Global data transfer rates expanded by a factor of more than 40 between 2005 and 2014. "The US-EU Privacy Shield Pact: A Work in Progress," Peterson Institute for International Economics, August 2016.

Threats to Other Key Agreements

As I arrived at my post in March 2014, it seemed that the entire well of US–EU relations had been poisoned by the fallout from the Snowden affair. The situation continued to worsen and it seemed that the *Schrems* judgment could be the final nail in the coffin. While the economic consequences were bad enough, the political consequences were even worse. The tensions over data privacy threatened the negotiations (in progress since 2013) to conclude a transatlantic free trade agreement (described in Chapter 4). They also threatened the 2012 US–EU Passenger Name Record (PNR) Agreement that governs the transfer to the Department of Homeland Security of information—including names, travel dates and itineraries and contact details about airline passengers traveling to the US. (In 2017, the European Court of Justice ruled that the Canada-EU PNR Agreement had to be amended because certain provisions for the handling of personal data were not limited to what was "strictly necessary.")

The tensions threatened to lead to problematic provisions in the GDPR under negotiation among the European Commission, the European Parliament, and the Council. One of these proposed provisions was the so-called anti-FISA clause. This clause prohibited a US company from complying with lawful orders from US courts, law enforcement, or regulatory authorities if those orders would result in the transfer of personal data of EU residents without the prior approval of a competent national data protection authority, unless the transfer was pursuant to an international agreement. That provision, thankfully amended, would have exposed these companies to an impossible conflict of laws. (The final text, however, is still problematic and is yet to be tested.) And since such international agreements were either too cumbersome or simply not available, the provision would have caused havoc to transatlantic cooperation in many areas such as law enforcement, antitrust, food and drug approvals, and financial services.

Two other major US–EU issues of common interest were at stake. Since 2011 we had been negotiating a Data Privacy and Protection Agreement (DPPA) to govern data exchange among US federal law enforcement authorities, on the one hand, and EU and member state law enforcement authorities, for the prevention, detection, investigation and prosecution of criminal offenses, including terrorism. Without such an agreement, data exchanges for these purposes would have to be scrutinized on a case by case basis to determine whether they complied with

EU data protection laws. That would have been far too complex and time-consuming and would have undermined our ability to combat increasing levels of transnational crime.

The tensions also threatened to reopen prior controversies about EU data protection safeguards in the 2010 US–EU Terrorism Finance Tracking Program (TFTP) that governs the transfer from SWIFT to the US Treasury of financial transaction data for counterterrorism purposes (especially the tracking of terrorism finance). SWIFT is a Belgium-based company that operates a worldwide messaging system used to transmit financial information among banking institutions. TFTP had been established after the terrorist attacks of September 11, 2001 as a classified program and then had been converted into an international agreement between the US and the EU in 2010.

Just before my arrival in Brussels, the European Commission had ominously asked for consultations and for a review and the European Parliament had called for the suspension of the program. Terminating the program would have had serious consequences. It has provided thousands of valuable leads to US and foreign (including European) governments that have aided in the investigation and prevention of many of the most violent terrorist attacks in the past decade. In the fall of 2013 and spring of 2014, the US Treasury and the European Commission worked diligently to document the value of TFTP and reassure critics that information was being transferred to the US in strict compliance with the agreement.

Different Perspectives on Privacy

More generally, the Snowden affair deepened the view in Europe that, with regard to data privacy, Americans are from Mars and Europeans are from Venus. I cannot count how many times Europeans, especially members of the European Parliament, would lecture me that Europeans consider privacy as a basic human right, while Americans do not. The strong feelings in continental Europe about data privacy are of course understandable in light of the recent history of autocratic rule, as well as human rights violations. Fortunately, the United States doesn't share that history; it has been graced with a democracy featuring a strict rule of law and checks on executive powers. But that doesn't mean that data privacy is undervalued, nor that the dangers of government surveillance are underestimated, in the United States, as discussed later in this chapter.

Both sides have long struggled with the difficult tension between the need for security, especially in light of the terrorist menace, and the need for privacy. This tension was dramatically highlighted in March 2016 when the FBI requested Apple to help it write software to break into an iPhone used by Syed Farook, a dead terrorist responsible for the massacre of innocent civilians in San Bernardino, California. The government had a strong case: The phone was government property because Farook had been a public employee. Apple's help was required because the files on the phone were encrypted and the files were important to solve a serious crime. But Apple (and many other companies that wanted to provide consumers comfort about the privacy of their communications) also had a strong reason to object: Agreeing to the request would embolden other governments around the world to make similar, if not broader and more frequent, requests in the future. In the end, the government found a way to access the files without Apple's help. Many European governments face this difficult balancing act.

It is true, however, that the cultures of privacy are distinct on either side of the Atlantic. In the United States, privacy is considered as primarily a question of liberty and is related to the rights of private property and free speech. The privacy right is intended principally to protect against *intrusions of the state*. In continental Europe, privacy is linked to the concepts of dignity and honor; every individual is deemed to have rights to his or her own image, name, and reputation. The privacy right is not only intended to protect against intrusions of the state, but also to protect against the *intrusions of the mass media or other private companies*.

One of the most notable transatlantic differences in the approach to privacy is the EU "right to be forgotten" that stems from a judgment of the European Court of Justice and is now enshrined in the GDPR. The case involved a Spaniard who complained when searches of his name on Google produced decade-old information in the Spanish press about the forced sale of his home due to social security debts. Arguing that the information was prejudicial to him and no longer relevant, he asked that Google's search results linking to the press articles be cut. The Court agreed on the basis that the Spaniard was not a person of public interest and therefore that his "right to be forgotten" prevailed over the public's right to outdated and irrelevant information accessed through Google search (albeit it did not compel deletion of the underlying press reports). There is no similar right in the United States. In a separate case decided in September 2019, the Court ruled that Google did not have to apply the "right to be forgotten" globally as demanded by France's privacy watchdog.

The United States has no equivalent to the concept of "informational self-determination" (the right to determine what to disclose about oneself) first elaborated by the German Federal Constitutional Court in 1983. The US and the EU strike a different balance between privacy and freedom of expression: while US courts tend to give greater weight to the Constitution's First Amendment guarantee of free speech when in tension with data privacy, EU courts tend to favor data protection over free speech.[30]

Notions of what should be considered private vary dramatically, of course, on either side of the Atlantic. As one expert has rightly observed, Europeans consider the American habit of talking about one's salary or net worth to be nearly the equivalent of "defecating in public." Americans are amused that Europeans seem so shy about talking about money, while having fewer inhibitions about taking off their clothes to sunbathe. Americans consider many practices in continental Europe to be contrary to privacy, including national ID cards; the authority of some governments to decide what names parents are permitted to give their children; the requirement (in Germany) to be formally registered with the police at all times; and the ability of some governments to conduct wiretaps with ease.[31] In the United States, commercial data may generally be processed unless some law prevents it; there is wide tolerance for industry self-regulation and market-based solutions. The EU, on the other hand, takes a more "precautionary" approach that does not require any showing of risk or harm in order to regulate data processing; consumer data may be collected only under strict limitations, upon specific legal grounds, and is subject to oversight by national DPAs.

One of the reasons why many Europeans do not view US data privacy laws as providing equivalent protection to their own is that the US does not have, unlike the EU, overarching pieces of legislation (such as the EU's 1995 Data Protection Directive, replaced in 2018 by the GDPR,

---

[30] The two approaches are detailed in James Whitman, "The Two Western Cultures of Privacy: Dignity Versus Liberty," *Faculty Scholarship* Series, Paper 649, 2004. http://digitalcommons.law.yale.edu/cgi/viewcontent.cgi?article=1647&context=fss_papers.

[31] Ibid., p. 1159. According to one study, telephones in France and Germany are tapped at ten to thirty times, and in the Netherlands and Italy at 130–150 times, the rate they are tapped in the United States.

and the 2002 E-Privacy Directive that provide high-standard blanket protections for personal data across all aspects of daily digital activities). This reflects the difference between civil law systems that feature unified codes and common law systems that feature a mixture of judge-made laws and diverse legislation. Indeed, the US privacy landscape is confusing and difficult to articulate because it is a complex web of constitutional law, sector-specific federal statutes, state statutes, and common law rules. Nonetheless, there is a comprehensive system in the United States to regulate and protect data privacy. It is backed by a broad and effective public and private enforcement in the commercial sector. There are substantial and effective safeguards, checks, balances, and independent oversight and legal redress relating to electronic surveillance conducted for national security and law enforcement purposes.

The idea of the citizen's fundamental right to privacy has been engrained in the US legal order for well over a century, well before that right was recognized in continental Europe. The US Constitution contains fundamental protections against searches and seizures carried out by the government of "persons, houses, papers and effects." These measures may only be carried out by warrants reviewed by judges requiring the government to meet a high burden of proof. The Supreme Court and federal courts have extended those rights to new technologies and new forms of communication.[32] The government may not take any measures interfering with the rights of free speech, press, religion, and association. Several federal statutes impose significant limits on what intelligence services may do. There are federal data privacy laws relating to the most sensitive categories of personal data, such as financial, medical, electronic communications, employment, insurance, and children's data. The Federal Trade Commission has wide-ranging powers to protect consumers by enforcing measures prohibiting unfair and deceptive practices, including those relating to data privacy.

Moreover, there are privacy laws enforced by attorneys general in each of the fifty states; many of the states, especially California, have passed legislation covering a wide range of activity, including unconsented use of

---

[32] Recent judgments have limited the government's ability to seize an individual's historical cell phone location information, to use thermal imaging technology to look inside a home, or to examine the content of a cell phone, without a warrant.

facial recognition, voyeurism, and misuse of data relating to voter registration and drivers' licenses. In 2018, California passed the broadest digital privacy law of any US state. The law, based on many of the same principles as the GDPR, may become a model for other states and could bring about tougher federal privacy laws. Just as significant as state laws have been the growth in the United States of corporate privacy officers who have become integral to risk management, data privacy codes of conduct in companies and across economic sectors, and active non-governmental organizations that publicize and bring legal actions to enforce data privacy rules.

While the US approach is certainly messier than that in Europe, it provides a level of data privacy protection that is "essentially equivalent" to that guaranteed in the EU legal order. That phrase, used by the European Court of Justice in *Schrems*, describes the threshold for determining whether a third country offers an adequate degree of protection to EU personal data. It means that the protections in the US need not be identical to those in the EU, but rather that they be "essentially equivalent"—in practice and effect, in substance rather than form. It also means that it is unnecessary to consider whether the US has an exact, or even close, equivalent to each and every EU data privacy right. It is the *entirety* of the protections afforded under the data protection regime that is relevant.[33] These conclusions provided the intellectual framework for the negotiations to replace Safe Harbor with Privacy Shield, and they also informed the judgments of US negotiators about how far to stretch to ensure Privacy Shield would survive legal challenge.

Negotiating the Deal

When US and EU negotiators sat down to negotiate a new deal, it was clear that we had to meet the requirements set forth in the judgment of the European Court of Justice. The most problematic area was

---

[33] The Court noted that a third country "cannot be required to ensure a level of protection identical to that guaranteed in the EU legal order." In deciding whether a third country's level of data protection is adequate, the European Commission should carry out a "global assessment." It may make an adequacy finding "even though the manner in which that protection is implemented may differ from that generally encountered in the European Union."

clearly going to be government surveillance. The Court had set forth several critical requirements. Surveillance measures must be based on clear and precise legal authority. There must be minimum safeguards against risks of abuse and unlawful access by public authorities. For example, the amount of data collected or retained must not exceed what is necessary to accomplish the purpose of the surveillance and cannot be generalized or indiscriminate; there must be effective executive, legislative, judicial and expert oversight of the measures; and the public should be informed about surveillance laws and have some opportunity to have legal redress.

The US negotiators urged that the totality of the data privacy protections before, during and after the acquisition of personal data had to be considered. The key was to consider the entire regime relating to surveillance, including its authorization, the practice of targeting "selectors" (such as e-mails and telephone numbers), the procedures aimed at limiting the acquisition, retention and dissemination of data, access by individuals to the raw data and the multiple layers of oversight to ensure compliance with procedures. The right to individual redress (such as to the courts) was an important, but not the determining, factor in and of itself.

US negotiators also stressed the importance of privacy rights "on the ground" rather than merely "privacy on the books." While evaluating the "essential equivalence" of the US and European data privacy regimes, US negotiators repeatedly urged their European counterparts to consider the reality of how these regimes were being enforced in practice, rather than simply what the law said on paper. As one exhaustive study concluded: "the EU legal order on surveillance reflects variety and wide discretion as to the necessity of surveillance and the safeguards to limit interference with rights and freedoms."[34] US data privacy rights should only be compared to an EU benchmark that reflects the range of discretion that exists in practice. The rules and procedures in the United States regarding the authorization and conduct of surveillance fall within the range.

US negotiators resisted any suggestion that US data privacy laws and practice had to be judged against the idealized version in EU law and court judgments, rather than the reality of European data privacy "on the ground." They were aware of the risk that the European Court of Justice

---

[34] Sidley Austin, "Essentially Equivalent: A Comparison of the Legal Orders for Privacy and Data Protection in the European Union and United States," January 2016, p. 4. https://www.sidley.com/-/media/publications/essentially-equivalent---final.pdf.

would hold us to that idealized standard; but, at the end of the day, there was no way that the United States would make legislative reforms to its intelligence laws to ensure 100% compliance with each and every EU data privacy right on paper. The political reality was that we and the European Commission had to accept at least *some* risk that Privacy Shield would be successfully challenged.

Despite all the challenges detailed above, the United States and the European Union managed to work through them. Legislative actions and executive branch reforms regarding data privacy during 2013–2015 played an important role in defusing transatlantic tensions caused by the Snowden leaks. The US and the EU negotiated a Privacy Shield Agreement that significantly improved Safe Harbor and in the process they deepened their mutual understanding of their data privacy regimes. The European Commission made a significant contribution by overcoming opposition from the European Parliament and by bringing the member states on board. The DPPA was concluded and the TFTP and PNR Agreements were safeguarded. These were remarkable achievements that set the foundation for important future work to build further data privacy bridges across the Atlantic.

Two legislative actions, both promoted by the Obama administration, were of particular significance. The first was the USA Freedom Act, passed by Congress with a large majority and on a bipartisan basis in June 2015. That legislation addressed the conclusion in the PCLOB's prior review of US data privacy laws that the government's bulk collection of "metadata"—including numbers calling and being called, and the date, time and duration of calls—was bad policy and not vital for national security. "Metadata" does not provide content of any conversations, identity of parties to conversations, or location information. Prior to the statute, NSA employees could query the metadata to obtain that detail once FISA Court judges have issued a general order authorizing the bulk collection; now the database can only be queried after judicial approval or in the case of a true emergency. Moreover, the "metadata" will be destroyed after five years.

These limitations on the bulk collection were significant to the Privacy Shield negotiations. In the EU legal order, even the initial acquisition of data involves the processing of that data and is therefore subject to data protection limitations. In the United States, on the other hand, the government does not consider the initial acquisition (conducted by automated means) to be processing and therefore subjects it to fewer limitations than the subsequent steps of storage and human consultation. Executive branch reforms announced by President Obama to US surveillance programs and subsequent legislative reforms in the Freedom Act proved that the United States would use bulk collection only when appropriate and with appropriate respect for individual privacy. That gave the European Commission comfort that Privacy Shield would not be successfully challenged in court because it failed to meet EU legal standards applying to bulk collection.

The Freedom Act provided that intelligence services could only query telephone numbers if they were no more than two steps removed from a number associated with a terrorist organization. It guaranteed the right of major Internet service providers (such as webmail and social network providers) to publish detailed statistics about the number of requests from the government to deliver information relevant to national security investigations. And it codified the administration's efforts to systematically declassify significant opinions of the Foreign Intelligence Surveillance Court whenever practicable and authorized the creation of a group of independent experts to brief the Court on important cases.

The Judicial Redress Act, passed by Congress with a large majority and on a bipartisan basis in early 2016, was the second key legislative reform. It sought to address the EU's longstanding complaint that the United States collects large amounts of personal data on Europeans but that US law does not grant them the same rights as US nationals to seek judicial review of complaints concerning misuse of such data. The discrimination rankled because rights of redress in EU data protection law are equally available to EU and other foreign nationals.

I am proud of my role in the passage of this statute. In May 2014, I flew to Washington to meet with Presidential Counselor John Podesta in the White House to explain why the issue had become of "totemic" significance in the general effort to restore transatlantic trust. John was the perfect person to lead an interagency effort to explore whether the discrimination could be fixed by legislation because he was the point man on privacy issues and big data in the White House and was an astute observer of transatlantic affairs. Most experts on legislative affairs at the White House thought that the chances of any legislation passing Congress at that time were low due to very contentious relations between the two political parties. It was unlikely that the administration would expend much political capital to promote legislation for which there was no apparent domestic constituency and that would be perceived as giving the Europeans a "present." But Podesta immediately appreciated how passage of the legislation could help unblock progress on many issues of transatlantic importance, including free trade, Privacy Shield and law enforcement.

After a very lengthy, and often contentious, interagency review, we managed to gain consensus in favor of new legislation to amend the 1974 Privacy Act. That amendment provides that citizens of certain designated foreign countries would now have the same rights as US citizens under the Privacy Act with regard to personal data transferred under the DPPA Agreement on data exchange between law enforcement authorities. Specifically, with respect to such data EU citizens are now able to access and correct information about themselves; seek and obtain administrative remedies where a request for access to, or correction of, information is denied or information is otherwise improperly processed; and seek and obtain judicial redress in US federal courts for privacy violations. In order to benefit from the Judicial Redress Act, a foreign country or regional grouping (like the EU) must not adopt data transfer policies that "materially impede" the national security interests of the US and must cooperate with the US on the exchange of commercial and law enforcement data.

On top of these legislative reforms, there were other important actions by the executive branch during 2013–2015 that enabled the US and EU to overcome the serious tensions around data privacy. Presidential Policy Directive (PPD) 28 of January 17, 2014 and the President's speech of the same day introducing it are historic documents.[35] They were the result of the recommendations of an experts' group on intelligence and communications technologies, constituted six months earlier, as well as consultations with the PCLOB.

PPD-28 created new limitations on the use of bulk collection of signals intelligence. US intelligence agencies could only use such data to meet specific security requirements: counterintelligence, counterterrorism, counter-proliferation, cybersecurity, protection of US and allied troops, and combating transnational crime, including sanctions evasion. In no event could signals intelligence collected in bulk be used for the

---

[35] See https://obamawhitehouse.archives.gov/the-press-office/2014/01/17/presidential-policy-directive-signals-intelligence-activities and https://obamawhitehouse.archives.gov/the-press-office/2014/01/17/remarks-president-review-signals-intelligence.

purpose of suppressing or burdening criticism or dissent, disadvantaging persons based on their ethnicity, race, gender, sexual orientation or religion; or affording a competitive commercial advantage to US companies. The last point was particularly relevant in the case of transatlantic relations because of the prior press reports that US and UK intelligence agencies had targeted the communications of foreign businesses and the European Commissioner in charge of antitrust policy.[36] Moreover, signals intelligence had to be as "tailored as feasible"; that determination should be based in part on the availability of alternative information sources, including diplomatic and public sources, that should be prioritized.

PPD-28 also defused the serious tensions caused by allegations that the NSA had been eavesdropping on the communications of foreign leaders, including German Chancellor Angela Merkel. In his speech, President Obama stated that:

> the leaders of our close friends and allies deserve to know that if I want to know what they think about an issue, I'll pick up the phone and call them, rather than turning to surveillance…I have made it clear to the intelligence community that unless there is a compelling national security purpose, we will not monitor the communications of heads of state and government of our close allies.

PPD-28 was also notable because it made the protection of privacy and civil liberties rights of persons *outside the US* an integral part of US surveillance policy. In his speech, the President noted that "people around the world, regardless of their nationality, should know that the United States is not spying on ordinary people who don't threaten our national security, and that we take their privacy concerns into account in our policies and procedures." PPD-28 provided that "All persons should be treated with dignity and respect, *regardless of their nationality or wherever they might reside*, and all persons have legitimate privacy interests in the handling of their personal information" (emphasis added). US intelligence activities must, therefore, include appropriate safeguards for the personal information of all individuals "*regardless of the nationality of the individual to whom the information pertains or where that individual resides*" (emphasis added).

---

[36] James Glanz and Andrew Lehren, "NSA Spied on Allies, Aid Groups and Business," *The New York Times*, December 20, 2013.

The directive also put into place express limits on the retention and dissemination of personal information about non-US persons collected by signals intelligence, comparable to the limits that apply to US persons. Importantly, signals intelligence about the routine activities of foreign persons may not be disseminated as "foreign intelligence" by virtue of that fact alone unless it is otherwise responsive to an authorized foreign intelligence requirement. PPD-28 did not require the intelligence community to apply identical procedures to information of US and foreign persons. Nonetheless, these were extraordinary changes because few, if any, spy agencies around the world constrain their activities beyond their borders; few provide any privacy rights to non-nationals within their borders.

While these legislative and executive branch actions were important to getting Privacy Shield across the finish line, significant enhancements to the prior Safe Harbor program were also fundamental. Critics alleged that many companies had made false claims about their compliance with the program and that enforcement had not been as robust as it should have been. For many years, critics had pointed out—with justification—that Safe Harbor needed to be updated and fleshed out with far more detail. It had been issued in 2000 and based on a 1995 EU Data Privacy Directive, practically at the dawn of the Internet age. The rules were simply not adequate in an era of exploding use of data, due in part to nearly ubiquitous mobile devices connected to the cloud, and due to the increasingly sophisticated tools of intelligence agencies grappling with the pressures of combatting more violent and transnational threats.

The Commission's Safe Harbor decision concluding that data transferred to the US pursuant to the program would provide an adequate level of protection consistent with EU law was all of three pages long. The European Court of Justice unsurprisingly concluded that the decision barely contained any reasoned analysis at all to substantiate its "adequacy" finding. Since that finding, the European Commission had not considered the evolution in the US legal system relating to the safeguards for privacy and data protection.

Responding to public pressures triggered by the Snowden revelations and amplified by the European Parliament and the national data privacy authorities' working group, the European Commission issued 13 recommendations to improve Safe Harbor. Eleven of these recommendations were commercially focused and not particularly controversial.

The Privacy Shield contains numerous improvements compared to Safe Harbor with regard to commercial transfers of data. These include stricter obligations on self-certified companies, for example, regarding notices and disclosures that they are required to provide, limitations on how long a company may retain personal data and the conditions under which data can be shared with third parties outside the Privacy Shield framework. They include more regular and rigorous monitoring by the Department of Commerce, including verifying the completeness of self-certifications, conducting periodic compliance audits and referring cases of abuse to the FTC. And they provide enhanced opportunities for EU persons to obtain redress.

The final two recommendations were far thornier because they concluded that restrictions on data privacy justified on the grounds of national security (and enabling US intelligence collection) had to be significantly tightened.

Through many tortuous rounds of negotiations, the European Commission's negotiating team pressed the United States to provide more and more information about how its intelligence collection works in practice. We realized, of course, that the Commission's "adequacy finding" would have to provide detailed reasoning about why US intelligence collection is consistent with EU fundamental rights. We were willing to provide information, but we certainly weren't going to alter intelligence practices or allow a direct negotiation between US intelligence services and the EU. The necessary information was therefore contained in letters from the General Counsel of the Office of the Director of National Intelligence to senior officials at the Department of Commerce (and annexed to the "adequacy finding").

The European Commission concluded on the basis of these submissions that US law contains significant limitations on such access, storage, and use (including dissemination) of personal data. It also explained why oversight and redress mechanisms provide sufficient safeguards that such data is protected from unlawful interference and risk of abuse. In particular, PPD-28 gave the European Commission comfort that the United States is applying principles that respect the EU law concepts of "necessity and proportionality" in the collection of intelligence: Targeted collection is prioritized, while bulk collection is limited to (exceptional) situations where targeted collection is not possible. When bulk collection is used, it is accompanied by safeguards to minimize the amount of data collected and to limit subsequent access to such data exclusively to the pursuit of legitimate national security purposes. The European Commission's review also detailed the various levels of executive, legislative, judicial, and independent agency oversight of intelligence activities.

Criticism of the Deal

Critics of Privacy Shield immediately pointed out that PPD-28 is an order from the president rather than legislation and, as such, may be revoked by any of President Obama's successors. While that is true, a presidential order still has the force of law, in the sense that it is binding on the intelligence services, until it is revoked or amended. Interestingly, the Trump administration has not done so despite having revoked many other directives of the prior administration. Critics also correctly pointed out that the two letters of the General Counsel merely reviewed existing US legislation and procedures and did not therefore amount to binding commitments. They reserved their strongest criticism, however, for the limited powers of the Ombudsperson at the US Department of State. The Ombudsperson is a new role that the United States agreed to create (with strong encouragement from me and the US Mission to the EU) in order to bolster individual rights of redress.

US and EU negotiators knew that Privacy Shield would be challenged before the European Court of Justice, sooner rather than later. A very strong case could be made that the rules and procedures governing the collection, and preventing the misuse, of data by intelligence authorities would meet the high standards of EU law; but it would be harder to show that the *remedies* available, in the event of breach, would meet those standards.

Many rights under the Constitution (including with regard to unlawful "search and seizure" under the Fourth Amendment) do not apply to non-US citizens. Although EU citizens do, in principle, have possibilities to seek judicial redress in US courts when they have been the subject of unlawful (electronic) surveillance for national security purposes, the European Commission concluded that the available causes of action are limited in practice. US federal courts have on occasion concluded that individuals (including foreigners) have "standing" (a judicial doctrine requiring a plaintiff to show sufficient direct interest to bring a lawsuit). But the European Commission worried that the doctrine is a significant obstacle for EU citizens seeking meaningful judicial redress.

There are other multiple avenues available to EU citizens, including under the Electronic Communications and Privacy Act, to seek judicial redress for unlawful surveillance.[37] But the EU considered them partial at best because it is unlikely that an EU (or other foreign) national would ever discover that he has been subject to US government surveillance. We needed to come up with some additional mechanism to provide a form of redress that would, on the one hand, be tolerable for our intelligence services and, on the other, satisfy EU requirements.

The Secretary of State, therefore, appointed an Ombudsperson at the State Department to ensure that individual complaints are properly investigated and addressed. In every case, the Ombudsperson will respond by stating that either US laws have been complied with or that any noncompliance has been remedied. A complainant does not have to demonstrate that his personal data have in fact been accessed by the US government (something that is obviously difficult to do). The Ombudsperson is entitled to rely on the cooperation of US intelligence authorities but remains independent from them. Secretary Kerry appointed as Ombudsperson an undersecretary that was already serving, under PPD-28, as a central point of contact for foreign governments wishing to raise concerns regarding US intelligence activities. The undersecretary was also responsible for keeping the European Commission abreast of changes in policies and procedures limiting access by intelligence and law enforcement authorities to personal data, as well as for participating in the annual review of Privacy Shield.

Critics have claimed that the Ombudsperson mechanism is insufficient to remedy the problem of inadequate judicial redress for EU citizens, according to standards of EU law to be applied by the European Court of Justice. Additionally, the role is enshrined in a letter from Secretary John Kerry to European Commissioner Věra Jourová and subsequently published in the Federal Register. It is not clear that a court would find such a letter to have any binding effect even though it is a communication at very senior levels of government. Critics have also argued that the Ombudsperson is not sufficiently independent of the executive branch; it does not constitute an independent tribunal; it is not permanent; it does not issue reasoned decisions or grant compensation; and it is not subject to judicial review. The powers of the Ombudsperson are limited: He or she will only confirm that a complaint has been properly investigated and

---

[37] The ECPA provides for criminal sanction and civil causes of action for "any person whose wire, oral, or electronic communication is intercepted, disclosed or intentionally used in violation of the Act."

that either US laws and procedures providing limitations and safeguards on intelligence collection have been satisfied or that any non-compliance has been remedied. Critically, the Ombudsperson will neither confirm nor deny whether the individual has been the target of surveillance nor will he or she confirm any specific remedy that has been applied.

These criticisms, however, fail to give due appreciation to the fact that the Ombudsperson mechanism is the first time ever that a country has created a body to deal specifically with complaints from foreign citizens regarding intelligence activities that affect them. I doubt that any EU member state, including the UK and France, will ever do the same.

The history of the Privacy Shield negotiation demonstrates that, despite the occasional frictions, the United States and the European Union were able to deepen mutual understanding of their data privacy regimes. As a result of the negotiations, the parties were able to put into place a new data exchange agreement that improved protections for EU citizens' data when transferred to the United States. In anticipation of an inevitable challenge before the EU courts, the European Commission was also able to articulate in detail why it considers that Privacy Shield and the US data privacy regime provide protections equivalent to those in the EU legal order. Privacy Shield has also been a commercial success, demonstrated by the fact that nearly 4000 companies (large and small) have certified their compliance.

Fortunately, the Trump administration has preserved Privacy Shield even though it is the product of the Obama administration. After entrusting a junior official within the State Department to the role of Ombudsman on a temporary basis, the Trump administration finally appointed an undersecretary on a permanent basis in June 2019. The two-year delay in doing so was one of the major criticisms of Privacy Shield in the first two annual reviews conducted by the European Commission. In late 2018, the administration also appointed members to the PCLOB, a critical oversight body discussed earlier and one of the key reasons why the European Commission had issued its "adequacy finding." The board had been operating without a quorum and had therefore been unable to function since early 2017. Its report on the implementation of PPD-28 provided the European Commission with confidence that the directive's privacy protections for non-Americans were being implemented across the US intelligence community. Moreover, the US Commerce Department has also increased its proactive oversight of the framework, including by conducting spot checks on companies to verify whether they comply with Privacy Shield principles. Finally, the Federal Trade Commission has also demonstrated a more proactive approach to enforcement.

Despite this good news, Privacy Shield will remain vulnerable to the possibilities that future presidents may dilute or even revoke PPD-28 and that they may fail to ensure that the Ombudsperson carries out its functions with independence and effectiveness. It will also remain vulnerable to the possibilities that privacy watchdogs like PCLOB do not receive the funding or manpower to carry out their functions or that Congress dilutes the privacy restrictions on intelligence surveillance that were put into place during the Obama administration. From the moment it was approved, Privacy Shield (and other mechanisms for transatlantic data privacy flows) has been the subject of numerous legal challenges.

Privacy Shield may not be a durable solution to the important task of building transatlantic data privacy bridges. At the time this book went to press, the EU courts were scheduled to deliver judgments that may have a significant impact on transatlantic data flows. In one case, the European Court of Justice is considering several questions referred to it by the Irish High Court in a second complaint filed by Maximilian Schrems (*Schrems II*). That complaint alleges that data transfers to the US using standard contractual clauses breach EU law. The Irish High Court had the benefit of hearing from many expert witnesses in US privacy law. Unlike the *Schrems* I case, the US government decided to intervene in *Schrems* II to try to set the record straight for the Irish High Court and subsequently for the EU courts. Although the Irish High Court's factual findings were nonetheless highly critical of US privacy practices and seemed likely to result in an unfavorable judgment, an opinion by the Advocate General suggests that the European Court of Justice may find standard contractual clauses to be valid. A second case brought by a French advocacy group challenging the legality of Privacy Shield was postponed until after the judgment in *Schrems* II.

US and EU negotiators felt that there is a strong basis on which to conclude that the provisions in Privacy Shield, coupled with US data privacy law, when seen in the aggregate and in practice, provide protections that are essentially equivalent to those in the EU. But there will be a risk that EU courts will find that some specific US law, most likely in the field of intelligence surveillance, falls short of EU law *on the books* rather than against an EU-wide benchmark that considers the reality of how many member states apply the law. As shown by the invalidation of Safe Harbor in *Schrems*, it is unlikely that the EU courts will be overly concerned with the commercial disruption caused by their privacy decisions. In the event that Privacy Shield is found wanting, the US and the EU will need to scramble once again to put into place a replacement agreement.

Building on Privacy Shield

While negotiating Privacy Shield was a significant achievement, it is a series of one-way explanations and commitments (especially noteworthy in the realm of intelligence gathering). The agreement is also limited to the US–EU dimension, rather than covering a broader geographic scope. Despite the significance of transatlantic data flows, data and the digital economy are becoming increasingly global.

The time is ripe for the US and the EU to build on Privacy Shield by negotiating a *two-way* agreement that enhances the alignment of their data privacy regimes. This would enhance the trust of consumers on both sides of the Atlantic in the digital tools of modern life. It would help build an integrated transatlantic digital economy and set global standards for data privacy. As argued in Chapter 8, the time is also ripe for a US–EU agreement on the access of our law enforcement authorities to electronic evidence stored abroad.

Recent events in the United States are bringing our data privacy regime into greater alignment with that of the EU. In 2015, the Obama administration proposed (but failed to win Congressional support for) a Consumer Privacy Bill of Rights Act that set conditions on the lawful processing of personal data. The purpose of the bill was to articulate in one document certain rights, such as the right to exercise control over the collection, retention and use of personal data; to have easily understandable information about privacy and security practices; to require that the collection, retention and use of personal data are carried out in ways consistent with consumers' intentions; to require secure and responsible handling of personal data; and to enable consumers to access and correct personal data. There were other attempts in Congress during the subsequent years to pass similar legislation.

The entry into force of the EU's GDPR in May 2018 helped to raise awareness in the United States of the need for such a bill of rights. GDPR requires any organization anywhere in the world that handles EU citizens' personal data to be transparent about how it collects, stores, and processes that data. Shortly after its entry into force, California passed a landmark data privacy law inspired by GDPR. Repeated revelations, involving many of the leading social media companies in the United States, of large-scale unauthorized access to personal data have only increased the sentiment that GDPR-type legislation is necessary at a federal level. The scandal in 2018 involving the purchase by Cambridge Analytica of tens of millions of people's Facebook profiles without their consent for political advertising purposes is perhaps the leading example. Even the FTC's record-breaking $5 billion fine against Facebook is not a substitute for a federal legislation.

When I was serving in my diplomatic mission, many CEOs of US tech firms complained to me bitterly that GDPR is an overly intrusive piece of legislation that is typical of EU bureaucratic overreach. They were calling for self-regulation or denying that any regulation is necessary. There were a few notable exceptions. A number of thought leaders on data privacy, such as Brad Smith, President of Microsoft, and Ginni Rometty, President and CEO of IBM, have long pressed for federal privacy rules that empower consumers to better control their data.

Now the giants of the US tech community embrace GDPR. Apple has long underlined its commitment to privacy. In 2018 Tim Cook, the CEO of Apple, called for a federal privacy law to prevent a "data industrial complex" from "weaponizing" personal information with "military efficiency." One year later Mark Zuckerberg, CEO of Facebook, a company that privacy advocates consider to be one of the key threats to personal data privacy, argued for a globally harmonized privacy and data protection framework in line with GDPR.[38] If passed, a US federal "Privacy Bill of Rights" would be another important step in bringing the US and EU data protection regimes closer together.[39]

US and EU regulators will need to cooperate ever more closely on data privacy. One critical area will be the interplay, and perhaps convergence, between data privacy and competition policy. There are many aspects to this area, including valuing (off-balance sheet) data for the purpose of jurisdictional thresholds for merger review, treating the accumulation of

---

[38] Mark Zuckerberg, "The Internet Needs New Rules," *The Washington Post*, March 30, 2019.

[39] Another step that would promote the alignment of US–EU data privacy regimes would be US ratification, after appropriate revisions, of the Council of Europe's Convention for the Protection of Individuals with regard to Automatic Processing of Personal Data. While the United States is not a member of this body, dedicated to promoting human rights, democracy and the rule of law in Europe, it is already a party to another Council of Europe convention on cybercrime.

valuable data as an indicator of market power, and determining when and how actors with market power may collect and use data.

Leading privacy experts from think tanks on both sides of the Atlantic have been trying to build "privacy bridges"[40] that do not require legislative change. These bridges merit consideration and some are both worthwhile and relatively straightforward. For example, the FTC and the EU Data Protection Board (that coordinates the EU's DPAs) should establish formal working relations and hold regular meetings. A Memorandum of Understanding could, for example, call on both sides to provide the other with advance notification of an intention to conduct specific policy analysis; to coordinate regulatory activity; and to promote cooperation on enforcement matters involving cross-border violations of data privacy law. Other proposals call for promoting common perspectives on privacy by fostering multi-disciplinary collaboration between data privacy experts and standardizing laws requiring the reporting of multinational data privacy breaches. The proposals also call for technology companies, privacy regulators, industry organizations, privacy scholars, civil society groups, and technical standards bodies to develop common mechanisms for individuals to express their privacy choices with regard to the collection, use, and transfer of their data.

A US–EU data privacy agreement would not be the first regional agreement of its kind. The Trans-Pacific Partnership (TPP) that the Obama administration sought to conclude, for example, included a chapter of binding provisions on electronic commerce. These provisions reflected core principles such as an open and free Internet (enabling consumers to access content and applications of their choice), unrestricted cross-border data flows (versus discriminatory and protectionist barriers), the prohibition of requirements to store data locally and the protection of innovation in products that enhance security and privacy (such as encryption). After the Trump administration withdrew from TPP, the other signatories proceeded with a new version that also included an e-commerce chapter.

The Asia-Pacific Economic Cooperation (APEC) group, encompassing 21 Asian-Pacific members constituting almost half of world trade,

---

[40] Privacy Bridges: EU and US Privacy Experts in Search of Transatlantic Privacy Solutions, 37th International Privacy Conference, Amsterdam 2015.

concluded a Privacy Framework in 2004. According to its recommendations, member states acknowledge and implement basic principles of privacy protection, while permitting variations reflecting their different legal systems, cultures, values, and privacy laws.[41] The APEC Privacy Framework was based on earlier Guidelines of the Organization for Economic Cooperation and Development (OECD), an organization of 35 economically developed countries. The OECD Guidelines, most recently updated in 2013, represent a consensus on basic principles that can be built into national legislation.

A US–EU data privacy agreement could be more ambitious than these regional agreements because the transatlantic region shares a common heritage of democracy, the rule of law and fundamental freedoms, as well as being the home of the most dynamic digital companies. TTIP would have been an opportunity to enshrine core principles, more ambitious than those in TPP, had we been able to conclude it.

One former colleague of mine at the National Security Council has proposed a Transatlantic Charter for Data Security and Mobility:

> Such a document might establish general principles that governments would observe as they analyse and deploy specific rules on data collection, handling and analysis. It would also encourage constructive engagement in these decisions from industry. While final agreement on such a charter by US and European policymakers would represent a signal achievement, the effort of seeking consensus on basic principles can in itself be helpful in establishing trust among governments that regulate data and companies that increasingly depend on data.[42]

Such a charter might require US and EU regulators to consult with one another when considering rules that might affect the firms or citizens of the other. In their consultations, they would explain how proposed rules align with the data privacy regime of the other and would undertake to minimize any contradictions. According to the charter, the parties would agree to promote an open and free Internet, and cross-border data flows; refrain from discriminating against digital transfers from other countries;

---

[41] APEC Privacy Framework. https://www.apec.org/Publications/2017/08/APEC-Privacy-Framework-(2015).

[42] Christopher Smart, "Regulating the Data That Drive 21st Century Economic Growth: The Looming Transatlantic Battle," Chatham House, June 2017. https://www.chathamhouse.org/publication/regulating-data-drive-21st-century-economic-growth-looming-transatlantic-battle.

ensure that government data be as open and available as possible; and permit data localization rules only in limited circumstances.

Firms could be encouraged to endorse the charter's principles and to develop industry sector-specific charters that would include codes of conduct and measures to improve standardization and interoperability of data privacy rules. One model for this proposal is the Memorandum of Understanding between the US Department of Health and the European Commission on the interoperability of health-related information and communication technology, products, and services. The MOU sets out a roadmap to facilitate the access, control, and portability of electronic health records.[43]

The charter would also encourage consultations among legislators and joint work among non-governmental privacy experts on such thorny issues as the interplay between privacy and cybersecurity (including encryption), how to distinguish between industrial and personal data (with the latter deserving a higher degree of protection), how and when to make data anonymous and therefore incapable of being used to identify individuals, and the circumstances in which individuals should be able to claim ownership of data relating to themselves. The charter could serve as a framework for joint proposals by the US and the EU at the G-7 and G-20 groups of advanced economies, as well as at the World Trade Organization.[44]

The gradual alignment of data privacy regimes in the US and the EU may eventually lead to bolder solutions. In the wake of the invalidation of Safe Harbor, Brad Smith, President of Microsoft, argued that data privacy is a fundamental human right and, as such, it should not change every time data moves from one location to another. Individuals should not lose their data privacy rights just because their data crosses a border; that is especially so when they are not aware of where their information is being

---

[43] Carl Bildt and William Kennard, "Building a Transatlantic Digital Marketplace: Twenty Steps Toward 2020," Atlantic Council, April 2016. http://www.atlanticcouncil.org/publications/reports/building-a-transatlantic-digital-marketplace-twenty-steps-toward-2020.

[44] In July 2016, the United States tabled a proposal at the WTO to update the General Agreement on Trade in Services to include a chapter on electronic commerce. The proposal included the following: prohibiting customs duties for digital products, establishing non-discrimination principles between foreign and domestic firms; allowing companies and consumers to move data as they see fit; preventing localization barriers; and barring forced technology transfers. At the time of writing, these proposals have not yet been agreed.

moved or stored by someone else. Smith made a simple, but far-reaching proposal that data privacy rights should travel with the data itself:

> If we're going to ensure that data…can move across the Atlantic on a more sustainable basis, we need to put in place a new type of trans-Atlantic agreement. This agreement needs to protect people's privacy rights pursuant to their own laws, while ensuring that law enforcement can keep the public safe through new international processes to obtain prompt and appropriate access to personal information pursuant to proper legal standards.[45]

That would mean that the US government would only have the right to demand access to EU citizens' personal information stored in the United States in a manner that conforms with EU law, and vice versa. Smith advocated in favor of a new transatlantic agreement that would create an expedited process for governmental entities on both sides of the Atlantic to access personal information that has crossed the Atlantic and belongs to the other's citizens. According to this process, a government could only request access to this data if lawful under its own laws; if the government in the citizen's country of nationality finds that the request is in conformity with local laws, it would authorize disclosure.

Such an agreement would have far-reaching consequences. It would mean that US law enforcement authorities could only compel US Internet service providers, for example, to deliver data relating to EU citizens if this were in perfect compliance with EU law, *even when the data is stored in the United States*. That is a significant step beyond the "essential equivalence" standard we observed in Privacy Shield. And it would require significant legislative changes that are highly unlikely in the areas of law enforcement and intelligence collection. Nevertheless, it would be worth considering whether to negotiate a US–EU pact on the minimum privacy standards that US and EU citizens and residents should enjoy vis-à-vis each other's foreign surveillance.[46] Although there are few limitations on US surveillance of EU nationals abroad, President Obama rightly stated that the United States cares about their privacy; this would be a concrete step to prove it.

---

[45] Brad Smith, "The Collapse of the US-EU Safe Harbor: Solving the New Privacy Rubik's Cube," October 20, 2015. https://blogs.microsoft.com/on-the-issues/2015/10/20/the-collapse-of-the-us-eu-safe-harbor-solving-the-new-privacy-rubiks-cube/.

[46] See David Cole and Federico Fabbrini, "Transatlantic Negotiations for Transatlantic Rights: Why an EU-US Agreement is the Best Option for Protecting Privacy Against Cross-Border Surveillance," in *Surveillance, Privacy and Transatlantic Relations*, ed. David Cole, Federico Fabbrini, and Stephen Schulhofer (Bloomsbury, 2017).

CHAPTER 6

The Digital Economy

On February 15, 2015, President Obama gave an interview to the technology news outlet Re/Code in which he made a statement that triggered immediate criticism from the European Union:

> ...sometimes [European] vendors...who, you know, can't compete with ours – are essentially trying to set up some roadblocks for our [internet] companies to operate effectively there...oftentimes what is portrayed as high-minded positions on issues sometimes is just designed to carve out some of their commercial interests.

The president was in Silicon Valley to participate in a White House Summit on Cybersecurity and Consumer Protection. His remarks in the interview were probably aimed at US technology firms with which relations had become strained in the wake of the Snowden revelations about US government surveillance. Some of these firms were alarmed that many European governments and consumers no longer trusted US firms to handle their data and were shifting their business to European competitors. While the context of the interview was important, the remarks were unfortunate. Many European concerns about US technology firms were sincerely held, and even legitimate, and not merely motivated by protectionism.

I had heard the same protectionist charge leveled against Europe so many times before. In the late 1980s, many observers warned ominously that the effort to create a Single European market without barriers to the free flow of goods, services, workers, and capital was in fact an effort to create a "Fortress Europe." According to this narrative, Europe would pursue an industrial policy, including regulations and standards that would discriminate against non-EU firms, as a means of nurturing European business champions.

To the contrary, the single market program dismantled barriers for EU and non-EU firms alike, deepened economic integration, increased European competitiveness, and made the EU into a global force for open, rules-based trade and investment. US firms have been great beneficiaries of this single market because they are unencumbered by historical, linguistic and emotional attachments. They were therefore naturally inclined to look at Europe, unlike some of their European competitors, as one big geographic area without internal borders.

The charges of protectionism and anti-Americanism have always been easy to make. When the European Commission found in 2015 that Ireland had to recover €13 billion (plus interest) from Apple for back taxes that it should have paid over a decade, Apple's CEO Tim Cook remarked that "It's total political crap...I think Apple was targeted here...[and] I think that [anti-US sentiment] is one reason why we could have been targeted."[1] Cook's prior meeting with Margrethe Vestager, European Commissioner for Competition Policy, had gone reportedly gone poorly.

The finding against Apple may explain why President Trump told European Commission President Jean-Claude Juncker at the G-7 summit meeting in Canada in June 2018 that "your tax lady, she really hates the US." President Trump had evidently forgotten the name of the "lady" or the fact that she was responsible for competition policy. When reporters asked her later about the comment, Vestager responded with her usual poise: "I've done my own fact-checking on the first part of the sentence, and I do work with tax and I am a woman, so this is 100% correct." But the second half of the sentence is "not correct," she added, saying: "I very much like the US."[2]

Trump's allegation was Fake News. His attack seemed based on the view that no regulatory authority of a foreign jurisdiction should have the temerity to tax, let alone regulate, US companies. The president seemed

---

[1] Interview with the *Irish Independent*, September 1, 2016.

[2] Magdaline Duncan, "Vestager: 'I do work with tax and I am a woman,'" *Politico*, July 18, 2018. "Trump told me 'You're a brutal killer,' EU's Juncker says," *Reuters*, June 14, 2018.

to think that only the US should investigate alleged tax and antitrust abuses by US tech firms, regardless of where that abuse occurs. This is a misunderstanding of how US and EU antitrust laws work. Both jurisdictions regulate activities such as mergers and alleged antitrust infractions, even by foreign companies, when they have effects on their territories. Given its long history of extraterritorial jurisdiction, the US is perhaps the last country that should complain about foreign countries exerting jurisdiction over US companies.

As a lawyer practicing EU antitrust law in Brussels during 1992–1994 and then subsequently as a government official and investor following EU issues, I never detected any evidence that the flag of the companies' headquarters influences EU competition decisions. Academic studies confirm this, specifically that there is no anti-American bias. In the most exhaustive analysis to date, covering over 5000 merger control decisions over 25 years, the authors could not find any evidence that the European Commission had intervened more frequently, or more extensively, in transactions involving a non-EU or US-based firm's acquisition of a European target.[3]

One dramatic recent example of how the flag of companies' headquarters does not determine the result of EU competition decisions was the decision of the European Commission in 2019 to block the merger between the German and French high-speed train manufacturers Siemens and Alstom. Despite intense lobbying at the highest levels of the German and French governments urging the creation of a European champion to compete with state-backed rivals from China, the European Commission insisted that the merger would harm competition in markets for railway signaling systems and very high-speed trains. If the European Commission is as political as some of its critics suggest, it would have heeded the pressure of the EU's most powerful members and would have cleared the merger.

Concerns About GAFA

Those looking for evidence of a concerted anti-American campaign against leading US technology firms in the fall of 2014 could point to some concerning developments, however. Government officials and the

---

[3] Anu Bradford, Robert Jackson, Jr., Jonathan Zytnick, "Does the European Union Use Its Antitrust Power for Protectionism?" April 3 2018. https://promarket.org/european-union-use-antitrust-power-protectionism/.

media were frequently referring to Google, Apple, Facebook, and Amazon in shorthand as "GAFA" in frequent warnings about the threat to Europe from US dominance in the digital economy. The fear only seemed to grow over time: *The Economist*, for example, carried two striking front covers in late 2017 and early 2018 that proclaimed "Social media's threat to democracy" (depicting Facebook's "f" trademark pointed like a pistol) and the threat from the "New Titans" (depicting the GAFA as giant robots eating every asset in their path).

The fear was understandable because Europe was feeling self-conscious about its failure to create many leading technology firms, especially online platforms, and because the wealth and market power of GAFA seemed threatening. Online platforms headquartered in the EU represent only a small fraction of the total global market capitalization of such platforms. Apple's cash reserves are larger than the GDPs of many European countries, and the market capitalization of GAFA exceeds the GDP of the French economy. Sometimes I wonder what Americans would feel if nearly all large players in the US digital economy were European. Wouldn't they feel slightly uneasy?

The well-connected German publishing industry appeared to be behind many of the repeated attacks on Google. In April 2014, Mathias Döpfner, head of Europe's largest newspaper publisher Axel Springer that owns Europe's best-selling newspaper tabloid *Bild* and the broadsheet *Die Welt*, penned an open letter to Google in which he alleged the company's total dependence on Google: "Google doesn't need us. But we need Google." Google was operating a business model that "in less reputable circles would be called a protection racket" because it discriminated against competitors in its search rankings.[4] He compared Google to Fáfnir, a character from a Norse myth that inspired Richard Wagner to compose *The Ring of the Nibelung*. The son of a dwarf king, Fáfnir, became so jealous of the family's treasure that he killed his father to take sole possession of it. Greed turned Fáfnir into a dragon, who guarded the treasure with fire and poison.

At the end of November 2014, the European Parliament overwhelmingly passed a non-binding motion that called upon the European Commission to unbundle search engines from their other businesses. (This

---

[4] Mathias Dopfner, "Why We Fear Google," *Frankfurter Allgemeine Zeitung*, April 17, 2014.

call was repeated in following years). While the motion didn't mention Google by name, Google was clearly the target. Eric Schmidt, Chairman of Google, called Secretary of Commerce Penny Pritzker to raise his concerns and numerous members of Congress fired off letters in protest.

Although the reaction was overdone because the resolution had no legal effect, I too was rather concerned about the general climate. The European People's Party issued a remarkable press release stating that "Even Uncle Google has to play fair...Europe must show its teeth against US giant groups...the Internet is not the Wild West." The press release was objectionable because it fanned the flames of envy about the success of US technology firms and alleged (without any proof) that they were acting in a lawless manner.

It would have been extraordinary, and unacceptable, for the US Congress to issue a resolution instructing the Department of Justice or the Federal Trade Commission to take specific action in an ongoing competition case. Yet the European Parliament had basically done just that by instructing a European Commissioner, who had taken office only a few months previously, on what measures to take in one of its investigations into Google's business practices. In several calls to the European Parliament and in my public statements, I said that in a state of law the accused should be found guilty only after, and not before, a proper trial. The resolution was misguided, moreover, because it would complicate efforts to conclude a transatlantic free trade deal by undermining the support for it from the US technology industry.

When some members of the European Parliament suggested that I was lobbying for Google, I replied that I had recently bought a T-Shirt with the message "I Don't Need Google: My Wife Knows Everything" emblazoned on the front. None of Google, the other GAFA companies or leading US technology firms ever asked me to lobby on their behalf at the time. Even had I been asked I would not have done so because it would have been counterproductive. Such lobbying would have confirmed suspicions that the US government takes its orders from Silicon Valley.

It would have been inappropriate for me to take sides between the US technology firms on the receiving end of the attacks and the US firms who were frequently bringing complaints against them to the European Commission. Most important, I felt that EU legal procedures deserve respect and should not be politicized. However, I did often publicly defend the principle that all US firms are entitled to an impartial and transparent hearing, based on objective facts, and that the playing field should not be tilted against them in order to give European competitors an advantage.

It is true that GAFA has been under fire in the EU for a long time. Google and Facebook (the "G" and "F") have alternated as the main object of criticism by regulators, the former for issues relating to its dominance in search, and the latter for issues relating largely to data privacy. But there is no evidence that this scrutiny reflects anti-Americanism.

Facebook has been subject to just as much criticism in the United States as in Europe over the past few years over Russian ads used to influence the 2016 US national elections and over the misuse of Facebook customer data by itself and third parties. In his testimonies before the US Senate and the European Parliament in 2018, CEO Mark Zuckerberg was subject to hostile questioning, especially about the ability of Cambridge Analytica, a data analytics firm, to use personal information harvested from more than 50 million Facebook profiles without permission to target US voters with personal political advertisements based on their psychological profile. In 2019, the Federal Trade Commission launched an antitrust investigation of Facebook (and Amazon).

Google has also had to appear before the US Senate investigation about social media influence in the 2016 national elections. In 2019, the Department of Justice launched an antitrust investigation into Google (and Apple). Attorneys general from 50 US states and territories have launched an investigation into Google's dominance in both search and advertising. There are many US firms concerned about Google's practices and some have brought complaints to the European Commission.

One consortium, including Oracle, Expedia, and Microsoft (before Microsoft subsequently dropped out following its settlement with Google), played an important role in convincing the European Commission to launch investigations into Google's practices in November 2010. The consortium alleged that Google was manipulating its online search algorithms to display search results from its comparison shopping product (called "Google Shopping") more prominently than results from its competitors. The Federal Trade Commission had decided unanimously in 2013 to terminate its two-year investigation into similar allegations when Google agreed to make several modifications to its business practices. Despite having decided in 2012 that Google's actions did not warrant a fine and despite having agreed a settlement with Google in 2014, the European Commission subsequently reversed course, proceeding with its investigation and fining Google €2.42 billion in 2017 in a decision that Google appealed to the European Court of Justice.

Several US firms also helped convince the European Commission to open a second investigation into Google in April 2015, leading to formal legal proceedings one year later. That investigation related to Android, the mobile operating system developed by Google. The Commission alleged that Google was restricting competition by requiring third party manufacturers of mobile devices to pre-install Google's search app and Chrome browser as a condition for licensing the Play Store (Google's App Store for Android). The Commission also alleged that Google prevented manufacturers from selling smart mobile devices running on competing operating systems based on Android open source code and that it provided financial incentives to these manufacturers and mobile network operators to exclusively pre-install Google search on mobile devices. It fined Google €4.3 billion in July 2018 in a decision that the company also appealed to the Court of Justice. Rather predictably, President Trump tweeted after the decision that "I told you so! The European Union just slapped a $5 billion fine on one of our great companies, Google. They truly have taken advantage of the US, but not for long!"

Taxation of the Digital Economy

Apple, another member of GAFA, has been in the European Commission's firing line for its taxation policies. Apple's highly technical dispute with the EU is worth reviewing in some detail because it raises fundamental issues of joint concern to the EU and the US about how US technology should be taxed. The perception has been growing in Europe and the United States that some of these companies, especially powerful and profitable ones, are able to pay low rates of tax by arbitraging the differences in national tax systems because of their ability to do business without a physical presence.

The European Commission's interest in Apple was triggered by public hearings held by the US Senate in May 2013 on tax avoidance by major US companies. That hearing was principally focused on the level of US tax paid by US multinationals from their international operations. However, the hearing also disclosed details on the amount of Irish tax Apple paid on its international revenues.

The EU's investigation concluded in August 2016 that Ireland had granted Apple illegal tax benefits, enabling it to pay substantially less Irish tax than other similar businesses from 1991 until it changed its tax structure in 2015 following a change in Irish law. During that period, Apple had organized much of its sales operations in Europe from Irish subsidiaries. In that way, Apple attributed much of its sales and profits from Europe and Asia to two of its Irish subsidiaries.

According to the Commission, two tax opinions issued by Ireland enabled Apple to attribute nearly all profits from sales in these Irish subsidiaries to "head offices" that existed only "on paper" (because they had no premises, assets, or employees).

Those Irish subsidiaries were incorporated in Ireland but managed and controlled in the United States. Apple was benefiting from a mismatch in tax laws: The United States considered the companies Irish because it determines tax residency on the basis of where companies are incorporated; Ireland considered them American because it determines their residency on the basis of where they are managed and controlled. The result was that much of their profits was not subject to Irish tax on the one hand and was deferred from US tax on the other (until the US ended tax deferral in enacting tax reform in December 2017).

The Commission concluded that Apple should have attributed to Ireland and paid 12.5% Irish corporate tax on all of its European profits derived from its Irish subsidiaries' sales into Europe and Asia. The difference between the amount of taxes that Apple should have paid and the amount it did pay in Ireland equaled €13 billion over the decade ending in 2014. Ireland therefore had to recover that amount from Apple (plus interest). Both Apple and Ireland appealed to the General Court in Luxembourg. A judgment was expected as this book went to press. An appeal and several more years of litigation appear likely.

The European Commission concluded that this tax arrangement was a hidden subsidy and that, as such, it distorted competition in a manner that contravened the "state aid" provisions (akin to anti-subsidy rules) in its competition laws. The practical effect of the subsidy, some critics claimed, was the payment to Apple of about €220,000 in cash annually for the creation of each of 6000 jobs in Ireland. Seen in that light, it was a questionable deal for Ireland.

Apple argued that the tax was due to the US and was deferred under US tax law. By the end of 2017, Apple had accrued $36 billion of deferred US taxes from its international business which became payable after US tax reform. Apple asserts that the European Commission's finding violates the basic principle in international tax law that profits are taxed where the value is created. "The vast majority of the value in our products is indisputably created in the United States – where we do our design, development, engineering work and much more – so the majority of our taxes are owed to the United States."[5]

While the retroactive recovery of unpaid taxes was a long-standing feature of the European Commission's "state aid" provisions, the gigantic size of the recovery request and several features of the decision made it noteworthy.

One such feature was the tension between the EU's ability to investigate the use of "sweetheart" tax deals under its competition laws, on the one hand, and EU member states' exclusive powers over taxation, on the other hand. The "state aid" provisions are a core tool of the European Commission to ensure that companies can compete in the single market on a level playing field. Even though Ireland stood to recover €13 billion (with interest), a huge amount for a country with a GDP of €280 billion, its government appealed because the decision challenged its taxing powers, a core element of sovereignty, and because it could undermine the long-term continued attractiveness of Ireland as a destination for foreign investment. Ireland was not the only EU member state to be concerned: Luxembourg, the Netherlands, and other member states had long offered international investors favorable tax treatment.

I believed then (as I do now) that Apple has a strong case. I contributed to a very detailed critique of the Apple decision that the US Treasury published on August 24, 2016.[6] It argued, for example, that the European Commission had departed from prior EU case law and Commission decisions, specifically in its analysis of when a company illegally benefits from "selective" tax advantages not available to other companies. The US government had strong doubts about whether Apple was really getting a unique "sweetheart" deal and whether other companies had been unable to request similar tax treatment. It questioned the European Commission's conclusion that a tax advantage can be "selective" merely because a multinational (rather than a national "standalone") company benefits from certain tax arrangements.

---

[5] "The Facts About Apple's Tax Payments," Apple Newsroom, November 6, 2017.

[6] "The European Commission's Recent State Aid Investigations of Transfer Pricing Rulings," US Department of the Treasury White Paper, August 24, 2016. https://www.treasury.gov/resource-center/tax-policy/treaties/Documents/White-Paper-State-Aid.pdf.

The interests of the US government in this case were not principally about Apple's specific situation. After all, Apple had skilled lawyers to defend it in EU courts. The government's concerns have been about the impact of the European Commission's decision on US-EU efforts to drive international consensus on key taxation issues (especially in the digital economy) and on the amount of US tax that it could recover from Apple if the EU's decision were upheld. The more Apple pays in Irish corporate income taxes, the less it will pay to the US.

Among these key taxation issues was the highly technical area of transfer pricing that lay at the heart of the dispute. Transfer pricing refers to the rules and methods for pricing transactions within and between enterprises under common ownership or control; transfer pricing determinations are usually governed by the "arm's length" principle that prices must be set as if the parties were independent from one another and reflect "market" conditions. The Treasury alleged that the European Commission was substituting its own "arm's length" principle derived from EU law for well-established international norms established (under US and EU leadership) by the OECD and the G-20.

The Apple decision appeared to undermine the basic principle that profits should be taxed where economic activities deriving profits are performed and where value is created; in the case of Apple, that was the United States, where its intellectual property is housed and where the essential research and development occurs. According to the Treasury, the European Commission was expanding its role as enforcer of competition and "state aid" law into a new role of a supranational tax authority that can review member state transfer pricing determinations without prior notice about how it would apply its powers.

The Treasury also argued that the European Commission's application of a novel "state aid" approach in a retroactive manner is inconsistent with the principles of fairness and the legitimate expectations of companies that rely on member state tax rulings. While the European Commission denied that the approach was novel, I thought that there were strong arguments as to why the decision should have had a prospective, rather than a retroactive, effect. With the comfort of Ireland's tax rulings, Apple had invested a significant amount of capital and had created many jobs in Ireland. Ireland had gotten the "benefit of the bargain" that it struck with Apple; it seemed unfair that Ireland should become a windfall beneficiary of €13 billion (plus interest) in back taxes after it had benefited from Apple's investment.

Surely, Ireland was well placed as a member of the European Union to understand whether or not its tax rulings were compatible with EU law. It was not persuasive to suggest, as the European Commission did, that Apple's extremely low effective tax rate should have put it "on notice" that the tax rulings were likely to contravene EU law. As a result of the decision, companies may no longer choose to give any weight to tax rulings granted to them by member states without getting a "good housekeeping seal of approval" from the European Commission.

The Treasury also pointed out that any repayment of back taxes by Apple would be considered as foreign income tax and hence creditable against Apple's taxes owed in the United States. The Treasury challenged the European Commission's assertion that Apple's offshore earnings, accumulating over many years to avoid paying US corporate taxation of 35% on remittance to the United States, would never be taxed in the United States; on the contrary, those earnings were simply *deferred* and would be repatriated as part of US tax reform. That is precisely what happened in 2018 when Congress passed the Tax Cuts and Jobs Act that imposed a one-off, obligatory 15.5% repatriation tax on foreign earned income.

Apple argued with justification that if the European Commission and EU member states don't like certain tax regimes, they should change them. And indeed that's just what Ireland did in 2013 when it modified its tax residency rules and eliminated the infamous "double Irish" tax loophole. Other countries, such as Luxembourg and the Netherlands, have also eliminated certain loopholes. Every company has an obligation to observe the law and to pay taxes that are legally owed, but not more. That amounts to appropriate tax planning, rather than tax evasion. Many companies, including some of the leading US online platforms, have been proactively changing their tax structures to comply with new laws and minimize the risk of public scrutiny.

The United States, like the European Union, is increasingly focused on the critical issue of how their tax systems can properly fund social programs, including pensions and protections of labor, health and the environment. This is especially the case in the EU due to its rapidly aging population and the rising burdens on its working-age population to support retirees. Tax systems need to ensure that multinational companies pay their "fair share" of tax and that countries do not engage in destructive tax competition by pursuing "beggar thy neighbor" policies. The challenge is considerable in the case of multinational companies that have significant intangible assets, such as intellectual property, as they have an easier time shifting profits to lower tax jurisdictions.

According to the European Commission, companies with digital business models pay an effective average tax rate of 9.5%, less than half the tax rate of businesses with traditional business models. That figure is strongly disputed, not only by many leading US technology firms but also by the authors of the EU study on which the figure is based. Most seriously, the European Commission averaged the tax rates IP-heavy companies enjoy in a range of countries, without acknowledging that US technology companies actually pay the majority of their income tax in the US, where rates are higher than in the EU.

The United States and the EU have a common challenge in updating current international tax rules that were designed for the "brick and mortar" economy and do not properly take into account business models in which companies can supply digital services in a country without being physically present there. There is a growing belief that too much tax is paid where these services originate and too little where they are consumed and users generate significant value. The European Commission therefore proposed in 2018 a comprehensive long-term solution that would impose tax on businesses where they have a significant digital presence, even if they do not have a physical presence. That presence would be deemed significant if revenues from the supply of digital services, or the number of online users or business contracts for digital services, exceed certain thresholds. This solution is intended to shape consensus at the OECD and then at global level.

Recognizing that this solution will require difficult discussions with global partners, especially the United States, including about the need to change bilateral double-taxation treaties, the European Commission also proposed a short-term solution that would impose a 3% tax on gross annual revenues in the EU on specific digital services. That blunt instrument would likely raise only €5 billion across the EU, while undermining multilateral efforts at tax reform. The proposal has fizzled out because of significant opposition from member states, not only the "usual suspects" of Luxembourg, the Netherlands, and Ireland (who host many digital companies' holding companies), but also other member states who are concerned about remaining or becoming high-tech hubs. Ursula von der Leyen, the current President of the European Commission, has favored the idea of an EU-wide digital services tax in 2020 if there is no global solution by then.

The risk of uncoordinated action on taxation of digital firms is real: Tired of the likely stalemate at the EU, several member states (including France, Italy, Spain, and the United Kingdom) have moved ahead with plans to impose tax on the revenues of digital companies, and more are likely to follow. That can only fragment the EU even further and lead to frictions with the United States. USTR has opened an investigation of the French proposed tax regime that could lead the US to impose unilateral tariffs against French imports under the 1974 Trade Act. President Trump threatened to do just that, before calling a truce with French President Macron until the end of 2020 in order to give time for negotiations toward a global agreement. In the meantime, the French tax will accrue but will not be payable. If a global agreement is not achieved, the tax under the French law would become payable and the EU would retaliate against unilateral tariffs by the US. As a result, transatlantic trade relations would be significantly impaired. A similar UK digital tax is also complicating negotiations toward a US-UK free trade deal. While the US has legitimate concerns about these and other digital tax regimes, it would be better to bring complaints to the WTO than to resort to unilateral trade measures. Technology firms should also ask themselves whether it would not be wise to work with (and improve) the EU proposed digital tax regime rather than to play whack-a-mole with multiple national tax regimes.

The EU's Digital Single Market

Just as some politicians and business leaders in the United States feared that the scrutiny of GAFA presaged some broader attack on US technology firms, some also feared that the European Digital Single Market (DSM) program would create barriers to US investment in favor of local incumbents. I never believed it would turn out that way, and it hasn't. The DSM made just as much sense and is likely to be just as positive for US interests, as the 1992 Single Market Program that largely eliminated obstacles to the free flow of goods, services, people, and capital within the EU. One can perhaps quibble with some of the specific proposals, the lack of sufficient prioritization or the focus on more regulation when less regulation or other tools (such as self-regulation) might be appropriate; but the real risk is that the EU does not move fast enough in its implementation.

When launching the program in the fall of 2014, President Juncker announced that "the Internet and digital communications can transform our economies as profoundly as the steam engine did in the 18th century or electricity did in the 19th century."[7] That sounded like hyperbole, but it reflected reality: The growth of digital technologies contributed roughly 30% to economic growth between 2001 and 2011. As the new Commission was beginning its mandate in the fall of 2014, it was self-evident that an insufficiently dynamic digital economy was one key reason why growth, productivity and job creation in Europe had lagged behind the US.

A study by the European Parliament's Research Service on "non-Europe" in the digital economy (i.e., the absence of a single rule book) showed that the creation of a DSM would increase economic output by between €35 billion and €75 billion euros per year, would raise EU GDP by 0.4% and would create 223,000 jobs by 2020.[8] Other studies showed that a deeper EU digital economy, harnessing the full potential of online services and digital infrastructure, could raise EU GDP by more than €500 billion euros. The boost to growth from a DSM would not be evenly distributed, however: The largest benefits would be concentrated in the so-called Digital Nine group of largely Northern European countries.[9] The impact of DSM, therefore, made nearly every other growth-boosting initiative (including a US-EU free trade agreement) pale by comparison.

It was very revealing that Germany chose to place its Commissioner, Günther Oettinger, as the head of the digital portfolio at the beginning of the Juncker Commission. Berlin clearly understood that this portfolio, despite its comparative lack of glamor (compared to the globe-trotting

---

[7] "Europe's Next Frontier: Creating Digital Jobs," http://juncker.epp.eu/my-priorities/digital.

[8] "The Cost of Non-Europe in the Single Market: Digital Single Market," European Parliamentary Research Service, September 2014. http://www.europarl.europa.eu/RegData/etudes/STUD/2014/536356/EPRS_STU(2014)536356_REV1_EN.pdf.

[9] The Digital Nine consist of Belgium, Denmark, Estonia, Finland, Ireland, Luxembourg, the Netherlands, Norway, and Sweden. One report in 2016 estimated that their growth rates until 2020 could be boosted by as much as 40%. Boston Consulting Group, "Digitizing Europe: Why Northern European Frontrunners Must Drive Digitization of the EU Economy," May 2016.

role of EU foreign minister that Italy was keen to claim), was the real epicenter of influence over the EU's economic future, including the competitiveness of the German economy. The importance of the issue extended far beyond the service economy but included the future of value creation in heavy industry, as the German automobile industry well understood. This industry was living in fear that US technology firms would dominate the value-added software of automobiles and relegate German automakers to the role of commodity metal-bashers with low margins. The fact that Tesla's market capitalization equaled that of Volkswagen and BMW combined in February 2020, despite selling far fewer vehicles, illustrated the concerns.

President Juncker identified the creation of a DSM for 500 million EU citizens—the creation of a single rule book replacing 28 different national regulatory regimes relating to digital services—as a top priority to stimulate cross-border sales, more choice of goods and services at lower prices, investment in new technologies, productivity gains, entrepreneurship and ultimately job creation. The more active regulatory approach in the EU compared to the US on issues relating to the digital economy is largely driven by the need to prevent market fragmentation and boost growth.

A DSM would enable individuals and businesses to access cross-border digital services irrespective of their nationality or place of residence, under conditions of fair competition and with the benefit of a high level of consumer and personal data protection. One of the reasons for Europe's sluggish economic performance has been the difficulty for consumers to buy and for small business to sell cross-border online; such transactions can be complex and expensive due to differing, and sometimes contradictory, consumer protection, data privacy, and contract laws. On top of these barriers, shopping habits are shaped by linguistic barriers and familiarity with home markets. As a result, only 15% of EU consumers buy online from another EU country, whereas nearly 44% do so domestically.

The DSM program covered a broad range of complex issues from its inception, ranging across many fields, including copyright, e-commerce, competition policy, online platforms, parcel delivery, telecommunications (including broadband services and radio wave spectrum management), data privacy, data flows, and cybersecurity.

One of the core reasons why the Digital Single Market is so important is that it can unleash private capital into the economy, especially in higher-risk and faster-growth technology sectors that have been held back by regulatory barriers and fragmented markets. While many actions lie with the member states, including reform of national tax, bankruptcy, and insolvency laws, the EU is making contributions in many areas, including the creation of a substantial pan-European venture capital fund of funds in 2018, the implementation of cross-border insolvency rules in 2017, and proposals to give small and medium-sized enterprises better access to financing through public markets.

The US government, including the US Mission to the EU, was watching closely as the European Commission rolled out sixteen detailed proposals grouped around three pillars of the Digital Single Market Program. The potential impact on US economic and political interests was (and remains) enormous.

The first pillar aims at promoting better access for consumers and businesses to online goods and services across Europe. One important initiative aimed at ending unjustified "geo-blocking." That term refers to discriminatory practices used by businesses in one member state to block or limit cross-border access to their online interfaces (such as websites and apps), as well as discriminatory practices to apply different conditions of access to goods and services sold by businesses online or offline to customers from different member states. Other initiatives aimed at making cross-border e-commerce easier and reforming European copyright law to reduce the difference in national copyright regimes, allow for wider public access to copyrighted works (including for educational and research purposes) and address the use of copyrighted content (such as news and music) by online firms. The initiatives also proposed the simplification of value-added tax regimes; the improvement in the efficiency and affordability of parcel delivery; a general investigation into the e-commerce sector to identify competition concerns; and a review of measures to boost cross-border access to broadcasters' services.

The second pillar aims at creating the right conditions for digital networks and innovative services to flourish. One initiative proposed measures to reinforce trust and security in digital services, notably concerning the handling of personal data. Other initiatives included a comprehensive review of online platforms that would cover issues such as the non-transparency of search results and of pricing policies, how such platforms use the information they acquire, the relationships between platforms and suppliers, and the promotion of platforms' own services to the disadvantage of competitors. The initiatives also proposed a review of rules on audiovisual media services (including a quota for European content in on-demand catalogs) and an overhaul of the EU's telecoms rules, including the more effective coordination of radio spectrum, the creation of incentives for investment in high-speed broadband and the creation of a more level playing field between "traditional" telecoms firms and "over the top" providers that distribute film, video and messaging content over the Internet.

The third pillar aims at maximizing the growth potential of the European digital economy by investing in information and communications technology (ICT) infrastructure and technologies such as cloud computing and big data, as well as research and innovation to boost industrial competitiveness. Proposals for action included important initiatives to promote the free movement of data within the EU and prevent unjustified data location restrictions for data storage or processing; to adopt common standards in priority areas, such as electronic health records ("e-health"), transport planning, mobile payments and energy efficiency; to study the emerging issues of ownership and access to non-personal data transmitted between businesses and generated by machines; and to ensure that more European citizens have the digital skills to seize the opportunities of the Internet and more governments harness digital tools to improve their public services.

The Digital Single Market is a vision that the US government and the vast majority of US business support and for good reason. Stronger European growth, resulting from a stronger digital economy and greater innovation, means more opportunities for investment and sales into Europe. Moreover, the DSM offers numerous opportunities for US and European businesses to collaborate and innovate. It also offers opportunities for the US government and the European Commission to adopt common, or at least compatible, policies that can set global standards for the digital economy. And if a DSM can contribute to the free flow of ideas, innovation, competitiveness, and lower youth unemployment, it will result in a more stable, peaceful, and democratic Europe.

There were, nonetheless, devils in the details. In my cables to Washington and my speeches to the US business community, I welcomed the DSM but added that we needed to keep a watchful eye on its development. There was the risk that certain powerful lobbies, especially in Germany and France, would seek to turn the DSM into a tool to advance their interests. Even within the European Commission, there appeared to be signs of conflict over the DSM's objectives.

Andrus Ansip, Vice President of the European Commission and Commissioner in charge of the Digital Single Market, had previously served as Prime Minister of Estonia, one of the most innovative countries in the world in the field of digital services. He was clearly committed to a non-discriminatory and lightly regulated EU digital market; his mantra was that the DSM should aim to create openness and opportunities, not obstacles. He also saw opportunities, not risks, in transatlantic cooperation. In nearly every meeting with visiting business leaders or US government officials, he would tell stories of how he grew up in Estonia listening to Voice of America and believing in the United States as a beacon of liberty.

Commissioner Oettinger, who reported to Ansip in the European Commission's structure but who carried significant weight because of the country he represented, was similarly supportive in front of an American audience. But when speaking to his home audience, especially the German publishing and automotive industries, his messages were different. He had, after all, been the Minister President of Baden-Württemberg, the headquarters of many iconic German car manufacturers. He would repeatedly stress that US technology firms were too large and powerful. European online businesses are too dependent on a few non-EU players, he warned. "This must not be the case again in the future." It was necessary, he claimed, "to replace today's web search engines, operating systems, and social networks with European ones."[10] Playing on European, especially German, emotions around data privacy, he warned that US online platforms like Facebook, Apple, and Google "will go to the member states where data protection is least developed, come along with their electronic vacuum cleaner, take it to California and sell it for money."[11]

German Minister of the Economy Sigmar Gabriel routinely described the DSM as a way for the EU to set its own globally accepted digital standards and to achieve market dominance against US "digital imperialists" in order to achieve "digital sovereignty." This Germanic view was often shared at the highest levels of the French government. Minister of the Economy Arnaud Montebourg warned that Europe risked becoming a "digital colony of the global internet giants."[12] More recently, French

---

[10] "Europe v. Google: Nothing to Stand On," *The Economist*, April 18, 2015.

[11] Tom Fairless, "Europe's Digital Czar Slams Google, Facebook," *The Wall Street Journal*, February 24, 2015.

[12] Juliette Garside, "From Google to Amazon: The EU Goes to War Against Power of US Digital Giants," *The Guardian*, July 6, 2014.

President Macron has also argued that France is fighting a battle for digital sovereignty. He has launched a $5.5 billion fund to help start-ups scale in key technologies.

I appreciated that many Europeans (and Americans) have real concerns about the digital economy that are as much cultural as they are economic. Many are not comfortable that critical decisions affecting their lives are being taken by powerful foreign companies without being able to shape them. For example, many Europeans are not happy with a deregulated model that permits abuses from privacy intrusions, decisions based on black-box algorithms, and winner-take-all outcomes.

Nonetheless, as ambassador I also frequently heard the narrative of a zero-sum DSM. According to this narrative, Europe could only lose if US technology firms (especially online platforms) flourished and, conversely, Europe could only "win" by handcuffing their US competitors. A climate of fear and envy was not what Europe needed. It was no good looking into the rear-view mirror and asking: "Why don't we have a Silicon Valley? Why haven't we created a Googlesmann, an Apfel or an Amazonne?" Silicon Valley is the result of many unique factors that will be extremely hard to replicate, including an ecosystem of talent, a culture of risk-taking, favorable tax, labor and bankruptcy laws, access to capital and a large, unified internal market.

Efforts to promote "digital sovereignty" through regulation to tilt the playing field against non-European companies, identify national champions through an industrial policy, and restrict data flows by forcing companies to store their data locally or in a European cloud are not what Europe needs to become competitive in a global digital economy. On the contrary, these policies would squander the transformative potential of big data analytics (the examination of large amounts of data to uncover hidden patterns, correlations, and other insights), the Internet of Things (the interconnection via the Internet of computing devices in everyday objects, enabling them to send and receive data) and artificial intelligence.

Europe needs to promote innovation through increased research and development, as well as to invest in ICT and broadband services and connectivity. According to one study, if four of Europe's six largest economies (France, Germany, Italy, and Spain) could raise their "digital density" (the level at which they consume, process, and share data) to the height of the United Kingdom, they could add roughly €200 billion to their economies. If those six countries could reach the level of "digital density" of the United States, they would increase their annual economic output by €460 billion.[13] Moreover, Europe needs to promote entrepreneurship and digital skills; around 40% of people in the EU workforce do not have adequate digital skills; 14% have no digital skills at all. And Europe needs to promote more liquid equity and debt capital markets and encourage entrepreneurship.

The problem with the zero-sum narrative of the DSM is that it is based on an overly gloomy assessment of Europe's achievements. The narrative doesn't give enough credit to many noteworthy start-up successes in Europe: During the period 2000–2014, Europe produced 40 technology companies worth more than $1 billion (so-called unicorns), only slightly less than the United States.[14] Founded in 2006, Dutch payments processing firm Adyen garnered worldwide attention when it launched an €7 billion IPO on the Euronext Amsterdam stock exchange in 2018. Sweden's Klarna, an online payments solutions provider, is planning an IPO that may be of similar size. There are many other examples, including household names such as Sweden's Spotify, France's Deezer, the UK's King Digital, and Germany's Zalando. There are flourishing hubs of entrepreneurial start-up talent in places like London, Berlin, Stockholm, and Paris (especially following the election of Emmanuel Macron as President of France).

Moreover, success in the digital economy is not only about creating or maintaining strong positions in the markets for search, e-commerce, and social networking. While these are high-profile, consumer-facing parts of the value chain, industrial, business-to-business, and back-office digital services, as well as the hardware and infrastructure that supports them, are no less important. The reality is that Europe is seizing the huge opportunities that digitalization offers in sectors as varied as financial services, including cryptocurrencies, insurance, health care, manufacturing, design, and engineering. The zero-sum narrative also ignores the fact that

---

[13] Paul Hofheinz and Michael Mandel, "Uncovering the Hidden Value of Digital Trade," The Lisbon Council, Issue 19/2015.

[14] Report by G. P. Bullhound, "European Unicorns: Do They Have Legs?" Independent Technology Research, 2015. http://www.gpbullhound.com/wp-content/uploads/2015/06/GP-Bullhound-Research-Billion-Dollar-Companies-2015.pdf?utm_source=Unicorns%20Report%20PR%2015.06.15&utm_medium=Pure360&utm_campaign=Unicorns%20Report%20PR%2015.06.15%20Pure360.

many European businesses, including thousands of small and medium-sized businesses, have benefited from participating in the ecosystems created by US digital firms.

I was also concerned that the DSM would give opportunities for narrow interest groups to press for over-regulation that would create, rather than eliminate, obstacles. To avoid that outcome, the interagency group established by the US government to analyze the DSM regularly stressed several high-level messages to the European Commission. Here are a few examples:

- The dynamic nature of the digital sector favors a cautious and technology-neutral regulatory approach to avoid unintended consequences that might stifle that dynamism.
- Continuing innovation is likely to be a stronger guarantee of fair competition than prescriptive regulations.
- The concepts of creative destruction and disruptive innovation are alive and well in the digital economy.
- Innovators will always be ahead of the regulators in finding new business models that displace incumbents by providing consumers more value and choice.
- Regulations are often out of date by the time they are implemented because they take many years to negotiate and implement; self-regulation should therefore be considered a faster and more flexible alternative.
- A strong position in the digital market is not necessarily synonymous with an abusive one and it is not necessarily a sustainable one. The costs and benefits to all relevant stakeholders should be carefully weighed before regulation is implemented.

When the DSM was announced, it rapidly became evident that the fault lines were mostly dividing US business interests, rather than splitting one side of the Atlantic from the other. US businesses had different views about the need to regulate online (largely US) platforms in order, for example, to ensure the fairness and transparency of search and the collection and usage of data. They differed about whether Internet platforms should compensate publishers for the use of short quotes of copyrighted news content ("snippets") and share with content creators more revenues derived from user-uploaded audiovisual content. They also differed about proposals to oblige online platforms to assume greater liability for illegal content (such as pirated music videos).

During my mandate in Brussels, online platforms were the regular subject of impassioned speeches and commentary that failed to recognize their many forms, each requiring specific and detailed analysis of benefits and harms. Early definitions were imprecise, applying to a vast array of online actors whose activities were far removed from those of the GAFA firms being targeted in the zero-sum narrative.

As one observer has rightly observed, "it is easy to be uneasy about Internet platforms" because they use vast amounts of data in mysterious ways and make enemies of incumbent firms that lobby for protection.[15] Many of the concerns raised about online platforms in the DSM are being debated in the United States, and the giant US platforms have plenty of US enemies that approved of the DSM's critical look. Although I didn't want to take sides, I was concerned that the issue of online platforms, above all others, could spin out of control due to its emotional content.

Under pressure from their publishing and telecommunications industries, the French and German governments were lobbying the European Commission to take broad action to curb the power of online platforms. The governments' key argument was that many large platforms had become critical gateways or "essential facilities"—akin to critical infrastructure like pipelines, rail, and ports—that required new legislation because existing legislation (including competition laws) was not "fit for purpose." The "essential facilities" doctrine has a long history in EU (and US) antitrust law and typically requires that a monopolist owning a facility essential to competitors must provide (if possible) reasonable use of that facility to such competitors if they are unable to duplicate it. The French and German governments argued that new legislation would be necessary because in the fast growing and constantly evolving technology sector it might be difficult to show either monopoly power or a competitor's inability to duplicate a platform.

One of the main problems with the effort to "do something" about digital platforms is that they come in so many varieties that a "one size fits all" regulatory approach makes no sense. Some, like Google and Facebook, monetize their free services to users primarily through advertising; some, like Uber, intermediate among various parties and charge a

---

[15] Joseph Kennedy, "Why Internet Platforms Don't Need Special Regulation," Internet and Technology Innovation Foundation, October 2015.

fee when they strike a deal; some, like Amazon and eBay, are open marketplaces that charge a fee when sellers find customers for their products; and some are "true platforms," such as cloud businesses and app stores.[16] Each of these models poses very different issues that require a different and nuanced response.

The European Commission has fortunately declined the invitation to extend the "essential facilities" doctrine to platforms. Rather than wield a sledgehammer, it seems more inclined to use a scalpel based on an in-depth look at the market. While it has remained convinced that existing antitrust law is capable of addressing most abuses in the online world, it has accepted the need for new legislation in certain areas. In 2015, the European Commission launched an investigation into the many forms of online platforms, including online advertising platforms, marketplaces, search engines, social media and creative content outlets, application distribution platforms, communications services, payments systems, and platforms for the collaborative economy. Its conclusions the following year acknowledged some of the important benefits of online platforms, such as revolutionizing access to information, efficiency gains, and increased consumer choice. They also recognized that simplifying, modernizing, and lightening existing legislation, rather than creating new legislation, might be the appropriate policy.

But the conclusions also highlighted concerns that such platforms impose unfair terms and conditions, such as unilaterally modifying the conditions for market access, including access to essential business data; unfairly promoting their own services to the disadvantage of suppliers with whom they compete; restricting suppliers' ability to offer more attractive conditions through other channels; and failing to provide transparency about tariffs, use of data, and search results. And the conclusions noted that while competition policy contains flexible tools that can be applied to online platforms, there may be instances where suppliers to platforms can be "disproportionately exposed to potentially unfair trading practices" even when the platforms are not dominant. A specific concern related to the dependence of small and medium-sized enterprises on a

---

[16] Cristina Caffarra, "'Follow the Money'—Mapping Issues with Digital Platforms into Actionable Theories of Harm." https://ecp.crai.com/wp-content/uploads/2019/09/e-Competitions-Special-Issue-Cristina-Caffarra.pdf.

small number of platforms that have access to "datasets of unprecedented size."[17]

The concerns from the investigation led the Commission to propose legislation in 2018 relating to business users of online "intermediation" services (that enable businesses to offer goods or services to consumers). This legislation aims, for example, to increase the fairness and transparency with which goods and services are ranked on search sites. It seeks to clarify the manner in which business users can request access to data held by online service providers and it requires such providers to justify restrictions on the ability of business users to offer the same goods and services to consumers under different conditions through other sales channels.[18]

The issues of transparency, fairness, discrimination, and data access in the online world are certainly worthy of careful scrutiny and debate. So is the frequently voiced concern about "network effects"—the phenomenon that the quality of goods or services improves as increased numbers of people or participants use them. The downside of such a virtuous circle is that economies of scale may be self-perpetuating and very rapid in the online world, thereby shutting out potential competitors. But such risks should be balanced against gains for consumers and business users.

BENEFITS FROM ONLINE PLATFORMS

These gains come in several forms, including improving the use of resources (such as by enabling the temporary use of assets), increasing competition and market efficiency, reducing transaction costs, and reducing asymmetries of information between buyers and sellers. Online platforms can help lower income and less privileged users because lower prices, access to information, more economic opportunities, and lower market barriers benefit them the most.

---

[17] Communication from the Commission to the European Parliament, the Council, the European Economic and Social Committee and the Committee of the Regions, "Online Platforms and the Digital Single Market: Opportunities and Challenges for Europe," May 25, 2016. https://eur-lex.europa.eu/legal-content/EN/TXT/PDF/?uri=CELEX:52016DC0288&from=EN.

[18] Proposal for a Regulation of the European Parliament and of the Council on promoting fairness and transparency for business users of online intermediation services of April 26, 2018. https://ec.europa.eu/digital-single-market/en/news/regulation-promoting-fairness-and-transparency-business-users-online-intermediation-services.

This is the case, for example, in the sharing economy for rides and accommodation. French President Emmanuel Macron has recognized that Uber has been one of the biggest employers of young (and often marginalized) people from minority backgrounds in the Paris region. The French job market (like many others in Europe) is polarized between insiders with secure long-term contracts and outsiders who live precariously from one short-term contract to the next. Uber identified and exploited a desperate need in Paris for rides, as anyone who has been stranded looking for a taxi in Paris knows all too well. In 2015, there were 18,000 taxis in Paris, fewer than in 1920, and the number did not adjust to meet demand at peak hours. This insufficient supply naturally led to high prices and an uneven level of service. That suited the founder of the private cab company G-7, who benefited from close relations with the pinnacle of French power and for years remained the only dependable, quality taxi service.

When Uber challenged the French labor law system built around contracts of indefinite duration, incumbent taxi drivers erupted in street violence. The French State publicly sided with them, but privately recognized that the sharing economy offered enormous flexible working opportunities and is the labor market's fastest-growing sector. The dysfunction in the French taxi industry enabled Uber to grow faster in France upon its launch in 2011 than in any other country in continental Europe. Uber has spawned numerous French copycats (including Heetch, Chauffeur-prive.com [rebranded Kapten] and Lecab.fr). As of 2015, around 50,000 people in France earn regular revenue from providing rides through online platforms. Many more do so through car-pooling platforms, such as through French "unicorn" BlaBlaCar. Fears that Uber would dominate the taxi industry have proven ill-founded, as competitors (including taxi companies themselves) are providing similar services, such as Lyft, MyTaxi, and Gett.

Travis Kalanick, the founder of Uber, was a genius in re-envisioning an entire industry to the delight of consumers. I have grown accustomed, like many of us, to the convenience of calling a car with a few taps on the screen of my smartphone and of paying for the ride through an automated debit to my bank card, as well as of receiving a summary by e-mail of the cost and itinerary of the journey. In my experience, Uber drivers almost always provide a high level of service, and I have rarely found one who is less than enthusiastic about earning extra cash in a flexible way.

Kalanick once described his opponent as "an asshole named Taxi." He used similarly colorful language when he slouched in a chair in my office and described European regulators. That is grossly unfair, as there are real public policy issues that require careful assessment (including the significant investment that taxi drivers have made to acquire their licenses and the degree of control that an online riding platform can exert over its drivers without converting them into employees).

Regulatory authorities and courts in the US are struggling with these and other issues, just as they are in Europe. In 2018, the California Supreme Court made it harder for Uber to qualify its workers as contractors rather than as employees. The following year the California state legislature codified and broadened that decision and decided that anyone deemed an employee must be afforded broad protection under labor laws.

An astonishing 12 million French people have Airbnb accounts, about 500,000 of them as hosts; Paris is Airbnb's leading destination, with about 65,000 listings. Naturally, not everyone is happy, including hotels, citizens concerned about tourist hordes in city centers and city administrations that want to crack down on unreported income. Barcelona, another top destination, was one of the early cities to curb the rapid growth in the supply of unlicensed short stay tourist accommodations. But the service has been a cash machine for hosts and has offered a more personal service increasingly desired by travelers.

Thanks to Google, I was able to research and fact-check my book from a terrace outside of Florence without ever going to a library. I am prepared to let Google collect some data on me as the hidden cost of that invaluable service; in any event, I can activate the "incognito" browsing mode within the Chrome browser if I want to surf the Internet without creating permanent trails of my activity, getting rid of my browsing history, cookies, site data, or other online data when I close the browser. Privacy settings enable me to choose what data gets saved and how long the data will be kept, as well as to delete my data altogether. Many other platforms have also made their privacy settings much easier to use. These positive developments are the results of legitimate concerns and pressure by consumers that they should remain in control of how their data is used and with whom it is shared.

While online platforms are, of course, capable of anti-competitive behavior and bad businesses practices, it is not evident why existing legal instruments available to injured parties and government regulators are insufficient to deal with actual harms. These platforms often face strong competition from incumbents, copycat businesses, and the ability of consumers to spend their money elsewhere. Perhaps the best guarantee against the risks of online platforms is to ensure an open and vibrant economy, one that encourages innovation and investment in ICT (especially broadband) and promotes the rapid scaling up of start-up ventures. There are many examples of online platforms like Alta Vista that used to be a dominant player in online search but disappeared when consumers flocked to more innovative and better alternatives.

One of the aspects often missing from the debate in Europe about the role of (mostly US) online platforms is that many European businesses have benefited from them. The launch of the iTunes App Store in 2008, for example, created an industry from scratch. According to a report prepared in 2014 for the European Commission, EU app developers earned €17.5 billion in 2013, a figure that was forecast to increase to €63 billion by 2018. The report predicted that the EU app developer workforce would grow from 1 million to 2.8 million over the same period.[19]

Amazon has enabled European small- and medium-sized businesses to sell billions of euros of their goods on the Internet, including cross-border within Europe and even across the Atlantic, for the first time. Amazon already employs around 83,000 people in Europe and is adding thousands more every year; since 2010 it has invested over €55 billion in infrastructure and operations.

According to a study by Deloitte in 2015 on Facebook's global economic impact, Facebook enabled, directly and indirectly, $51 billion of revenue and 783,000 jobs in the EU.[20] Thanks to the Grow with Google program, over three million people across Europe acquired new digital skills between 2015 and 2017; of these, 188,000 found a job or started a business within 14 weeks after their training. Thousands of European micro-entrepreneurs have launched their own YouTube channels and are making six-figure salaries annually. There are many other examples.

---

[19] Mark Mulligan and David Card, "Sizing the EU App Economy," Gigaom Research, February 2014. https://ec.europa.eu/digital-single-market/en/news/sizing-eu-app-economy.

[20] Deloitte, Facebook's Global Economic Impact, January 2015. https://www2.deloitte.com/content/dam/Deloitte/uk/Documents/technology-media-telecommunications/deloitte-uk-global-economic-impact-of-facebook.pdf.

Conflict over Copyright

In addition to the issue of online platforms, there were a few other issues in the DSM that divided US businesses. Following the European Commission's announcement in 2014 that it was planning its first big update of copyright rules since 2001, US content creators (especially in the music industry) joined with their European counterparts in a battle against (mostly US) Internet platforms about the correct balance between the need to share digital content, on the one hand, and the rights of content creators to be compensated fairly and incentivized to do their jobs, on the other.

The Directive on Copyright in the Digital Single Market that was ultimately passed after furious debate in 2019 will enter into force in 2021 when member states implement it into national law. The final text, far more balanced than the prior proposals, includes a provision requiring Internet platforms (especially Google News and Facebook) to obtain a license to use snippets of news articles. Hyperlinks and "very short extracts," however, are excluded. News publishers have long argued that the news and other journalistic content is one of the main things that people search for online; such content has value and its distribution should be prohibited without a license, just as is the case with music, film, and books.

Google and the publishers claim that the other is getting the better of the bargain: Google states that it doesn't sell advertising alongside news and that the publishers benefit from the traffic it sends to their sites (8 billion clicks per month to EU news publishers); the publishers claim that most readers of online news only read the snippets with few clicking on the links that take them to the publishers' websites (where the traffic would generate advertising revenue).

There is no doubt that the state of the print industry is precarious everywhere, including in Europe. According to PriceWaterhouseCoopers, print revenues at Europe's newspapers and magazines declined by €14 billion between 2010 and 2014, while digital revenues rose by €4 billion, leaving a €10 billion hole. A broad coalition of European newspaper and magazine publishers, especially Axel Springer in Germany, enjoyed enormous influence in shaping public opinion. The US print industry has had similar concerns about the use of its content by online platforms.

Critics of the EU's legislative proposal on copyright argued that the parlous financial state of the print industry was due to factors unrelated to the use of news snippets. The industry's business model was simply becoming out of date. For years, the industry had made money by being the central one-stop-shop for information about news and much else besides, such as movie listings and classified ads. With the emergence of many other information sources, including proliferating television, cable, online sites, and social media, that business (and associated advertising revenues) had shriveled. For years, the print industry had given away content for free in the hope of being able to monetize it through larger audiences, higher ad revenues and (eventually) paid subscriptions. But that had not worked out because audiences became accustomed to free content.

Critics also argued that the option of publishers to demand a fee could turn out to be counterproductive. They could point to two concrete examples. When the Spanish government had introduced a similar (mandatory) law in 2014, Google had simply shut down Google News in Spain. While readers continued to go directly to the Web sites of large newspaper and magazine publishers, the business of smaller news sites and blogs that rely on traffic from news aggregators and search engines declined. When Germany passed a similar (voluntary) law in 2012, Google responded by carrying news of only those publishers who agreed to be featured on its site for free. Those who refused saw their traffic plummet and eventually backed down.[21]

The US music industry also joined with their European counterparts in clashing with (mostly US) Internet platforms over provisions of the Copyright Directive concerning the liability of online platforms for pirated audio content uploaded by their users.

The US music industry had become increasingly disillusioned with the "safe harbor" provisions of the 1998 Digital Millennium Copyright Act (DMCA). Those provisions shield online service providers from liability for the activities of their users that infringe copyright as long as those providers are nothing more than neutral hosting providers (in other words purely passive intermediaries). One of the conditions of the safe harbor is that they implement "notice and takedown" procedures to remove content if they have knowledge of copyright infringing material, for example, because of notice from the owner of the content or of the copyright.

---

[21] Matthew Karnitschnig and Chris Spillane, "Plan to Make Google Pay for News Hits Rocks," *Politico*, January 28, 2018. The impact of the law in Spain is detailed in http://www.aeepp.com/pdf/InformeNera.pdf.

The DCMA, the music industry claimed, has proven to be completely ineffective. The "safe harbor" provisions, the music industry believes, are being interpreted too broadly, essentially providing protection to online sites that play an active role in curating or generating advertising revenues that monetize user-uploaded content. The provisions give digital platforms an unfair negotiating advantage in determining royalty rates for the use of copyrighted content. Moreover, according to the industry, the "notice and takedown" procedures don't work. Of the hundreds of millions of DMCA notices sent to Google (the owner of YouTube), the vast majority relate to songs that have already received a prior notice (before being uploaded again).

The problem of pirated content is significant: The vast majority of music revenues comes from digital distribution (mostly from subscriptions). Online platforms have been major distributors of music and user-uploaded content services such as YouTube are a main source of music consumption. YouTube has argued that it has paid billions in royalties to the music industry (more than $3 billion in 2019 alone) and that the money represents "value added" because YouTube helps the recording industry monetize those consumers (80% of the total) who are not willing to pay for music.

As the music industry had been unable to amend the DMCA despite declining revenues (at the time) due to piracy, it looked to the EU with hope when it announced its intention in 2014 to re-assess similar "safe harbor" rules established under EU law in 2000.[22] Many European songwriters, artists, and firms also lobbied heavily to defend their interests. The industry urged the EU to replace the "notice and takedown" procedures with a requirement on online platforms to implement effective "staydown" technologies—typically by means of software that automatically filters uploads—to detect whether content they are hosting contains copyrighted audiovisual material. Whereas YouTube already does this with its Content ID software, some smaller online companies objected that effective software is expensive, that they could not assume the legal risk of being liable for the wrongdoing of their users and that they would therefore have an incentive to block as much as possible.

The music industry believed that tougher requirements on online platforms to remove infringing copyrighted material would also strengthen the hand of the music industry in demanding more compensation for

---

[22] Revenues of the recorded music industry in the United States have been recovering since 2015, including (in part) by streaming services. https://www.riaa.com/u-s-sales-database/.

the use of its content, thereby reducing what it perceived to be a mismatch, or "value gap," between the royalties that online platforms extract from paid-for subscription audio-streaming services (such as Spotify and Deezer) and from online sites like YouTube that generate advertising from content uploaded by their users.[23] The final text of the Copyright Directive is a compromise, granting online platforms like YouTube an exemption from copyright liability only if they make best efforts to implement "takedown" and "staydown."

While there were issues in the DSM on which US business was divided, the DSM also posed a few risks on which US businesses had an almost uniformly negative view. These risks included a requirement on streaming-video providers (like Netflix and Amazon Prime Video) to dedicate at least 30% of their on-demand catalogs to European content. They opposed, but failed to prevent, the insertion of this requirement in the revised Audiovisual Media Services Directive. The US entertainment industry (especially film and TV studios) did succeed, on the other hand, in partnering with like-minded European industries to prevent overbroad restrictions on "geo-blocking" that would interfere with their ability to distribute content on a territorial, rather than pan-European, basis (e.g., through exclusive licenses with the online platforms of Europe's national broadcasters).

"Geo-blocking" needs to be distinguished from "data portability." The latter term refers to the ability of consumers to access their online (copyrighted) content when they travel in the EU in the same way they access them at home. For instance, when a French consumer subscribes to CanalPlay films and series from an online service, the user will be able to watch them in France, or when he or she goes on holidays to Croatia or on a business trip to Denmark. The US content industry did not oppose the ability of European consumers to access their content throughout Europe, and the regulation entered into force in 2018.

---

[23] According to IFPI, a trade association that represents the recording industry worldwide, the main user uploaded content services have around 900 million music users globally, compared with 68 million users for music subscription services such as Spotify or Deezer (that do not invoke the "safe harbour" provisions). The "value gap" is the difference between the €16 of average yearly revenue per user Spotify (the market leader in Europe in paid-for subscription audio-streaming services) generates for record producers versus the less than €1 of average yearly revenue per user YouTube generates for record producers. Figures as of May 2016.

When the campaign against "geo-blocking" was first announced, it appeared to assume that all forms of "geo-blocking" are unjustified and it targeted access to copyrighted and uncopyrighted products and services. As time went on, finer distinctions were made about what practices should be prohibited and which permitted. Certain forms of geo-blocking were clearly unjustified when applied in the context of uncopyrighted goods and services. It was clearly unacceptable, for example, for a Belgian customer who finds an attractive deal for a refrigerator on a German Web site to be unable to order the product and collect it at the seller's place of business; or for a Bulgarian consumer who wishes to buy hosting services for her Web site from a Spanish company to be unable to order these services at the same price as a Spanish consumer; or for an Italian family visiting a French theme park to be unable to take advantage of the same family discount on the price of the entry tickets offered on the theme park's French Web site.

Copyrighted material was very much targeted in early opposition to "geo-blocking." In his manifesto laying out his priorities upon election as President of the European Commission, Juncker emphasized that consumers should be able to "access services, music, movies and sports events on their electronic devices wherever they are in Europe and regardless of borders."[24] The Juncker Commission considered discriminatory practices interfering with that ability as a significant cause of consumer dissatisfaction and as a contributor to fragmentation of the internal market. Vice President Ansip went even further, declaring that such practices are a violation of the fundamental rights of European citizens to be treated the same wherever they are located.

That view challenged the existing means of distributing digital copyrighted content in Europe. Whereas consumers can purchase physical products (such as CDs and DVDs) throughout Europe, they can't always buy comparable online content because digital distribution rights have been licensed on a national basis. That means that consumers who want to watch movies or TV shows online are limited to the content that they are permitted to see in their home country. Netflix libraries may differ from one country to another, for example, in cases where a series is already licensed to the online platform of a local broadcaster. Apple has multiple

---

[24] See Jean-Claude Juncker's "Priorities" page of his official website: http://juncker.epp.eu/my-priorities.

iTunes stores around the EU and charges differing prices depending on the consumer's residence.

European content producers and broadcasters resisted Ansip's pressure. An executive for European broadcaster TF1 spoke plainly: "Pan-European licenses are not a viable business model for TV broadcasters since television markets are either national, regional or even local."[25] He went on to note that even Netflix realized this, leading it to invest in local stories with local actors. European film producers strongly backed this line.

In the United States, by contrast, most licenses for digital content cover the entire territory (except, for example, with regard to some live sports broadcasts). However, as US government experts explained to EU officials on several occasions, this has much more to do with culture and language than it does with any legal restriction. Legally speaking, content providers in the United States are free to make decisions about territorial coverage based on commercial demand, free from any government mandate to license nationwide. Indeed, US antitrust authorities point out that territorial limitations on copyright licenses "may serve procompetitive ends by allowing the licensor to exploit its property as efficiently and effectively as possible."[26]

Like their European counterparts, US content providers, especially the film and television industry (among the largest US exporters), were also concerned that applying a prohibition on "geo-blocking" to audiovisual content would undermine their flexibility to negotiate distribution deals at a member state, multi-state or pan-European basis—choices shaped by Europe's remarkable diversity of languages, cultures, consumer preferences, and purchasing power.

For smaller producers the risk was existential. Making content, such as films and TV series, is a risky activity, largely because of the need to commit funds up front (i.e., at the pre-production phase). Reducing the financing risk requires distributors and broadcasters to contribute toward production costs; but they are only willing to do so in return for territorial exclusivity. Smaller players with shallower pockets are especially sensitive to the risk of losing access to that critical financing model.

---

[25] Per Strömbäck, "You cannot force the creation of a European "ghost" market for transmission rights," *Netopia*, October 19, 2016. https://www.netopia.eu/cannot-force-creation-european-ghost-market-transmission-rights/.

[26] US Department of Justice and the Federal Trade Commission, "Antitrust Guidelines for the Licensing of Intellectual Property," January 12, 2017. https://www.ftc.gov/system/files/documents/public_statements/1049793/ip_guidelines_2017.pdf.

Mandatory pan-European licensing would interfere with the ability to sell content in different formats (theatrical, DVD, home entertainment, pay-TV) at different times and price points to maximize returns. And it would reduce the incentive to invest in the development of customized content for local markets, including dubbing films into local languages and developing original content for local markets. Some studies (funded by the content providers) have concluded that prohibiting "geo-blocking" of audiovisual content would lead to higher prices and a reduction in the amount, quality, and diversity of content production. Consumers in lower income member states would be hurt because they would pay a (higher) common EU price rather than a lower price set on the basis of national purchasing power.[27]

US content providers were joined by their European counterparts in making these arguments with the EU institutions. Their successful lobbying campaign removed copyright-protected content (including films, TV shows, music streaming services, e-books, online games, and software) from the Geo-Blocking Regulation that entered into force at the end of 2018. But these exclusions will be reviewed at the end of 2020.

In summary, the DSM has identified key ways for the EU to reduce its digital fragmentation and, as a result, to grow faster. It has been, and deserves to be, supported by US business and the US government. There have been very few instances where US business has had a unified and critical view of its proposals. Now that the DSM is largely on its way by 2020, the question is: What comes next? The answer is a renewed focus on transatlantic digital cooperation.

TRANSATLANTIC DIGITAL COOPERATION

I recently saw a world map that shows the intensity of Internet connectivity. Most of Europe and much of the United States were colored in bright red to show intense connectivity. Whereas some other parts of the world were also depicted in red, such as East Asia, India, Malaysia, Indonesia, and the East coast of Australia, the rest of the world was depicted in black

---

[27] "The Impact of Cross-Border Access to Audiovisual Content on EU Consumer," Oxero and O&O, May, 2016. https://www.oxera.com/getmedia/5c575114-e2de-4387-a2de-1ca64d793b19/Cross-border-report-(final).pdf.aspx.

to show weak or absent connectivity.[28] The message from the map was clear: The United States and the European Union are natural partners in addressing the opportunities and challenges of the digital age. The statistics bear out what the map suggested. Over 80% of EU households have broadband connection (versus roughly 70% in the US), and 80% of EU citizens have smartphones connected to the Internet (similar to the US). Over 90% of European businesses are online (similar to the US).[29]

Transatlantic data flows are the highest in the world. They are 50% higher than the data flows between the US and Asia in absolute terms, and 4 times as large on a per capita basis. The US and the EU are each other's largest partners in digital trade. The US exports roughly $200 billion in digitally enabled services to Europe and imports about $120 billion of such services from Europe, generating a trade surplus in this area of about $80 billion. And demonstrating the interconnectedness of US and European industries, over half of digitally deliverable services imported by the US from the EU were used in the production of US products for export, as well as vice versa.[30]

With the growth in mobile computing and the advent of the Internet of Things, big data analytics, and cloud computing, transatlantic data flows are projected to grow substantially over the next decade. But this growth will depend on whether the US and the EU can work together to promote flexible, interoperable standards for these services, high-speed Internet access, and Internet-friendly rules. It will also depend on whether they can address a number of privacy and security issues to maintain the confidence of ordinary citizens, businesses, researchers, and innovators.[31]

---

[28] Pamela Engel, "This World Map Shows Every Device Connected To The Internet," *Business Insider*, September 14, 2014. https://www.businessinsider.com/this-world-map-shows-every-device-connected-to-the-internet-2014-9.

[29] Statistics date from 2016. "Transatlantic Digital Economy and Data Protection: State of Play and Future Implications for the EU's External Policies," European Parliament Committee on Foreign Affairs (AFET), July 1, 2016. http://www.europarl.europa.eu/RegData/etudes/STUD/2016/535006/EXPO_STU%282016%29535006_EN.pdf and http://www.telecompetitor.com/pew-u-s-smartphone-ownership-broadband-penetration-reached-record-levels-in-2016/.

[30] Daniel Hamilton and Joe Quinlan, *The Transatlantic Economy 2019* (Johns Hopkins University SAIS, 2019), p. ixx. https://transatlanticrelations.org/wp-content/uploads/2019/03/TE2019_FullStudy.pdf.

[31] The growth in the global digital economy is also projected to be rapid. It is estimated that by 2021 global internet traffic will be 127 times the volume of 2005. "Cisco VNI

It is clear that the Internet and the digitalization of *everything* are revolutionizing the economy and society globally. Cheap new communications technologies feature accurate sensors and enormous computing capabilities that are bringing more and more people and things online. These developments are not only relevant in the sector of high tech; they are fundamentally reshaping traditional industries like health care, finance, transport, agriculture, energy, and even retail. This point was driven home to me on one of my last visits to Seattle, the headquarters of Amazon and Starbucks.

Like many of us, I have long enjoyed the convenience of ordering books and a wide range of other goods and receiving delivery within two days (on the Amazon Prime service) with just a few clicks. While we may be concerned about the future of physical bookshops and the high street, the reality is that online shopping for books and other goods saves us the hassle of driving to a shop, looking for a book (and perhaps not finding it), waiting in line and paying in cash or by card, and then driving back home. Amazon is also investing in bricks-and-mortar bookstores, not just driving them out of business. Amazon's stores make sense because the company knows more than any competitor about reading habits, even in the specific catchment area of every store, so that it can ensure that there is the right inventory. And, of course, it can also sell its wide range of other products, especially electronics such as the Kindle and Alexa.

I dropped in to experience one of the AmazonGo grocery stores that allow consumers to download an app, wave a barcode at a turnstile to walk in, select grocery items and simply walk out without waiting at a checkout counter. This is thanks to the company's Just Walk Out technology that automatically detects when products are taken from shelves (and not returned), as well as keeping track of them in a virtual cart. Within seconds of my departure, a useful summary of my purchases appeared on my iPhone. Amazon has managed to completely reimagine the grocery shopping experience thanks to advanced digital technology.

On that trip to Seattle, I also dropped into one of the Starbucks Reserve stores. Seconds after I walked in, a smiling attendant approached me with a small tablet in hand to inquire what I would like to order.

Forecast and Methodology 2016–2021," Cisco, September 15, 2017. The size of the "digital universe" (the data created and copied every year) will grow nearly 20 times during 2015–2025 to 180 zettabytes (or 180 *trillion* gigabytes). "Data Is Giving Rise to a New Economy," *The Economist*, May 6, 2017, citing IDC, a market research firm.

I was able to customize my order from numerous options for my cappuccino and pastry. After a few taps of his stylus on the tablet to note my choices (that were electronically communicated to the baristas), the attendant invited me to take a seat in a comfortable leather chair and said that my order would be brought to me. Starbucks has managed to reimagine the experience of ordering a coffee thanks to digital technology.

Consumer experiences like these shape our views about the utility of the digital economy. But it is elsewhere that the really life-changing developments will occur. Many experts believe that the Internet of Things, more commonly known as the "Industrial Internet" in Europe, will soon outstrip the value of the consumer Internet and will reshape the global, including especially the transatlantic, digital economy in profound ways in nearly every area of commercial activity. According to McKinsey, the IoT could add as much as $11 trillion per year to the global economy in nine different areas of application, most significantly in factories and cities.[32]

Reliance on data generated by sensors has been a long-standing feature in industry. IoT is new, however, because it features the ever-closer marriage of the digital and physical worlds through a combination of network connectivity, super-fast computing, the ubiquitous placement of cheap sensors on objects, and sophisticated data analysis techniques, known as big data, that allow insights to be derived from vast pools of data.

Around the world, there are estimated to be around 50 billion connected devices—including heavy machinery, vehicles, and home appliances—embedded with sensors and software that enable them to capture and communicate data. In the automotive industry alone, it is projected that 250 million (or one in five) cars worldwide will be connected to the Internet by 2020. Only a sliver of the "digital exhaust" generated by connected devices is actually used; of that amount, most is applied for the purposes of detection and control (i.e., maintenance of assets), rather than optimization and prediction of performance, where the real value lies.

IoT is capable of delivering efficiency gains across a wide range of sectors. Although consumer-facing applications such as personal health monitors and home appliances garner significant publicity, business-to-business applications are forecast to generate the bulk of the value. Of

---

[32] "The Internet of Things: Mapping the Value Beyond the Hype," McKinsey Global Institute, June 2015.

the total value that the IoT may generate, McKinsey estimates that about 40% will come from factories and work sites, with transport and urban infrastructure accounting for a further 30%.

The use of IoT is expected to boost productivity, as well as living standards, substantially in the same way the Industrial Revolution and the Internet Revolution did. Although US labor productivity grew at 2% during the period 1995–2013, roughly double the rate in Europe, both sides of the Atlantic have struggled since then to grow productivity at a faster rate. If IoT could double productivity, then over the next twenty years it could raise average incomes by 25–40% above the current trend. It is hard to overstate what is at stake for both sides of the Atlantic: the competitiveness of our economies; our ability to pay for our high standards of environmental health and consumer protections; our ability to fund pensions for our swelling ranks of retirees; and even our ability to protect our democracies from the attack of populists and demagogues who are increasingly darkening our political landscapes.

Many companies on both sides of the Atlantic, especially in industrial sectors, are racing to seize the opportunities and are fundamentally reshaping themselves in the process. GE, like its European competitor Siemens, has been transforming itself into a "digital industrial" business. That has not only meant recharacterizing the company, but also focusing on data as a source of enormous value generation. As Jeff Immelt, former CEO of GE put it, a modern locomotive is not just a means of freight or passenger transportation; it is a "rolling data center."[33] Thanks to Predix, its software platform for managing and analyzing industrial data, GE is striving to become as much a software and analytics company as an industrial firm.

Europe is well placed to benefit from the Internet of Things. IoT applications may add $2.8 trillion to European GDP by 2030. European industry has significant technological assets to build on, including leadership in industrial robotics and factory automation, embedded digital systems, enterprise and design software, and 3D- and laser-based manufacturing. It has an installed base of over half a million large machines with rotating parts that can be made more efficient.

At the 2016 Hannover Fair, I saw many examples of how US and European businesses are partnering to reap the benefits of IoT and big

---

[33] Ed Crooks, "General Electric: Post-Industrial Revolution," *Financial Times*, January 12, 2016.

data. For example, I saw how IBM and John Deere are piloting new technology in Europe that increases efficiency in the production of client-customized tractors and troubleshoots manufacturing problems. IBM has also teamed up with Siemens to develop a technology-solution that allows building owners to gauge a building's performance and better forecast operational budgets. It also provides better predictive analytics for fault detection and diagnosis so that potential problems can be addressed before they emerge. I saw how Microsoft and Rolls Royce are partnering to improve aircraft efficiency and on-time performance through data analytics. Armed with up-to-date information about how an engine is performing during a flight, mechanics are ready to start on repairs as soon as the plane arrives at the gate.

One of the great opportunities and challenges facing policy-makers on both sides of the Atlantic today is how to promote a transatlantic partnership on IoT. Both the US and the EU are addressing the promise and challenges of self-driving cars, for example. The United States is working to help create consistent state regulations on autonomous vehicles across the United States and speed along testing of such vehicles. Similarly, the EU member states and the European Commission are working on developing common traffic and transport rules and a common digital communication system, so that cars in Europe can "talk" to one another and travel seamlessly across national borders. And both sides of the Atlantic are investing in Smart Cities, where digital technologies provide better public services for citizens, better use of resources, and less impact on the environment. This focus is appropriate in light of the fact that nearly 70% of the global population will live in urban areas by 2050.

A main focus of our transatlantic agenda should be to deepen the transatlantic digital economy by analyzing the prospects and challenges together, as well as implementing complementary solutions. Policy-makers bear significant responsibility to establish a regulatory context that facilitates the Internet of Things, while dealing with key economic and legal issues, including data privacy and data security, intellectual property rights, legal liability for the harmful outcomes of automated systems, the displacement of certain manual work by greater automation, and the risk that social and economic inequalities will exclude certain groups from the benefits of accessing data. We should be cautious about regulating on the basis of speculative concerns, rather than known, demonstrated risks.

The full economic potential of the Internet of Things can only be captured if the US and the EU continue to adopt policies that support expanded high-speed Internet access and the free flow of data. Although the European Commission has earmarked significant capital to research so-called fifth-generation ("5G") telecommunications technology and has promoted a faster pan-European strategy for its rollout, Europe suffers from fragmented markets, complicating the ability of operators to see a compelling business case for investment, and a lack of an EU strategy toward the usage of spectrum. Instead of there being several large pan-European fixed and mobile operators, multiple (often sub-scale) players compete in each country. EU competition laws have prevented consolidation from happening based on concerns about price increases. In the United States, by contrast, three large players (AT&T, Verizon, and Comcast) have been racing toward nationwide coverage with download speeds of around 400 Megabits per second. China, South Korea, and some other parts of Asia are also moving fast.

The US and the EU should be making cooperation on 5G a priority. Such cooperation would focus on interoperability, namely through common standardisation and spectrum harmonization. Together they can drive further work in international bodies such as the International Telecommunication Union to set a global vision for 5G. The future of telecommunications and computing infrastructure connecting billions of users and trillions of devices will rely on whether they are successful.

The EU has successfully provided regulatory certainty around the free flow of data. The Regulation on the free flow of non-personal data in the European Union, passed in 2018, removes all restrictions imposed by member states' public authorities on the geographical location for storing or processing non-personal data, unless justified on grounds of public security. The next step should be to ensure the free flow of data between the EU and the US.

Some Digital Challenges We Face

There are many challenges ahead. In addition to the transatlantic divergences about data privacy, described in Chapter 5, three are particularly significant. The first is that the IoT ecosystem will employ hardware and software from many different vendors. The ability of these devices and systems to work together is critical to realize the full value of IoT applications. Without interoperability, at least 40% of the potential benefits of the Internet of Things will not be realized.[34]

It would be detrimental to tie the IoT ecosystem prematurely to burdensome or conflicting standards coming from different jurisdictions. Collaboration in the development of international standards enables technological innovation by defining and establishing common foundations upon which product differentiation, innovative technology development, and other value-added services can be developed.

This collaboration is possible when standards are developed in organizations that are transparent in their decision-making and open to participation by all interested stakeholders. The development of open and voluntary standards, led by the private sector with active government participation, is more likely than government-led mandatory regulation to address issues with the speed and flexibility required in a fast-changing Internet environment and, therefore, to meet the needs of industry and government. Input from all experts, regardless of where they are based, should be welcomed.

The second major challenge will be for the US and EU to deepen their collaboration on cybersecurity. The Internet highway connects an increasing number of devices and is therefore becoming increasingly vulnerable to those seeking to disrupt it, steal data or influence the outcome of elections. As one report points out, "Cyberattacks are becoming more prevalent, more sophisticated and – in an era of networked cars, medical devices, and appliances – increasingly capable of causing significant and potentially physical harm."[35] Moreover, US and EU ICT networks are interconnected and face cyber threats that are global in origin, indifferent to national borders and common to both sides of the Atlantic. The US and EU have increasingly collaborated to establish stronger frameworks to protect critical infrastructure and data-rich assets from, and improve resilience to, cyber-attack and espionage. Both sides of the Atlantic have adopted similar pieces of cyber legislation.[36]

---

[34] "The Internet of Things: Mapping the Value Beyond the Hype," McKinsey Global Institute, June 2015.

[35] "Building a Transatlantic Digital Marketplace: Twenty Steps Toward 2020," Atlantic Council, April 2016.

[36] The Network Information Security Directive (the NIS Directive) in the EU, and the National Institute of Standards and Technology Framework for Improving Critical Infrastructure Cybersecurity in the US (the NIST Framework). The US and the EU have been discussing cyber issues since the launch of the US-EU Working Group on Cyber

The third major challenge will be to prevent the misuse of the Internet by international terrorist groups and those who propagate online racist and xenophobic hates speech. Leading Internet companies (such as Facebook, YouTube, Twitter, Microsoft, and Instagram) have agreed on a voluntary basis to work in an EU Internet Forum including governments, EU agencies, and academics to remove online terrorist content and to respect a Code of Conduct on Countering Illegal Hate Speech Online. Although the companies have made significant progress in satisfying the stringent obligations relating to the detection and effective removal of content, the European Commission introduced a Recommendation in March 2018 that included operational measures to remove illegal content more swiftly and effectively.[37] It has warned that additional steps, including the proposal of binding legislation, might be required. The US government should look carefully at the lessons from the EU's approach to determine how to attack the same challenge domestically.

The US and the EU have the skills, the technology, and the industrial base to drive a third innovation revolution, following the industrial and ICT revolutions. Each leads in specific fields: the United States in the Internet of Things and data analytics, the EU in quantum computing and telecommunications.[38] The Digital Nine group of digital frontrunners in the EU is particularly well placed to exploit the opportunities of the digital economy.

Thanks to the high degree of transatlantic digital integration, the US and the EU have the opportunity to define the architecture and rules of the evolving digital world. They have a shared stake in building a global digital marketplace based on openness, dynamism, and innovation. Ambitious chapters on information and communication technology (ICT) services and e-commerce in a US-EU free trade agreement would be important steps toward this goal. Both sides tabled proposals during the TTIP

Security and Cybercrime in 2010, formalized in the US-EU Cyber Dialogue launched in 2014.

[37] https://ec.europa.eu/digital-single-market/en/news/commission-recommendation-measures-effectively-tackle-illegal-content-online. Under the Code of Conduct, Internet companies were (as of February 2019) removing an average 72% of illegal hate speech notified to them. About 89% of the notifications were being assessed within 24 hours and between 70 and 80% were estimated to be satisfactory removal rates.

[38] G20 Innovation Report 2016, Organisation for Economic Co-Operation and Development, November 4, 2016. http://www.oecd.org/innovation/G20-innovation-report-2016.pdf.

negotiations, but little progress was made.[39] In addition to restarting negotiations to conclude a transatlantic free trade agreement with strong provisions on e-commerce, the US and the EU have the opportunity to revive and shape stalled World Trade Organization talks to define modern rules governing e-commerce and cross-border data flows. These rules have not been updated since the Internet was in its infancy.

Cooperating with the EU on the global digital agenda is important for the United States for several reasons. The EU's regulatory activism on digital issues impacts the interests of many US businesses, most obviously in Europe, the largest market for US investments and digital exports. This activism also has an impact abroad, outside of Europe. The recent case of the GDPR is a good example: Well over one hundred countries have adopted data protection laws broadly modeled on the EU approach. And this activism also has an impact in the United States. Some multinational US firms have adopted the GDPR as their data privacy standard, either out of conviction that it has become the de facto global gold standard or because it is too difficult to maintain multiple data privacy standards. Leading US Internet platforms have also tailored their global terms of service to conform with the voluntary codes of conduct on hate speech that they have signed with the EU.

At times it may appear that there are divisions between the US and the EU on digital policy. These differences are marginal compared to the commonality of views between them, especially compared to the rigid command-and-control approaches to digital policy in China and Russia. Both countries appear determined to assume sweeping powers over the Internet and the collection, storage and use of data. By contrast the US and the EU are innovation-driven economies, with shared interests in spreading the rule of law, robust intellectual property protection, and sensible regulation.

Regulation in the EU of the digital economy, often impacting US firms and core US interests, are neither manifestations of anti-Americanism nor (except arguably in the case of taxation) of profound differences. Both the US and the EU are grappling with difficult issues such as: How should

---

[39] However, the US and the EU have negotiated Trade Principles for Information and Communication Technology Services that set forth some of the key principles on ICT that could be reflected in a bilateral free trade agreement. http://trade.ec.europa.eu/doclib/docs/2011/april/tradoc_147780.pdf. Rules on e-commerce are also an important feature of the ongoing negotiations toward a Trade in Services Agreement (TISA) at the WTO. Such rules might cover issues such as the conclusion of contracts by electronic means, electronic trust authentication and electronic signatures.

digital companies, among the largest and most profitable companies in the world, be taxed so that they pay their fair share? Do online platforms and data-rich companies pose specific challenges for antitrust policy that has been shaped in a pre-digital age? Should our copyright laws be updated to strike a different balance between the need to promote innovation and the diffusion of knowledge, on the one hand, and the incentivization of artists, writers, and journalists, on the other? What responsibilities do online platforms have to ensure that they do not host illegal material uploaded by their users?

In some cases, the EU has taken a more proactive approach than the US, inspired in part by US investigations (as in the Apple tax case) and by complaints brought by US firms. The EU has taken antitrust action against Google for behavior that the FTC cleared (although at the time of writing the Department of Justice has announced an investigation into Google). The EU has reformed its copyright laws to give publishers and content owners greater leverage against online platforms to require stronger action against pirated content and to pay higher compensation. Whereas several EU member states and the EU itself have passed laws criminalizing hate speech and imposing penalties on online platforms for hosting such content, the United States has not done so because of the guarantee of free speech in its constitution.

The political guidelines for the current European Commission indicate that the EU will continue with its proactive approach. Priorities include an EU-wide digital tax (if there is no global solution by 2020) and a new Digital Services Act that will "upgrade" regulations governing digital platforms, services, and products.[40] Margrethe Vestager has been appointed a senior "Executive Vice President" of the European Commission to lead the EU's efforts in these areas, along with her prior competition portfolio. The European Commission may well continue to set global standards in the digital economy, including standards affecting the responsibility of online platforms to remove illegal content, similar to what has happened for privacy in the case of GDPR. EU courts are promoting the global application of EU law. In one recent judgment, for example, the European Court of Justice ruled that nothing in EU law prevents national courts from requiring online platforms to search and delete duplicate posts of illegal content worldwide.

---

[40] Ursula van der Leyen, "A Union That Strives for More: My Agenda for Europe." https://ec.europa.eu/commission/sites/beta-political/files/political-guidelines-next-commission_en.pdf.

The Digital Services Act also appears aimed at overhauling the EU's current rule book—largely contained in the 20-year-old E-commerce directive—governing the liability of online platforms for hate speech, other illegal content (such as child pornography and incitement to violence) and political advertising. A new centralized EU regulator may be created with significant powers over a large swathe of the digital economy, including Internet service providers, search, cloud services, and social media platforms. The Act might contain some far-reaching provisions such as a requirement that platforms subject their algorithms to regulatory scrutiny and comply with mandatory "notice and take down" orders forcing them to remove illegal content. Not only would the Act have a considerable impact on major US companies in Europe, it might also help shape regulatory outcomes in the US and around the world.

US businesses go to Brussels to litigate issues that will have an important impact on their business operations in Europe. They also do so in the hope of establishing EU norms that will apply in the United States and beyond. For example, new EU copyright rules that enhance the bargaining power of news publishers to demand payment for the use of news snippets or of music companies to demand more compensation for content uploaded by users on online platforms might eventually lead Congress to amend the "safe harbor" in the Digital Millennium Copyright Act. If it does so, however, the balance struck among competing interests is likely to be different than the one in the EU's Copyright Directive.

In the area of taxation, the transatlantic rift threatens to grow wider. Actions by the EU and its member states to impose taxes on digital companies, based on their revenues wherever they have an online presence (even without a physical presence), could lead to similar action by other countries around the world. More than 110 countries have agreed to review the international tax system, parts of which have been rendered obsolete by the digital economy. There is deep disagreement about whether the EU approach is fair. The United States and other countries (including within the EU) have consistently opposed the creation of a different standard for Internet companies in which gross taxes are levied on revenue. The profound disagreement could undermine what has been a coordinated, global effort to crack down on tax avoidance. Worse still, it could help ignite a transatlantic trade war.

A global approach would be preferable, but the reality is that reaching global consensus is very (perhaps too) time consuming. The reality is that Europe will act soon, if not at EU level then at member state level. The question is whether US digital giants would be better off with one consistent set of pan-European rules that they can help craft or with multiple inconsistent national rules.

The EU's proactive approach toward regulating the digital economy may also be explained by the fact that the EU, especially the European Commission, is widely perceived as having the tools to address public concerns in a swift and decisive manner. The EU institutions are widely criticized as incapable of responding to concerns about safety, migration, economic growth, and so forth. But on some issues of economic regulation, particularly competition law and state aid law, the EU is often perceived as more effective than the member states and, indeed, as the sole vehicle to apply pan-European solutions.

The EU's proactive approach on the digital economy, moreover, reflects the EU's essence as a rules-based organization whose function, in large part, is to write and enforce regulations. As the guardian of the EU treaties and like any other bureaucracy, the European Commission has a natural predilection to regulate. EU policy-making does not reflect the widely shared conviction in the United States about the ability of self-regulating markets to solve problems; to the contrary, it reflects the view—strongly held in at least a few key member states—that the market is a jungle that needs to be tamed and that government intervention is often necessary to ensure that narrow private interests do not hijack the broader public good. Despite the rise of populism in Europe, there is still a greater respect there for top-down solutions crafted by bureaucracies, and less trust in market-based solutions, than in the United States.

In order to influence the EU's regulatory agenda, US firms need to engage with EU institutions early (i.e., at the stage of strategy papers and early proposals) because significant changes in EU regulations become rapidly less likely following internal agreement among the main legislative actors. Where possible, they need to partner with like-minded European allies. I witnessed frequently when I was in my post that strong and early engagement of this kind can help moderate European policy while ensuring greater compatibility across the Atlantic.

There are several critical areas—including artificial intelligence, blockchain, and cryptocurrencies—where regulation is still in its early stages and where the US and EU need to cooperate to ensure consistent regulations. Where regulations are inconsistent, they need to minimize the negative impact on the transatlantic digital market. Because of a change of policy under the Trump administration, for example, there is widespread skepticism that the "net neutrality" principles will be enforced in the US to the same extent as in the EU. According to those principles, Internet service providers should enable access to all content and applications regardless of the source and without favoring or blocking particular products or Web sites. It is important for the US and the EU to remain aligned on both regulation and enforcement to promote an efficient transatlantic digital marketplace for content and services. It is also important for the US and the EU to remain aligned regarding global "internet governance"—specifically the transition from an Internet largely under US control to the creation of a multi-stakeholder system that ensures that decision-making about the Internet does not fall under the control of governments.

One of my distinguished predecessors, Bill Kennard, has proposed twenty concrete steps in five areas to create a "transatlantic digital single market stretching from Silicon Valley to Tallinn."[41] One valuable recommendation is the creation of a US-EU Digital Council, directed by a senior official on the White House staff and a senior member of the European Commission. This council would play the same role in the digital sector as the US-EU Energy Council (described in Chapter 9) plays in the energy sector. It would serve as a platform for high-level discussion of critical regulatory issues and as an early warning system for regulatory divergences. It might prepare joint impact assessments of measures planned by either the US or the EU that have a clear and substantial impact on the transatlantic digital economy. Its mission would be to enhance the coordination of existing transatlantic digital dialogues[42] and to break down bureaucratic silos.

It is in the interests of the United States that the DSM succeeds quickly. There are some areas in which the US can impart to Europe its learnings about how to create a dynamic digital economy. These include the development of innovation clusters, improving access to capital, and stimulating entrepreneurship through more flexible tax and labor policies. Even

---

[41] Carl Bildt and Bill Kennard, "Building a Transatlantic Digital Marketplace: Twenty Steps Toward 2020," Atlantic Council, April 2016.

[42] The dialogues are the Information Society Dialogue, the Cyber Dialogue and the Transatlantic Economic Council. The Innovation and Investment in the Digital Economy Dialogue, launched in 2016 by Secretary of Commerce Penny Pritzker and European Commissioner Günther Oettinger, had only one meeting.

more significant would be an effort by the EU to disseminate the practices of the Digital Nine to the rest of the member states.

If the EU and the US do not work faster to strengthen their digital economies and to align their regulatory frameworks, they will be left behind by their competitors in Asia (especially China). Only by building a partnership, based on the two largest economies of the world and a population of 800 million consumers, can the US and Europe ensure that they retain leadership in this critical area.

Given its own challenges of being left behind in the race with Asia to exploit the opportunities of big data, the Internet of Things and artificial intelligence, the US has a fundamental interest in partnering with the EU because they share largely identical values about society and technology. Moreover, their combined consumer market is a far stronger base from which to compete with China in attracting investment and promoting innovation. The digitization of our economies is no longer a choice; it is an imperative. A deeper transatlantic digital market would not only help ensure that the US and the EU capture the benefits of higher growth rates and standards of living but would also help set the rules for the digital economy globally.

Part II

Security Ties

CHAPTER 7

Sanctions

The United States and the European Union have cooperated on a broad range of foreign policy issues around the world. These issues have not just focused on specific countries but have also been cross-cutting, such as the promotion of human rights, democracy building and good governance. With respect to one specific foreign policy tool, sanctions, I really saw the power of what these two essential partners can do together.

Nearly every week during my diplomatic mission, a staff member would inform me that "We have another SVTC on sanctions against Russia in the SCIF." The US government loves acronyms and I had to learn many of them, including these two, on the job. I would regularly participate in Secure Video Tele-Conferences on sanctions in the Sensitive Compartmented Information Facility of the US Embassy. The facility was a claustrophobic, windowless room in which highly classified information could be discussed without fear that others, including the Russians, were eavesdropping. To ensure secrecy, it was strictly prohibited to enter with any electronics, including mobile phones.

The split screen video would show SCIFs in different parts of the US government, including the National Security Council, the State Department, the Treasury Department, the Defense Department, our intelligence services, and our embassies in Ukraine and Russia. Some of the most important of these meetings were held at "deputies" level that deputy secretaries or their substitutes would attend. Ably chaired by my old friend and Deputy National Security Adviser Antony Blinken, the calls would start with briefings from two of the State Department's most experienced career diplomats, Ambassador Geoff Pyatt in Kyiv and Ambassador John Tefft in Moscow. I would brief the group on whether the EU was likely to implement similar measures and at the same time as our own.

Russia's annexation of Crimea in early March 2014 and its instigation of a separatist conflict in south-east Ukraine confronted the US and the EU with one of the most serious crises in Europe after World War II. Although it was clear that neither would elect a military response, it was far less clear whether they would be able to craft a joint non-military response that would convince Russia to change course. The US and the EU had already been cooperating on extensive sanctions against Iran since at least 2006; significantly enhanced in 2012 with an oil embargo and measures to cut off Iran's banks from the global financial system, these sanctions were already showing their results by the time I took up my post.

The success of the United States and the European Union in implementing, renewing and enforcing nearly identical and extensive sanctions against Russia after its annexation of Crimea and against Iran to curb its nuclear weapons program is one of the most extraordinary (yet underappreciated) recent achievements of their relationship. Whereas each one acting alone would have likely failed to change the behavior of Russia and Iran, they magnified the effectiveness of their policies by cooperating intensively.

The predominant role of the US dollar in global trade and the centrality of the US financial system in facilitating global financial transactions have afforded Washington enormous power to sanction foreign companies and individuals. Specifically, the US government derives significant leverage from the fact that all dollar-denominated transactions, including most oil trading, must pass through dollar-clearing accounts in the United States.

In the case of both Russia and Iran, even Washington can't carry out effective sanctions over the long term without the European Union. One key reason is that the EU has much deeper economic ties with Russia and Iran compared to the United States. EU-Russia trade was eleven times larger than US-Russia trade before the US and the EU began to impose sanctions in March 2014. Moreover, the EU imports roughly one-third of its oil and 40% of its gas from Russia. Whereas the United States had largely terminated its trading relationship with Iran by 2011, the EU imported roughly €12 billion of goods from Iran, including 600,000 barrels of oil per day (18% of the country's total oil exports) on the eve of tougher coordinated US-EU sanctions in 2012.

While unilateral US sanctions can certainly inflict significant pain in the short term, as has been the case with the additional Iran sanctions imposed by President Trump, they risk splitting the alliance and undermining their own objectives over the longer term. Yes, dealing with the EU on sanctions can be slow and sometimes painful because its deeper economic exposure to some countries (including Russia and Iran) makes it understandably more cautious than the United States. But when it finally does act, despite its burdensome bureaucratic procedures, it has an impact.

The United States and the European Union are the world's first and second most prolific users of sanctions, respectively. If they were not to coordinate their sanctions, business and investment with the targeted country would flow to the one with the laxer policies. That would, of course, cause complaints among the companies losing business and create transatlantic friction. Efforts by the United States to force EU firms to adopt sanctions against a third country, including through extraterritorial "secondary sanctions" that threaten to withhold access to the US market or prevent the use of US-source goods and intellectual property, have often failed in the past.

History clearly demonstrates that sanctions are hard to implement successfully. It is hard to sustain political and popular support for economic penalties against a third country, especially one that carries weight in the international economy. While there is rarely a clearly identifiable "constituency" for the relatively intangible benefits of long-term sanctions, there will always be a vocal and motivated lobby of businesses affected by sanctions that will seek to remove them. The difficulty of transatlantic, let alone international, coordination on sanctions has often convinced leaders that the effort is simply not worth it.

The United States and the European Union have often disagreed about the utility of broad unilateral sanctions regimes, such as Washington's decades-long embargo against Cuba and extraterritorial "secondary sanctions" that threaten to withhold access to the US market. But they largely agree that sanctions should seek to be non-punitive and targeted at changing the behavior of a country, entity, or individual responsible for violating

Fig. 7.1 Secretary Kerry and Ambassador Gardner meet European Commission President Juncker in Brussels, Belgium to discuss sanctions and other matters (© 506 collection/Alamy Image Bank, 25 March 2016)

international norms. Both the US and the EU seek to inflict minimal collateral damage on innocent people in the targeted country, on their own economic interests or on the global trading or financial system.

The complexity of coordinating international sanctions inevitably led to differences between the US and the EU about the timing, targets, and content of sanctions against Russia and Iran (Fig. 7.1). In both cases, Washington was repeatedly out in front calling for quicker, broader, and tougher action. In the case of sanctions on Russia, Vice President Biden stated:

> It was America's leadership and the president of the United States insisting, often times almost having to embarrass Europe to stand up and take economic hits to impose costs.[1]

---

[1] Remarks at the John F. Kennedy Forum, October 3, 2014. https://obamawhitehouse.archives.gov/the-press-office/2014/10/03/remarks-vice-president-john-f-kennedy-forum.

I witnessed some of the US efforts to stiffen the spine of some wobbly EU member states, especially during the very frequent visits to Brussels of my friend Dan Fried, Sanctions Coordinator at the State Department and former colleague in the Clinton White House. Dan traveled indefatigably to the main European capitals to share information, build trust, and align sanctions. The United Kingdom played an important role in guiding us through the complexities of the EU sanctions process.

European Council President Donald Tusk was a critical ally in spine-stiffening exercises. His courage and moral compass, demonstrated ever since his activities with the Solidarity movement opposing authoritarian rule in Poland in the 1980s, proved to be important assets. While some member states thought he overstepped his brief on occasion, I thought that it takes a Pole to understand the Russians.

The Crimean crisis that erupted shortly before my diplomatic mission began was not just a professional focus of mine for three years. It was of intense personal interest. I had studied Russian for seven years at high school and at university and had spent significant time in the Soviet Union pre- and post-Gorbachev as a student at Leningrad State University and then as an intern in the US Embassy in Moscow and at the Institute of US and Canada Affairs of the Soviet Academy of Science. I had worked as a lawyer in an international law firm in Moscow and then helped GE Oil & Gas with its Russian projects. I felt I knew a little about the Russian psyche.

In the months leading up to my diplomatic mission, I had been fixated by the images of Ukrainians, from all walks of life, who were braving the freezing cold and risk of death by snipers to demonstrate in Kyiv's Maidan Square. One of my proudest moments was when the US Mission to the EU sponsored the screening of "Winter on Fire," a documentary about those events. The crisis had started with Russia's refusal to accept the Ukrainian people's right to choose their own destiny as part of the European family, including signing a free trade and association agreement with the European Union. I felt that they were fighting for the same inalienable rights as the American patriots during the Revolutionary War or as the Balts and the Central and Eastern Europeans during their struggle for liberation from the Soviet yoke. In my first July 4 celebration in Brussels, I told the crowd that: "Freedoms are not free. They need to be defended. And those who wish to be free deserve our support."

A Conversation in the Kremlin

In order to appreciate fully the extent of the US-EU achievement in coordinating sanctions on Russia, it may be helpful to imagine a conversation between Vladimir Putin and Russian Foreign Minister Sergei Lavrov soon after the Kremlin's decision to send special operations forces to occupy critical installations in Crimea in late February 2014.

The dialogue might have gone something like this:

> *LAVROV*: Mr. President, I am pleased to report that all is going according to plan. Crimea will soon be reunited with Mother Russia where she has always belonged. The useful idiots in the Western media are repeating disinformation that our forces are unknown militia operating autonomously and that the government in Kyiv is dominated by Fascists who are committing atrocities against the Russian-speaking population.
>
> *PUTIN*: Thank you, Sergei. It is time to undo Khrushchev's criminal decision to cede Crimea to Ukraine in 1954. Yeltsin, that drunken fool, was also a criminal to allow Ukraine to become independent in 1991. It is absurd that Ukraine pretends to be an independent country. We must not only absorb Crimea but also take back southeast Ukraine and—who knows—even move on Kyiv itself? At a bare minimum, we must ensure that the entire country remains weak and divided, as well as outside NATO and the EU. We cannot tolerate an independent, stable, successful and democratic Ukraine on our borders! The hypocritical West will say that we are breaching international law, while conveniently forgetting that they grabbed Iraq for its oil reserves and NATO interfered in Kosovo. [Putin takes a long, reflective pause] Do you see any risks?
>
> *LAVROV*: Mr. President, our enemies are good at playing a strong hand poorly, while we know how to play a weak hand well. The United States will push for sanctions, but Europe will come up with excuses for not acting. They were unable to take coordinated action against us after we thrashed the Georgians in 2008. If Washington pushes for extraterritorial secondary sanctions against Europe, as President Reagan did in 1982 to prevent European firms from participating in the construction of the Siberian oil pipeline, or as the US Congress did in 1996 to force Europe to adopt sanctions against Cuba and Iran, the EU would likely respond with counter-sanctions and "blocking statutes" that prohibit European courts and companies from complying with US law. We would benefit hugely from a split in the transatlantic alliance.
>
> *PUTIN*: But what is the risk that the EU will actually get its act together and cooperate with Washington?

LAVROV: I can put your mind at ease. Remember that the 28 members of the EU must act unanimously to implement sanctions. Just think how easy it will be to pressure the Cypriots whose banks depend on the money of our oligarchs, or to influence the Greeks, our orthodox brothers, who are furious with EU-imposed austerity measures, or to convince our Hungarian friend Viktor Orban who sees you as a role model? The Italians will not want to endanger their sales of luxury fashion, or the French their sales of cheese and wine, or the Germans their sales of cars and machine tools. Unlike in the United States, where the president has significant powers to set sanctions policy and the executive branch executes, the European Commission must consult extensively with the member states. The member states' national administrations are responsible for interpreting the sanctions. They can do that sometimes rather flexibly. They are tasked with spotting and punishing violations, but they can also turn a blind eye.

PUTIN: But what if the EU 28 do agree unanimously on sanctions?

LAVROV: Even if they do, Mr. President, remember that they would be of limited impact if they are not followed by similar sanctions imposed by Canada, Japan, Switzerland, Norway, South Korea, Australia and others. Even if those countries do participate, the EU 28 must renew the sanctions every six months, each time by unanimity! That gives us numerous opportunities to divide and conquer. A few days before each renewal date we can dangle the carrot of a "negotiated solution" and a truce in front of their noses. Once the US and Europe start believing in a diplomatic process, they will be hooked. The public and the press will demand that no diplomatic stone is left unturned. Europe and the US will bend over backwards, thinking that you are a rational chess player. They will telegraph their intentions in an open debate, allowing us to plan well ahead of time. You should play a different game—blackjack perhaps—and double down at every turn. You should be unpredictable. They do not have an appetite for risk.

PUTIN: What if they do impose sanctions? Is there any risk that these could be problematic?

LAVROV: Even if they do so, they will focus on visa bans, asset freezes and an arms embargo that are minor inconveniences. The wives of some oligarchs won't be able to shop at Harrods, visit their houses in Knightsbridge and send their little Sashas to private schools in the UK and the US, but this is not a significant issue. Designations of people and companies in EU sanctions lists can easily be challenged before the EU's highest court for lack of evidence, just as the Iranians have done successfully. Sanctions against our broader economy are unlikely; even if implemented, the measures will be targeted and will not pinch us where it really hurts— exports of natural resources, especially oil and gas, and our need to raise money in Western capital markets. They will never, ever resort to the "nuclear option" of forcing SWIFT to cut Russian banks from the international financial messaging system.

PUTIN: You are right. The US and the EU can successfully pressure a country of minor importance, like Iran, but Russia is a different story. Our economy is more than three times the size of Iran's and it is far more integrated with the world economy. Russia sells vastly more energy to the world than Iran does. We can't be isolated like Iran.

LAVROV: Of course. But the United States will push the EU and its allies to punish us.

PUTIN: If they have the balls to implement broad sanctions against our energy companies and banks, I can intimidate them. We can flood the separatist militia in Ukraine with weapons and provide them with training. We can annihilate Ukrainian Army positions with our long-range artillery from just inside our borders. The US and Europe will never equip Ukraine with military hardware, even of the defensive kind. Our military will prevail. But, Sergei, we must be careful to prevent information about deaths and injuries of our troops from becoming public.

LAVROV: Of course. Mr. President, you can propose a new law making the deaths of Russian soldiers in special operations during peacetime a state secret. The soldiers shall receive no military honors and shall be buried in unmarked graves.

PUTIN: Excellent. We can also crater the Ukrainian economy by forcing enormous costs of conflict on Kyiv; Gazprom can raise prices for the supply of natural gas to Ukraine or we can simply shut off all supply and make the Ukrainians freeze in their beds. There is no way that the IMF, the US and Europe will step into save the Ukrainian economy. But, Sergei, what is the risk of sanctions against our key economic sectors?

LAVROV: Mr. President, I can put your mind at ease. Such sweeping sanctions are highly unlikely, especially in Europe. The cost of lost exports, and of our own counter-sanctions, will have to be evenly distributed across all EU 28 member states. There will be endless controversy about which member states are bearing a disproportionate burden. We will, of course, seek to promote a transatlantic split by encouraging the narrative that Europe is paying the price for sanctions while the United States is getting off without a scratch.

PUTIN: So all I need to do, as the ancient Chinese philosopher Sun Tzu observed, is to wait by the river long enough to see the bodies of my enemies float by. The best part of this plan is that the Russian people will shower me with praise for being a strong leader and making Russia respected once again on the world stage.

So just how clever were Putin and Lavrov when we look back on what occurred? While they did get some bets right, on the whole they were proven disastrously wrong. The United States and the European Union did remain unified during a lengthy period of implementing and renewing increasingly restrictive sanctions. The EU was galvanized into following US so-called sectoral sanctions against the Russian economy's energy, financial, and arms sectors after Russian-backed separatists shot down a Malaysian Airline plane filled with European nationals on July 17, 2014. When European Commission President Juncker had warned Putin at the G-8 meeting in Brisbane, Australia, in November 2014 not to attempt to split the transatlantic alliance because he would surely fail, Putin had confidently replied: "I won't fail." Well, he did.

What Russia Guessed Right

Putin and Lavrov were certainly correct in guessing that the immediate reaction to the annexation of Crimea would be tepid at best. President Obama and EU leaders issued the ritual condemnations, of course. I was seated in the front row of the packed press conference following the US-EU Summit at the end of March 2014 during which European Council President Herman van Rompuy stated that the annexation was "a disgrace in the 21st century and we will not recognize it."[2] Leaders on both sides of the Atlantic called for a de-escalation and a peaceful resolution of the crisis. They announced their support for the territorial integrity, sovereignty, and independence of Ukraine and called on Russia to immediately withdraw its troops to areas where they had been stationed. As of early March, they instituted and quickly implemented some visa bans and

---

[2] Remarks by President of the European Council Herman van Rompuy Following the US-EU Summit, March 26, 2014. https://www.consilium.europa.eu/media/23895/141919.pdf.

asset freezes of limited impact. They threatened unspecified "additional and far reaching consequences" if Russia took further steps to destabilize the situation in Ukraine, essentially writing off Crimea's annexation as a *fait accompli*.

The meeting of the G-8 leaders scheduled for mid-June in Sochi was canceled, substituted with a G-7 only meeting in Brussels. The EU-Russia summit and bilateral meetings between EU member states and Russia were also canceled. But importantly, Russia's participation in the G-8 was only suspended temporarily, not terminated. My suggestion to the NSC staff that the G-7 be held in Kyiv was rejected as being too aggressive. To my amazement, Putin was invited to participate in the commemoration of the World War II Allied landings in Normandy on June 6. Putin also hobnobbed with world leaders at the G-20 meeting in Brisbane as if business had returned to normal. When I had called on Van Rompuy during my "letters of credential" ceremony at the beginning of my diplomatic mission, he had aptly observed that Europeans "are not in a fighting mood" and wanted stability with its Russian neighbor above all else. While the United States is lucky not to have Russia as a neighbor, it was also not in a fighting mood. The stark reality was that the US and Europe would never care about Ukraine as much as Russia, and therefore would not go to war over it.

Putin and Lavrov were also right that EU member states would have very different views of Russia and that sustaining unanimity would be very challenging. The United Kingdom was the member state most philosophically aligned with our position. I was on the phone several times per week, sometimes several times per day, with the UK's permanent representative to the EU Sir Ivan Rogers during the crisis in order to understand the EU's position and to plot next steps. Sweden, the Baltic states, Poland, and Romania were also dependably aligned with the US desire to toughen sanctions.

On the other side of the spectrum, Greece repeatedly opposed sanctions, perpetually arguing for a soft approach and watering down communiqués and proposed sanctions lists. Prime Minister Tsipras visited Putin in Moscow May 2014 and again in April 2015, breaking the EU consensus not to hold bilateral discussions. Foreign Minister Nikos Kotzias repeatedly argued that EU sanctions were counter-productive. Panos Kammenos, a leading figure in the governing coalition, said that Western NGOs provoked the crisis in Ukraine and that a *coup d'état* overthrew the legitimate government. Energy Minister Panagiotis Lafanazis, leader of the hard-left faction of the governing coalition, described EU sanctions as "totally unacceptable" and repeated that Greece "had no differences with Russia."[3] (One of the ironies of Greek affinity for Russia is that Russia nonetheless tried in early 2019 to scupper Greece's ultimately successful efforts to resolve a highly contentious dispute with Macedonia about its name.)

Greece was not alone. Cypriot President Nicos Anastasiades said Cyprus had "grave doubts" about Europe's policy toward Russia. Cyprus allowed Russia to use its ports and won improved terms for a $2.5 billion Russian loan.[4] Prime Minister Victor Orban said the EU was shooting itself in the foot and signed an agreement with Putin for Russian companies to supply two nuclear reactors, including a Russian state loan of up to €10 billion to finance nearly all of the project. The Bulgarian, Slovak, and Czech governments were scarcely more supportive.[5] These countries' total dependency on Russian gas was only a partial factor; Poland and Lithuania were sanctions hawks despite being in the same position.

In between this group of sanctions sceptics and the group of sanctions supporters stood other states that were unpredictable. Germany and France slowly took a tougher line against Moscow over time. Italy was keen to protect the export success of Italian business (including fashion and food) in the Russian market and seemed especially protective of ENI, its oil major that had significant agreements with Rosneft to explore oil fields in the Barents and Black Seas. Prime Minister Renzi repeatedly attacked German Chancellor Merkel for invoking European solidarity to approve sanctions that would hurt Italy, while approving the Nord Stream II pipeline that would benefit German business and exacerbate European gas dependency on Russia. The Netherlands were supportive of sanctions, but Prime Minister Rutte seemed to be mindful of Dutch business interests, especially those of Shell Oil headquartered in The Hague.

---

[3] Sam Jones and Courtney Weaver, "Alarm Bells Ring over Syriza's Russian Links," *Financial Times*, January 28, 2015. https://www.ft.com/content/a87747de-a713-11e4-b6bd-00144feab7de.

[4] Andrew Higgins, "Waving Cash, Putin Sows EU Divisions in an Effort to Break Sanctions," *The New York Times*, April 6, 2015. https://www.nytimes.com/2015/04/07/world/europe/using-cash-and-charm-putin-targets-europes-weakest-links.html.

[5] Gergely Szakacs, "Europe 'Shot Itself in Foot' with Russia Sanctions: Hungary PM," *Reuters*, August 15, 2014. https://www.reuters.com/article/us-ukraine-crisis-sanctions-hungary/europe-shot-itself-in-foot-with-russia-sanctions-hungary-pm-idUSKBN0GF0ES20140815.

Putin and Lavrov were correct that many Europeans, encouraged by ample Russian disinformation, considered that only Europe, not the United States, had a "dog in the fight" because of its geographic position and economic ties with Russia. Why should the United States shape the response to Russian annexation in Crimea when it was so far away?

There were many answers to that question. It was not just the case that the United States cares about the ability of people to determine their destiny, the importance of international law and the sanctity of internationally recognized frontiers. The United States (along with Russia and the United Kingdom) had given security assurances to Ukraine under the Budapest Memorandum of 1994 under which Ukraine had agreed to give up its nuclear weapons stockpile. As the leading world power, the United States also had a unique interest in ensuring that its credibility and power not be questioned by others, especially the Iranians, the North Koreans, and the Chinese, who were probing Washington's willingness to stop their destabilizing actions.

Many Europeans believed that Europe was paying the price of the sanctions while the United States was getting away cost-free, if not even benefiting from them. It is true that the EU was more exposed than the United States to a reduction in trade with Russia: The EU and the US were Russia's fourth and 23rd largest trading partner, respectively, before sanctions were imposed. EU exports to Russia during 2014–2016 dropped by 21%, but this was due, perhaps in large part, to an economic downturn in Russia caused by a slump in the international oil price and the devaluation of the rouble, neither of which was due to sanctions or counter-sanctions. The sanctions-induced export losses for the EU have been estimated at 11% during the three years.[6]

The burden on EU member states was very unevenly distributed, with some (including those complaining most loudly) not suffering much real pain and others, including many of the sanctions hawks, suffering relatively more seriously. Roughly one-fifth of the EU's exports of fruits and vegetables went to Russia, with some sectors (such as Polish apple exports) particularly badly hit. But the EU budget softened the blow and many of these exporters successfully redirected their exports to other markets. In 2017, the European Commission estimated the damage to the

---

[6] "Russia's and the EU's Sanctions: Economic and Trade Effects, Compliance and the Way Forward," European Parliament Research Service, 2017. http://www.europarl.europa.eu/RegData/etudes/STUD/2017/603847/EXPO_STU(2017)603847_EN.pdf.

European economy of the sanctions and countersanctions at a very modest 0.3% and 0.4% of GDP in 2014 and 2015, respectively.

The United States also took an economic hit, suffering a drop in US exports to Russia of 17% during 2014–2016, only slightly less than the drop in EU exports. Although the impact on the EU was greater in the first two years, the impact on the US was significant in 2016. Moreover, some large and politically influential firms took big hits. Exxon Mobil, for example, was forced to terminate its partnerships with Rosneft to drill in the Arctic, Western Siberia, Russia's Far East, and the Black Sea at a cost of $1 billion. US energy firms complained bitterly that the EU "grandfathered" its oil companies' existing contracts in existence at the time the sanctions were announced to allow them to continue, whereas the US had insisted on immediate termination. Significant US exports of oil and gas extraction and maintenance equipment to Russia were also hit.

Putin and Lavrov were also right in believing that the United States and Europe would not (at least during the Obama administration) arm Ukraine to help it defend itself. At the Munich Security Conference in February 2015, Chancellor Merkel had voiced a view shared by many European leaders: "I cannot envisage any situation in which improved equipment of the Ukrainian army will lead to a situation in which Putin is so impressed that he will lose militarily."[7] That was true, but it wasn't really the point. Arming the Ukrainians could have changed Putin's risk calculus and it certainly would have cost him the ability to deny that the body bags coming out of south-east Ukraine contained Russian soldiers. Taking the option of arming Ukraine with lethal weapons off the table made Putin's decisions much simpler.

President Obama never formally took the option off the table, but it was pretty clear even from the earliest days of the conflict that it just wasn't going to happen. I participated in many video conference calls in which our key policy-makers debated and rejected the option of sending lethal arms, such as anti-tank missiles, to Ukraine. At an address before the joint houses of Congress in September 2014, Ukrainian President Petro Poroshenko had pointed out that "Blankets and night vision goggles are also important but one cannot win the war with blankets."[8] By the fall,

---

[7] Bret Stephens, "From Munich to Munich," *The Wall Street Journal*, February 9, 2015.

[8] Dan Roberts, "Ukrainian President Makes Emotional Plea to Congress for Greater Military Aid," *The Guardian*, September 18, 2014.

Washington had finally started sending modest amounts of non-lethal aid, such as short-range counter-mortar equipment, patrol vehicles, boats, and surveillance equipment. But the refusal to send more sophisticated equipment, such as long-range radar and tactical surveillance drones, had already proven to have devastating consequences. When Ukrainian government forces reversed some earlier losses of territory to Russian-backed separatists in early July 2014, Russian forces operating just inside the Russian border conducted sustained and intensive artillery attacks that turned the tide once again.

Under rising Congressional pressure, President Obama signed the Ukraine Freedom Support Act in December 2014 that authorized, but did not require, the president to provide increased military assistance, including of the "lethal" kind, to Ukraine. But the president was not inclined to do so, partly under significant pressure from European leaders who believed that this would worsen the conflict and destroy efforts by Germany, France, and the EU to broker a settlement. In repeated meetings at the European Commission and the European Council, I was warned that any US unilateral decision to arm Ukraine with lethal weapons would risk splitting the transatlantic alliance and would fracture Europe internally, even if it might be welcomed secretly in several member states.

That fear was overstated. The decision of the Trump administration in 2018 to give significant military assistance, including the sale of lethal weaponry, to Ukraine strained but did not split the alliance. Nonetheless, in 2014–2015 it was clear that the European public had no desire to resolve the conflict militarily. A 2015 opinion poll by the Pew Research Center had indicated that most Europeans opposed sending arms to Ukraine and that they would not fight for it; shockingly, the poll demonstrated that a majority would not even come to the defense of a fellow European NATO member if attacked.[9] In light of that reality, US-EU agreement to ratchet up pressure with sanctions was even more important.

Putin and Lavrov were right that Europe was enamored with process. I wish I had a euro for every time I heard an EU official, and the permanent representatives of the EU member states, speak about the need for "caution," "restraint," and "dialogue." When I heard one of them

---

[9] Katie Simmons, Bruce Stokes, and Jacob Poushter, "NATO Publics Blame Russia for Ukrainian Crisis, but Reluctant to Provide Military Aid," *Pew Research Center*, June 10, 2015. https://www.pewresearch.org/global/2015/06/10/nato-publics-blame-russia-for-ukrainian-crisis-but-reluctant-to-provide-military-aid/.

say with an earnest expression that "we need to move from a logic of confrontation to a logic of cooperation," I felt like reaching for an air sickness bag. It was certainly true that we needed to keep the diplomatic track open as there was no military solution to the conflict and in order to keep the public on both sides of the Atlantic on our side as we increased the pressure on Moscow. But I sometimes felt that many Europeans were engaging in dangerous self-delusion about the likelihood that diplomacy alone would yield results. Innumerable meetings were held among representatives from France, Germany, Ukraine and Russia (the "Normandy Format"); from the EU, the US, Ukraine and Russia (the "Geneva Format"); and from Ukraine, Russia, the Organisation of Security and Cooperation in Europe and the breakaway separatist "People's Republic" of Donetsk and Luhansk (the "Minsk Format").

The Minsk Protocol signed in mid-September 2014 set forth a detailed twelve-point plan, including an immediate cease-fire in the Donbas region of Ukraine and critical provisions that heavy weaponry had to be withdrawn from the "line of contact" and that "illegal armed groups and military equipment as well as fighters and mercenaries" had to be withdrawn from Ukrainian territory. But the protocol was almost instantly violated, mostly by the Russian side. After the complete collapse of the protocol by January 2015, Germany and France helped to broker a new package of measures (called "Minsk II") that were meant to stop the fighting on terms acceptable to both sides. Little of this arrangement has been implemented, principally because Russia has refused to exert its clear influence over separatist forces. While the United States supported these efforts at a peace process, many of the officials in the Obama administration were convinced that Russia actually wanted to keep the conflict simmering in order to exert the maximum destabilizing influence over the future of Ukraine.

The reality was that on both sides of the Atlantic we were bending over backward to appease Moscow. For example, European Commission President Jean-Claude Juncker sent an extraordinary letter to Putin in November 2015 in which he expressed his "regret" that closer EU-Russia ties had not been able to develop over the past year. "I can assure you that the European Commission will be a helpful partner in this process," he wrote. Moscow rejected his proposal of closer trade ties between the EU and the Eurasian Economic Union, a grouping for former Soviet states dominated by Moscow.[10] Juncker also observed that "One doesn't provoke a bully" and that "We must make efforts towards a practical relationship with Russia…we can't go on like this." I thought that language very unfortunate because it neglected how it would be heard as a sign of weakness in Moscow.

Some high-level officials in the Obama administration also repeatedly urged that we express to Putin a desire to de-escalate and offer him "off-ramps" that would offer him a face-saving way out of the crisis. I thought the concept of an "off-ramp" completely ignored the realities we faced with Putin. During the regular SVTCs on Russia sanctions, I regularly agreed with my friends, Victoria Nuland, the Assistant Secretary of State, and Dan Fried, the State Department's coordinator for sanctions, both of whom had significant experience dealing with Russia and were sanctions hawks. They argued that only sustained pressure, increased if necessary and combined with continued Ukrainian resistance, would ever convince the Russians to settle the conflict in the Donbas. Vice President Biden was refreshingly clear-minded, repeating in the US and to European counterparts that the threat had to be faced up front; the real choice was "paying now or paying double later."

Putin and Lavrov were also right that the US and the EU would focus their initial response on travel bans and asset freezes. In March 2014, both sides imposed these measures on a relatively small number of individuals. The sanctions lists included officials who were either Crimean separatist leaders or Russians who had taken a direct role in the annexation of Ukrainian territory. During the month of March, both the US and the EU added individuals, including prominent targets like the former Ukrainian President Viktor Yanukovych and Dmitry Rogozin, the Deputy Prime Minister of the Russian Federation, to their lists. Of course, none of this deterred Putin from orchestrating a referendum in Crimea that unsurprisingly resulted in an overwhelming show of support for independence and Russian recognition of Crimea as an independent state.

The one sentence in the US executive order that might have raised some concern in Moscow related to the intention of targeting individuals wielding influence in the Russian government, including their personal assets. That warning might have led some Russian oligarchs to move their assets to places less exposed to subsequent sanctions.

---

[10] Andries Sytas, "EU's Juncker Dangles Trade Ties with Russia-Led Bloc to Putin," *Reuters*, November 12, 2015.

At the US-EU Summit on March 26, President Obama urged the EU to pick up the speed and intensity of its sanctions, observing that the United States was ready to impose tighter sanctions. He urged the EU to act imminently, not in the multi-week timeframe the EU side had in mind. However, the EU's next round of sanctions announced one month later didn't go much further than the prior one. Although the EU list included 15 more individuals, including most significantly the Chief of the General Staff of the Russian armed forces and the head of the GRU, Russia's largest foreign intelligence agency, the EU failed to follow the United States' example of sanctioning any Putin "cronies" or Russian entities. The US administration used the term "cronies" to denote confidantes and supporters of Putin who had amassed their wealth through opaque dealings and with his support.

This was primarily due to heightened concern in the EU institutions about the vulnerability of such sanctions to legal challenges before the European Court of Justice. The concern was well-founded because numerous targets of EU sanctions, including Ukrainians and Russians, were successfully challenging their inclusion. The core of the EU's difficulty was that, having no intelligence-gathering capabilities of its own, it needed to rely on information provided by the member states. Neither the US government nor key member states with the relevant intelligence, especially the United Kingdom, were keen to share classified information with the EU. There was no way, moreover, to introduce such information before the EU courts in a restrictive manner to persons with security clearance. The result was that some of the "designations" amounted to little more than Internet search results and second-hand information. After suffering some embarrassing defeats before the courts, the EU changed the rules of procedure to allow restricted access to confidential information. It also started basing its "designations" on the *status* of the targets rather than their *conduct* because the former required less evidentiary support.

The EU kept adding more separatist leaders to its lists in mid-May and mid-July and banned the import of goods from Crimea at the end of June. When the EU finally got around to imposing sanctions on entities in mid-May, it was to target two expropriated Crimean energy companies of minor significance. The signing at the end of June of the EU-Ukraine Association Agreement, including a free trade agreement, was a far more significant event. Even though the agreement did not guarantee eventual EU membership, it was hugely significant because the Kremlin's pressure on the Yanukovich regime not to sign it had precipitated the demonstrations in Kyiv that led to the end of his regime and because it was an important step westwards both economically and politically.

There were two highly significant measures, short of sanctions, that the US and the EU regrettably failed to take. The first was to release damning information about corruption at the highest levels of the Russian government. According to some estimates, including one by the CIA in 2007 (and subsequently revealed by officials who had read them), Putin's fortune amounts to around $40 billion. Some lawmakers in Congress discussed requiring the Obama administration to make these estimates public, but that never happened.[11] Putin's oligarch supporters would have been very annoyed at having their dirty laundry displayed in public. The second measure the US regrettably failed to take was to reveal information about the identities of Russian soldiers dying in combat. The Russian State had gone to extraordinary lengths to keep this information a secret in order to prevent an erosion of public trust.

What Russia Guessed Wrong

Fortunately, Putin and Lavrov got much more wrong than they got right. While making some tactical gains, they committed strategic blunders that will set back Russian interests for many years. Russian aggression made my job of promoting US-EU relations so much easier. By seizing Crimea, he rekindled the love lost during the transatlantic discord over data privacy in the wake of the Snowden revelations.

Russian threats proved to be counterproductive. In a phone call in late August 2014, Putin had told then European Commission President José Manuel Barroso that Russia could occupy Kyiv in two weeks if he wanted. In November 2014, he defended the Molotov-Ribbentrop non-aggression pact that carved up Poland between Nazi Germany and the Soviet Union.[12] The annexation of Crimea and the frequent incursions into Scandinavian and Baltic airspace by Russian jets convinced some

[11] Peter Baker, "Sanctions Revive Search for Secret Putin Fortune," *The New York Times*, April 27, 2014.

[12] Andrew Roth, "Putin Tells European Official That He Could 'Take Kiev in Two Weeks'," *The New York Times*, September 2, 2014. Tom Parfitt, "Vladimir Putin Says There Was Nothing Wrong with Soviet Union's Pact with Adolf Hitler's Nazi Germany," *Telegraph*, November 6, 2014. https://www.telegraph.co.uk/news/worldnews/vladimir-putin/11213255/Vladimir-Putin-says-there-was-nothing-wrong-with-Soviet-Unions-pact-with-Adolf-Hitlers-Nazi-Germany.html.

European states to increase their defense spending, reinvigorated NATO and led the United States and its allies to move troops and weapons closer to the Russian border. Moreover, Gazprom's threats to turn off the natural gas spigot promoted progress toward a European Energy Union, including the diversification of energy supplies and improved energy infrastructure permitting the free flow of gas. That diminished Russia's ability to use energy supplies as a weapon against Europe. As a result of Russian actions in Crimea and south-east Ukraine, the number of Ukrainians having positive views of Russia declined precipitously. Like Ukraine, Moldova and Georgia wanted to move ever closer toward Europe. And that is just a short list.

Although very well-funded Russian media outlets, such as the international television station RT (Russia Today) and the Sputnik news agency did enjoy a broad following, even in the US and Europe, Russia's grotesque disinformation at home undermined the credibility of Russia's entire public relations campaign. Russian state-owned media reported that the Ukrainian government planned to put Hitler's face on its paper money and that Ukrainian nationalists had crucified a Russian child in Slovyansk, south-east Ukraine, after the Ukrainian Army expelled Russian-backed separatists from the town.

Putin and Lavrov were also wrong that unanimity among the EU 28 would fracture. Greece, Cyprus, Hungary, and some other member states complained bitterly about the sanctions but never risked shattering EU solidarity in the knowledge that they benefited so much more from the EU than from close ties with Russia. During the fraught negotiations between Greece and the EU over a debt bailout, Moscow must have been tempted to offer Athens cheap loans in return, perhaps, for a Greek veto of sanctions against Russia or a naval base in Greece. But that never happened. Hungary could cozy up with Moscow in return for cheap energy and financing for its nuclear power plant, but it would never endanger its EU membership because 6% of its GDP stemmed from EU transfers.

There inevitably were tensions among the EU 28 before the expiration of each six-month sanctions period. A minority of member states argued for longer periods or in favor of pre-emptively rolling over the sanctions before their expiration. The majority argued that the six-month periods gave the EU flexibility to respond to events on the ground. But the reality was that the periods gave Moscow numerous opportunities to fracture EU solidarity. One repeated debate within the EU, encouraged by Moscow, was whether sanctions should *partially* be lifted in return for *partial* compliance with the Minsk Protocol. Washington and the majority of the EU 28 fortunately nipped in the bud each effort to pursue this *à la carte* approach. The sanctions were regularly rolled over.

EU solidarity did come into question in an area few would have anticipated: the EU-Ukraine free trade agreement. In September 2014, Putin nearly convinced several EU member states to remove all tariff preferences for Ukraine in the agreement in return for a ceasefire. Not only did this put the lie to Russia's claim that it was a non-combatant and had no influence over the separatists, there was no evidence that trade preferences or regulatory requirements in the agreement would seriously impact the modest amount of Russia's non-energy exports to Ukraine.

Although the free trade agreement entered into "provisional application" in January 2016 pending ratification by all EU member states, it was once again threatened by the results of a Dutch referendum on the agreement in April. The referendum had been called because the opponents had barely cleared the low 300,000 signature threshold and then had managed to gain 61% of the votes among the one third of the Dutch electorate that voted. The result was that two and a half million voters, often voting for reasons entirely unrelated to the free trade agreement, endangered an agreement that had been ratified by every other member state. It was a huge propaganda win for Russia that portrayed the vote as a rejection of Ukraine. Fortunately, the Dutch Senate finally ratified the agreement in May 2017 after the EU heads of government had clarified that it would not have any impact on Ukraine's aspirations to join the EU, access EU labor markets or receive financial or military support.

Putin and Lavrov were wrong in believing that the US and the EU would not help Ukraine meet its energy and financial needs. As described further in Chapter 9, in April 2014 Gazprom canceled Ukraine's natural gas discount agreed the previous December, jacked up prospective prices and cut off gas supplies to Ukraine in June after trilateral talks (including the EU) had failed. US and EU energy experts reported from their technical meetings in Kyiv that there might not be sufficient gas supply during the coming winter, despite price hikes and lower demand in the Donbas industrial region affected by the conflict. But the experts helped develop an emergency plan, including the provision of mobile power generators for schools and hospitals, technical assistance to improve the exploitation of existing Ukrainian oil and gas resources, and support for enabling the "reverse flow" of gas from Slovakia, Poland, and Hungary to Ukraine. At the end of October 2014, EU Energy Commissioner Günther Oettinger brokered a gas supply deal between Kyiv and Moscow that depended in part on EU financial guarantees.

The US and the EU, moreover, stood by Ukraine financially as its economy reeled from the cost of the conflict, the loss of industrial production, reduced trade and investment, and runaway inflation. The economy contracted 7% in 2014 and even more in 2015. With a widening budget shortfall, dwindling international currency reserves, a worsening public debt to GDP ratio, and difficulty to raise capital, Kyiv was facing a real crisis. But the IMF stepped in quickly at the end of April 2014 to approve a $17 billion two-year package of support, including immediate disbursement of $3 billion that unlocked further credits from other donors of $15 billion. That package was replaced in March 2015 by another $17.5 billion credit line, giving immediate access to $5 billion. The United States provided $2 billion in loan guarantees, while the EU disbursed €1.6 billion under its "macro-financial assistance" program, during 2014–2015. All the programs were conditioned on Ukraine continuing on its path of economic reform.

Putin and Lavrov were wrong that sanctions on individuals would be minor nuisances. Already in late March, the US started targeting members of Putin's inner circle, including not only high-level government officials but also Putin "cronies". These included some very wealthy and powerful people: Vladimir Yakunin, the Chairman of the state-owned Russian Railways; the Rotenberg brothers who had amassed a multi-billion fortune through significant state contracts; and Gennady Timchenko, one of Russia's richest oligarchs, a confidante of Putin and a founder of Gunvor, one of the world's largest independent commodity trading firms involved in the oil and energy markets.

The sanctions notice released by the US Treasury contained a highly significant sentence: "Putin has investments in Gunvor and may have access to Gunvor funds." The message to Putin was clear: We know where you hold your wealth and we may go after it. In late March, the US also sanctioned Bank Rossiya, one of the country's largest banks and the personal bank for senior officials, including members of Putin's inner circle.

In late April, the US went further by sanctioning more Putin "cronies," including Igor Sechin, the head of Rosneft, Russia's leading state-owned oil company, and Sergei Chemezov, the head of Rostec, the Russian state-owned company overseeing high-tech industries. The US also sanctioned many companies belonging to the Rotenberg brothers and Timchenko. By the end of July, the EU not only added more senior Russian officials to its sanctions list, including the head of the FSB security service, the main successor agency to the KGB, and Putin's first deputy chief of staff, but finally added three Putin "cronies," including Arkady Rotenberg and two main shareholders of Bank Rossiya, whom the United States had targeted earlier.

These measures against Putin's cronies were not mere pinpricks that prevented oligarchs from yachting in St. Tropez and skiing in Courchevel with their well-paid escorts. They created serious complications for the targeted individuals in accessing their assets and in using international financial institutions to manage them.

Putin and Lavrov were wrong to think that the US and the EU would not impose sectoral sanctions. They did so and were successful in coordinating similar sanctions by the key developed economies and allies of the EU and the US, including Japan, Canada, Norway, Switzerland, and Australia. That was an extraordinarily time-consuming and technically challenging feat in light of the varied interests of the countries involved and the time pressure of responding to rapidly unfolding events.

The US imposed the first round of sectoral sanctions on July 16, 2014. These sanctions, by far the most significant to date, prohibited "US persons and persons within the United States" from providing medium and long-term financing for some of Russia's largest companies in the financial and energy sectors. These companies included Gazprombank, a financial institution and subsidiary of the behemoth Gazprom, the largest natural gas company in the world; VEB, a development bank and payment agent for the Russian government; Novatek, Russia's largest independent natural gas producer; and Rosneft. Eight Russian arms firms were also on the list. But Gazprom itself would not be named as it was considered a "nuclear option" that Europe would never support. Most EU member states, as of July 16, were very hesitant to engage in sectoral sanctions out of concern that they might hinder a peaceful resolution to the conflict and have serious consequences for the EU's trading and investment relations with Russia. Events on the following day changed everything.

On July 17, Russian-backed and Russian-trained separatists in southeast Ukraine fired a Russian-made surface to air missile at an aircraft that they thought was a Ukrainian military aircraft but was instead a Malaysian

Airline flight from Amsterdam bound for Kuala Lumpur. The tragedy cost the lives of 298 people, including 193 Dutch, 10 Britons, and 4 Belgians. The separatists prevented international monitors, including from the OSCE, from promptly accessing the site. According to eyewitness accounts of the immediately subsequent events, some of the debris was removed and the bodies were stripped of their wallets and personal effects, before being left to rot in the fields. A joint investigative team established by the Netherlands and Australia (that lost 28 citizens) formally held Russia accountable in May 2018 after a lengthy inquiry. I remember seeing extremely convincing evidence of Russia's culpability in the early months after the disaster. Some of this was shared with the EU and the member states.

As always, a change in Germany's position, specifically that of Chancellor Merkel, was pivotal to a change in the EU's policies. As her spokesman argued, "a completely new situation has emerged which makes further measures necessary…only…a substantial package would enable the German government and the EU to send a clear, strong signal to Russia."[13] Once Berlin decided to overrule the concerns of German industry that had the most to lose from tough sanctions, the group of EU sanctions hawks clearly had significant weight and clear momentum. France and even Italy agreed that much tougher actions were required.

The EU immediately announced that the EIB would suspend funding for projects in Russia. The European Bank for Reconstruction and Development, majority-controlled by the EU, the EU member states and the EIB, similarly announced the end of Russian investments a few days later. Both institutions had significant lending operations in the country.

Although the EU was more reluctant than the US to consider broad sanctions, US officials had worked closely for months with their counterparts in Brussels and European capitals to design targeted sectoral sanctions. This allowed the EU to move relatively quickly (for EU standards) to align with US sectoral sanctions in the financial, armaments, and energy sectors by the end of July. The sanctions restricted the ability of Russian state-owned banks to issue new medium and long-term debt or new equity in the EU's capital markets; the former was particularly impactful as those banks had relied on the EU to raise billions in initial public

---

[13] Jack Ewing and Peter Baker, "US and Europe Set to Toughen Russia Sanctions," *The New York Times*, July 28, 2014.

offerings and roughly half of their bond issuances.[14] The sanctions also prohibited the import or export of arms from or to Russia, banned the export of dual-use goods and technology for military use in Russia and restricted the export of certain energy-related equipment and technology to Russia. Specifically, export licenses of energy-related equipment and technology destined for deep water oil exploration and production, arctic oil exploration or production, and shale oil projects in Russia were banned. The EU measures steered clear of the natural gas sector because of the EU's high dependency on Russian gas supplies.

The United States took similar measures in the financial, energy, and armaments sectors in late July and early August. It restricted the ability of three major Russian financial institutions, including VTB, Russia's second-largest banking group, to raise new medium and long-term debt or new equity in the US capital markets. In addition, it blocked the assets of Russia's largest shipbuilding company. Most significantly, it imposed controls on the export of certain items for use in exploration or production from Russian deep water, Arctic offshore or shale projects with the potential to produce oil or gas.

The US and the EU took their most dramatic coordinated action on sanctions of the entire crisis in mid-September. Washington now prohibited all new debt financing over fourteen days to the five Russian banks it had already targeted and added Sberbank, Russia's largest bank, to the sanctions list. The EU announced similar measures against the five banks, except that it imposed a thirty-day threshold for new debt financing. The US also prohibited the provision of *any* goods, services (not including financial services), and technology for unconventional energy exploration to Gazprom as well as its subsidiary Gazpromneft, Lukoil, Surgutneftegas, and Rosneft which already had restricted access to the US capital market. The EU announced similar measures against the first three.

In addition to the sectoral sanctions against the Russian financial sector, the combined impact of the sanctions applying to debt capital raising and the sale of oil and gas equipment in the Russian energy sector was highly significant. Russia is the third largest producer of oil after Saudi Arabia and the United States. Sales from oil and gas accounted for roughly

---

[14] According to a European Commission assessment, Russian state-owned financial institutions raised $16.4 billion through IPOs in EU markets between 2004 and 2012, and in 2013 alone raised €7.5 billion in bonds.

two-thirds of total Russian exports and around half of the Russian federal budget in 2014–2015. The energy sanctions limited Russia's ability to compensate for depleting onshore Siberian deposits by developing offshore unconventional oil and gas exploration.

The subsequent sanctions announced by the US and the EU over the following months and even years of the crisis involved extensions and tightening of the pre-existing sectoral sanctions, additions of some firms and individuals (especially "cronies") to whom visa bans and asset freezes would apply, and more restrictive provisions regarding trade and investment in Crimea. But the bulk of the meaningful sectoral sanctions were already in place.

While US sanctions could have gone much farther, that would have risked a split in US-EU unity and therefore a huge victory for Russia. More severe US sanctions could have also resulted in a financial crisis in Russia, imposing pain especially on the most vulnerable members of its society, including pensioners and the poor. One of the key lessons of the transatlantic cooperation on Russia sanctions is that it is far better to moderate the sanctions than to risk such a split. Congressional legislation in 2019 that requires the Trump administration to sanction companies (including European ones) that help Gazprom complete the Nord Stream II natural gas pipeline has aggravated the transatlantic split.

It is hard to isolate the impact of the US and EU sanctions from other phenomena weighing on the Russian economy, especially the steep decline in oil prices during the crisis. But most estimates conclude that there was a significant impact and that it contributed to Russia's longest recession in decades. In 2016, the IMF estimated that US and EU sanctions were costing Russia 1.5% of its GDP per year, potentially rising to 9% over the long term. The sanctions certainly did contribute to rising inflation and government bond yields, significant capital outflows, and the inability of major state-owned firms to finance their operations. Sanctions also contributed to a steep fall in foreign direct investment, a worsening budget deficit that required running down reserves to finance government spending, the downgrading of Russian sovereign debt to barely over junk status and massive Russian Central Bank intervention in the currency markets to defend the depreciating rouble. Moreover, the sanctions may have set back Russia's efforts to modernize its military and its energy sector. According to an in-depth study conducted by the State Department's Office of the Chief Economist, moreover, the average sanctioned company lost about one-third of its operating revenue, over one-half of its asset value, and about one-third of its employees relative to their non-sanctioned peers.[15]

Putin and Lavrov must have been taken by surprise by the extent of the sanctions that were imposed. By the fall of 2014, their risk calculus must surely have changed. Sanctions on Russia clearly didn't lead Russia to withdraw from Crimea or to stop supporting the separatists in southeast Ukraine. But those were never realistic expectations to begin with. The sanctions may well have deterred more aggressive actions that would have broadened the conflict and caused far more destruction, injuries, and deaths. Russia did not use the 20,000 troops assembled near the Ukrainian border to press an overwhelming military advantage. Instead, following the imposition of the sectoral sanctions by the US and EU, Russia bowed to the increasing economic and diplomatic pressure by returning to the negotiating table. While falling far short of its objectives, the resulting Minsk I and II agreements helped to ensure that the armed conflict in Ukraine did not escalate further. The sanctions also had an important signaling effect, both for Russia and more widely for other autocratic regimes around the world, that the violation of basic norms of international law has consequences.

SANCTIONS ON IRAN

The United States and the European Union not only cooperated on Russian sanctions; their coordinated and extensive sanctions brought Teheran to the negotiating table to restrict Iran's nuclear program after many years of weaker US, United Nations and international sanctions had failed to do so. One can imagine a conversation between Mahmoud Ahmadinejad and a senior adviser on the eve of tougher US-EU sanctions in early 2012, when he was still President of Iran and the US and EU were starting to tighten their Iranian sanctions.

They might have thought that a united front between the US, EU, and key allies would be hard to put into place and nearly impossible to maintain over time. They might have doubted that the EU would agree to sanctions not authorized at the United Nations, where Russia would always wield a veto. They might have taken comfort, for example, from

---

[15] Daniel Ahn and Rodney Ludema, "Measuring Smartness: Understanding the Economic Impact of Targeted Sanctions," US Department of State Working Paper 2017-01, December 2016. https://www.state.gov/documents/organization/267590.pdf.

the fact that the EU and Iran had a strong trading relationship: the EU was Iran's largest trading partner, accounting for almost one-third of its total exports and around one quarter of its oil exports, with several EU member states (including Greece, Italy, and Spain) sourcing a significant percentage of their total oil imports from Iran.[16] Significant European commercial interests were also at stake. France's Total had defied US sanctions in 1997 when it signed a $2 billion contract with Iran's national oil company to develop the giant South Pars field in the Persian Gulf that holds the world's largest natural gas reserves. Iran owed Italy's ENI $2 billion for prior oil deliveries in early 2012.[17]

Ahmadinejad and his senior adviser might have hoped that Greece would be the Achilles heel of the EU's sanctions regime because of its economic weakness and reliance on very favorable financial terms for its oil purchases from Iran. They might have considered that history is littered with examples of failed oil embargoes. They might have reasoned that the international oil market is so large, so complex and features so many major purchasers (including China, India, and Turkey) and so many means of payment, including barter, that Iran would have options to sell its oil, either publicly or secretly outside the traditional banking system, even if the EU, Japan, and South Korea stopped buying (as the US had already done). And they might have believed that the EU and the US would not be willing to increase their dependency on Russia and Saudi oil or risk higher prices at the pump.

For these and other reasons, Ahmadinejad and his senior adviser might have concluded that there was little risk of continuing with Iran's covert nuclear weapons program and that it could perpetually procrastinate and pontificate rather than sit down at the negotiating table with the US and the EU. In 2012, Iran's Supreme Leader Grand Ayatollah Ali Khamenei confidently predicted that:

> other countries [aside from the US and Israel] have either been forced to go along with sanctions or they are just doing it as a ceremonial gesture...these conditions will not continue.[18]

---

[16] Greece, Italy, and Spain sourced 30%, 14%, and 12% of their oil imports from Iran, respectively.

[17] "L'Iran nega 2 miliardi $ all'Eni. «L'embargo non ci preoccupa, venderemo ad altri il nostro petrolio»," *Il Sole 24 Ore*, January 7, 2012. https://st.ilsole24ore.com/art/finanza-e-mercati/2012-01-07/liran-nega-miliardi-embargo-130448_PRN.shtml.

[18] "Leader Meets Government Officials," *Khamenei.ir*, July 24, 2012. http://english.khamenei.ir/news/1654/Leader-Meets-Government-Officials.

This proved to be a serious miscalculation: The US and EU implemented and renewed crippling sanctions during 2012–2015 that succeeded in bringing Teheran to the negotiating table. The negotiating process culminated in the so-called Joint Comprehensive Plan of Action (JCPOA) in July 2015 that subjected Iran's nuclear program to strict controls in return for a partial lifting of sanctions.

The coordinated US-EU sanctions program accomplished what US-led sanctions were unable to achieve on their own. While the three decades of US sanctions against Iran during 1979–2008 constrained Iranian growth and created inconveniences, the effects were hardly catastrophic and even partly beneficial to Iran as they had created transatlantic tensions and had led to import substitution, the development of domestic industries, and alternative trade relationships.

Starting in 2003, France, Germany, and the United Kingdom (the so-called P3) started negotiating with Iran on behalf of the European Union following the revelation that Iran had been secretly constructing a uranium enrichment facility and a heavy water production plant. Both of these were clear signs of an intention to develop the nuclear weapons capability that Teheran had long denied. The P3 offered numerous incentives to Iran, such as strengthened commercial ties, technical support in the energy sector (including for the civilian use of nuclear power), and EU support for Iran's accession to the WTO.

The negotiations appeared to be making headway in 2004 when Iran agreed to freeze nuclear fuel enrichment and reprocessing, as well as nuclear research and development, and to accept intrusive verification by the International Atomic Energy Agency (IAEA). But the negotiations collapsed in 2005 following the election of Ahmadinejad as President of Iran when it became clear that he would not accept any restrictions on Iran's nuclear program. His threats and offensive language, especially his denial of the Holocaust and threats to annihilate Israel, reinforced the widely held view that Iran posed a serious danger to world peace. In late 2005, the IAEA found Iran to have breached its non-proliferation obligations and submitted a full report to the UN Security Council to consider further action.

During 2006–2010, the Security Council became the most visible actor in the international efforts to curb Iran's nuclear program. By combining sanctions (including against Iranian banks for supporting terrorism) with diplomatic efforts, the United States put pressure on France, the

United Kingdom, Russia, and China, the other four permanent members of the Security Council, and Germany (the "P5+1") to get tough. During 2006–2010, the Security Council passed six resolutions, including four that applied sanctions, to curb Iran's nuclear program, especially fuel enrichment and reprocessing. Ahmedinejad's dubious re-election victory and violent suppression of pro-democracy protests in 2009 increased the pressure on the United Nations to act. The UN resolutions were critical, not only because of their content but especially because they provided international legal cover for the EU to implement its own sanctions.

While Russia cooperated in approving Security Council measures against Iran, it did so hesitantly and after extracting concessions. The cooperation may be explained in part by the "reset" of the strained US-Russian diplomatic relations sought by President Obama at the beginning of his term in 2009. New evidence that Iran's government had falsely denied the existence of secret uranium enrichment facilities in Iran, including one in a heavily fortified underground facility, may have also raised concerns in Moscow about the imminent specter of a nuclear-armed Iran and conflict in the Middle East. Most importantly, Iran's cheating on its IAEA commitments convinced the European members of the P5+1 that they must implement their own sanctions against Iran.

The Europeans' stronger stance contributed to the passage of a UN Security Council resolution on sanctions in 2010 that was more restrictive than the prior three: It subjected Iran's financial sector to international sanctions on the grounds that Iranian financial institutions handled oil profits that the government used for proliferation efforts. Although the four Security Council resolutions fell short of sweeping economic sanctions because of Russian and Chinese opposition, and therefore had little dissuasive effect, they did provide international legal justification for subsequent action. By 2011, the "reset" was already in trouble and Russia now openly questioned the intelligence assessments about Iran's nuclear capability, as well as the need for further sanctions. Once again, Moscow seemed more interested in supporting Iran as a counter-weight to US regional influence in the Middle East and the Caspian Sea.

Both the US and the EU made the UN a key focus of their Iran sanctions efforts during 2006–2010. They regularly added to the UN sanctions, including lists of sanctioned entities and individuals, as well as descriptions of goods, services, and technologies that could not be provided to Iran on the ground that they might promote its program to develop weapons of mass destruction. Both the US and the EU moved well beyond UN sanctions starting in 2010 after roughly a decade of failed negotiations with Iran to stop its nuclear weapons program.

Over the next few years, President Obama worked with Congress to pass sweeping legislation that tightened existing sanctions on Iran and implemented new ones. The legislation and related presidential executive orders restricted the importation of Iranian goods, targeted the Iranian shipping, shipbuilding, port, and automotive sectors, expanded the list of "dual use" goods with potential military or security applications subject to an export ban, and added many names to the list of sanctioned individuals. Over the next few years, the president issued executive orders that sanctioned Iranian entities and individuals for engaging in serious human rights abuses and punished firms for helping Iran evade US sanctions. The EU passed very similar legislation.

Until 2010, the EU refrained from imposing punitive sanctions on Iran that diverged from those of the UN. The collapse of the P3 talks, Ahmedinejad's rhetoric, the persistent evidence of Iranian lying to UN inspectors and the inadequate nature of UN sanctions changed that policy. Six major EU decisions followed in the next two years that implemented sweeping sanctions against Iran, many of them similar to what the United States was doing.

TARGETING IRAN'S FINANCIAL AND ENERGY SECTORS

The two areas of focus for the US and the EU were Iran's financial and energy sectors. The first objective was to isolate Iran from the international financial system, something that the United States was uniquely well qualified to achieve because of its predominant role in the global financial system. US legislation and executive orders prohibited any US firm or individual from conducting business with Iranian banks, including the Central Bank of Iran, and enabled the Treasury Department to block any foreign financial institution from accessing the US financial system if it processed a wide range of illicit transactions with Iran, such as facilitating Iranian petroleum exports. The Treasury Department designated Iran's entire financial sector as a "money laundering" operation and President Obama froze all the assets of the Iranian government and financial institutions in the United States. All US banks and most foreign banks stopped dealing with Iranian financial institutions altogether because the risk of being frozen out of the United States market was too high. In order to squeeze Iranian oil-related operations that sought to skirt the

US financial system, new US legislation sanctioned any entity transacting in Iranian Rials or providing precious metals to Iran.

A key part of US success in applying financial sanctions against Iran (and other countries) has been to convince private financial institutions to "self-censor," that is to overcomply with sanctions rather than run any risk of regulatory cost or reputational harm.

Although the US carries greater weight than the EU in the international financial system, the EU took a critically important financial measure in March 2012. The EU prohibited the Brussels-based SWIFT to continue providing specialized financial messaging services to EU-sanctioned Iranian banks. This step was highly significant as Iranian banks suddenly found themselves shut out of the world economy. At the time it took this step, SWIFT was handling daily payments estimated at more than $6 trillion. Nineteen banks and 25 affiliated institutions from Iran were exchanging millions of cross-border payments using SWIFT.

SWIFT's action to disconnect Iranian banks from its system was one of the biggest points of contention between the US and the EU. Initially, both EU member states and SWIFT's board of directors were wary of turning the financial messaging service into a sanctions tool. EU member states understood that disconnecting Iranian banks would deliver a serious blow to the lucrative business ties that many small and medium-sized enterprises had with their Iranian counterparts. Recognizing that such a step would be a major pressure point for Iran, however, the EU ultimately agreed to the US request.

The second target of US-EU sanctions was to squeeze Iran's energy sector that provided Teheran with 80% of its export earnings and two-thirds of its government revenues. US and EU measures further restricted investments in Iran's petroleum, petrochemical, and natural gas industries, including the supply to Iran of related goods, services, or technology. The measures also penalized any individual or firm providing underwriting, insurance, and reinsurance for goods, services, or projects related to those industries. South Korean and Indian refineries of Iranian crude oil that relied heavily on European and US insurance were impacted especially hard. As a result of these measures, Iran's energy sector was starved of funds for modernization. Few companies were prepared to insure, lease, or sell tankers to Iran and the Iranian tanker fleet became very expensive to operate. In order to exploit Iran's insufficient refinery capacity, the sanctions also targeted the sale of gasoline and refined petroleum products to Iran.

But one major area of EU-Iranian commercial relations remained untouched: the EU was still permitting the importation of Iranian oil and gas into the EU. On the eve of 2012, Iran was exporting 2.5 million barrels of crude oil per day, making Iran the world's third largest exporter, and was earning around $95 billion per year. These exports represented more than three-quarters of Iran's total export earnings and most of its government revenues. Europe was Iran's second largest customer, buying about one quarter of its oil exports.

Perhaps the most important moment in US-EU cooperation on Iran sanctions came in January 2012 when the EU agreed to ban the purchase, import, and transport of Iranian crude oil, petroleum products, and related finance and insurance. In order to provide struggling European economies reliant on Iranian oil imports, such as Greece, enough time to find alternative suppliers, the sanctions provided for a six-month grace period. The EU sanctions were subsequently tightened to include an embargo on importing Iranian natural gas and a prohibition on EU nationals and firms to transport or store Iranian oil or participate in the construction of Iranian oil tankers and cargo vessels. US-EU restrictions on the provision of any financial transactions related to Iran's oil exports, such as letters of credit, left the remaining importers with no choice but to use local currencies, gold, or other commodities.

Among the key reasons why the US and the EU were able to take coordinated action to squeeze Iran's oil exports is that Saudi Arabia agreed to replace the lost Iranian oil export volume, oil production from Iraq had increased substantially, and the United States was beginning to experience a massive expansion in oil production thanks in part to hydraulic fracturing and other technological advances.

The EU's oil embargo imposed severe economic pain on Iran. EU oil imports shrank from around 600,000 barrels per day in 2011 to essentially zero by the second half of 2012. At $95 per barrel, that equated to a loss of $21 billion per year for Iran. Moreover, the policy of the US to provide countries six-month renewable waivers from sanctions only if they steadily decreased oil imports from Iran was having an effect: Major non-EU importers of Iranian oil, especially China, India, South Korea, Japan, and Turkey decreased their imports over the course of 2012 by 550,000 barrels per day. The total impact of these measures was to deny Iran access to over $150 billion over the 2012–2015 period.[19] Even the proceeds of continuing sales to non-EU importers were locked up in offshore escrow accounts and could only be accessed for limited (humanitarian) purposes.

Not only were Iran's current oil export revenues impacted, but so were the future prospects of its oil industry. At the end of 2011, Iran's Oil Minister stated that Iran needed $300 billion in order to stem or reverse the steep decline in production rates in Iran's aging fields. Starved of export proceeds for maintenance and renewal of oil fields, as well as advanced technology to access more challenging deposits, Iran was unable to maintain oil production. In theory, Iran could have sought to substantially increase its natural gas production as it had barely started to do, despite having the second largest proven deposits in the world. But it lacked the means to do that as well. In short, Iran faced the prospect that sanctions would severely mortgage its energy future.

The economic impact of the joint US-EU sanctions on Iran became clear by the end of 2012. With its oil revenues diminished and its banks largely cut off from the global banking system, Iran's economy suffered. Central bank reserves plummeted, with holdings of foreign currency declining by about $100 billion. The economy shrank in 2012 (for the first time in two decades) by 7.4%, after modest growth in the preceding two years. By the spring of 2014, its economy was estimated to be 15–20% smaller than it would have been had it remained on its pre-2012 growth trajectory. The value of the Rial declined by over half against the dollar and inflation rose significantly, peaking at 40%, between January 2012 and January 2014. With the value of many assets diminishing so quickly, Iranians began to purchase and hoard dollars, gold, and even cars. By the fall of 2012, food prices for key staples had risen so much that they had become unaffordable for many Iranians. Public discontent with rising inflation and the inability of many companies to pay workers' wages boiled over into unusual public riots.

Even as the EU moved to tighten its sanction regime against Iran in 2012, the strength of that regime came under pressure in EU courts as sanctioned Iranian individuals and entities brought lawsuits before the EU courts in Luxembourg. The concern of the United States was so great

---

[19] Anthony Cordesman, Bryan Gold, and Chloe Coughlin-Schulte, "Iran—Sanctions, Energy, Arms Control, and Regime Change," Center for Strategic & International Studies, January 2014. https://csis-prod.s3.amazonaws.com/s3fs-public/legacy_files/files/publication/140122_Cordesman_IranSanctions_Web.pdf.

that I decided to attend oral arguments at the European Court of Justice (ECJ), the supreme court of the EU on matters of EU law, on September 10, 2014, in joined cases involving two Iranian banks on the sanctions list. The EU was appealing a decision by the lower EU General Court that had upheld the banks' challenge to their listings and the EU's freezing of their assets. Not only did I want to judge for myself the risks that the EU sanctions regime might buckle, but I also wanted to send a signal that Washington was keenly interested in the outcome.

The advocates of the EU withered under questioning from the judges who appeared unconvinced that the unclassified evidence put before the court proved the banks' involvement in Iran's nuclear and ballistic missile program. In my meetings with the President and Vice President of the Court that same day, I learned that there was no EU doctrine of broad deference to executive discretion in foreign policy matters, as in the United States. In those limited areas of the EU's common foreign and security policy where the EU courts had jurisdiction, such as sanctions policy, judicial review must ensure that EU fundamental rights (such as the right to a proper defense at trial) are observed. The Iranian banks subsequently won their appeals at the ECJ.

The EU sanctions regime against Iran did survive most of the legal challenges, however, for the same reasons noted above with regard to the sanctions regime against Russia, including a change in the EU courts' rules of procedure to allow the introduction of confidential information in court and a shift to designating individuals and entities based on their status rather than their actions.

Because of the accumulated and intensifying effects of the US and EU sanctions, Iran eventually bowed to the pressure and sat down with the P5+1 and the EU to sketch out an interim agreement limiting its nuclear program in return for a partial lifting of sanctions. In July 2015, that agreement took its final shape in the form of a Joint Comprehensive Plan of Action requiring Iran to accept international monitoring of its pledge never to "seek, develop or acquire" nuclear weapons. After the IAEA verified that Iran had fulfilled certain key promises, such as reducing its stockpiles of fissile material and centrifuges, the JCPOA entered into effect in January 2016.

Although US and EU sanctions unrelated to Iran's nuclear program (such as those related to its human rights violations) remained in place, the most punishing sanctions imposed on Iran were lifted as a result of the agreement: roughly half of Iran's $115 billion in foreign held reserves were unfrozen; Iran was now able to export oil once again and trade, including with Europe; foreign firms were free to invest in Iran's oil and gas industry; and Iran was reconnected to the global banking system, including to SWIFT.

The hard-fought transatlantic unity that was maintained during the sanctions program against Iran has been under strain because of the radically different policy of the Trump administration toward the JCPOA. President Trump has called it the "worse deal ever" despite the fact that the IAEA and even the State Department repeatedly confirmed that Iran was living up to its obligations. After unilaterally withdrawing the United States from the agreement in May 2018, the administration re-imposed all the nuclear proliferation-related sanctions that had been previously lifted and pressured SWIFT into disconnecting Iranian banks once again from the global banking system. European firms and individuals now face the threat of US secondary sanctions for engaging in business transactions with Iranian companies. The Trump administration also withdrew all waivers from previous sanctions on Iranian crude oil imports granted to Iran's largest customers. On its face, this strategy has borne fruit: Iran is shut off from world financial flows and is struggling to sell its oil (even if China appears prepared to keep buying in secret).

But there is no evidence that undermining the JCPOA is succeeding at making Iran into a more responsible international actor. On the contrary, it seems that Iran is determined to play even more of a spoiling role as it comes under pressure. Furthermore, US unilateralism regarding Iran sanctions has a long-term cost to the transatlantic alliance. The EU has dusted off its "blocking statute," first introduced to prevent secondary sanctions under the Clinton administration, that threatens European businesses with legal action if they comply with US sanctions. The statute is likely to have modest practical effect because most European companies, especially larger ones, will naturally privilege their continued access to the US market over access to the Iranian market. But it nonetheless serves a political purpose in signaling to Washington the EU's profound resentment at extraterritorial policies and in signaling to Teheran the EU's good-faith efforts to keep the JCPOA alive.

More seriously, the US decision to leverage its dominant role in international financial markets to unilaterally pressure SWIFT into disconnecting Iranian banks, despite EU objections, will fuel efforts by certain countries to find alternatives to SWIFT that are independent from the US banking system and are therefore immune to US sanctions. While such a system may well take time to implement, there can be little doubt that such an alternative will eventually be found.[20] Similarly, US threats against foreign banks that handle any payments related to transactions that are permissible under the JCPOA have led France, the United Kingdom and Germany, the three European signatories of the nuclear deal (along with the EU), to establish a barter system that is compliant with US sanctions. The system enables European and Iranian companies to do business with one another without exchanging payments directly. So far, its effect is more symbolic than practical as it has facilitated a tiny amount of humanitarian aid to Iran in semi-secrecy. But it may evolve into something more substantial. Both Russia and China have long sought to diminish their dependence on the dollar and the US financial system and are therefore eager to join.

It is worth noting that the new president of the European Commission, Ursula von der Leyen, has instructed Valdis Dombrovskis, commissioner in charge of deepening Economic and Monetary Union, as well as financial services, that he should work toward strengthening the role of the euro as a "strategic asset" and that he should help ensure Europe is "more resilient to extraterritorial sanctions" (especially from the United States).[21]

The Trump administration's approach of maximizing US short-term leverage, no matter what the cost to the transatlantic alliance and the long-term consequences for US foreign policy leverage, stands in stark contrast to the sanctions policies pursued under the Obama administration and prior administrations. One of the lessons from prior experience that guided the Obama administration's approach toward both the Russia and Iranian sanctions is that sanctions will only succeed long term if key allies are on board. The EU may not be the easiest ally to deal with because of its complexity, slow decision-making, and predilection for compromise, even in the face of aggression. Unlike the United States, it will never be willing to engage in secondary sanctions, even when it would

---

[20] According to one of the key architects of the financial sanctions against Iran, "With SWIFT's messaging format available for free, the system can be replicated outside the system that SWIFT manages. These imitations are not as efficient or secure as SWIFT's system, but they are workarounds that will no doubt evolve and improve over time." Juan Zarate, *Treasury's War: The Unleashing of a New Era of Financial Warfare* (Public Affairs, 2013).

[21] Mission Letter from Ursula von der Leyen to Valdis Dombrovskis, September 10, 2019. https://ec.europa.eu/commission/sites/beta-political/files/mission-letter-valdis-dombrovskis-2019_en.pdf.

have the power to do so. But its economic importance gives it unique assets that must not be overlooked.

The influence of the United States will only persist if it wisely husbands, but does not abuse, its unique power. As the *Financial Times* rightly put it:

> global banking is [not] a US fiefdom that Mr Trump can control without incurring significant costs. Imposing his will on Swift will increase the chances that alternative communication systems will gather support around the world…The US, by bulldozing its allies, will have weakened a key element in its own strategic arsenal.[22]

A related lesson from the sanctions against Russia and Iran is that transatlantic efforts can only be successful if they are rooted in mutual trust. If either the US or the EU believes that the other is not negotiating in good faith, then the chances of success are minimal. Trust must be carefully nurtured, and it can disappear in a flash. The United States should be playing the long game. As the old Zulu adage goes, "If you want to go quickly, go alone; if you want to go far, go together."

Acknowledgements The author would like to acknowledge the assistance of Ole Moehr in the preparation of this chapter.

---

[22] "Global Banking Is Not an American Fiefdom," *Financial Times*, May 18, 2018.

CHAPTER 8

Energy Security

On October 27, 2014, senior government and business representatives from Lithuania, the United States, and the European Union gathered at the port of Klaipeda, Lithuania, to welcome the arrival of a ship measuring three football fields in length. The vessel converts natural gas, supercooled and condensed into a liquid for safe storage and transport, back into the burnable gaseous variety.

The vessel, aptly named *The Independence*, is capable of re-gasifying approximately 4 billion cubic meters (bcm) of liquefied natural gas (LNG) per year, nearly twice Lithuania's total annual gas needs, and enables Lithuania to meet nearly all gas demand in neighboring Latvia and Estonia. Whereas Lithuania's consumption of natural gas was satisfied entirely by Russian imports before 2014, the vessel now enables Lithuania to free itself entirely from these imports because LNG trades flexibly and globally.[1] Once an "energy island" cut off from the intra-European gas supplies other than East-West flows from Russia, the Baltic states can now buy energy from multiple suppliers and through different routes. Given Moscow's history of price gouging vulnerable customers and using gas as a political weapon to promote its political objectives in Europe, this change of outlook is highly significant.

Years before the delivery of *The Independence* the United States had helped Lithuania finance technical preparations for a LNG facility that

---

[1] The European Commission, 2014 Country Report on Lithuania. https://ec.europa.eu/energy/sites/ener/files/documents/2014_countryreports_lithuania.pdf.

would increase the country's sources of energy supply. The significant up-front costs to build the onshore infrastructure were partly financed by loans from the European Investment Bank and Lithuanian government guarantees approved by the European Commission. Significant annual payments are required to lease and operate the vessel until Lithuania acquires it in 2024. But the project paid for itself in the first year when Gazprom quickly responded to Lithuania's purchase of LNG from Norway with a 23% discount on future supplies. Most significantly, the terminal cut in half Gazprom's share of Lithuania's gas market. This share has been declining ever since the project's completion as the terminal has taken LNG shipments from around the world, including the United States.

The inauguration of *The Independence* in Klaipeda is a neat illustration of how the European Union and the United States have worked together to reduce European energy insecurity.

Neither Europe nor the United States is a stranger, of course, to the perils of energy insecurity. The oil embargo of 1973–1974, imposed by the Arab members of the Organization of Petroleum Exporting Countries against the United States and several European countries that supported Israel during the Arab-Israeli War, elevated the issue of energy supply to a fundamental foreign and security policy concern on both sides of the Atlantic.

The oil embargo, resulting in a fourfold price increase for oil, led the US and Europe to create the International Energy Agency (IEA) as part of the Organization for Economic Cooperation and Development. The original focus of the agency was to promote cooperation in securing the energy supplies of industrialized nations. One early action toward that end was to create a regime for oil stockpiling, burden-sharing mechanisms in case of supply-side shocks, and regular mutual consultations on energy security.

While the oil embargo was a wake-up call, efforts to improve European energy security have largely focused on ensuring secure supplies of gas rather than oil. The principal reason for this is that oil is a widely traded commodity in global spot markets in which prices are fixed by the free market interplay of supply and demand. It can be imported into Europe from many sources and through many means of delivery. By contrast, gas has been mainly sourced from a few suppliers (especially Russia, Norway, and Algeria) through long-term bilateral contracts and almost exclusively through fixed infrastructure (mostly pipelines) that require years and billions of euros to build. Although Russia sells about four times more oil than gas to Europe in value terms, it has much less leverage to withhold supplies or to set arbitrarily high prices in the oil market. Even in the relatively rare instances in which Russia has disrupted oil supplies, such as when it shut down the Brotherhood pipeline in 2007 over a pricing dispute with Belarus, downstream consumers in Europe have been largely unaffected because they could quickly access alternative supplies elsewhere.

RUSSIA'S USE OF ENERGY AS A WEAPON

Russia frequently insists that it is a dependable energy supplier. To borrow a line from Shakespeare's *Hamlet*, "Methinks the lady doth protest too much." The reality is that Russia has a well-established track record of using gas exports as a tool, sometimes even as a weapon, to promote foreign policy objectives. Studies differ in their estimates about how often that has occurred. One has identified 15 instances in which Russia has exploited its power of price and/or physical delivery of gas (and occasionally oil) to pressure former Soviet states and countries in Central and Eastern Europe, especially in the middle of political tensions; countries that have complied with Russia's foreign policy agenda have benefited, moreover, from lower prices than those that have not. Another study has concluded that Russia has cut off gas (and occasionally oil) exports on at least 40 occasions between 2000 and 2006 alone.[2]

The use of the energy weapon has differed widely. For example, Russia imposed an oil and gas embargo on the Baltic states in the early 1990s in an effort to crush their independence movements. After Russia cut off gas supplies to Ukraine in 1993, then-President Leonid Kuchma agreed to allow Russia to retain most of the Black Sea naval fleet in return for the cancelation of debt related to gas imports. More recent examples that

---

[2] Gabriel Collins, "Russia's Use of the Energy Weapon in Europe," Baker Institute for Public Policy, Issue Brief, July 18, 2017. https://www.bakerinstitute.org/media/files/files/ac785a2b/BI-Brief-071817-CES_Russia1.pdf. Agnia Grigas, "Legacies, Coercion and Soft Power: Russian Influence in the Baltic States," Chatham House Briefing Paper, August 2012. Grigas cites Robert L. Larsson, Russia's Energy Policy: Security Dimensions and Russia's Reliability as an Energy Supplier, Swedish Defence Research Agency, March 2006. https://www.chathamhouse.org/sites/default/files/public/Research/Russia%20and%20Eurasia/0812bp_grigas.pdf.

have served to propel energy security to the very top of Europe's foreign policy concerns are Russia's interruption of gas supplies to Ukraine in 2006, 2009, and 2014—all strategically leveraging the winter months when the maximum pain could be inflicted.

On January 1, 2006, Gazprom reduced gas shipments to Ukraine after months of clashing with Naftogaz, Ukraine's national oil and gas company, over the terms of gas supply and transit. Consumers of Russian gas further west in central Europe suffered lower supplies until Gazprom turned the spigot back on. While the disruption lasted only one day and available storage capacities could easily make up for the shortfall, the shot across the bow caused alarm. The interruption of gas supplies in January 2009, also over debt and contract terms, was far more serious as it lasted three weeks and resulted in a 20% decline in the gas reserves of the EU. Eighteen EU countries lost their Russian gas supplies entirely. In Ukraine, Slovakia, Romania, Bulgaria, and several Balkan states that had no or few other alternatives of gas supply, citizens suffered and even died in underheated apartments. The domino effect on downstream consumers of gas transiting Ukraine extended into France and southeastern Europe. These two crises made painfully clear to the EU just how important it is to ensure greater diversification of suppliers and supply routes, increased interconnection among Europe's network of gas pipelines, as well as better and more coordinated efforts to plan for and respond to similar events.

Russia continued to use the gas weapon in December 2013 as a tool to ensure that Ukraine remained within the Russian sphere of influence. One of the main reasons why Ukrainian President Viktor Yanukovych abruptly changed his mind about signing an association agreement with the EU is that Vladimir Putin offered to have Gazprom supply Ukraine with gas at a one-third price discount. When Yanukovych was ousted and Ukraine veered back toward the EU as a result of the popular protests, Putin withdrew the offer. Following its annexation of Crimea and occupation of the Donbas through Russian-backed militants, Moscow canceled an agreement reached with Ukraine in 2010 extending Russia's lease on the Sevastopol naval base in return for discounted Russian gas exports. As a result, Kyiv faced a near doubling of Russian gas prices and an additional drain of billions of euros. In addition, Moscow demanded the immediate repayment of Ukraine's substantial debts related to gas imports that had accumulated over many years. The termination of coal deliveries from Donbas to the rest of Ukraine and the loss of gas fields in the northern Black Sea aggravated the energy shock to an economy already suffering from the conflict. The EU's efforts at mediating a settlement between Ukraine and Russia relating to gas supplies failed in mid-June when Moscow once again turned the spigot off.

The immediate impact of the crisis was limited because Ukrainian gas reserves were high (due to the unseasonably warm winter of the prior year) and Ukrainian national gas production was sufficient to cover demand during the summer months. It was clear, however, that Ukraine would face a crisis during the critical winter months and peak heating season. EU member states, coordinated by the European Commission, raced during the normally sacrosanct summer holidays to conduct stress tests to determine national levels of vulnerability and appropriate responses to continued gas supply disruptions. EU mediation finally succeeded at the end of October due in large part to the able diplomacy of Günther Oettinger, the EU's commissioner responsible for energy. Thanks to the EU's agreement to act as a guarantor of Ukraine's commitments, the deal resulted in a compromise between the draconian price increase demanded by Russia and the low price sought by Ukraine, as well as a rescheduling of Ukrainian debt for past supplies.

Russia's depiction of the conflict as a mere commercial dispute was clearly false. Russia had routinely shown forbearance toward Ukraine for past unsettled debts and had offered low prices in return for political advantages, before radically changing tack when those advantages were no longer offered. Russia's use of energy-related levers, such as changes in gas price and/or supply, in response to geopolitical events (such as those in Ukraine), fatally undermined Moscow's claim to be a reliable energy partner. Russia's claim to uphold international legal norms was also undermined when Gazprom ignored an international arbitration court's ruling largely in favor of Naftogaz in February 2018 and cut gas deliveries to Ukraine once again.

The Diverging Prospects of US and European Energy Markets

While Europe's dependence on Russian energy is in large part a natural result of its geographical location and the convenience of purchasing cheap gas from a neighbor, it also reflects geological factors and policy choices.

European energy production has been falling sharply due to a gradual depletion in oil and gas reserves. The decline in gas production has been steep, especially in the North Sea, and in the Netherlands, both of which have served as important alternatives to Russian gas. The Dutch government has announced that production from the giant Groningen onshore field, Europe's largest gas field, will end by 2026 because of environmental and safety concerns.

Europe's technically recoverable shale gas reserves, concentrated in Poland, France, and Ukraine, are nearly as large as those in the United States and could account for roughly one-tenth of global reserves. But many factors are holding back the exploitation of these reserves. The EU does not have common policies in place regarding hydraulic fracturing or "fracking," aside from non-binding recommendations of the European Commission about "minimum principles" applying to exploration and production. Fracking is a process of injecting liquid, often water with a mixture of chemicals, at high pressure into subterranean rocks to force open existing fissures.

Numerous EU member states ban or severely limit fracking. Even where it is permitted, accessing the shale reserves is far more complicated than in the United States due, in large part, to higher population density, weaker public support, less favorable geological conditions, and property rights over sub-surface minerals that limit incentives for investment. Shale gas (and oil) production in Europe will only make a modest contribution, therefore, to offset declining domestic production.

Natural gas and oil account for about 23% and 36%, respectively, of the EU's total energy needs. While their combined share has been declining and will continue to decline over coming years, it is nonetheless projected to remain high at roughly 50% for the next decade. The EU's dependency on imported oil is projected to rise slightly to 90% (from 87%) and on imported gas to 80% (from 65%) over the same period. While liquidity of global oil markets reduces the EU's vulnerability to oil supply disruptions, the combination of the increasing use of natural gas in the energy mix, increased import dependency, and the legacy of fixed pipeline infrastructure as the dominant means of supply present a significant challenge.

That is particularly the case because Russia supplies 40% of the EU's natural gas imports, well ahead of Norway and Algeria, and will probably supply even more in the coming years. While imports of LNG from Qatar, Algeria, Nigeria, Australia, and the United States are growing, these will continue to account for a small share of natural gas consumption. Russian gas can and even should continue to play an important role in European energy supplies. But the EU and the US share the conviction that it should do so only as part of a diversified energy mix.

Europe has also been hit by several energy-related developments that have undermined the competitiveness of European industry. Climate change policies, including high feed-in tariffs to promote renewable energy, resulted in higher energy costs. Until relatively recently, continental European gas prices in long-term contracts remained linked to the price of oil (rather than to pricing at gas hubs as is common today) and therefore did not decline with the world supply glut of gas. The US shale revolution, moreover, significantly reduced the cost of manufacturing, drew investments away from Europe to the US, and damaged European competitiveness.

On top of this challenging energy outlook, the EU faces the problem that its member states have rather diverging perceptions about what should be done to improve energy security. Many have pursued largely national policies, with little regard for pan-European interests and the need for solidarity.

Until recently, the United Kingdom has appeared little interested in EU energy policy as it exploited its oil and gas reserves from the North Sea. France has been a champion of nuclear power, in contrast to many other member states. Ignoring objections from the EU and fellow member states, Hungary recently awarded Rosatom, a Russian state-owned power conglomerate, a contract to build and provide nuclear fuel to two Russian-designed reactors without public tender and financed the purchase nearly entirely with a loan from Vnesheconombank, a Russian state-owned development bank. Germany has shown an unparalleled degree of comfort in the EU with its dependency on gas imports from Russia. Its decision to terminate by 2022 the use of nuclear power, widely considered an ideal green energy bridge to a renewable energy future, will increase its reliance on hydrocarbons. And Germany's recent decision to achieve "carbon neutrality" (a net zero carbon footprint) by 2050, a key focus of its increasingly powerful Green Party, will require a very significant reduction in the use of dirty lignite coal that accounts for roughly one-third of its energy needs. Most EU member states have supported the carbon neutrality goal, but several others (especially Poland) that have relied on cheap coal to power their electricity generation may resist.

The energy security landscape in the United States during the past decade has evolved in a dramatically different direction to that in the EU. The US has experienced a revolution that boosted domestic energy production, significantly reduced oil and gas imports, and lowered energy-related costs of manufacturing.

The boom in US domestic oil production in the past decade has been remarkable: From 5.5 million barrels per day in 2011 to 12.5 million barrels per day in 2019, an increase that exceeds the annual oil production of Kuwait and the United Arab Emirates combined. As a result, US net oil imports (imports minus exports) as a percentage of total consumption have fallen (as of 2018) from about two-thirds to about 11%, the lowest percentage since 1957. Net imports have fallen to just over 2 million barrels per day. These dramatic shifts led the United States in 2015 to repeal its 40-year-old crude oil export ban and have resulted in downward pressure on global oil prices and OPEC's diminished influence.

A similarly dramatic evolution occurred in the US natural gas market. In 2005, the United States was the world's largest importer of natural gas, relying on imports for 16% of its consumption. According to government projections that year, import volumes would nearly double in the next decade, requiring the construction of many LNG import terminals. Yet within that period natural gas production rose by 50% and imports had dramatically *fallen*. By 2015 net imports had shrunk to only 5% of total consumption and almost none of those imports came from LNG. The idle import terminals were reconfigured to serve as export terminals. Just a few years later, in 2017, the United States became a net natural gas exporter for the first time in sixty years.

The change in US oil and gas fortunes was due principally to three technological innovations: more accurate seismic imaging that provides companies better information about where to drill; better horizontal drilling, a practice that involves drilling in different directions to access more of the reservoir; and cost effective, large-scale fracking.

The United States has experienced a boom in the past decade in the extraction of oil and gas from shale rock formations through fracking. The boom has been due to many factors. Shale formations are plentiful and located in sparsely populated areas that are easy to access. Moreover, the majority of wells are drilled on private land where consent is easy to obtain. Other factors include advanced drilling technology and conducive environmental and tax legislation. As of 2019 shale oil production represented roughly one-half of total US oil production and shale gas production represented roughly two-thirds of total US natural gas production.[3]

US Support for European Energy Security

Improving energy security in the United States over the past decade has deepened its concerns about European energy *insecurity*. These concerns are not new. Alarmed about growing European reliance on Soviet energy supplies, for example, the Reagan administration imposed and then, under significant pressure from European allies, ultimately lifted sanctions in 1982 on European companies participating in the construction of an oil pipeline linking Siberia to European markets. US concern about European energy insecurity has also been marked by cooperation with Europe. In the late 1990s and early 2000s, for example, the US and the EU promoted the diversification of European energy supplies by supporting the Baku–Tbilisi–Ceyhan oil pipeline bringing Azeri crude to European markets.

Why should the United States care about whether European energy insecurity? The reason is that energy insecurity translates into political and economic insecurity. When Europe is energy insecure, the United States, not just Europe, bears the consequences. If European energy consumers lose their access to stable and affordable energy supplies, they may reduce their investments and hire fewer workers, curbing economic growth. That would have an indirect but important impact on US investment in and exports to Europe, both of which are important contributors to the US economy. Moreover, European energy security is intrinsically tied to Europe's stability. A Europe that is energy insecure lives in the perpetual fear of supply interruptions or politically motivated price changes and would therefore be exposed to blackmail, manipulation or at least pressure to conform to the demands of dominant energy suppliers. Specifically, weakness in standing up to Russian pressure could divide and weaken NATO and the EU, both essential partners of the United States

[3] See the US Energy Information Administration website: https://www.eia.gov/tools/faqs/faq.php?id=847&t=6 (shale oil); https://www.eia.gov/tools/faqs/faq.php?id=907&t=8 (shale gas); and https://www.eia.gov/outlooks/aeo/data/browser/ (projections).

in addressing military, political, and economic issues of regional and even global significance.

Some European countries were either completely dependent (in the case of the Baltic states and Finland) or highly dependent (in the case of Austria, Slovakia, the Czech Republic, and Bulgaria) on Russian gas supplies when the Crimean crisis broke out. In some cases, those supplies were not only the only available source of imports but also represented a significant share of total energy consumption. Losing energy imports representing 10–20% of energy consumption literally overnight would cause serious economic and social problems. Fear of that risk obviously clouds a country's independent policy-making.

For example, when US diplomats tried to convince EU member states to join the tough US-EU sanctions regime against Russia in 2014, the Baltic states and Poland offered robust support despite their vulnerability to reduced Russian gas supplies, while most of the other member states were lukewarm. Amos Hochstein, a friend and former colleague when he served as the State Department's most senior executive on energy issues during President Obama's second term, has described the lukewarm reaction he got from several heads of state as follows:

> How can I talk about sanctions on Russia after Crimea if they turn off the heat in the dead of winter? That's not an argument in the abstract...look at Ukraine. They did it in '09; they did it in '14. Why would they not do it to me? And what are my alternatives? So...if the United States wants my country's support on these issues that have nothing to do with energy, you're going to have to help me figure this out. I cannot be that victim.[4]

Those heads of state were, of course, right to be concerned. Russia's decisions to cut off gas supplies to Ukraine were wake-up calls for the United States as well. They dramatically increased the attention that US diplomacy reserved to energy issues. Under Secretary Clinton, several small units at the State Department that dealt with energy affairs were merged into a full-fledged Bureau of Energy Resources led by an Assistant Secretary. That bureau would, within several years, be staffed with about one hundred professionals around the world. The 2015 National Security Strategy, the last one issued by the Obama administration, reflects

---

[4] Speech at the 2nd Washington Oil and Gas Forum, Cosmos Club, June 9, 2016. https://2009-2017.state.gov/e/enr/rls/258436.htm.

the conviction that not only the nation's energy security, but that of our allies as well, is a key component of national security.

The Russian decisions to cut off gas to Ukraine were also important motivations behind the creation by the US and the EU of an Energy Council in 2009. The objective of the council was to ensure a dedicated bilateral channel of communications between high-level officials on transatlantic energy cooperation, especially related to European energy security. While energy had naturally featured in their relations before that time, both sides felt in light of geopolitical events that energy should be treated separately as a high-profile issue with regular follow-up.

The council meetings, held annually under the Obama administration (but less frequently during President Trump's term), bring the US secretaries of state and energy together with their numerous EU counterparts (the High Representative for Foreign Affairs, the Vice President of the European Commission in charge of Energy Union, the Commissioner for Climate Action and Energy and a representative of the rotating EU presidency) to discuss a wide range of topics. For example, the council has often discussed the promotion of transparent and secure global energy markets, including through the diversification of energy sources, regulatory cooperation to encourage efficient and sustainable energy use and the identification of priorities to promote research into clean energy technology. The meetings of the principals are supplemented by regular interaction by senior officials in four working groups. Neither the US nor the EU has a similar energy council with any other country.

The significance of the council is not captured by the rather formalistic meetings or the turgid communiqués that follow them. The council shines a spotlight on energy issues of common concern, especially European energy security. It has served as an important forum for the US and the EU to track the EU's progress toward creating an Energy Union, consisting of common policies to diversify fuel sources, energy supplies, and import routes and aimed at creating an integrated, open, and competitive internal energy market based on non-discriminatory free market rules.

While the Trump administration has continued the Obama administration's focus on European energy diversification, this appears to be motivated principally by the desire to exploit the economic potential of plentiful US LNG and reduce the trade deficit with Europe, rather than as a means for Europe to diversify its energy supplies for its own good. The main focus of the 2019 US-EU Energy Council was to host a business forum of more than 500 energy executives to discuss the future of US LNG supplies to Europe.[5]

In order to avoid the imposition of US car import duties, the EU has been eager to show that it is a good customer for US energy exports. At a meeting with President Trump in July 2018, President Juncker stated that the EU intended to increase its purchases of LNG from the United States significantly. The decision to buy LNG in Europe lies in the hands of private parties and not the European Commission, of course. Nonetheless, the European Commission has trumpeted the fact that EU purchases of LNG following the meeting appear to be on a steeper upward trajectory than they were before the meeting.

THE VISION OF AN ENERGY UNION

A few weeks after my arrival in Brussels in March 2014, Donald Tusk, then Poland's Prime Minister, penned a deliberately provocative article in the *Financial Times* proposing a European Energy Union that would reduce Russia's "stranglehold" on Europe's energy.[6] The overwhelming focus of the article on energy security reflected the author's Polish perspective, shared by the overwhelming majority of the Central and Eastern European member states that joined the EU in 2004 and 2007. Those states felt that the EU's energy policy had prioritized climate policies over energy security. As these states had long felt vulnerable to Russia because of their dependence on imported Russian gas, they insisted that at least equal attention should be paid to energy security.

Tusk argued for a more coordinated European approach to Russia in the energy sector. The argument was not new, of course. Partly due to the Russian cutoff in gas supplies to Ukraine in early 2006, the European Commission's first significant policy paper on energy security published that year had made the same argument. Not enough had been done, however. Even the Commission's efforts to compel member states to be

---

[5] Richard Morningstar, Andras Simonyi, Olga Khakova, and Irina Markina, "European Energy Security and Transatlantic Cooperation: A Current Assessment," Atlantic Council Issue Brief, June 2019. https://www.atlanticcouncil.org/images/publications/European_Energy_Security_and_Transatlantic_Cooperation.pdf.

[6] Donald Tusk, "A United Europe Can End Russia's Energy Stranglehold," *Financial Times*, April 21, 2014. https://www.ft.com/content/91508464-c661-11e3-ba0e-00144feabdc0.

more transparent about their energy supply contracts with Russia had run into resistance and had demonstrated that many of those contracts were incompatible with EU law.

Perhaps the most provocative of Tusk's ideas was his proposal to centralize EU gas purchases through a single buyer to offset Russia's power as Europe's predominant gas supplier. Tusk pointed out that the EU member states already purchase uranium for their nuclear power plants through the European Atomic Energy Community. The idea was problematic for several reasons, however. Establishing a buyer cartel in response to a supplier quasi-monopoly is not compatible with the EU's guiding principle that the internal market should be governed by free competition and free movement of goods and services. It was also unclear whether the idea would apply to non-Russian gas suppliers or whether a buyer cartel would be effective when the buyers had few supply alternatives.

Tusk's article barely mentioned Gazprom, Russia's energy behemoth that produces about 500 bcm of natural gas per year (around 12% of global gas output) and exports about 40% of that to Europe. State-owned since 2005, Gazprom is Russia's largest energy-exporting company and underwrites about 13% of the state budget, thereby enabling many of the Kremlin's activities that are antithetical to the interests of the EU and the United States. The company was very much at the core of Tusk's concerns, however, because it was the main reason why Russia exercised a "stranglehold" over EU energy as the dominant, and sometimes exclusive, supplier. In April 2015, after a four-year investigation into Gazprom, the European Commission's anti-trust department reached its provisional conclusion that the firm was abusing its dominant position in breach of EU law by pursuing a strategy of partitioning gas markets along national borders in eight Central and Eastern European EU member states.

I had hoped during my term as ambassador to see the EU impose fines on Gazprom of 10% of its €100 billion revenues, as the EU had the power to do. After all, the European Commission had been levying multi-billion euro fines on many US tech firms, such as Google, Intel, and Qualcomm, for alleged abuses of their dominance. There was no question that for years Gazprom had forced vulnerable gas customers to pay billions more than they should have. Although the European Commission disappointingly decided to settle the case in 2018 without imposing a fine, the terms of the settlement eliminated some of the key tools Gazprom had used to exercise its stranglehold. For example, Gazprom accepted binding obligations to remove restrictions preventing customers from re-selling gas across borders; to facilitate gas flows to and from parts of Central and Eastern Europe that remained isolated from other member states due to the lack of interconnectors; and to offer customers prices that reflect benchmarks at European gas hubs rather than reference higher oil indexes.[7]

Gazprom has also suffered a defeat at the WTO in its efforts to fragment European gas markets and gouge European consumers. In August 2018, a WTO panel unanimously rejected Russia's complaint that EU gas market rules in its Third Energy Package (TEP) were discriminatory and broke WTO law.

Many of the ideas in the Tusk article were fleshed out in the EU's first energy security strategy paper of May 2014 and then by the legislative program of the EU's Energy Union launched under the Juncker Commission in November. The objective of the Energy Union is ambitious: to replace a fragmented European energy landscape characterized by uncoordinated national policies and market barriers with a more centralized internal energy market where energy flows freely. Since his appointment in December 2014 as president of the EU Council, Tusk was able to play a key role in ensuring that energy security remained a top priority of the EU during his five years in office.

The EU's Energy Union has been broader than Tusk's primary focus on energy security. It has also included measures to create a fully integrated internal energy market, moderate energy demand by promoting energy efficiency (above all in the transport and building sectors), reduce the reliance on fossil fuels, lower emissions, and stimulate research, innovation, and competitiveness in low-carbon technologies.

The Energy Union builds on the prior so-called TEP, implemented in 2011, that provides the core legal architecture governing the EU's internal energy market in gas and electricity. In addition to providing detailed rules, the TEP established independent national regulatory authorities to implement them and serve as watchdogs over the national energy markets.

---

[7] "Antitrust: Commission imposes binding obligations on Gazprom to enable free flow of gas at competitive prices in Central and Eastern European gas markets," European Commission Press Release, May 24, 2018. https://ec.europa.eu/commission/presscorner/detail/en/IP_18_3921.

The TEP has liberalized and promoted competition in the energy sector. It includes, for example, the requirement to separate energy supply and generation from the operation of transmission networks. If a single company operates a transmission network and generates or sells energy at the same time, it is likely to have an incentive to obstruct competitors' access to infrastructure, thereby preventing fair competition in the market and leading to higher prices for consumers. TEP regulation therefore requires network operators (with a few exceptions) to grant energy companies non-discriminatory access to their infrastructure. That means that they must offer the same service to different users under identical conditions. At the urging of the United States, the EU also included in the TEP a prohibition of so-called destination clauses that prevent customers of gas suppliers from re-selling to customers in other countries. This proved to be of crucial significance in enabling Slovakia, Hungary, and Poland to argue that the "destination clauses" in Gazprom's supply contracts could not legally prevent them from re-selling gas to Ukraine in 2009.

The TEP has also resulted in other important achievements, such as "network codes" that enhance cross-border cooperation among firms operating pipelines and grids. These codes form a legally binding set of common technical and commercial rules governing access to and use of European energy networks. Moreover, it has resulted in rules to promote open and fair retail markets by protecting the rights of European energy consumers. Suppliers are required to assume pro-consumer obligations relating to transparent billing, the contents of supply contracts, the length of time that consumer data may be retained, and the ability of consumers to switch suppliers quickly and easily.

Although the Energy Union has been broader in scope than what Tusk proposed, several of his key proposals regarding energy security have been implemented. For example, he advocated a phased approach toward having EU member states jointly negotiate energy contracts with Russia. The first step would be to strip "secret and market-distorting clauses" from existing supply contracts before implementing a template for all new gas contracts and then giving the European Commission a role in all new contract negotiations. EU member states were not prepared, however, to centralize power with the European Commission over bilateral inter-governmental energy supply contracts. Nonetheless, it was clearly unsatisfactory that existing rules only allowed the European Commission to review such contracts *after their signing* and didn't give it the power to address their numerous deficiencies with EU law. Amended rules implemented in 2017 required member states to submit new contracts to tougher scrutiny *before their signing* to ensure that they are both compatible with EU law and not harmful to the EU's energy security.

The Tusk article also argued that in countries most vulnerable to energy supply cutoffs the EU should provide three-quarters of the financing needed to build critical infrastructure, such as gas links and storage capacity. While Tusk's proposed level of direct EU subsidy for national energy infrastructure has not been achieved, the EU has provided significant financial assistance. Energy infrastructure projects that have been identified as "projects of common interest" by the European Commission and essential to the completion of the European internal energy market are eligible for financial support from the Connecting Europe Facility (CEF), an EU fund for pan-European infrastructure investments. The CEF has earmarked roughly €5 billion during 2014–2020 for energy-related projects, a rather modest amount compared to the €200 billion required according to European Commission estimates. However, roughly a quarter of the €315 billion European Fund for Strategic Investments, an initiative launched in 2015 by the European Commission and the European Investment Bank to mobilize private financing for critical cross-border infrastructure, has also flowed to the energy sector. Thanks to this infrastructure, the European Commission projects that all EU member states, except for Malta and Cyprus, will have access to three sources of gas by 2022.

Other proposals in the Tusk article have been fleshed out as part of the EU's Energy Union. The EU has promoted the coordination among member states of their national energy policies, including with regard to contingency planning and risk assessments, and has improved the ability of the EU to speak with one voice on international energy policy matters. It has helped to implement "solidarity" mechanisms that boost emergency fuel reserves and guarantee intra-EU deliveries of alternative fuel to vulnerable consumers (such as hospitals and schools) in member states whose energy supplies are disrupted.

Tusk also emphasized the importance of reaching out to partners outside of Europe to provide new sources of energy. EU member states, supported by financing and technical assistance from the European Commission, as well as important diplomatic support from the United States, have made substantial strides to achieve this objective.

Diversifying Energy Supplies with LNG

Lithuania hasn't been the only European country wishing to reduce its energy dependency on Russian gas. Thanks to about €220 million in EU funds, Poland opened an LNG terminal in 2015 at Świnoujście, not far from Szczecin, a city made famous by British Prime Minister Winston Churchill in 1946 when he proclaimed that "From Stettin in the Baltic to Trieste in the Adriatic, an iron curtain has descended across the Continent." After an extension in 2019, again financed largely with €120 million in EU funds, the terminal has a regasification capacity of 7.5 bcm per year, almost half of the country's total natural gas consumption. Before the terminal was constructed Poland was importing about two-thirds of its natural gas from Russia.

As natural gas has represented a relatively small percentage of its total energy consumption, Poland was not as exposed as Lithuania to the risk of Russian energy blackmail. But Poland was sufficiently concerned, especially after Russia's annexation of Crimea, to spend €1 billion on the terminal. Over the past few years, it has been signing long-term LNG purchase agreements with exporters from the US, Norway, and Qatar. These supplies, supplemented by gas from an EU-financed pipeline under the Baltic sea linking Poland to Norway's gas fields, may enable Poland to cease imports from Gazprom when its agreement comes up for renewal in 2022.

Not far from the Iron Curtain's terminus in Trieste, Croatia is expecting to complete a floating LNG terminal with a capacity of 2.6 bcm per year on the northern Adriatic island of Krk by 2021 (if sufficient downstream purchase agreements can be secured). That represents most of Croatia's total consumption of gas, roughly 70% of which used to be imported from Russia. Both the EU and the United States have been eagerly promoting this project for many years with technical assistance, diplomatic engagement and (in the case of the EU) about €120 million in financing. Not only would the project free Croatia from dependency on Russia, it would also provide landlocked countries in Southeastern Europe with alternative sources of gas.

Even Germany, which has not had the same concerns about relying on imported gas from Russia, is planning to complete by 2022 two LNG facilities, one as an onshore terminal at Brunsbüttel on the Elbe River with a capacity of 5–8 bcm per year and the other as a floating vessel (like *The Independence*) at Germany's only deepwater port in Wilhelmshaven with a capacity of 10 bcm. Together those terminals represent a regasification capacity that is a sizeable chunk of the gas that Germany imports from Russia per year.

As a result of all this construction of LNG terminals, the EU is expected to have by 2022 a total regasification capacity of around 232 bcm, more than half of the total EU imports of natural gas in 2018. The desire of some EU member states, especially in Central and Eastern Europe and the Balkans, to build new LNG terminals may appear puzzling when existing terminals in Europe have been operating (as of 2019) at about 30% of their capacity. The high level of spare capacity has reflected the stagnant demand for natural gas in the early 2000s, partly due to cheap coal and subsidized renewables, as well higher prices for LNG in Asia that have drawn LNG exports away from Europe. The reason for the construction of new terminals is that many of the existing terminals have been located (until recently) in western and southern Europe, especially Spain, France, and Italy, rather than in the countries where it has been most needed. Before 2015 many countries behind the former Iron Curtain continued to be tied exclusively to long-distance Russian gas pipelines and therefore cut off from the network of intra-regional European gas supplies.

The United States is currently the third-largest exporter of LNG in the world, behind Australia and Qatar. According to the IEA, the US may become the largest exporter by 2024. In recent years, most of US LNG shipments have been directed to Asia and Latin America where prices have been higher. Compared to the roughly 550 bcm of annual natural gas demand in Europe and European imports of roughly 120 bcm of LNG, US annual LNG shipments to Europe of roughly 10 bcm per year are a drop in the ocean. But LNG shipments to Europe have grown rapidly in absolute terms and relative to total shipments since they began in 2016. Natural gas companies from the UK, France, and Spain have rushed to contract LNG from the handful of export terminals on the US Gulf Coast. Strongly motivated to diversify gas supplies and delivery routes, Poland has placed several large long-term orders. During the first quarter of 2019, an impressive 30% of all US LNG exports arrived in the EU.

The real significance of US LNG shipments to Europe goes well beyond the volume. The explosion of US natural gas production has caused a global LNG supply glut by displacing significant volume that would have been consumed in the United States onto the global market. Even modest US LNG exports to Europe, coupled with the prospect of rapid growth of these exports over time, have strengthened the negotiating leverage of European importers with Russia. Studies have shown that US LNG exports to Europe could result in significant wealth transfers from Russia to European consumers by virtue of reduced contract prices.[8]

Diversifying Energy Supplies with New Routes and Sources for Piped Gas

The search for new gas sources and routes has focused on the Caspian Sea region. Azerbaijan, Turkmenistan, Kazakhstan, and Uzbekistan represent 11% of proven world gas reserves and are therefore critical to the EU's long-term energy security. Efforts to improve energy diversification have included, perhaps most notably, the development of a "Southern Gas Corridor" (SGC) linking the giant Shah Deniz field in Azerbaijan to Europe. The SGC, in operation as of early 2020, consists of three separate pipelines: The first, the South Caucasus Pipeline, links Azerbaijan to Georgia; the second, the Trans-Anatolian Pipeline (TANAP), traverses Turkey; and the third, the Trans-Adriatic Pipeline, connects TANAP to Greece and Albania before crossing the Adriatic Sea to Italy.

Sustained US and EU diplomatic engagement contributed to the success of the SGC. In 2018, the European Investment Bank approved a loan of $1.5 billion, its largest loan to an energy project in its history, for the construction of the third leg of the pipeline. EU recognition of the pipeline as a "project of common interest" made it eligible to benefit from streamlined permitting, preferential regulatory treatment and significant financing from the EU's Connected Europe Facility.

Admittedly, the project is not a game changer as it will do little in itself to diminish Europe's energy dependence on Russia. The initially projected capacity of 16 bcm of gas per year is about half of what European planners had anticipated. About 6 bcm is earmarked for Turkish demand, leaving only 10 bcm for Europe (roughly equivalent to only 1.7% of total annual gas consumption). But it is significant nonetheless as it brings non-Russian gas to Europe by pipeline for the first time in many

---

[8] "Made in America: The Economic Impact of LNG Exports from the United States," Deloitte Center for Energy Solutions, 2013. https://www2.deloitte.com/insights/us/en/industry/oil-and-gas/made-in-america-the-economic-impact-of-lng-exports-from-the-united-states.html.

years. Its significance would be greater if it provides new routes to southeastern Europe and the Balkans, regions that have hitherto been "energy islands." The new routes could be in the form of interconnectors enabling gas to flow from Greece to Bulgaria (and its neighbors) and from Albania to Croatia (and its neighbors).

Diplomatic efforts to promote the SGC and its interconnectors under the Obama administration have continued under the Trump administration. Indeed, the latter provided a rare waiver from its tougher sanctions on companies doing business with Iran in order to enable continued development of the second phase of the Shah Deniz project in which Iran's national oil company has a minority stake.

In addition to developing new sources of energy supply and new delivery routes, the United States and the EU have had some success in blocking projects that would increase European reliance on Russian gas. Perhaps the principal example was Gazprom's South Stream project that would have transported gas from Russia across the Black Sea to Bulgaria and eventually Austria. Why was Russia willing to spend about €40 billion when additional gas export volume could be accommodated with increased throughput in existing pipelines? The answer is that with 63 bcm of planned capacity, nearly equal to the entire volume of gas that transits Ukraine, the pipeline would have enabled Russia to undermine Kyiv's negotiating leverage regarding transit fees (accounting for roughly €2 billion or 3% of GDP per year) and would have increased the dependence of downstream customers, especially in Central and Eastern Europe and the Balkans. Although several EU energy and pipeline construction firms had economic interests in the project, most member states supported the European Commission's decision to block the project because it violated EU energy market rules.

This victory may be short lived, however, if Russia succeeds in selling more gas to Europe through Turkey. Gazprom's Blue Stream gas pipeline that links Russia and Turkey under the Black Sea before connecting to Bulgaria already handles up to 16 bcm of gas per year, largely for Turkey's domestic market. The completion of additional pipelines from Russia to Turkey, known as Turkish Stream, might have the same negative impact as South Stream on Ukrainian transit fees and European energy independence if they bring additional Russian gas to European consumers. Under conditions of equal access to third parties, an additional pipe would create more options for the consumer. But as Gazprom is the only company in Russia allowed to export piped natural gas and is not required to provide equal access to its pipes outside the EU, unlike European operators subject to EU law, Turkish Stream will not create more consumer optionality.

Compared to the battle over South Stream, the one over the Nord Stream pipeline has been far more controversial. The Nord Stream I pipeline under the Baltic Sea linking the Leningrad region to Greifswald in Northern Germany halved the percentage of Russian gas exports to Europe that transit through Ukraine from about 100% prior to the pipeline's inauguration in 2011. Nord Stream II, a second pipeline running alongside the first, would double the original capacity to 110 bcm. Gazprom (supported by leading energy companies in Western Europe) has underwritten the €10 billion bill to construct the pipeline despite the fact that its existing pipelines from Russia to Europe are only 60% utilized. The reason is that the project is as much politically as economically motivated. Nord Stream II would increase Gazprom's share of the German gas market from 40% to 60% and would concentrate roughly three-quarters of Russian gas exports to the EU through a single route, thereby offering Russia a valuable choke point at which to disrupt supplies.[9]

Ukraine has been the transit route for nearly half of all Russian gas exports to the EU. Combined with a multi-line Turkish Stream, Nord Stream II would enable Russia to service its European customers while circumventing Ukraine entirely. Gazprom has publicly announced that this is its intention as soon as possible after 2020. It is not at all clear how Ukraine would recover from the blow of losing €2 billion per year in transit fees. When Chancellor Merkel sought assurances from President Putin that Russia would continue to export gas through Ukraine's pipelines even after the completion of Nord Stream II, Putin replied that Russia would do so if that made economic sense.[10] That was obviously far from the assurance she was seeking.

---

[9] Written Testimony of Deputy Assistant Secretary of State John E. McCarrick of the Bureau of Energy Resources before the Senate Foreign Relations Committee's Subcommittee on Europe and Regional Security Cooperation, December 12, 2017. https://www.foreign.senate.gov/imo/media/doc/121217_McCarrick_Testimony.pdf.

[10] Claire Jones, Guy Chazan, and Kathrin Hille, "Merkel and Putin Discuss Syria and Ukraine at Landmark Meeting," *Financial Times*, August 18, 2018. https://www.ft.com/content/08f7f0c4-a303-11e8-8ecf-a7ae1beff35b.

Germany has insisted on proceeding with Nord Stream II despite an outpouring of criticism from many EU member states and the European Commission itself. During EU discussions on Russian sanctions in 2015, Italian Prime Minister Matteo Renzi argued that Germany was subordinating the EU's collective diplomacy to German economic interests. Other countries have also been angered by the apparent contradiction between the termination of South Stream and the continuation of Nord Stream II. The reason why Germany has been able to endorse Nord Stream II is that it is an entirely undersea pipeline originating outside the EU and making landfall in Germany, whereas South Stream would have transited several EU member states. EU energy market rules clearly applied only to the latter until they were modified in 2019. Those rules include provisions requiring ownership "unbundling" (essentially the separation of companies' generation and sale operations from their transmission networks), third-party access, and non-discriminatory tariffs. As amended, the rules now apply to all offshore pipelines. But since member states may ask for derogations in case of existing (rather than future) pipelines, Germany has so far been able to safeguard Nord Stream II.

The Obama administration worked intensively with the European Commission and supportive EU member states to question the rationale for Nord Stream II. Over the past three years, the Trump administration raised the pressure substantially on Germany and the project's commercial backers. At a NATO summit in July 2018 President Trump attacked Chancellor Merkel for allowing Germany to be "totally controlled" and "captive to Russia" because of its reliance on Russian gas and questioned why the United States should spend billions defending European countries that handed billions to Russia in business deals.[11]

In a rare sign of bipartisan consensus, the US Congress approved sanctions in December 2019 on companies and governments working on the project. Germany has strongly criticized the legislation, arguing that it is unacceptable interference in national sovereignty, and has vowed to proceed. When international contractors suspended work on the project because of the sanctions, Gazprom announced that it would complete the pipeline alone. The decision of Denmark to allow the pipeline to cross its seabed suggests that the project appears likely to be completed. The key

---

[11] Jonathan Lemire and Jill Colvin, "Trump Rattles NATO, Knocking Its Value, Assailing Germany," AP News, July 12, 2018. https://apnews.com/e863b9f08c1d48fc94c75030cdfcae46.

question is whether the pipeline's negative impact can be minimized by ensuring that it operates under EU energy market rules and that Ukraine continues to serve as a country for the transit of Russian gas.

While the tactics and the rhetoric of the Obama and Trump administrations on this issue differ sharply, they display a higher degree of continuity than in nearly any other area of US policy toward the EU. Opposition to Nord Stream II may be influenced by the desire of the US government to promote US LNG exports. Yet that in no way diminishes the main (valid) criticisms that the pipeline weakens Central and Eastern Europe by making the region less relevant for gas transit, undermines Ukraine's reform program, and retards the EU's energy diversification goals. It is not correct to state that both Russian and US energy exports to Europe are state controlled. Unlike Russia that can direct Gazprom to do what it wishes, US LNG exporters are free to pursue their own market interests. The biggest champions of US LNG exports are in fact European governments, such as Poland and the Baltic states.

Both the Obama and Trump administrations have shared the view of many prior Democratic and Republican administrations that energy security is a core element of foreign policy and national security and that promoting European energy security is in the US national interest. I applaud this and hope the bipartisan approach continues.

Ensuring the Free Flow of Gas and Electricity Within the EU

The United States has also supported the EU's efforts to ensure that gas and electricity flow freely in every direction to where they are needed. While more progress has been made in the gas sector in the past decade, significant steps are also taking place in the electricity sector.

As noted above, many countries in Central and Eastern Europe, especially Ukraine, have suffered the consequences of the fact that Russian gas has (until recently) flowed only East to West. Those countries would have been in a far better position had they been able to access supplies from their neighbors. Gas pipeline interconnections and "reverse flow" (i.e., bi-directional flow) capabilities are helping to address the problem. The free flow of gas does not mean that Russian gas will be replaced with other sources. In many instances, the same Russian gas will continue to transit through European pipeline networks, but through different routes. That additional flexibility is a guarantee that Russia cannot exploit the use of its pipeline network to apply selective pressure on downstream consumers.

The Baltic states, once an "energy island," are being increasingly integrated into the European gas and electricity network. The Baltic Energy Market Interconnection Plan (BEMIP) has included multiple projects to this end. A gas pipeline interconnector between Poland and Lithuania aims to connect the Baltic and Finnish gas networks with the continental European gas network by the end of 2021. Another gas pipeline interconnector between Finland and Estonia, completed in 2019, connects the Finnish gas network with the continental European network. BEMIP also includes a submarine power cable between Lithuania and Sweden, a submarine power cable between Estonia and Finland and an electricity link between the Baltic transmission system (integrated with that of Russia and Belarus) and the continental European transmission system. As a result of these and other projects, the Baltic states are now among the best interconnected regions of Europe.

Poland is emerging as a gas hub, thanks to the completed LNG terminal in Świnoujście and a future gas pipeline from Norway to Poland that is expected to bring 10 bcm per annum of Norwegian gas to Poland and other Central European and Baltic countries. Thanks to about €300 million in EU funding, a gas interconnector between Poland and Lithuania is expected to begin operations in 2021. Poland is also working on gas interconnectors with Lithuania, Ukraine, Slovakia, and the Czech Republic. These developments would provide a secure alternative to Russian gas from Nord Stream. Hungary, Slovakia, and Poland have introduced "reverse flow" capabilities on the pipeline supplying them with gas from Russia through Ukraine. Hungary has built interconnectors with Croatia, Romania, Slovakia, and Bulgaria (through Serbia). The Eastring gas pipeline, whose first phase is projected to be completed around 2025, would tie western European gas hubs to the Balkans by connecting Slovakia with the external border of the EU in Bulgaria. A proposed Ionian-Adriatic gas pipeline would transport gas from Albania, through Montenegro and Bosnia and Herzegovina, to Croatia. Interconnectors between Greece and Bulgaria and between Bulgaria and Serbia are also planned.

Promoting the flow of gas southwards from the new LNG terminals in Poland and Lithuania, and the flow of gas northwards from the new LNG terminal in Croatia, is a major strategic priority of the Three Seas Initiative, comprising twelve Central and Eastern European member states whose territories lie between the Baltic, Black, and Adriatic seas. The forum gathers heads of state and ministers annually to discuss regional economic development and the interconnectivity of transport, digital and energy infrastructure, focusing especially on the promotion of gas pipeline interconnectors.[12] In addition to drawing on EU funds, the members have launched an investment fund with a €5 billion budget that aims to stimulate up to €100 billion in new projects. The Trump administration has lent high-level support for the initiative, including a speech by the president at the 2017 summit in Warsaw and a promise by Energy Secretary Rick Perry to catalyze investments identified by the initiative.

Central and Eastern Europe is not the only region in Europe where gas and electricity interconnections are moving ahead. For many years, the Iberian Peninsula has been isolated from the European electricity system, largely due to French reluctance to enable Spain to export excess electricity generated from renewable energy. Whereas the EU aims for each member state to reach a minimum 10% interconnection level with its neighbors (to be raised to 15% by 2030), Spain has been stuck at well below that. Due to France's recent change of heart and the EU's significant financial backing of a Franco-Spanish subsea power cable under the Bay of Biscay, Spain (and Portugal) will no longer be isolated from the European electricity grid. Despite regulatory hurdles, the EU continues to push for a gas pipeline across the Pyrenees that would double gas transport capacity between France and Spain.

Helping Ukraine Strengthen Its Energy Sector

The EU and the US have cooperated on numerous dimensions of the EU's Energy Union that seek to enhance energy security through diversifying routes and sources of supply and promoting the free flow of energy within the EU.

---

[12] James Shotter, "Three Seas Seeks to Turn Tide on East-West Divide, *Financial Times*, November 22, 2018. https://www.ft.com/content/2e328cba-c8be-11e8-86e6-19f5b7134d1c.

In addition to this cooperation, the EU and the US have worked together to improve Ukraine's energy security. The stakes could not be higher: If Ukraine is not energy secure, it cannot enjoy political stability, and if it is politically unstable, it will be vulnerable to Russian domination. That would represent a failure of the EU's effort to project stability in its neighborhood and a major setback for transatlantic efforts to promote a united, prosperous, and democratic Europe.

Following the Russian annexation of Crimea and the instigation of a separatist movement in the Donbas in March 2014, Ukraine not only lost a significant part of its coal deposits, offshore Black Sea oil reserves, and its power generating assets, but also faced the possibility of reduced natural gas supplies from Russia. US and EU experts raced against the clock to help Ukraine to prepare contingency measures for the upcoming winter. Naftogaz wanted to buy significant quantities of gas but didn't have strong enough credit to do so because of its financial troubles. Amos Hochstein and European Commission Vice President Maroš Šefčovič led an intensive effort to put into place a lending mechanism through the European Bank for Reconstruction and Development to enable Naftogaz to do so.

I recall the concern of the experts from the US Department of Energy who regularly passed through the US Mission to the EU to report on progress in their work with the Ukrainian government. The emergency plans included decisions about how to allocate energy supplies to different parts of the economy, maximize domestic energy production, reduce demand, increase storage of gas, and increase "reverse flows" of gas from Ukraine's neighbors.

Even while the upcoming winter in Ukraine was the overriding concern, the US and the EU have also had to work on a longer-term plan to modernize and diversify Ukraine's energy sector. The European Investment Bank and the European Bank for Reconstruction and Development have provided significant loans to help Ukraine finance the costs of doing so.

Reforming a country's energy sector is a tough challenge in the best of times. Doing so under severe time pressure in a country of 45 million people straining under the significant financial and human costs of conflict, struggling to address endemic cronyism and corruption (especially in the opaque energy sector), and shouldering the legacy of Soviet-style infrastructure is a herculean task. Most of Ukraine's power generation assets will reach the end of their life cycle during the next decade and will need to be decommissioned or upgraded. Those assets will have to be integrated with the EU's power system and meet EU environmental standards, both of which will require significant investment. In light of the devastating consequences of the Chernobyl disaster, caused by a faulty Soviet nuclear power plant, US and EU experts have also been engaged with Kyiv to introduce modern safety practices and technology into Ukraine's operating nuclear reactors.

One of the challenges US and EU experts faced was to help Ukraine increase its domestic oil and gas resources in order to reduce the country's dependency on imports. The conflict in eastern Ukraine had largely driven out the few large international energy companies that had braved the administrative red tape and chronically dysfunctional nature of Ukraine's energy sector. The remaining domestic and smaller international firms did not have the financial and technical means required to exploit the country's significant reserves, especially of gas. The country has Europe's third-largest deposits of shale gas, but these are largely difficult to reach and hence expensive to exploit.

During the critical early years of the conflict, domestic gas production declined to about three-fifths of the country's needs. US and EU experts helped Ukraine weather the storm by increasing its gas storage capacity and accessing gas from its neighbors through "reverse flow" agreements. As a result, Ukraine was able to stop importing gas from Russia as of 2015. The experts also helped Ukraine with the longer-term project of making the energy sector more professional and transparent, improving the regulatory structure to provide greater incentives for foreign investors, accessing modern technology to increase extraction from existing conventional wells, and exploiting the country's significant shale resources. Ukraine aims to become self-sufficient in gas by 2022, a dramatic turnaround from the pre-war period in which Ukraine was importing about 45 bcm per year. Moreover, investment in the Ukrainian renewable energy sector has increased substantially due to reforms in regulations and attractive feed-in tariffs. As a result, the renewable energy share of total energy consumption tripled from about 4% in 2014 to 12% in 2020.

Part of the reason why Ukraine can now meet its energy consumption needs without requiring significant foreign imports is that domestic demand has been reduced dramatically. Some of this reduction was due to the loss of energy-intensive industries in the Donbas and the economic downturn caused by the conflict. But much of it has also resulted from the efforts of Ukraine, assisted by the EU and the US, to lower demand.

According to the US Energy Information Administration, Ukraine is one of the least energy-efficient countries in Europe; it uses about two to three times more energy per unit of economic output than even its direct neighbors in the EU. Efforts to lower demand have included the phased reduction in extremely generous energy subsidies for gas, heating, and electricity that represented about 7.5% of GDP in 2012. Residential consumers have faced significant price hikes, but the poor and vulnerable have received offsetting direct payments. In 2016, the Ukrainian government was spending roughly seventy times more on subsidies for public utilities than on energy efficiency. The US and the EU have advised the government on how to reduce that gap by planning a modernization program, including proper insulation, for buildings owned by federal, regional, and local entities. The gap between production of energy and demand has also been reduced by urgent measures to lower very high loss rates on electricity transmission lines and repair leaky pipelines.

Just as important as the technical measures to boost production and lower consumption outlined above was the advice of the EU (with assistance from the US) to the Ukrainian government on urgent regulatory reform. Ukraine is obliged to implement the EU's energy laws, including the TEP, as one of the requirements of its membership in the Energy Community. Founded in 2005, this international organization brings together the EU and eight non-EU countries in Southeastern Europe and the Black Sea region to create an integrated pan-European energy market. As a result, Ukraine has undertaken numerous reforms, such as the structural reform of the gas and electricity market; "unbundling" of supply and generation assets from the operation of transmission networks; and the creation of an independent regulator. Among the recent achievements of these reforms, Ukraine implemented an Electricity Market Law in 2019 that introduced more open competition and non-discriminatory participation in the electricity market. Now companies have freedom to buy and sell electricity, consumers have greater choice of electricity suppliers, tariffs reflect actual costs, and transmission and distribution grids can be accessed by third parties on transparent, market terms.

A major part of this work has involved cleaning up Naftogaz. Representing 14% of Ukraine's budget revenues, it has long been exploited by politicians as a tool of patronage and corruption. Work toward ensuring professional and independent management, as well as transparent accounting meeting international standards, has advanced significantly, but it is still not complete. It is essential that the US and the EU continue to encourage the Ukrainian government to finish this work so that Ukraine can finally enjoy the benefits of a competitive energy market and a democracy that is clean and efficient.

FUTURE AREAS OF US-EU ENERGY COOPERATION

My diplomatic mission reaffirmed my conviction that energy cooperation should be a priority for US-EU relations because of its spillover effects on economic, political, and security relations and because there are so many areas in the energy sector where the US and the EU could be doing more together.

Shortly after my arrival in Brussels in 2014, I pushed for an additional five-year extension of the 1998 US-EU Agreement on Scientific and Technological Cooperation. The agreement provides an official framework for cooperation in a very wide range of research areas, including in non-nuclear energy and materials science. I also collaborated with the dynamic EU Commissioner for Research, Science and Innovation, Carlos Moedas, to simplify the participation of US research institutions in the European Commission's €80 billion Horizon 2020 research and innovation fund. The very low participation rate of US institutions in Horizon 2020 projects, due to several technical legal obstacles, made no sense to either of us, especially when those institutions were not actually seeking funding from the EU.

During my diplomatic mission, I had the pleasure of traveling several times to Ispra, Italy, to visit the EU's Joint Research Centre (JRC), one of Europe's leading research campuses. In 2008 the JRC had reported to the European Commission that due to the use of illegal software (so-called defeat devices) there was a significant discrepancy in diesel vehicle emissions between testing and road conditions. EU member states did not act on the European Commission's further investigations, and it was only when the US Environmental Protection Agency charged Volkswagen in September 2015 with violations of the Clean Air Act that the "Dieselgate" scandal broke out.

But the reason for my visits had nothing to do with automotive manufactures' cheating of laboratory emissions tests. I wanted to learn more about the collaboration between the JRC and the Department of Energy's Argonne National Laboratory in Illinois on electric vehicles' interoperability with smart grids and charging stations. Smart grids, an essential building block of a more energy-efficient future, are essentially energy networks that can automatically monitor energy flows and adjust to the changes in energy supply and demand accordingly. Interoperability refers to the notion that any electric vehicle and supply equipment should be capable of being plugged in anywhere and anytime without disturbing energy networks. This is a critical element in the effort to prepare for a cleaner energy future in which more electric vehicles circulate on our roads. The collaboration between the two labs also seeks to define global product standards for electric vehicle interoperability with smart grids and charging stations with the objective of minimizing trade barriers and facilitating adoption of new technology.

The US and the EU have also collaborated effectively on energy efficiency. The ENERGY STAR Agreement, signed in 1991 by the European Commission and the Environmental Protection Agency, promotes the use of a voluntary label and a consistent set of performance standards for the energy efficiency of office equipment on both sides of the Atlantic. By helping manufacturers avoid the burden of complying with multiple labeling programs, the agreement has increased the global supply of and demand for energy-efficient office equipment. The agreement expired in February 2018 and should be renewed.

The communiqués of the US-EU Energy Council have repeatedly mentioned many other areas of collaboration, but practical progress has been too slow. One priority area should be research into storage solutions for renewable energy. The main obstacle preventing faster expansion of renewables is no longer their cost (wind and even large-scale solar power is already cheaper than coal and gas), but rather their intermittency since the wind and sun don't always blow or shine. Electricity grids have difficulty handling significant electricity loads from renewable energy sources because of their volatility. A critical component to addressing intermittency is the improvement of distributed storage solutions, such as batteries, pump storage (reservoirs), and electric vehicles themselves, so that excess energy can be stored when produced and then released when needed.

Batteries would be a particularly fruitful area of cooperation as the EU has made this a major priority since launching the European Battery Alliance in October 2017. The group, consisting of several EU member states, the European Commission and the European Investment Bank, as well as industrial and research partners, seeks to build a strong and competitive European battery industry. The European Commission has authorized, pursuant to its rules on subsidies, seven EU member states to contribute roughly €3.2 billion to finance the project. The Department of Energy and the US car manufacturing industry, among others, are also focusing on the same objective. The US and the EU should explore whether it makes sense to join forces.

The US and the EU should also continue to prioritize collaboration on methods of capturing carbon dioxide emissions (usually at power plants and factories) for subsequent underground storage so that they will not enter the atmosphere. While the technology and sufficient storage sites are available, the high cost and concerns about carbon dioxide leakage are slowing the speed of implementation. With growing evidence that the earth's climate is warming at an alarmingly increasing rate, it is critical to accelerate our ability to prevent carbon dioxide from being emitted in the first place and to remove it once it is already in the atmosphere.

As described above, one of the reasons for the divergence between the US and the EU in terms of energy security is the decision of the US to encourage the exploitation of shale oil and especially shale gas reserves, whereas many EU member states have banned it. Some member states, including Poland, and critical non-EU member states, such as Ukraine, are interested in developing their shale reserves. The US has unparalleled experience in defining a regulatory framework that promotes shale projects. Fortunately, it is sharing that experience with foreign governments through the Unconventional Gas Technical Engagement Program of the US Department of State. This program deserves continued support. While the program could theoretically undercut US "energy dominance" in shale and US LNG exports to Europe over the long term, it is far more important that the US encourages European energy security.

The US and the EU should also focus their collaboration on combatting the risk of cyber-attacks on energy infrastructure. This risk is far from theoretical and can result in devastating consequences for energy production and public safety. Although many such attacks remain confidential, there are numerous well-publicized cases such as the attacks on Ukraine's power grid, Iran's nuclear facilities, and Saudi Aramco's computer systems. In 2018, the US Department of Homeland Security and the FBI declared that Russian-backed hackers had embedded malware into a range of US power plants and had gained remote access into energy sector networks.

The US and the EU should continue to align their diplomatic efforts at expanding energy supply options for Europe. Very large reserves in the eastern Mediterranean—between 5 and 8 trillion cubic feet of natural gas recently discovered off the coast of Cyprus and about 19 trillion cubic feet in one field off the coast of Israel—have the potential to be game changers if significant production is (eventually) destined for export, including to Europe. While the development of Cyprus's offshore reserves are complicated by the ongoing conflict with Turkey and the transportation of gas to Europe from the Israeli reserves are beset by political and technical challenges, the US and the EU should do their utmost to provide private energy operators with as much confidence as possible to invest in these projects.

Energy has the potential to be a powerful force for peace, not only in Europe but around the world. One good example is a recent agreement whereby Israel will export up to 7 bcm of natural gas per year to Egypt. This deal, worth $15 billion, is arguably the most significant one these neighbors have ever concluded since they made peace in 1979.

Finally, the United States should be clear that European energy security is about more than just selling US LNG to Europe, as much as this contributes to reducing the over-reliance of certain EU member states on Gazprom or other suppliers. When the US engages in aggressive commercial promotion, it undermines the credibility of its message and the effectiveness of its diplomacy to promote a competitive and integrated energy market in Europe—an objective that is even more important than reducing the transatlantic trade imbalance.

CHAPTER 9

Law Enforcement Cooperation

Twenty minutes prior to my scheduled 8:40 a.m. departure on a highspeed train from Brussels to Paris on March 22, 2016, one of my bodyguards from Belgian State Security informed me that there had just been an explosion at the Brussels airport. As the cause of the explosion and the damage were still unknown, I decided to board the train and continue with my scheduled speech and meetings with the French government on the Transatlantic Trade and Investment Partnership agreement that the US and the EU were negotiating.

After only one hour, however, the scale of the calamity was already clear: At just before 8 a.m., terrorists had detonated two bombs near the check-in counters of Delta and American Airlines, killing and wounding many. Among the dead, as I was to discover later, were the spouse of an employee at our Embassy to NATO and Ambassador André Adam, former Belgian ambassador to the United States, whom I had first met in the Oval Office during the presentation of his credentials to President Bill Clinton in 1994. The two bombs were so powerful that they blew the roof off the main terminal. As a result, much of the airport was shut down for many months, diverting many flights to other Belgian airports and requiring the use of makeshift tents for security screening and check-in. A third bomb had been detonated just after 9 a.m. in the tunnel between the Maalbeek and Arts-Loi metro stops in Brussels, a key artery of the metro system and one used by many employees of the US Mission to the EU and the US Embassy to Belgium.

© The Author(s) 2020
A. L. Gardner, *Stars with Stripes*,
https://doi.org/10.1007/978-3-030-29966-8_9

Finding myself in Paris during the afternoon of March 22 with all air and rail links to Brussels severed, I hitched a ride with a friend to the Belgian border, where the Embassy driver and my bodyguards picked me up. That evening in Brussels, my colleagues, Denise Bauer, US Ambassador to Belgium, and Doug Lute, US Ambassador to NATO, and I received a briefing that made clear the gravity of the situation: Three suicide bombers from the Islamic State of Iraq and the Levant (ISIL) had detonated homemade nail bombs, killing thirty-two people and wounding more than 320 in the deadliest act of terrorism in Belgium's history. The country was in a state of emergency and the three US embassies were in lock-down. Although all embassy personnel had been accounted for during the successful operation of our emergency procedures, there was obviously significant concern among our staff and their families. The compound containing the US embassies to Belgium and the EU already looked like a heavily protected bunker but plans to erect large gates before one of the entrances were nonetheless accelerated.

Unfortunately, these attacks were not the first of their kind in Belgium or in Europe. Terrorist attacks in Madrid in 2004 and in London in 2005 had killed 192 and 52 people, respectively, with thousands more injured. Between 2010 and 2016, over 300 people were killed by terrorists in the EU. Just under three months after my arrival in Brussels in 2014, a terrorist attack affected me personally and convinced me to make US–EU law enforcement cooperation a key priority of my diplomatic mission. On May 24, a French national of Algerian origin who had returned to Europe after fighting with radical Islamists in Syria walked into the Jewish Museum and randomly opened fire with a Kalashnikov rifle, killing four people. The museum, which I had visited several times, is a stone's throw from the Sablon district where I had lived for three years in the mid-1990s and is a few minutes walking distance from the US Mission to the EU.

During January 5–7, 2015, French nationals of Algerian descent, members of the Al-Qaeda terrorist group, carried out three attacks on the satirical magazine *Charlie Hebdo* (that had carried polemical cartoons, including about Islam), as well as on police officers and a kosher supermarket. In mid-February 2015, a Danish national of Palestinian descent murdered two people at a café and a synagogue in Copenhagen. On July 14, 2016, in a terrorist attack for which ISIL claimed responsibility, a Tunisian resident of France deliberately plowed a 19-ton cargo truck into a crowd of thousands along the Promenade des Anglais in Nice as they were celebrating Bastille Day, killing 86 people and injuring 458 others. In August of that year, a heavily armed Moroccan aboard a high-speed train from Amsterdam to Paris attempted a terrorist attack but was thwarted by six passengers including three Americans (two of whom were off-duty members of the Armed Forces). But the worst was yet to come.

On November 13, 2015, three groups of nine men, mostly French and Belgian nationals of Arab descent, conducted six separate suicide bombings and mass shootings in central Paris, including at the Stade de France stadium and the Bataclan concert hall, that killed 130 victims and wounded 413. At least six of the killers had apparently fought with ISIL in Syria and two had apparently re-entered Europe through Greece in early October along with vast refugee flows from Turkey. Following these attacks, the worst acts of violence in France since World War II, France declared a state of emergency and three-day period of mourning, temporarily shut its borders and called in 1500 soldiers to maintain order in Paris. France invoked the Lisbon Treaty's mutual assistance clause that requires EU member states to offer aid with "all the means in their power" to another member state that is the victim of armed aggression on its territory. The scenes of empty Paris streets, patrolled by heavily armed troops, were out of a bad sci-fi movie about the end of the world. The following January, it was moving to see at least 3.7 million people take to the streets in France, including 1.6 million in Paris, to show solidarity with the victims and France.

I was watching the events from Brussels with extreme concern. Brussels was already on a state of high alert since the shooting at the Jewish Museum. Salah Abdeslam, an accomplice and a brother of a suicide bomber in the Paris attacks, was on the run and thought to be back in Brussels. On the evening of November 13, Belgian police were carrying out multiple late-night raids to find him as the Prime Minister, Charles Michel, warned of imminent Paris-style attacks. The metro, schools, shops, and offices, including those of the European Union and the US embassies, were shut. An advertisement on the front cover of a Belgian weekly rather unhelpfully encouraged its readers to "think about your will." Even the staff at the US Mission to the EU who had previously been posted to tough places like Baghdad and Kabul were beginning to show the strain. Many would avoid all public places, including restaurants and theaters for many months, and would consult a US government psychiatrist stationed in Brussels.

I was well protected by bodyguards and a heavily armored vehicle that was supposed to withstand a roadside bomb, a rocket-propelled grenade and machine-gun fire. But I was troubled that the vehicle was easily identifiable as one of four similar SUVs in Brussels used by two of the three US ambassadors (Doug Lute, the Ambassador to NATO, had successfully swapped his suburban for a more low-key model) and by the Israeli ambassadors to the EU and Belgium. I was not comforted by the fact that the residence featured an underground panic room with three-inch-thick steel doors that the previous owner, a Russian oligarch, had installed. I hoped that it would never come in handy.

Like others at the embassy, I was beginning to suffer from the stress. In one unnerving incident, I was pulled out of the front row of a very public event by my security detail and brought back to the residence because of an apparent threat to my safety. My wife and I did leave the residence alone, albeit rarely and mostly on weekends, in order to maintain some privacy. As we were driving on one of these occasions through the Soignes forest next to our residence, I had a momentary panic attack as a car sped up behind us from nowhere, overtook us in an abrupt manoeuver and then slowed down. I realized just how quickly we were being engulfed in a collective psychosis when my wife's five-year-old nephew, on a visit from Madrid in late March 2016, started running through the forest shouting in Spanish "Run, the Jihadis are after us!"

The terrorist attacks kept coming throughout 2016, including in Germany, a country that had been left almost unscathed. On July 18, an ax-wielding teenager from Afghanistan wounded five people aboard a train in Würzburg. Six days later, a Syrian refugee blew himself up outside a wine bar in Anspach, injuring 15 people in Germany's first suicide bombing. And on December 19, a Tunisian failed asylum seeker deliberately drove a truck into a crowded Christmas market next to the Kaiser Wilhelm Memorial Church in Berlin, leaving 12 people dead and 56 others injured.

Common Themes Emerge

In the course of multiple discussions about the attacks with my staff from the Department of Homeland Security and Department of Justice, several common themes emerged.

One obvious point is that they all featured at least one international element. For example, Mehdi Nemmouche, the perpetrator of the Jewish Museum attack in Brussels, was a French national who had previously traveled to Syria and back to France through several countries, using a method known as "broken travel" to avoid detection. The attacker on the high-speed train from Amsterdam had lived in Paris, Vienna, Cologne, and Brussels; he had traveled from France to Belgium to obtain firearms and to board the train. The terrorist at the Kosher supermarket in Paris had met his accomplices in Spain, traveled to Turkey, sent his wife to Syria, and bought weapons in Belgium that had been manufactured in Slovakia and exported by a Slovenian company. Given these international characteristics of terrorism, it became abundantly clear that deeper cooperation among EU member states and even globally, especially between the EU and the US, is essential.

Another common theme is that most of the terrorists were second or even third generation EU citizens of immigrant Arab families who had been born and/or had grown up in Europe where they had been radicalized. As EU citizens, these terrorists had EU passports and therefore were able to travel freely within the Schengen area without being subject to any passport or identity checks. Whereas non-EU nationals arriving in Europe by legal means were normally subject to rigorous checks, EU nationals re-entering Europe were subject to minimal checks to establish identity and to verify travel documents. Some of the terrorists had also exploited the chaos at various European frontiers caused by the massive influx of refugees.

Furthermore, most of the terrorists were already known to at least one of the EU security services. According to press reports, Nemmouche was known to French authorities as a serious criminal and Foreign Fighter in Syria. Ayoub El Khazzani, the perpetrator of the attack on the high-speed train to Paris, was known to Spanish authorities as being connected to Islamic radicals. All of the terrorists involved in the terrorist attacks in Paris in November 2015 were known to the French authorities as having fought for ISIL and were being monitored. Anis Amri, the perpetrator of the attack on the Berlin Christmas market, had been officially classified by the German authorities as a potential terrorist. According to press reports, Amri's intercepted communications showed that he had volunteered to be a suicide bomber and that he had links to a radical preacher who had recruited people to fight with ISIL in Iraq and Syria. Amri had been under near-constant police surveillance, and even placed in a detention center for eventual deportation, before being released and then going underground. In these and other cases, there was not enough information to prosecute the suspects of a crime.

Although information about the terrorists was often known, it was not always shared effectively among security services. Eight months before the suicide bombings at the Brussels airport, for example, Turkish police had arrested Ibrahim El Bakraoui, one of the terrorists, near the Syrian border for his Jihadi connections. He was also on the FBI's watch list. After learning that El Bakraoui was a Belgian citizen, the Turks had contacted the police liaison officer in Belgium's Istanbul consulate to inform him that El Bakraoui would be deported in several weeks. The liaison officer passed the information to Belgium's federal police, but the latter failed to insert his name into the Schengen Information System (SIS), a European border control and law enforcement database. That was a major failure, especially as Belgium had been warned by foreign intelligence services that ISIS was planning to bomb the Brussels airport and metro system.[1]

As a result of the failure, El Bakraoui was able to board a flight to Amsterdam, where he promptly disappeared because the Dutch authorities were unaware that he was a dangerous suspect. The Belgian authorities had no way of knowing when he returned home because there are no border checks within the Schengen area of free movement. The Brussels bombings might have been averted had the Belgian police inserted Abdeslam's name as a foreign terrorist fighter rather than as an ordinary criminal in the SIS. Had that occurred, the French gendarme who checked Abdeslam at the Franco-Belgian border the day after the Paris attacks would have alerted the authorities about a possible terrorist suspect and not released him.

The terrorist attacks shared other features. They shone an uncomfortable spotlight on the fact that existing information tools were not being used to their maximum effect. Of the estimated 6000 EU citizens who had traveled to Syria and Iraq to join ISIL and other extremist groups, EU member states passed less than one-third of those names to Europol, the EU's agency for law enforcement cooperation, for inclusion in its Focal Point Traveller anti-terror database. Most of the information about foreign fighters came from a handful of member states, indicating that many others were free riders; many member states were rarely consulting the

---

[1] "No Poirots: Belgium's Security Problem," *The Economist*, April 2, 2016. https://www.economist.com/europe/2016/04/02/no-poirots.

database. The habits of national security services to work bilaterally on a "need to know" basis with trusted partners, rather than on an EU-wide "need to share" basis, were deeply ingrained and hard to change.

Moreover, most of the attacks were low-tech and required little advance planning or financial resources. The Brussels airport bombings were carried out with suitcases full of an unstable white explosive powder known as triacetone triperoxide that can be made with household chemicals (apparently including drain cleaner and nail varnish remover). Some of the attacks used the destructive force of trucks plowing into crowds; some of them used handguns, rifles, knives, and explosive vests. The terrorists had either acted alone, even if they had collaborated with others, or had acted in small groups.

Many of the terrorists had been previously suspected, and even convicted, for serious crimes. For example, Nemmouche has a long criminal history, including arrests for armed robbery, theft and vandalism, and had spent five years in prison prior to his attack on the Jewish Museum. One of the perpetrators of the Charlie Hebdo attack had been convicted of terrorism and sentenced to three years in prison. Amri had served four years in Italian jails for crimes, including arson, prior to his attack on the Berlin Christmas market. It was clear that the likelihood of a terrorist suspect carrying out an attack was much higher if he had a prior record of serious crime. Security and intelligence services, therefore, had to have the full picture of an individual's prior record and needed access to all relevant databases. Unfortunately, the EU had multiple databases, each built up for a separate purpose, that had to be consulted separately (when the EU's rigorous data privacy laws allowed).

Most uncomfortably, especially for those of us living in Brussels, was the fact that Belgium appeared to play a supporting role in nearly every one of the attacks. Some of the attacks had been carried out there; some of the perpetrators were Belgians; and even when they were not Belgians, they benefited from planning, accomplices and weapons purchases in Belgium.

Some of the officers in the US embassies started calling Brussels "Jihadi Central," capital of Belgistan, a "failed state." (President Trump later called Brussels a "hellhole.") These descriptions were insulting and inaccurate. Belgium is a peaceful, wealthy and vibrant democracy that is a pleasure to live in. It is also an important partner of the United States on law enforcement matters. Nonetheless, it is undeniable that many features of the country have made it uniquely attractive to terrorists. At least one-quarter of Brussels' inhabitants are Muslim, making the city the most Muslim capital in Europe. Nearly every attack with a Belgian connection had a link to Molenbeek, a majority Muslim district in Brussels. Molenbeek features many characteristics that have made it an ideal recruiting ground for Islamic extremists: widespread poverty, high unemployment, especially among the substantial youth population, high crime rates, and a transient population. In the words of a former US counterterrorism official, "What Islamic State offers them, in a nutshell, is a fast track from zero to hero."[2] Efforts at integrating Muslims in Belgium, many of whom are second or third generation immigrants, have met with mixed success. Some other European cities and countries had similar difficulties. But it was certainly striking that Belgium supplied more Foreign Fighters to Syria than any other European country on a per capita basis.

Some public reports estimated in 2016 that roughly 335 Belgians had gone to fight in Syria and Iraq. While some were killed or stayed, about 117 were estimated to have returned. These were just a subset of the roughly 670 terrorist suspects on the Belgian Federal Police's consolidated list. There was no way that the roughly 600 members of the Belgian State Security could keep track of all of them because it requires between 10 and 20 agents to provide round-the-clock surveillance of each suspect. The Belgian State Security was already overstretched in its main job of providing protection for top members of the Belgian government and the EU institutions, visiting dignitaries and some resident diplomats (like the US and Israeli ambassadors).

What made this challenging situation even worse was the extremely complex patchwork of governing bodies in the country: three regions and three linguistic communities, six separate parliaments and 589 communes with significant decision-making powers (usually attributed to larger political entities in other countries). Brussels, with just 1.2 million inhabitants, is composed of 19 communes, each with its own mayor, and is policed by no less than six different forces. By contrast, New York City, a metropolis of 8.5 million, has one mayor and one police force. No wonder that Abdeslam decided to return to Molenbeek, where he was able to reside with family and friends for roughly four months before being

---

[2] Matthew Levitt, "My Journey to Brussels' Terrorist Safe Haven," *Politico*, March 27, 2016.

apprehended. He was even seen at the barber getting his hair cut and at a shop buying clothes without anyone thinking it necessary to notify the police. According to press reports, he was apprehended about 500 meters from the house where authorities believed he had helped plan the Paris attacks.

EU Efforts to Improve Security

The pan-European, indeed global, nature of the terrorist attacks in 2014–2016 highlighted in stark terms the importance of the EU accelerating and deepening efforts to improve European security, alongside the member states. These efforts had begun well before the attacks. Europol, originally founded in 1994 as the EU's agency to combat drugs, was refashioned into the EU's agency to counter serious crime in 1999. Another agency, called Eurojust, was founded in The Hague in 2002 to facilitate coordination among judicial and prosecutorial authorities in cases involving cross-border crime.

The attacks in the US on September 11, 2001, provided the impetus for several important EU measures. For example, the EU introduced a common definition of terrorism (lacking entirely in some member states) and harmonized national criminal laws related to terrorism. Thanks to such legislative harmonization, terrorists and their accomplices are no longer able to avoid apprehension merely by fleeing from one EU member state to another with different laws. The EU also established a common list of terrorist groups. (The US and EU lists feature minor differences, for example, with the former designating the entirety of Hezbollah, and the latter designating just its military wing, as a foreign terrorist group).

Furthermore, the EU facilitated the cross-border apprehension of suspects following arrest. Following the entry into force of a European Arrest Warrant in 2004, law enforcement authorities from a member state where a crime has occurred are able to apprehend suspects located in another member state without delay rather than wait many months, if not years, to do so. It was thanks to this tool that the UK and Belgian authorities were able quickly to bring back from Italy and France the perpetrators of the bombings in London in 2005 and the attack on the Jewish Museum in 2014. The terrorist attacks in Madrid in 2004 led the EU to establish a Counterterrorism Coordinator to act as a bridge between the competent

EU institutions and member states' agencies in the field of counterterrorism. In 2011, the EU also formed a Radicalisation Awareness Network to connect practitioners from around Europe to explore strategies to counter radicalization and violent extremism.

The attacks of 2014–2016 prompted the European Commission to propose a series of measures to enhance security in the EU. Legislation on combating terrorism, adopted in 2017, established new terrorism offenses and stiff penalties for traveling within, outside or to the EU for terrorist purposes (to join the activities of a terrorist group or with the purpose of committing a terrorist attack); organizing and facilitating such travel, including through logistical and material support; training or being trained for terrorist purposes (such as in the making or use of explosives or firearms); inciting, promoting or glorifying terrorism, whether offline or online; and providing or collecting funds with the intention or the knowledge that they are to be used to commit terrorist offenses.

A related package of measures passed in 2017–2018 aims to further limit the ability of terrorists to operate. These measures include tighter controls on and penalties for the acquisition and trafficking of high-capacity weapons, the access to chemical substances often used to make homemade explosives, document fraud and money laundering. The new rules provided authorities greater power to freeze and confiscate assets belonging to terrorists, as well as gain speedy access to and use financial information in criminal investigations. In 2018, the European Commission proposed legislation on "E-evidence" that will make it easier and faster for a judicial authority in one member state to obtain electronic evidence (including e-mails, text, or messages in apps) directly from a service provider—such as an electronic communications service provider, hosting service provider, social network, or online marketplace—in another member state. At the time of writing, the proposal had not yet been approved.

During the past decade, the EU has also taken important steps to enhance the identity checks on people crossing the EU's external frontiers by air, land, and sea. These checks are important because it is hard to maintain security within the EU if the external frontiers are porous. One of the most important reforms of the past decade has been to ensure that EU citizens are thoroughly checked against all EU databases when they cross an external frontier, just like third country nationals. This is especially significant in light of the number of European-borne terrorists.

One of the critical debates in the European Parliament during my diplomatic assignment related to the passage of an EU-wide Passenger Name Record (PNR) system. PNR data, supplied by passengers at the time of booking and checking in and then stored in airlines' reservation systems, consists of information such as passenger name, travel dates and itineraries, seat number, baggage, contact details (phone number and e-mail address) and means of payment. When supplied to national authorities, the data can be very useful in detecting suspicious air travel patterns and other indicators that may identify potential terrorists. The reason is that terrorists depend on travel to receive training and indoctrination, to case their targets and to carry out their attacks. Every time terrorists board a plane or cross a border, they give law enforcement authorities a chance to detect and capture them. The problem, of course, is that about 70 million travelers fly between the United States and the EU every year. Terrorists represent a needle in a haystack. To find the needle, one needs to gather and analyze a lot of data.

PNR data is one important tool. Border protection authorities can use PNR data to check travelers' names against watchlists of known or suspected terrorists. Since terrorists often use false identities or otherwise try to conceal themselves, PNR can reveal hidden connections (such as a common e-mail address) between known terrorists and their unknown associates. Had investigators used this simple technique, they could have uncovered the ties among all 19 of the 9/11 hijackers. PNR data can also be used to spot potential terrorists based on their travel patterns, especially if they use convoluted routings to avoid detection. International cooperation between countries that collect and share PNR data is essential to uncover this technique. Finally, PNR data can be used to identify perpetrators and their accomplices after an attack takes place.[3]

The United States has been using PNR data since 1992. US privacy laws provide robust safeguards against the misuse of personal information, contrary to the preconceived notions of many Europeans. For example, those laws limit when and with whom that information can be shared, the circumstances in which individuals may request access to their records, and the purposes for which that data may be used. Despite the utility of PNR data, legislation to establish an EU system languished for many years, principally due to concerns in the European Parliament about its compatibility with EU data privacy rules. In the meantime, some EU

---

[3] Speech by Ambassador Nathan Sales, Coordinator for Counterterrorism, "Counterterrorism, Data Privacy, and the Transatlantic Alliance," German Marshall Fund, July 19, 2018.

member states had their own PNR systems, but they were not harmonized or interconnected.

During my frequent trips to Strasbourg for the European Parliament's plenary sessions, I tried to convince as many parliamentarians as possible that an EU PNR system was an important anti-terrorism tool. Some of the parliamentarians were data privacy ayatollahs, reserving their righteous indignation for the quantity of PNR data that the authorities could collect and for the period they could retain it, rather than for the slaughter of civilians at the hands of terrorists.

Some parliamentarians favored a requirement that PNR data should be deleted once a traveler's visit ends; others were prepared to accept that such data be retained, but only for several months.[4] That would have prevented law enforcement from protecting the public or prosecuting the perpetrators of terrorist attacks. Take the case of Ra'ed al-Banna, a Jordanian citizen, who arrived at Chicago's O'Hare airport from Amsterdam on July 14, 2003. Although he had a valid passport and US visa, customs officials decided to fingerprint him and put him back on a plane to Jordan because his PNR data and his answers seemed suspicious. Nearly two years later, he drove a car into a crowd in an Iraqi town, detonated a powerful bomb and killed 132 people. Had PNR data on al-Banna not been collected and scrutinized in the United States, the atrocity might well have been committed on US soil. There are many similar cases to this one.

As I followed the tribulations of the EU PNR legislation caused by data privacy concerns, I couldn't help feeling that Europe was fighting a battle with one hand tied behind its back. Authorities from the EU and the member states had the tools to provide the security that citizens so desperately wanted but were often unable to use them. I often heard the objection that an EU PNR system would not have prevented any of the recent terror attacks of 2014–2015. That was purely speculative; while no one expected it to be a silver bullet, all serious counterterrorism experts expected it to be helpful. The attacks in Paris and Brussels were instrumental in raising public pressure on the European Parliament to stop dragging its feet. French Interior Minister Bernard Cazeneuve was clear in his statement to fellow ministers at the end of November

---

[4] In the United States, PNR data are held in an active database for up to five years, before being "depersonalized" (made anonymous) and transferred to a dormant database, where they can be held for a further ten years.

2015: "[PNR] is absolutely indispensable to combat terrorism. Not a single French citizen or EU citizen will understand why the European Parliament will continue blocking this essential tool."[5] In April 2016, the European Parliament finally approved a system that requires airlines to supply national authorities with PNR data for international flights entering or departing the EU. All EU member states have availed themselves of the additional possibility of requiring airlines to provide this data for intra-EU flights as well.

THE REFUGEE CRISIS

The porousness of the EU's external frontiers was highlighted during the refugee crisis of 2015, in which roughly 1.2 million refugees poured into Europe in the space of several months. The sudden wave was due in large part to the fact that many Syrian refugees had depleted their savings and had lost hope of returning to their homes because of a civil war in Syria that continued unabated. At the same time as the United Nations food aid programs were being cut, the refugees noticed that parts of Europe were open to their arrival. In particular, Chancellor Angela Merkel had put out a welcome mat and refused to impose any cap on asylum seekers. That decision, taken without prior coordination with other EU member states, would foreseeably place enormous strains on EU solidarity.

Europe had already been facing significant humanitarian crises in the preceding few years, mostly due to flows of economic migrants from Northern Africa. In the fall of 2014, Pope Francis had called on Europe to prevent the Mediterranean from becoming a "vast migrant cemetery." But the 2015 crisis was different because of its scale and because it principally involved refugees rather than economic migrants. For several months, it seemed as if the EU was at long-term risk of losing control over who was entering and monitoring the identities of hundreds of thousands of people circulating freely within the EU.

Two horrific events highlighted the fact that the refugee crisis was above all a humanitarian tragedy. In August 2015, Austrian border police found an abandoned truck contained the decomposing corpses of 59 men, eight women and four children (including a baby girl less than

---

[5] Zoya Sheftalovich and David Meyer, "Deal Close on EU Passenger Name Records," *Politico*, November 30, 2015. https://www.politico.eu/article/deal-close-on-eu-passenger-name-records/.

one year old). The victims were migrants who had fallen into the hands of migrant smugglers in their desperation to flee horrific conditions in Syria, Iraq, and Afghanistan. The victims had apparently suffocated and had been dead for two days when the discovery was made. The truck had attracted the suspicion of the border police because of decomposing body fluids dripping from the vehicle. As shocking as this was, the discovery was simply a drop in the ocean of human trafficking, often conducted by organized criminal groups.

In September 2015, the front pages of many newspapers in Europe carried the image of a three-year-old Kurdish boy face down on a beach. He had drowned attempting to reach the Greek island of Kos and had washed ashore near the internationally renowned resort of Bodrum. Any parent, indeed any human being, could not help but feel a sense of revulsion, shame, and anger at the smugglers who were treating humans like animals and risking their lives by putting them in unsafe vessels.

One week later in Strasbourg, I watched European Commission President Juncker deliver his annual State of the Union address to a packed hemicycle of parliamentarians. In the address, he made a moving reference to the humanitarian disaster caused by the refugee crisis. It practically reduced me to tears as I recalled that my grandparents had once been refugees:

> We can build walls, we can build fences. But imagine for a second it were you, your child in your arms, the world you knew torn apart around you. There is no price you would not pay, there is no wall you would not climb, no sea you would not sail, no border you would not cross if it is war or the barbarism of the so-called Islamic State that you are fleeing.[6]

The refugee crisis was far more destabilizing for Europe than the preceding financial crisis because it was so much more tangible and emotional. Thousands of people saw first hand the endless lines of desperate people entering their villages. Even those not directly affected worried about whether the human tide would ebb and what consequences it would have on Europe's culture. Images of refugees being loaded onto German train wagons or handing over their valuables to border guards in Denmark brought back uncomfortable reminders of the past.

---

[6] State of the Union 2015: "Time for Honesty, Unity and Solidarity," Strasbourg, September 9, 2015. http://europa.eu/rapid/press-release_SPEECH-15-5614_en.htm.

The refugee crisis triggered concerns that serious criminals and even terrorists would hide among the refugees to enter the EU and undermine its security. Unfortunately, those concerns tended to overwhelm other, more positive, humanitarian and economic considerations. The vast majority of those fleeing the Syrian civil war, for example, were simply fleeing ghastly conditions in search of a better life. These refugees also represented a major opportunity for Europe, if handled properly, to address its demographic challenge and to revitalize economic growth. In parts of Europe, populations are aging so fast and the birth rate is so low that the age pyramid is inverting rapidly, such that fewer people of working age at the bottom of the pyramid are supporting many more pensioners at the top. Without an influx of young people, for example, Germany's population was projected to decline to 65 million from 82 million by 2060 and its pensioners were projected to rise from one-fifth of the population to one-third.

Even though a relatively small percentage of the refugees were highly skilled, they represented a potential source of talent. In my public comments on the refugees during my diplomatic mission, I frequently reminded my audiences that of the 98 high-tech firms in the Fortune 500, 45 were founded by immigrants or their children; examples include Sergei Brin of Google, Steve Jobs of Apple and Hamdi Ulukaya, the founder of the billion-dollar Chobani yogurt company, who arrived in the United States as a penniless Kurdish immigrant.

Policing the EU's External Frontiers

At the same time, however, it was impossible to deny that the porousness of the EU's external frontiers did pose a security risk to Europe and even to the United States. The fact that several of the perpetrators of the Paris attacks of November 2015 had entered Europe with falsified Syrian passports with the refugee streams only heightened this concern. The mixed record of some European countries, including Germany, in finding employment for immigrants also raised the question of whether there would be hundreds of thousands of young, marginalized and frustrated males ripe for terrorist recruitment.

The difficulty of policing the EU's external frontiers had already been in evidence for several years. Italy had been pleading for more help from its fellow EU member states to deal with massive refugee flows from Northern Africa. It bore the brunt of a costly naval rescue operation on its own for one year until an EU operation managed by Frontex, the EU's border security agency, took over in November 2014. But the limitations of Frontex were manifest: It was underfunded, with a budget of only about €100 million (at the time); it relied on voluntary contributions from EU member states; it had few staff and little equipment; and it had a limited right to carry out border management and search and rescue operations. *The Economist* exaggerated only slightly when it wrote that Frontex "cannot do much more than fingerprint and count migrants as they pass through a country."[7]

Italy continued to be on the front lines and justifiably complained of insufficient EU solidarity. EU heads of state would routinely make declarations of support during their summits but wouldn't loosen their purse strings. Many EU member states simply didn't feel directly affected by the crisis and were only too happy to let Italy (and Greece) deal with it. Frontex received only a modest budget increase to €114 million in 2015, but the agency was spread even more thinly when it deployed officers and vessels to several Greek islands to help the Greek authorities cope with the massive refugee flows from Turkey. Borders along the Balkan Route from Greece into Croatia, Slovenia, Hungary, and Austria were also being overrun.

The legislative centerpiece of the EU's asylum system, the Dublin Regulation, was clearly exacerbating the situation because it required applications for asylum to be processed in the first country of entry. The huge problem with the system is that it undermined pan-European solidarity by contradicting the principle of burden-sharing. It allowed other countries that did not want immigrants to return them to the countries where they originally arrived. That may have been sustainable in an age of limited flows of asylum seekers arriving by air, but it was unfair and unsustainable in an age of vast migration flows arriving by sea or land.

As they faced the burden of the refugee crisis largely alone, Italy and Greece, the two principal frontline states, preferred to ensure that the refugees moved along as quickly as possible to their final destinations (usually Germany and Sweden) rather than to process their asylum applications as required under the Dublin Regulation. At first the countries on the Balkan Route tried to stem the flow of refugees with fences, before encouraging them to move northwards. For a while, it seemed

---

[7] "A Real Border Guard at Last," *The Economist*, December 16, 2015.

that frontiers would reappear among many EU member states and that the Schengen area of free movement was in trouble. The destruction of Schengen, European Commission President Jean-Claude Juncker warned, would not only be a body blow to the EU's self-esteem, but would also presage the demise of the euro and the single market. If the "temporary" re-introduction of border controls within the EU turned out to be permanent, warned the Bertelsmann Foundation, the EU would suffer €470 billion euros in lost economic output over a ten-year period.[8]

The US government and the US Congress were watching the situation with alarm, not only because of the human cost, but also because of the dangers of serious splits among EU member states and a potential unraveling of the EU itself. Moreover, they were concerned that many of the terrorists, radicalized in Syria and Iraq, had EU passports and could therefore benefit from visa-free entry into the United States under the Visa Waiver Program (VWP). After all, Zacarias Moussaoui, one of the September 11 hijackers, was a French citizen and Richard Reid, who had tried to blow up a plane by detonating his shoe in flight, was a British citizen. Both had traveled to the United States under the VWP.

Five of the 28 EU member states (Bulgaria, Croatia, Cyprus, Poland, and Romania) do not benefit from the VWP because they have fallen short of the statutory requirements. Those five have repeatedly urged the European Commission to withdraw visa-free travel for US citizens until they are included in the program. During the negotiations on a Transatlantic Trade and Investment Partnership agreement, Romania had threatened to block eventual ratification if the US did not give its citizens visa-free travel; it successfully pressured Canada to lift its visa restrictions as a condition to ratifying the Canada–EU Free Trade Agreement in 2016.

The US government repeatedly explained that the requirements of the VWP were established by statute; only Congress could amend them (something it was clearly not willing to do) and the executive branch could not simply waive them. As I reminded my interlocutors, several of the five member states were close to meeting the requirements and would probably do so soon. Eliminating US visa-free travel to Europe

---

[8] Dr. Michael Böhmer, Jan Limbers, Ante Pivac, and Heidrun Weinelt "Departure from the Schengen Agreement: Macroeconomic Impacts on Germany and the Countries of the European Union." https://www.bertelsmann-stiftung.de/fileadmin/files/BSt/Publikationen/GrauePublikationen/NW_Departure_from_Schengen.pdf.

would simply lead Congress to eliminate all European visa-free travel to the United States, a step that would have a serious impact on transatlantic tourism and business flows. Moreover, I explained that the refugee crisis and the porousness of Europe's borders did pose legitimate concerns for the United States.

I argued that the EU should therefore acquiesce in the inevitable tightening of VWP conditions in order to save the VWP. That tightening occurred in early 2016 when the US Congress overwhelmingly approved amendments to withhold visa waivers from any person (with certain exemptions) who had traveled to Syria, Iraq, Iran, Sudan, Libya, Somalia, or Yemen on or after March 1, 2011; EU dual nationals of most of these countries were also denied visa waivers, meaning that they had to apply for a visitor visa at a US consulate. The amendments also required all countries participating in the VWP to issue electronic passports and machines capable of reading them at all ports of entry. It threatened to terminate participation of any EU country that failed to share counterterrorism information or to screen travelers against relevant EU and Interpol databases on criminals and terrorists.

In December 2015, the European Commission proposed a proper European Border and Coast Guard (EBCG) to take over from, and improve upon, Frontex. The EBCG was approved in record time and became operational in October 2016. The plans for the agency have called for a budget of over €300 million (significantly exceeding the Frontex budget) and a permanent staff of 1000 by 2020. Member states have agreed to commit a total of at least 1500 field agents to a reserve pool of guards prepared to protect external frontiers within days of a request to do so. According to these plans, the agency would have access to a pool of equipment, including vessels, helicopters and patrol vehicles, owned by EU member states or by itself. The goals of the agency include monitoring and managing borders, collecting personal data and transferring it to Europol, coordinating relief efforts, and conducting search and rescue operations, either at the request of a member state or, in certain urgent situations, even when a member state is unwilling or unable to act.

These plans became even more ambitious by the end of 2018, when President Juncker announced in his annual State of the Union address a proposal to expand the EU border guard force to 10,000 and to grant it powers to bear arms and use force to police frontiers, as well as to return refugees to their home countries when their asylum applications fail. If the plan is approved, the force would even be able to deploy in non-EU third countries with their permission. This would represent a dramatic extension of EU powers in one of the most sensitive areas of member state sovereignty and, therefore, one of the boldest steps in the history of European integration. Some Brexiteers found this to be an outrageous usurpation of powers by the EU. On the contrary, it is a step that member states have urged the EU to take for the simple reason that pan-European challenges like refugee flows and the protection of external frontiers demand a pan-European response.

In order to ensure control over its external borders, it has been necessary to regulate the flow of refugees and migrants at their source. The EU has deployed a naval force to neutralize established refugee smuggling routes in the Mediterranean. A report issued by the House of Lords in 2017 concluded that irregular migration into Europe on the central Mediterranean route had increased and that the operation had led to greater migrant deaths at sea. However, a deal Italy struck with Libya in February 2017 to train, equip, and fund the Libyan coastguard in return for Libya preventing departures of migrants to Europe appears to be successful. Another deal the EU struck with Turkey in 2016 to provide financial assistance and to ease visa restrictions in return for Turkey stemming the westward flow of migrants to Europe has also prevented a repetition of the 2015 migration crisis. Critics of the deal allege that the EU and its member states have arguably had to compromise their principles when striking deals with countries with poor human rights records.

In order to re-establish control over the EU's external frontiers, the European Commission has also rightly focused on the functionality of the EU's many databases and information sharing systems. Each has been established with distinct objectives in mind, such as law enforcement and immigration control. The SIS, the most widely used information system for border management and security in Europe, contains information on suspected criminals, forged identity documents, and stolen firearms, vehicles, and property. The Visa Information System contains information on visa applications by third country nationals who require a visa to enter the Schengen area. The Eurodac system contains fingerprints of asylum applicants and third country nationals who are found to have crossed the external borders of the Schengen area unlawfully.

The terror attacks in Europe revealed that these (and other) systems did not always capture the type of information that could prove useful in investigations and sometimes were difficult to search. The member states were not consistently populating the systems with the required information or even consulting them methodically. The identities of Schengen area citizens were subject to minimal checks (such as to verify the authenticity of passports) at external borders, unless they were known to be a risk; some member states were not even carrying out proper checks on third country nationals. The systems could only be queried for the specific purpose with which they were designed and not for general criminal investigatory purposes. Moreover, the conditions for access were overly strict and all (or even several of them) could not be searched at one time (a feature of obvious utility under time pressure).

The failure of some member states to register and fingerprint refugees, as well as to share fingerprints among other member states, were also causing blind spots for law enforcement. Although countries on the EU's external borders were legally obliged to save and share all fingerprint data of refugees upon arrival, some were not doing so consistently. In late 2015 Greece was even refusing to take possession of 300 Eurodac fingerprinting machines on some of their islands closest to Turkey, citing problems with Internet connections and staff training, and was refusing the deployment of Frontex staff to reinforce its borders. Although it seemed odd at first, it was perfectly logical that Greece preferred the refugees to move onwards to their final destinations than to "own" the problem by installing the machines. Greece's refusal also seemed to be an attempt to gain leverage in its tense negotiations with the EU about its financial bailout: give us a better deal, Athens seemed to be saying to Brussels, or we can flood the EU with refugees. The situation became so serious that the European Commission sued Greece for its failure to respect its Eurodac obligations and even threatened to suspend Greece from Schengen, a step that would have trapped refugees in Greece and would have turned the country, in the memorable phrase of the Greek deputy minister for migration, into a "cemetery of souls."[9]

Transit states were subject to different obligations than those of frontier states. Whereas Austria could take fingerprints of the hundreds of thousands of refugees entering the country to check for a criminal record, it was not legally allowed to save and share that data in the overwhelming majority of cases where the migrants wanted to move elsewhere to claim

---

[9] Andrew Byrne, "Athens Hits Back at EU Plan to Isolate Greece Over Migrants," *Financial Times*, January 25, 2016.

asylum.[10] Even where fingerprints were inputted into the Eurodac fingerprint database, law enforcement officials often had difficulty meeting the strict conditions for access. Worse still, the Eurodac database was not connected to comprehensive pan-European databases on criminals. The combination of the failures of frontier states and the flawed legal regime meant that the EU had no trace of hundreds of thousands of refugees once they had crossed the EU's external frontiers. The head of Germany's federal office for migration admitted that there were up to 400,000 people in the country whose identities were unknown to the authorities. 130,000 asylum seekers had simply "disappeared."[11]

Over the past few years, the EU has been developing large-scale centralized IT tools to improve the functionality of existing border management and law enforcement information systems. Under new EU rules, these systems are interconnected, interoperable, and searchable simultaneously through a central portal. The rules facilitate the ability of border guards to establish whether an individual's name or fingerprint appears in one of the many EU databases. Member states are now making greater use of centralized border management and law enforcement systems—not only those established and operated by the EU such as Europol, but also those established and operated by Interpol and the decentralized systems implemented by the member states.

Finally, a new Entry-Exit-System, operational by 2020, will compile biometric data and travel history records relating to third country nationals entering the Schengen area for short-stay visits. The data will be stored in a central database that can be consulted by border and visa authorities, Europol and national law enforcement authorities. The system will enable those authorities to identify persons overstaying their visas and suspects in terror-related investigations. By 2021, a new European Travel Information and Authorization System (ETIAS), similar to the US ESTA, will apply to all visitors from countries who do not need a visa to enter the

---

[10] "EU Rules Prevent Sharing of Refugee Fingerprints," *Euractiv*, February 23, 2016. https://www.euractiv.com/section/global-europe/news/eu-rules-prevent-sharing-of-refugee-fingerprints/.

[11] "Germany Reports Disappearance of 130,000 Asylum Seekers," BBC, February 26, 2016. https://www.bbc.co.uk/news/world-europe-35667858.

Schengen Zone. The ETIAS database will enable Frontex to conduct electronic checks of such visitors against a list of wanted persons before they travel to Europe and to detect potentially dangerous visitors according to certain criteria.

US–EU Cooperation

All of these measures will enhance Europe's security. But the European Union, and its member states, recognize that they cannot ensure strong borders or combat serious crime and terrorism on their own. Many EU member states have long enjoyed strong bilateral police and judicial cooperation with the United States; some, like the UK, are rather protective of their special relationship and occasionally prickly about US–EU collaboration. Nonetheless, EU institutions, including the European Commission and Europol, have also been strengthening international law enforcement cooperation with Washington since the early 2000s. The United States has recognized that the security of the EU has a direct impact on its own security and that US–EU cooperation enhances bilateral law enforcement relationships with EU member states. While the United States has the good fortune of having large oceans to its east and west and is bordered by friendly countries, it cannot remain in splendid isolation from increasingly transnational threats, such as cybercrimes, drug trafficking, child sexual exploitation, terrorism, and migrant smuggling.

The terrorist attacks of September 11, 2001 prompted the US and EU to deepen pre-existing dialogues at cabinet and working level on police and judicial cooperation. These dialogues have covered a host of issues, including counterterrorism and countering violent extremism, terrorist financing, tracing of firearms and explosives, migration and border controls, cybercrime, and cargo security.

The US and the EU also have entered into several international agreements relating to security. In 2001 and 2002, the US and Europol signed several agreements to facilitate the exchange of information, to promote cooperation on combating serious crime and to authorize the exchange of liaison officers. In 2004, another agreement enabled US customs officers in several EU foreign ports to pre-screen maritime cargo containers bound for the United States. A subsequent agreement on the mutual recognition of each side's "trusted trader" programs facilitates customs procedures for certain shippers.

Two US–EU agreements from 2003 harmonized and made more effective the bilateral accords that already existed between the US and individual EU member states on extradition and mutual legal assistance. Both contain important provisions that enhance information sharing and prosecutorial cooperation. For example, the extradition agreement clarifies the kinds of offenses that justify extradition, facilitates the exchange of information and transmission of documents, and sets rules for determining priority in case of competing requests for extradition. The US–EU Mutual Legal Assistance Treaty (MLAT) allows, among other things, the prompt identification of financial account information in criminal investigations; the acquisition of evidence, including testimony by means of video conferencing; and authorizes the participation of US criminal investigators and prosecutors in joint investigative teams in the EU. The US–EU MLAT also served to establish for the first time mutual legal assistance between the US and some member states that had recently joined the EU.

US–EU agreements on the supply of EU PNR data to the US, the protection of data privacy regarding the transatlantic exchange of law enforcement information, and US access to interbank financial messaging data of European companies have made important contributions to transatlantic security.

The US–EU PNR agreement, reached in 2004 and repeatedly revised to address data privacy concerns in Europe before finally being ratified in 2012, also stemmed from the joint desire to investigate and thwart terrorist attacks through the sharing of information. It requires European airlines to supply PNR data to the US Department of Homeland Security's Bureau of Customs and Border Protection within 15 minutes of a plane taking off. The agreement seeks to heighten transatlantic security while enabling the continued flow of visitors and respecting data privacy. The US–EU PNR agreement contains data privacy protections that go beyond those required by US law, including the use of encryption and strict administrative controls to limit access to PNR data, and the notification of travelers when their PNR data is disclosed or accessed improperly. The EU has welcomed the fact that the United States has proactively shared analytical information obtained from PNR data with EU member states and Europol.

The second agreement, the Data Privacy and Protection Agreement (DPPA), described in Chapter 5, was ratified in 2016. The agreement covers all transatlantic personal data exchanges for law enforcement purposes. It is known as an "Umbrella" agreement because it complements existing agreements between the US and EU member state law enforcement authorities, creates harmonized data protection rules, and sets a high level of privacy protection for future agreements in the field.

The third and most significant agreement, the US–EU TFTP Agreement, provides the legal framework under which the US Treasury may access and subsequently process financial messaging data held in the EU by a Brussels-based consortium of international banks, called the Society for Worldwide Interbank Financial Telecommunication, for the purpose of investigating, detecting or prosecuting terrorism. Simply put, the SWIFT network is the communication backbone of the formal financial system; it handles most of the millions of daily international interbank messages exchanged among 11,000 financial institutions in more than 200 countries. The messages contain information about banks involved in transactions, account holders, contact information, amounts transferred, and times of payments.

The agreement was first concluded in 2007 after revelations during the prior year that the US Treasury had been secretly issuing subpoenas to access SWIFT data since 2001 under its classified Terrorist Finance Tracking Program (TFTP).[12] Under the TFTP Agreement, Europol assesses whether Treasury's data requests are necessary for the fight against terrorism and its financing. Europol also verifies that each request is tailored as narrowly as possible to minimize the amount of data provided in order to comply with EU data privacy laws. The agreement was amended to satisfy certain EU data privacy concerns but was voted down in the European Parliament in early 2010, before being further revised and approved in mid-2010 (thanks in large part to the effective advocacy of my predecessor Ambassador Bill Kennard and the personal appeals of Vice President Joe Biden).

The TFTP Agreement has proven to be a valuable tool in terrorism-related investigations because it enhances the ability to map terrorist networks by tracking terrorist money flows. US authorities have made extensive use of their ability under the agreement to provide TFTP information to EU and member state authorities. To the rather considerable irritation of certain member states, this is information that they cannot obtain directly from SWIFT themselves. Although there have been repeated proposals to create an EU TFTP equivalent, they have been shot down by

---

[12] Eric Lichtblau and James Risen, "Bank Data Is Sifted by US in Secret to Block Terror," *The New York Times*, June 23, 2006.

data privacy hawks concerned about giving governments another avenue of obtaining personal information. Furthermore, some member states have worried that an EU TFTP would be the first step toward granting the EU more powers in intelligence gathering, a jealously guarded national domain. It is rather ironic that the United States helps the EU enhance European security by obtaining information the EU can't obtain itself, even though the information is held in Europe by a European company.

Another striking feature about the TFTP Agreement is that its scope excludes intra-EU payments. The reason for the exclusion has been that information about such payments is more likely to concern European citizens and therefore more likely to affect European data privacy rights than international payments information. The problem is that many European terrorists, like those behind the recent attacks in Europe, live, work and travel in Europe, and only conduct financial transactions in Europe. While the TFTP information that the United States provides to Europe contains important leads gleaned from international financial transactions, the terrorists' financial dealings in Europe remain a black hole.

As of November 30, 2018 the US has shared more than 50,000 TFTP-derived leads with European authorities and EU member state governments. These leads have prevented some terrorist attacks and have assisted the investigation of many others. The US Treasury Department has made a few examples public. They include the August 2017 terror attack in Turku, Finland; the August 2017 attack on La Rambla, Barcelona; and the April 2017 attack in Stockholm. Moreover, the US provided roughly 800 leads based on SWIFT information to Europol and European counterterrorism authorities in response to the attacks in Paris and Brussels. Some of them were provided in real time as the attacks were still under way. SWIFT information has also helped to prevent other attacks, as well as uncover EU-based recruitment of terrorist fighters in Syria and international financial support of terrorist organizations. Despite repeated allegations, especially in the immediate aftermath of the Snowden allegations, that the US Treasury has abused its powers under the agreement, regular US–EU joint reviews have concluded that the agreement is operating as intended.

The Contribution of Europol

The day after the terrorist attacks in Brussels, I traveled to Europol in The Hague to speak at a meeting of law enforcement officials from the EU member states and the United States on the importance of deepening transatlantic counterterrorism cooperation. During my speech, the photos of recent victims of terrorism on both sides of the Atlantic were flashed on the screen behind me. Later that day, I stood next to Rob Wainwright, the director of Europol, as he addressed the entire staff of the agency in the atrium and asked for a minute of silence out of respect for the victims. The mood was somber but resolute. As I looked out on the crowded atrium, with representatives of law enforcement authorities from 42 countries, I thought to myself that Europol represents international cooperation at its finest. The whole will always be greater than the sum of its parts when countries band together to provide mutual assistance and share information to save lives and prosecute criminals.

Europol is perhaps not as well-known as Interpol, an international body founded in 1923 with the aim of promoting police cooperation among its 192 members, but it has been steadily growing in significance. Its international profile certainly benefited from the fact that the film *Ocean's Twelve*, released in 2004, featured a Europol investigator (played by Catherine Zeta-Jones) who is on the trail of main character, Danny Ocean (played by George Clooney). Its growing size and responsibilities over the past decade are due in part to the terrorist attacks mentioned earlier; but it is primarily due to the vision and drive of Rob Wainwright, who led the organization between 2009 and 2018.

With a budget of about €125 million and a staff of 1200, Europol focuses on organized crime, terrorism, and other forms of serious crime that affect two or more member states and that require a "common approach by the member states owing to the scale, significance and consequences of the offences."[13] Even two decades after its founding, Europol falls short of German Chancellor Helmut Kohl's vision of a European FBI with sweeping powers. It relies on member states for information and cooperation, and it does not have enforcement powers, such as the

---

[13] COUNCIL DECISION of 6 April 2009 establishing the European Police Office (Europol). https://eur-lex.europa.eu/legal-content/EN/TXT/PDF/?uri=CELEX:32009D0371&from=en.

power to arrest suspects. *Ocean's Twelve*'s depiction of Europol was erroneous because it does not engage in operational police work.

Europol has had to deal with the view of the larger EU member states, especially the UK and France, that the EU does not have the legal authority to provide the intelligence work that traditional secret services do (even though there is a small EU unit that does intelligence analysis of issues based on information provided by member state intelligence services). Since 2002 all the intelligence agencies of the EU 28, as well as those from Norway and Switzerland, have met informally outside the EU legal framework as the Counter-Terrorism Group to improve intelligence cooperation. Nonetheless, the EU has demonstrated that Europol and many EU databases usefully supplement the work of member states' intelligence services.

Europol's contributions are significant: It serves as an information hub that gathers criminal intelligence from member states, third countries, and other sources and subsequently disseminates that information through a secured communications network. It is also a center of law enforcement expertise that generates strategic reports (such as threat assessments), and a support center for law enforcement operations in the member states (especially complex cross-border operations against high-value targets).

Europol's strong relationship with US law enforcement authorities took time to establish. When Wainwright, a former intelligence analyst at MI5, Britain's domestic intelligence service, first met Robert Mueller (then director of the FBI) soon after his appointment to Europol in 2009, Mueller seemed skeptical of the value that Europol could deliver. Mueller made it clear that the FBI wasn't interested in multilateral cooperation; the only thing that mattered, according to him, was bilateral cooperation. At that time, Europol had only been in existence for a decade and had few credentials and limited means. Moreover, Europol had yet to prove that it could safely collect and store intelligence without data breaches (something that it has succeeded in doing). Mueller probably was unimpressed with Europol because of its lack of enforcement powers and its reliance on the willingness of member state law enforcement authorities to share information. As the member states have increasingly used Europol as a provider of analysis and a clearinghouse of information, the desire of the FBI and other US law enforcement authorities to cooperate with Europol has grown.

Today Europol's reputation is well-established on both sides of the Atlantic because of its work in many areas such as cybercrime, drug trafficking, child sexual exploitation, terrorism, and migrant smuggling. Europol houses liaison officers from the law enforcement agencies of all EU member states, more than a dozen non-EU countries (including the United States), EU agencies such as Eurojust, and non-EU organizations such as Interpol. On each of my visits to Europol I sat down with some of the 40 liaison officers from eleven US law enforcement agencies posted there.[14] Despite some turf battles between these agencies, they have played a very constructive role in Europol's work and also benefit from Europol's expertise. Every year Europol supports approximately 500 cases involving US authorities, of which 50 are classified as being "high impact." Europol also has two senior liaison officers working in Washington to ensure a reliable point of contact for US law enforcement authorities.

Cybercrime continues to grow as an area of US–EU law enforcement cooperation. Europol's European Cybercrime Centre (EC3), established in 2013, has quickly established itself as a major player in forensics, strategy, and operational support to combat transnational cybercrime. Its Joint Cybercrime Action Task Force focuses on high-tech crimes (such as malware and identity theft), transnational payment fraud, crime on the Dark Net, and online child sexual exploitation. By hosting police officers temporarily seconded by EU member state law enforcement authorities and non-EU authorities (including the FBI and the US Secret Service), the task force pools national intelligence related to a specific cybercrime case.

The Dark Net is an anonymous network within the part of the World Wide Web that is not discoverable by means of standard search engines. It is difficult to police because it anonymizes a user's real Internet Protocol (IP) address by routing traffic through many servers. It can only be accessed using specific software such as TOR (an acronym for The Onion Router). TOR alone is used worldwide by over 750,000 people on a daily basis, with over 2 million directly connected users (half of whom are in Europe) and hosting over 45,000 domains.

The Dark Net was developed to protect freedom and privacy but is being misused by criminals to trade anonymously in a wide range of goods

---

[14] The law enforcement agencies are: Immigration and Customs Enforcement, Customs and Border Protection, the Federal Bureau of Investigation, the Drug Enforcement Agency, the Food and Drug Administration, the Secret Service, the State Department's bureau of diplomatic security, the Internal Revenue Service, the Bureau of Alcohol, Tobacco and Firearms, the Transportation Safety Administration and the New York Police Department.

and services such as drugs, firearms, fraudulent documents, counterfeit goods and currency, human trafficking, stolen personal data, and malware. As a significant part of its activity relates to hosting platforms engaging in illicit activity, the Dark Net has become one of the main engines of organized crime in the EU.

The widespread use of lightly regulated virtual currencies as a means of payment between vendors and clients complicates the task of tracing transactions and seizing assets. The most widely used virtual currency, bitcoin, enables pseudonymous (but not anonymous) transactions. The cryptographic addresses of the sender and the recipient of transactions are recorded on a publicly accessible ledger (called a "blockchain"). Although these addresses are not linked to real-life identities, it is possible to unmask the true identity of senders and recipients of bitcoin transactions with sufficient investigative resources.

Unfortunately, new virtual currencies offer a high degree of anonymity by using decentralized systems (without a central server or central supervisory body), combining multiple transactions, hiding the amount of each transaction, and obscuring the origin and recipient of funds. Although there have been few known instances of virtual currencies being used to finance terrorism, that may soon change because terrorists like the anonymity that the new currencies provide. By avoiding the use of traditional financial messaging, these virtual currencies will undermine the ability of the US and the EU to extract useful information from SWIFT through the TFTP Agreement.

In November 2014, EC3 coordinated an operation involving the FBI, the Immigration and Customs Enforcement (ICE) bureau of the Department of Homeland Security, and 21 countries in taking down the "Silk Road 2.0" Dark Net marketplace that was being used by thousands of dealers in drugs, firearms, and dangerous contraband. The operation led to multiple arrests of vendors and the administrators of the marketplace, as well as the seizure of bitcoins, cash, drugs, and gold. The operation also led to the shuttering of hundreds of other online marketplaces. While the takedown of a Dark Net marketplace was not new (the FBI had already acted against the predecessor Silk Road website in 2013), the operation was noteworthy because of its multinational character and speed. What would have taken years to organize without Europol was accomplished in several months.

In June 2017, EC3 was at the center of another multinational operation involving the FBI, the US Drug Enforcement Agency, and the Dutch national police. The operation shut down two of the three largest Dark

Net marketplaces that dwarfed the size of Silk Road and facilitated a major underground criminal economy affecting the lives of thousands of people around the world. The AlphaBay and Hansa marketplaces enabled the trading of over 350,000 illicit goods (especially drugs and firearms) among 200,000 members and 40,000 vendors. The value of transactions conducted through them since their creation in 2014 was conservatively estimated at $1 billion.

With the technical and forensic support of EC3, Dutch national law enforcement took covert control of the Dutch servers of Hansa, the third largest Dark Net site, and then monitored the activity of its users without their knowledge. At the same time, the authorities shut down AlphaBay, the largest darknet site, and waited until its users flocked to Hansa to continue trading. After gathering valuable information about the names of buyers and transactions, the operation shut Hansa down as well, and led to arrests and seizures of servers, cryptocurrencies, and intelligence that will lead to further investigations. Once again, Europol had proven its worth as a hub of transatlantic law enforcement information exchange, analysis, and cooperation.

Drugs are increasingly traded online on various platforms, including on the Dark Net. The drug market remains the largest criminal market in the EU. The retail drug market has been conservatively estimated to be worth about €24 billion per year and to account for up to 0.6% of the GDP of many EU member states. The reality is that the market is much, much larger. More than one-third of the organized criminal groups in the EU are involved in the production, trafficking, or distribution of drugs and derive billions of euros of profits from such activities. More than two-thirds of such groups involved in the drug trade are simultaneously involved in other criminal activities. The harm caused by the drug market extends well beyond drug use; it includes the financing of other criminal activities (including terrorism) and corruption.

On one of my visits to Europol, the head of the drugs unit emphasized the growing health risk from synthetic opioids, such as fentanyl derivatives. As I was about to pour a packet of sugar into my morning coffee, he made me sit up by pointing out that fentanyl is 30 times more potent than heroine and that a packet of that size contains thousands of doses, each of which can quickly poison and even kill an individual. Because of their psychoactive effects, such as causing euphoria, these opioids are frequently used as replacements for heroin, cocaine, and other illicit drugs. They are not controlled by international drug conventions and can therefore be manufactured and traded relatively freely in many countries. Organized crime groups therefore consider the opioid market to be a relatively low-risk and high-profit opportunity.

Hundreds of new synthetic compounds have been detected in the past few years alone. These synthetic opioids are typically manufactured by Chinese pharmaceutical and chemical companies, shipped to Europe either in bulk by air or sea cargo or in smaller quantities by express mail services, and subsequently sold through physical shops or online. There is an increasing risk that some of this traffic will flow onwards to the United States where opioid addiction is an alarming health problem. About 47,600 Americans died from overdosing on opioids such as fentanyl in 2017, up from 5000 in 2014. Europol will be a key partner of US law enforcement authorities in tackling this threat.

Another important area of work for the Joint Cybercrime Action Taskforce is transatlantic cooperation to combat online child sexual exploitation. In February 2015, the liaison officer representing the Department of Homeland Security at the US Mission to the EU informed me that law enforcement agencies on both sides of the Atlantic, including Europol, had assisted Romanian police in arresting a Romanian woman who had been sexually abusing her two-year-old daughter, filming the abuse and posting the content online. The woman's two children, who were found in the house search, were handed over to child custody services. I felt so revolted that I requested a full briefing.

The case arose when the National Center for Missing and Exploited Children (NCMEC) received a report of suspected child sexual abuse on their CyberTipline, a reporting tool for the public and Internet service providers (ISPs) to report child pornography. NCMEC is a private, non-profit entity based in the United States that serves as a national clearinghouse and resource center for victims, families, law enforcement and the public on issues relating to missing and sexually exploited children. ISPs are required by federal law to report child pornography that comes to their attention. Many also take proactive steps to detect and disrupt its redistribution by using technology like Microsoft's PhotoDNA. That technology creates a unique digital "signature" for a digital photograph, like a fingerprint, that calculates the essential characteristics which can then be compared against other photos to find copies, even when they have been resized or otherwise altered. Microsoft has provided PhotoDNA for free to NCMEC, law enforcement authorities, and many other organizations, including technology companies, to combat child exploitation.

NCMEC examined the report and immediately forwarded the information to the ICE Homeland Security Investigations liaison officer at Europol. Although the case was just one of tens of thousands of referrals made by ICE through Europol to EU member states every year, it was especially urgent because of the age of the victim. EC3 immediately launched an investigation, analyzed and cross-checked the data, and forwarded an intelligence package to Romanian authorities. The suspect was arrested within four days of Europol receiving notice of the case, a remarkably short period. I found the case particularly intriguing when I was told about the sophisticated tools employed to narrow the geographic search for the culprit; it was the presence of just a few objects in the background to the photographs that enabled law enforcement to focus on Romania and eventually the city of Sibiu in Transylvania. The success in that case helped launch a broader initiative called "Trace an Object" in which Europol posts images of objects on its Web site and solicits the public to help identify their origin.

In February 2017, US and European law enforcement authorities, including Europol, concluded a two-year investigation into Playpen, the world's largest pedophile ring on the Dark Net with over 150,000 users. The Playpen site enabled users to browse for a wide range of videos and photos of boys and girls, including toddlers, under different categories, such as incest and various fetishes. The investigation was one of the largest and most complex ever undertaken in its field. The FBI used malware to hack into Playpen's website and server and then track and identify its users. As a result of the investigation, the FBI convicted Playpen's founder to 30 years in prison and law enforcement authorities around the world arrested nearly 900 of its members, including 368 in Europe.

Under its "Angel Watch" program, furthermore, the ICE bureau of Homeland Security Investigations provides annually hundreds of alerts to Europol and EU member states about US child sex offenders traveling from the United States so that appropriate actions can be taken under national laws. A small but increasing number of EU member states provide ICE with similar alerts regarding European child sex offenders traveling from Europe to the United States.

Europol's reputation as an effective law enforcement agency is also due to its actions in the field of counterterrorism. A European Counter-Terrorism Centre (ECTC) serves as a platform for EU member states to pool and share information, as well as coordinate operations, relating to foreign terrorist fighters, firearms trafficking, and the financing of terrorism. The ECTC is also developing a strong working relationship with the US National Counterterrorism Center as it becomes abundantly clear that the defeat of transnational terrorism requires a regional or global approach rather than one focused on bilateral cooperation.

Alarmed by the trend of European Islamist jihadists who were traveling to Syria and Iraq (and sometimes back to Europe) to engage in acts of terrorism, in 2014 the ECTC launched a dedicated database, now part of the broader European Information System (EIS), to enable EU member states to collect, analyze, and share information on their recruitment and movements. The response from most member states was initially lukewarm: Europol received information (largely from just five member states) on roughly 2000 suspects, one-third of the 6000 EU nationals that member state security services suspected of being so-called foreign fighters. As of 2018, Europol estimated that one-third of the fighters died in fighting, one-third may have returned to their home countries, and one-third was still unaccounted for.[15]

At the time of the Brussels attacks in March 2016, Europol had about 4000 intelligence entries relating to terrorism; two years later the figure had more than doubled to 8600. The EIS is now consulted millions of times per year. Importantly, the database is also linked to Europol's organized crime database, enabling cross-matching of information and the establishment of links between investigations. As many of the terrorists who have attacked Europe had prior criminal records, this is an important contribution. Several US law enforcement agencies have signed agreements to participate in the ECTC's efforts to combat the "foreign fighter" phenomenon.

The ECTC has also provided operational support to EU member states during investigations launched in the wake of terrorist attacks. Within an hour of the attacks in Paris in November 2015, for example, the ECTC set up a taskforce staffed with 60 Europol officers (joined by US law enforcement) to assist the French and Belgian investigations. Combining its own data with information provided by the member states, information from the US TFTP, and other sources, Europol provided thousands of leads to

---

[15] Giulia Paravicini, "Europe Is Losing the Fight Against Dirty Money," *Politico*, April 4, 2018. https://www.politico.eu/article/europe-money-laundering-is-losing-the-fight-against-dirty-money-europol-crime-rob-wainwright/.

those investigations and contributed to the disruption of future attacks. The role of the ECTC has continued to grow after the Paris attacks. In 2017, it helped in 439 counterterrorist operations in Europe, up from 127 the year before.

The terrorist attacks of early 2015 underlined once again the malignant role of online terrorist propaganda. Jihadist groups have implemented a sophisticated Internet and social media campaign to recruit followers and glorify terrorism. Although not all terrorist attacks have been entirely due to online content, there is no doubt that some of the attackers were influenced by what they saw online. Some were persuaded by online content to join Islamist fighters in Syria and Iraq and some returned to commit atrocities in Europe. Others did not need to travel and were radicalized and instructed on weapon-making in the comfort of their own homes. Responding to the call of EU member states to address this phenomenon, the ECTC launched an Internet Referral Unit (IRU) in mid-2015 to provide operational support and analysis to the EU member states on online terrorist propaganda, as well as to identify and refer such content to ISPs and social media platforms for subsequent removal.

A related initiative called the EU Internet Forum brings together representatives of EU member state interior ministries, EU agencies, the Internet industry and other stakeholders to reduce accessibility to terrorist content online. The major platforms participating in the Forum, including Google, Facebook, Microsoft, and Twitter, have created a shared database containing tens of thousands of known items of terrorist content and are increasingly developing automated tools for their speedy detection and removal (even when re-uploaded onto different sites). Moreover, the platforms agreed with the European Commission on a "Code of Conduct on Countering Illegal Hate Speech Online" to tackle the spread of such content, including terrorist propaganda and xenophobic or racist hate speech. The code has been a success. As of 2019, all companies that signed the code (including all the large Internet firms) were assessing 89% of flagged content within 24 hours and removing about 70% of it.[16]

Europol has also coordinated multiple multinational operations by law enforcement authorities, including from the United States, to disable key media outlets affiliated with the terror group ISIS. One such operation in April 2018 took down the Amaq News Agency website, the primary

---

[16] European Commission Factsheet, February 2019. https://ec.europa.eu/info/sites/info/files/hatespeech_infographic3_web.pdf.

mouthpiece of and multi-lingual propaganda source about the group's activities worldwide. The operation resulted in the seizure of digital evidence and servers that later helped to identify both the administrators of ISIS websites and potentially radicalized individuals.

While the EU Internet Forum led to significant improvements in the removal of terrorist content online, the European Commission and EU member states felt much more could be done and faster. In March 2018, the European Commission proposed a set of voluntary recommendations to Internet companies about actions they should take to curb terrorist content online. According to the recommendations, the companies should remove terrorist content within one hour of notification and should implement proactive measures, including automated detection tools, to remove the content and prevent its reappearance. By the end of 2018, however, the European Commission abandoned the self-regulatory approach and proposed binding legislation, passed in 2019, on the removal of terrorist content within one hour of notification. This was partly driven by the fear that in the absence of EU-wide action many member states would pass their own national legislation.

Europol has also emerged as an important forum for US–EU cooperation on the combat against migrant smuggling. Europol established the European Migrant Smuggling Centre (EMSC) in early 2016 in response to the unprecedented wave of migrants that overwhelmed Europe during the prior year. Migrant smuggling is a fast-growing and highly profitable multi-billion-euro criminal activity, deriving revenues from charging illegal migrants extortionate fees to facilitate their travel into Europe. The goal of the center has been to assist EU member states, through information exchange and operational support, to target and disrupt the financing and conduct of sophisticated criminal networks involved in migrant smuggling. The deployment of EMSC staff to southern Italian ports and Greek islands near Turkey has made an important contribution, especially in the detection of fraudulent documentation and in conducting checks against criminal databases in the event that Frontex and national authorities have concerns during their initial screening.

The United States has a keen interest in disrupting migrant smuggling, not only because of the horrific conditions suffered by migrants at the hands of unscrupulous criminal groups, but also because of the danger that migrants may be able to benefit from visa-free travel from Europe to the United States. Although there is no clear evidence that terrorists have systematically used migrant flows to enter Europe, it is indisputable that some have done so. Reflecting these concerns, ICE and US Customs and Border Protection have joined a special joint operations team established by EMSC to combat illegal migration organized by criminal groups across the Mediterranean.

Prospects for Further Collaboration

I draw several conclusions from my engagement with law enforcement issues during my diplomatic mission in Brussels. First, the EU institutions have made an important contribution to European security, both at the EU's external borders and within its territory. Member states retain a key role in this regard, of course, but they can't achieve their goals without an increasingly unified approach. Second, US–EU law enforcement cooperation is also essential, not only to European security but to the security of the US homeland as well. Serious crime and terrorism are increasingly transnational in terms of the organization, recruitment, and financing that make them possible. Bilateral law enforcement cooperation between the United States and individual EU member states will remain a critical tool in combating serious crime, and terrorism, but US–EU cooperation will continue to gain in importance.

Despite the many areas of US–EU relations that have suffered a setback during the Trump administration, law enforcement fortunately continues to be an area of fruitful cooperation. For example, the US and the EU have recently collaborated to reduce the risk that terrorists could exploit portable electronic devices (such as tablets, laptops, and phones), chemicals, and powders to disrupt air travel, while minimizing undue burdens on the industry and passengers. There are several areas where we could go even further. One important opportunity would be to conclude a US–EU agreement to facilitate law enforcement authorities' access to electronic evidence held in each other's jurisdiction. The aim should be to conclude such an agreement far faster than the US–EU PNR Agreement or the Umbrella Data Privacy and Protection Agreement that took eight and six years, respectively.

A US–EU Agreement on access to "e-evidence" is necessary because personal devices, digitalization, the Internet, and high-speed communications are transforming crime and law enforcement. Transnational crime (much of it facilitated by the Internet) is on the rise and much of the related evidence is in electronic form, stored in places unrelated to the location of the crime. The Department of Justice and the European

Commission have both noted a significant recent increase in cross-border requests for electronic evidence.

The existing method of requesting assistance through an MLAT is not fit for purpose. Most of the mutual legal assistance treaties entered into between the US and the EU member states are so dated that they do not contemplate electronic evidence and do not provide strong procedural protections (such as judicial oversight) or data privacy rights. The average period required to fulfill MLAT requests is ten months because they must be transmitted from one central authority to another and then to foreign prosecutors and, in some instances, to courts. Often the requests must be translated and interpreted by the foreign government. And if the central government's law enforcement authority transfers the request to a local authority for action, the latter may well place a higher priority on its own investigations.

This delay is increasingly unacceptable in a world in which electronic evidence can be moved, manipulated, or deleted at lightning speed. As a result, governments around the world are increasingly requiring electronic service providers to store evidence locally. And they are seeking alternative means of acquiring evidence, such as asserting extraterritorial jurisdiction or making "voluntary requests" to foreign cloud providers and telecommunications companies, resulting in an increased likelihood that such firms will face a conflict of laws.

The MLAT system sometimes doesn't make sense because it requires foreign governments to meet US legal requirements rather than satisfy their own (often satisfactory) due process requirements, even when the case is national. Why compel a Belgian investigative magistrate to show "probable cause" to access an e-mail sent by a Belgian suspected jihadist to another Belgian suspected jihadist to plan an attack in Belgium simply because the e-mail is stored in a US server?

The passage of the Clarifying Lawful Overseas Use of Data (CLOUD) Act in the United States in 2018 was an important step toward modernizing US laws requiring acquisition of electronic evidence and toward enabling cross-border cooperation with foreign governments. The act allows federal law enforcement to compel US-based technology companies via warrant or subpoena to provide requested data stored on servers regardless of whether the servers are in the US or abroad. That rendered moot a long-running legal battle between Microsoft and the US government in which Microsoft resisted requests by the FBI, in the course of a drug trafficking investigation, to hand over e-mails of a US citizen that were stored on one of Microsoft's servers in Ireland.

The CLOUD Act is also significant because it authorizes the executive branch to enter into international agreements with foreign governments whose countries guarantee certain basic standards of due process and data privacy rights that are equivalent to those found in US law. These agreements enable national law enforcement authorities to request electronic service providers to deliver electronic evidence located in the other party's territory, a far quicker and simpler route than afforded under the MLATs.

The first such signed agreement between the United States and the UK will enable British law enforcement authorities to obtain electronic data such as e-mails, texts, and direct messages from US service providers—such as Google, Facebook, Twitter, and Microsoft—in criminal and national security investigations involving UK citizens. The UK must respect its own laws in doing so and it may not obtain records of any US citizen that might surface in an investigation. US law enforcement authorities have reciprocal rights under the agreement to obtain information from UK companies. The UK has apparently received assurances that information provided to the US under the agreement will not be used in cases involving the death penalty.

The US government faces the key question of whether to replicate the template of the US–UK executive agreement purely on a bilateral basis. For example, it may decide to pursue similar agreements with the other members of the "Five Eyes" intelligence-sharing alliance (Australia, New Zealand, and Canada). With regard to Europe, the US government must choose whether to negotiate with certain "trusted" member states or with the EU as a whole. Although the EU 27 have given the European Commission a mandate to negotiate on behalf of all of them, the US Department of Justice has harbored some reservations about this approach, principally because of concerns about the degree of due process protections in certain member states, such as Hungary and Poland.

Those concerns are overstated because of the robust protections under EU law, especially the EU Charter of Fundamental Rights and the General Data Protection Regulation, as reinforced by the recent regulation on electronic evidence. There are strong reasons justifying a US–EU agreement. Most important, it would provide an opportunity to begin establishing an international norm for cross-border access to evidence stored in the cloud that would be consistent with law enforcement needs and a high level of fundamental rights protection. An agreement could always provide additional safeguards of fundamental rights, beyond those found in EU and US law. And if there is credible evidence that a state does not provide sufficient protection of these rights, the agreement could be curtailed or suspended pending review.

The need for such an agreement is particularly important in light of the EU's own proposed "E-evidence" legislation that enables member states to compel telecommunications service providers to deliver information held in other EU member states or outside the EU when the information relates to serious crimes committed under their own laws. Before agreeing to sign an "umbrella" agreement with the EU and then detailed executive agreements with individual member states, the Department of Justice would have to conclude that EU law requires member states to satisfy minimum standards relating to data privacy, human rights, and due process. That would be a rather ironic mirror image to the situation the United States faced during the Privacy Shield negotiations described in Chapter 5.

The US and the EU also need to deepen their coordination in the fight against money laundering and the financing of terrorism. The challenge is massive and far from being addressed adequately. According to Wainwright, professional money launderers are running billions of euros of illegal drug and other criminal profits through the banking system with a 99% success rate. Despite banks spending tens of billions of euros on compliance, law enforcement authorities are seizing only a tiny fraction of criminal assets.[17] One of the issues holding back progress is the absence of an EU-wide body to coordinate the work of the national Financial Intelligence Units, the agencies that receive and analyze information relating to these crimes. Another issue is that there is no central database to store information: A decentralized computer network provides an information exchange between the agencies. Europol has frequently convened cryptocurrency exchanges, payment processors, and digital wallet providers as well as authorities from EU member states to assess ways to crack down on the use of digital assets for money laundering.

One important way for the US and the EU to deepen their campaign against money laundering and terrorist financing is to build on

---

[17] Giulia Paravicini, "Europe Is Losing the Fight Against Dirty Money," *Politico*, April 4, 2018. https://www.politico.eu/article/europe-money-laundering-is-losing-the-fight-against-dirty-money-europol-crime-rob-wainwright/.

the Europol Financial Intelligence Public–Private Partnership, a public–private partnership launched in December 2017. The partnership brings together experts from large international banks (including from the United States) and officials from law enforcement and the Financial Intelligence Units of EU and non-EU states. Its purpose is to build a common intelligence picture and understanding of the threats and risks, as well as to facilitate the exchange of intelligence related to on-going investigations.

While there are many uncertainties about the future of US–EU relations, one thing is certain: More and smarter cooperation on law enforcement will be increasingly necessary to confront well-financed and well-organized threats to our common security. Advancing transatlantic coordination will require identifying and working to eliminate obstacles whenever possible. For example, the exclusion of intra-European payment information from the TFTP Agreement should be terminated as this gives European terrorists significant scope to evade detection.

The departure of the UK from the EU presents a risk to the effectiveness of Europol because the UK has been a major contributor to (and beneficiary of) its work. It will be important for the UK to be as tightly involved in Europol's work as possible, including maintaining their access to Europol databases. If the UK is treated like a "third country" such as Russia, or even the United States, the operational effectiveness of Europol and US–EU law enforcement cooperation could suffer.

CHAPTER 10

Military and Security Cooperation

When I arrived in Brussels in March 2014, I assumed that military cooperation would be an insignificant feature of the US–EU relationship. I knew that we were cooperating on a wide array of foreign policy areas with security dimensions, including sanctions against Iran and Russia, the promotion of good governance, human rights and anti-corruption around the world, foreign aid and humanitarian assistance, climate change, and energy security. But I was surprised to note the range and depth of the US–EU military and broader security relationship and to realize the significant potential for further progress.

My negative preconceived notion about the military relationship was largely due to my memories of the EU's inability to deal with two major crises on its very doorstep. I was working as an intern in the European Commission when Jacques Poos, Luxembourg's Foreign Minister and President of the EU's Council, declared solemnly on the eve of Yugoslavia's civil war in 1991 that European governments had a special responsibility to act. "This is the hour of Europe," he said. "It is not the hour of the Americans."[1] Alas, that proved to be wide off the mark. It was only thanks to US airpower and diplomacy that the bloodshed stopped several years later and that a peaceful resolution emerged through the Dayton Agreement.

---

[1] Alan Riding, "Conflict in Yugoslavia: Europe Sends High Level Team," *The New York Times*, June 29, 1991. https://www.nytimes.com/1991/06/29/world/conflict-in-yugoslavia-europeans-send-high-level-team.html.

Belgian Foreign Minister Mark Eyskens gave a far more accurate, and equally widely quoted, summary of the situation in early 1991 when he said that "Europe is an economic giant, a political dwarf, and a military worm."[2] The EU's political and even military influence grew in the subsequent two decades, but Europe's efforts in 2011 to prevent dictator Muammar Gaddafi from committing crimes against humanity in Benghazi indicated once again the need for US military support. The NATO-led operation, largely conducted through air strikes in which France and the UK played leading roles, could not have succeeded without significant US intelligence, surveillance, and reconnaissance capabilities, as well as smart munitions and air-to-air refuelling.

THE EU's MILITARY AND CIVILIAN SECURITY OPERATIONS IN AFRICA AND BEYOND

During my frequent meetings with leading US military commanders I heard rather positive assessments of the EU's military and security contributions in Africa. David "Rod" Rodriguez, the four-star general and Commander of the United States Africa Command (AFRICOM) from April 2013 to August 2016, was one notable supporter. Headquartered in Stuttgart, AFRICOM was established in 2007 and is the most recent and perhaps least well known of the six US regional "combatant commands." Responsible for US military activities and relations with 53 African nations and several African regional security organizations, it was thrust into the limelight during the 2011 Libya operation, the attack on the US consulate in Benghazi in September 2012 that resulted in the deaths of US diplomats, and once again in October 2017 when four US troops were tragically ambushed while on patrol in Niger while helping the government fight Islamist terrorist organizations.

General Rodriguez, a physically imposing, battle-hardened, and frequently decorated officer directed very large and well-equipped military operations. I couldn't help being surprised that he would consider the EU's military and civilian missions, employing only 2000 civilians and slightly more than 3000 military staff, as anything more than sideshows. As of 2017, AFRICOM has 6000 military personnel spread across the

---

[2] Quoted in Craig Whitney, "Gulf Fighting Shatters European's Fragile Unity," *The New York Times*, January 26, 1991. https://www.nytimes.com/1991/01/25/world/war-in-the-gulf-europe-gulf-fighting-shatters-europeans-fragile-unity.html.

continent, with significant presences in Djibouti, home to the only US permanent military base in Africa and a key base in surveillance and combat operations against al Qaeda and other terrorist organizations (4000); Niger (800) and Somalia (400).

The EU's military and civilian missions are conducted under its Common Security and Defence Policy (CSDP), part of its Common Foreign and Security Policy (CFSP). The Lisbon Treaty, the equivalent of the EU's Constitution, provides that the EU may draw on civilian and military assets on missions outside the EU in accordance with the principles of the Charter of the United Nations. The missions include disarmament operations, humanitarian and rescue missions, military advice and assistance, conflict prevention and peacekeeping, and crisis management, including peacemaking and post-conflict stabilization. "All of these tasks may contribute to the fight against terrorism, including by supporting third countries in combating terrorism in their territories."[3] The EU carries out those tasks with the unanimous approval of the EU Council (representing the member states) and with assets provided by the member states. Civilian CSDP missions and operations are financed through the EU budget, with current expenditure running around €350 million per year. Common costs of military missions and operations fluctuate between €80 and €150 million per year and are financed outside the EU budget by all member states. Most of the costs are borne directly by member states participating in the missions and operations following a "costs lie where they fall" principle similar to that of NATO.

Of the EU's sixteen ongoing military and civilian operations conducted under its CSDP, nine are in Africa. Of the six ongoing military missions, five are in Africa. Two are maritime operations: The first is an anti-piracy maritime operation off the Horn of Africa and the other a maritime operation off the coast of Libya to disrupt migrant smuggling and human trafficking routes. The maritime operations can detain people, destroy illegal assets, and use force to implement their mandate within rather restrictive rules of engagement. There are also training, institution-building, and law enforcement operations in Somalia, Mali, and the Central African Republic. There have been other military operations (now terminated) in Chad and the Democratic Republic of the Congo.

Of the EU's ten ongoing civilian operations, four are in Africa: in Niger, Mali, Somalia, and Libya. There have been others in Sudan, Guinea-Bissau, and the Democratic Republic of the Congo. General

---

[3] Articles 42–43 of the Treaty.

Rodriguez believed that these military and civilian operations make a real contribution to security and stability on the continent, especially to the safety of shipping; the disruption of networks for the smuggling of people, weapons, and narcotics; and the fight against Islamist terrorist groups such as Boko Haram in West Africa, al-Shabaab in Somalia, al Qaeda, and the Islamic State of Iraq and Syria (ISIS). The EU has also invested heavily in promoting the economic and political resilience of fragile African states, including through political engagement and significant development assistance (as described in Chapter 12).

During the decade beginning in 2007, the most significant of these operations was the anti-piracy mission off the Horn of Africa to protect vulnerable commercial shipping from Somali pirates. That waterway is strategically important because it is often the shortest route in and out of Europe through the Suez Canal; the alternative route around the Cape of Good Hope is significantly longer and more expensive. The problem of piracy in this region was highlighted by the award-winning film *Captain Phillips* starring my favorite actor, Tom Hanks. In April 2009, the captain of the *Maersk Alabama* ignored numerous warnings to mariners to stay at least 600 nautical miles from the Somali coast. The ship, loaded with relief supplies bound for Kenya, was boarded by Somali pirates 300 nautical miles from the coast and the captain was taken prisoner for five days, before being rescued by the US Navy. The piracy was leading not only to armed attacks and the taking of hostages, but also to significant costs to merchant shipping because of ransom payments, security precautions, and higher insurance premiums.

The EU launched its anti-piracy naval force a few months before the incident with the *Maersk Alabama*. It has had the challenging task of patrolling 8.7 million square kilometers of sea—an area almost the size of Europe and covering the Red Sea, the Gulf of Aden, and a large part of the Indian Ocean—with up to seven surface combat vessels and several marine reconnaissance aircraft. NATO has had a similar anti-piracy mission that has worked closely with the EU; other countries (including from China, Russia, and Korea) have contributed vessels.

The EU and NATO missions have been unquestionable successes: Whereas 736 hostages and 32 ships were being held by pirates at the height of Somali piracy in early 2011, almost no hostages or ships have been held and few attacks have occurred in the past few years. While there were a few other reasons for the decline in piracy (including the requirement of insurance companies that vessels steer well clear of the Somali coast), the naval mission has been a key factor. Importantly, the anti-piracy operation has cooperated with other naval forces in the area and the shipping industry in the fight against piracy.

In addition to the maritime mission, the EU has managed an onshore military mission in Somalia since 2008 to cooperate in training Somali soldiers and advising the Somali armed forces. The United States has cooperated with the mission by paying for salaries of thousands of Somali troops, as well as providing food, fuel, uniforms, and other necessities. Since 2012, the EU has also managed an onshore civilian mission in Somalia to assist federal and regional authorities to develop coast guard and maritime law enforcement. Moreover, the EU has covered nearly all of the costs—over €1 billion over the past decade—of the African Union's Mission to Somalia, a peacekeeping force of roughly 8000 men. To the West, the EU has worked through the African Union to finance a Multinational Joint Task Force, including Cameroon, Niger, and Chad, that combats Boko Haram's threat to regional stability. That is in addition to significant development assistance (worth over several billion euros per year) to address the root causes of radicalism by creating jobs and improving agricultural practices, physical security, basic social services, and infrastructure.

Elsewhere on the continent, the EU has military training missions in the Central African Republic and Mali to train and advise the armed forces of those countries, including in counterterrorism. These are, to put it mildly, pretty dangerous places to be, as the armed attacks on the EU's military mission headquarters in Mali made clear in 2016 and 2019.

The EU's naval operation off the coast of Libya has disrupted refugee smuggling routes and performed the humanitarian mission of saving the lives of refugees in the south central Mediterranean. This operation began during the migrant crisis of 2015 during which the sea route from Libya to Italy was one of two main corridors used by just under 100,000 refugees per month to reach Europe. Traffic along that route remained high at over 100,000 per year in 2016 and 2017 before declining significantly over the subsequent years. Further progress has been hampered by the inability of Libyan leaders and the international community to bring Libya's warring factions together in a government of national unity. The EU's maritime mission and Italy have had some success in reducing migrant flows by helping regional and local Libyan authorities to develop a more effective coastguard that now stops most smugglers' ships from leaving the coastline. The EU remains concerned about conditions in detention centers for migrants in Libya; the continuing conflict around Tripoli has made conditions even worse.

The EU's civilian missions in Mali and Niger have focused on helping those countries combat the smuggling of weapons, narcotics, and humans. And the EU has been a significant provider of humanitarian and development assistance in many other African countries, including Ethiopia, Burkina Faso, and Sudan.

Why did General Rodriguez have a high opinion about these missions? Put simply, if the EU were not present in many African countries with its military and civilian operations, the political and economic conditions in the region would deteriorate further. That would result in greater instability, terrorism, famine, warfare, and an increase in refugees seeking European asylum (a phenomenon fueling European populism). These consequences would eventually demand a costly response, including by military forces, from the United States. In many of the African countries cited above, the EU (and its member states, especially France, Belgium, and the United Kingdom) simply has better local knowledge than the United States. General Rodriguez also appreciated the EU's unique mix of military and "soft power" tools, including diplomacy, trade, and development assistance. Without the investment in strengthening the resilience of unstable African states, there would be greater need to spend blood and treasure on military conflict. Furthermore, the EU's security activities mesh well with the strategic reorientation of the US military toward a lighter and more nimble military footprint, a concentration on a few key theaters like Afghanistan and Iraq, and a greater focus on training and equipping partner countries to enable them to be more self-sufficient.

The EU's military and civilian missions under CSDP are also making valuable contributions in many areas outside of Africa, including in the Balkans. Since 2004, for example, the EU replaced a NATO-led multinational peacekeeping force deployed to Bosnia Herzegovina after the Bosnian War. The EU's military mission there oversees the military implementation of the Dayton Agreement and provides a secure environment in the country. Importantly, the mission is able to rely on the "Berlin Plus" arrangements agreed in 2003, whereby the EU is able to access NATO assets and capabilities for EU-led operations.

Since 2008, the EU has managed a major civilian mission in Kosovo that promotes the rule of law, multi-ethnic democracy, and the fight against corruption. It also supports the implementation of the agreement between Serbia and Kosovo, Serbia's former province, brokered by the EU in 2013 to normalize relations after Kosovo declared independence in 2008. The United States has contributed to that mission by providing police officers, prosecutors, and judges. It has also played an important role in supporting the Special Investigative Task Force charged with investigating and prosecuting alleged war crimes and other criminal behavior conducted by former members of the Kosovo Liberation Army. The EU (and especially the Netherlands) has supported the specialist court established in The Hague to hear these cases.

The EU also exerts significant influence in the Balkans through financial and technical assistance, as well as by holding out the prospect of accession in return for reform. Montenegro, North Macedonia, Albania, and Serbia are candidates to become new EU members (although several EU member states have recently blocked opening accession talks with North Macedonia and Albania). So-called Stabilisation and Association agreements with these countries establish a free trade area and identify common political and economic objectives that encourage reform and regional cooperation. If it weren't for the EU's military and civilian involvement, it is quite possible that the historic achievement of the Dayton Agreement would have unravelled long ago, possibly into another armed conflict.

It is of vital importance that the EU continues to deliver on its promises of eventual EU membership to those candidates that fulfill the criteria. Internal EU reform is indeed necessary before new members are welcomed into the club. But that doesn't mean that a pathway to membership, or some form of closer relationship, over a period of time cannot be maintained for promising candidates. Even if membership remains a distant prospect for some, it would be a mistake to slam the door after candidates have cleaned up their houses. Doing so would leave a dangerous vacuum that would be filled by Russia, China, and militant Islam.

There are also CSDP missions in the Middle East and in the former Soviet Republics. The EU is often derided as not being a key player in the Israel–Palestine conflict. But it certainly makes a significant contribution, and wields influence, through its checkbook. A civilian mission was set up in 2005 to monitor the critical border crossing point between the Gaza Strip and Egypt. Unfortunately, the mission has not been able to operate since the Hamas takeover of the Gaza Strip in 2006 and has been limited since then to providing advice on border management. Another CSDP mission provides support to the Palestinian police and criminal justice systems. The EU provides significant financial assistance to the Palestinian Authority to pay for salaries, pensions, and allowances. Without this assistance, the rule of law in the Occupied Territories could collapse, with dire consequences for the region.

The EU also provides significant financial assistance to the United Nations Relief and Works Agency, an international relief organization that provides education, health care, and social services to more than 5 million Palestinian refugees in Jordan, Lebanon, Syria, the Gaza Strip, and the West Bank. Together with its member states, the EU provides significant humanitarian assistance to those affected by the war in Syria, both inside Syria itself and in Jordan, Lebanon, and other countries hosting refugees. Elsewhere in the Middle East, the EU provides advice to the Iraqi government on civilian aspects of its security strategy.

A previous civilian mission in Afghanistan assisted the government during 2007–2016 in building and training a police force that operates under a rule of law, including a respect for human rights. The EU has committed over €1 billion euros (on top of member states' financial contributions) for a wide range of goals in Afghanistan, including police training, justice sector reform, health, and border management.

In the former Soviet Republics, the EU provides a monitoring mission in Georgia along the border to help ensure the durability of the EU-mediated peace agreement that brought an end to the war with Russia in 2008. In Ukraine, a police advisory mission has been in place since 2014 to assist in security sector reform. In Ukraine and Moldova, the EU helps border and customs agencies combat customs fraud, drug smuggling, and human trafficking, particularly in Transnistria.

THE EU's COMMON FOREIGN, SECURITY AND DEFENSE POLICY CAN SUPPORT US INTERESTS

In all of these cases, the EU advances not only its own common defense and security policy, but also that of the United States. It has been because of this clear harmony of interests that the US and the EU signed a Framework Agreement on the participation of the US in EU crisis management operations in 2011. That agreement enabled US civilian participation in the missions in Congo, Kosovo, and Somalia mentioned above. In addition, there have been increasing staff-to-staff consultations between the EU Military Staff, on the one hand, and AFRICOM and the US European Command (EUCOM), on the other.

During my tenure, EUCOM and the EU Military Staff signed an administrative agreement to facilitate cooperation and the exchange of information between the organizations. I encouraged the Pentagon to make an exemption to National Disclosure Policy to enable the disclosure of US classified military information to the EU. And, most importantly, I contributed to the conclusion of an Acquisition and Cross Servicing Agreement that enables the US Department of Defense to provide (and charge for) logistics support, supplies, and services to EU military operations. Importantly, the agreement does not obligate the United States to sell equipment when it does not approve of the mission. Despite my encouragement, however, the US and EU have not yet put in place a Basic Exchange and Cooperation Agreement to enable the exchange of geospatial information between the US National Geospatial Intelligence Agency and the EU Satellite Centre; that is a pity as it would have helped the EU in many of the missions described above, especially in Africa.

Over the past few decades, there have inevitably been some commentators in the United States who have warned that a stronger EU common foreign policy, including a defense and security policy, will lead to frictions with the United States. With regard to foreign policy, the fear is that a common policy will inevitably be at the lowest common denominator in order to achieve consensus among member states with different histories, cultures, and views of the world. In some areas, such as the Middle East, the European view has diverged persistently from the US view, thereby complicating Washington's objectives.

It is, of course, more convenient to have the EU simply play along with whatever the United States decides. But that is certainly not what partnership is all about. A real partnership of equality is so much more powerful because it contributes to the effectiveness of US foreign policy in the overwhelming number of cases where the interests of the US and EU coincide. The real problem of the EU's foreign policy for the United States, at least before the changes implemented by the Lisbon Treaty, was that it was uncoordinated, slow, and ineffective. With regard to security policy, some commentators have voiced concerns about proposed measures that might undermine NATO, the bedrock of the transatlantic security relationship. But these concerns have usually been misplaced or at least overstated.

I collaborated with my mentor and former US ambassador to the EU, Stuart Eizenstat, in 2010 to write an article in *Foreign Affairs* in which we praised the Lisbon Treaty's useful features. One of them was the creation of the post of High Representative of the Union for Foreign Affairs and Security Policy, essentially a foreign minister in all but name. Federica Mogherini of Italy, one of my sister's oldest Italian friends, proved to be a highly competent High Representative and earned the admiration of Secretary John Kerry, including for her work on the thorniest issues of Russian sanctions and the Iran nuclear negotiations.

The High Representative also serves as Vice President of the European Commission during her five-year term. She is responsible for chairing and setting the agenda for various configurations of council meetings in which ministers in charge of foreign affairs, defense, and development participate. And most important, she speaks for the EU on matters of foreign and security policy when the member states have agreed by consensus (which is overwhelmingly the case). That replaced the unworkable pre-Lisbon situation in which the member state holding the presidency of the EU in six-monthly rotation would chair the meetings and speak for the EU.[4]

In our article, Eizenstat and I warned that the EU might still struggle to ensure a consistent foreign policy, partly because the rotating presidency continues to chair and set the agendas for monthly Council meetings on "general affairs"—which include some issues having international significance, such as the accession of new members to the EU, humanitarian aid, climate change, energy security, and economic and monetary policy. The concern was misplaced as the High Representative and the relevant commissioners in charge of these policy areas have worked closely together. We also warned that the Lisbon Treaty's creation of a new post, a President of the European Council (the body that represents the heads of government of the member states), might cause confusion and conflict with the High Representative because the former is tasked with representing the EU on issues of foreign policy with presidents and prime ministers of non-EU countries. But that has not occurred because of the close coordination between the two officials. Indeed, the position of President of the European Council has enhanced the ability of the EU to engage in long-term agenda-setting in foreign policy.

---

[4] Anthony Luzzatto Gardner and Stuart E. Eizenstat, "New Treaty, New Influence?" *Foreign Affairs*, March–April 2010.

Another key innovation of the Lisbon Treaty was the creation of an European External Action Service, an EU foreign ministry in all but name. Like the title of High Representative, this name reflects the aversion in some member states (especially the UK) to the idea that the EU should behave like a state with wide-ranging diplomatic relations. The EEAS is a highly professional corps of roughly 4500 officials in Brussels and in 143 delegations in countries and international organizations worldwide. The delegations represent the EU, not just the European Commission, as past delegations did. That means the delegations (rather than the embassy of the country holding the rotating presidency of the EU) represent the EU in non-EU countries. They cooperate with and supplement, but do not replace, the diplomatic missions of the member states around the world.

The Lisbon Treaty made clear that neither the High Representative nor the EEAS affects the "responsibilities and powers of each member State in relation to the formulation and conduct of its foreign policy, its national diplomatic service, relations with third countries and participation in international organizations." In other words, EU foreign policy decision-making remains inter-governmental rather than supranational. Nonetheless, the EEAS has developed a broad and deep expertise on foreign policy and has facilitated the emergence of an EU-wide foreign policy perspective. It has unquestionably enhanced the EU's credibility, continuity, and communication on the global stage.

In one important respect, Eizenstat and I were right: The Lisbon Treaty has not yet addressed the problem of the EU's over-representation. As we noted, the EU's claims to be a single, coherent actor are undercut by the high number of European officials in attendance. At the three US–EU Summits I attended with President Obama, the President of the European Commission, Jean-Claude Juncker, the President of the European Council, Donald Tusk, and the High Representative, Francesca Mogherini, were present and spoke for Europe. At meetings of the G-20, the EU is represented by the presidents of the European Commission, the European Council, the European Central Bank, as well as leaders from six different member states (four as G-20 members and two as guests).

The EU's Response to Growing External Security Challenges

The EU's search to develop and project a coherent foreign and security policy has taken on added urgency over the past decade. Europe's security has rarely looked so precarious as Russia seeks to threaten it militarily or destabilize European societies. These objectives are readily apparent in Russia's occupation of two provinces in Georgia, annexation of Crimea, occupation of Southeast Ukraine and repeated incursions into the airspace and territorial waters of EU member states. They are also reflected in its efforts to undermine European elections and support extremist groups, spread disinformation to sow disaffection with democracy, and interfere in the choices of several Balkan countries to move closer to the EU and NATO.

Europe's security has also suffered from the instability and internal conflict of its neighbors. A devastating civil war in Syria triggered massive refugee flows into Europe from the eastern Mediterranean. Desperate economic conditions in Africa, exploited by terrorist and criminal gangs, triggered massive refugee flows into Europe from the southern Mediterranean. These flows not only stretched the ability of the main European destination countries to absorb them, but also tested European solidarity to the breaking point. On top of all these threats, Europe has had to cope with repeated terrorist attacks on European soil, Turkey's continued drift toward authoritarian rule, and the effort by Beijing to use its economic leverage to prevent unified EU policies toward China.

Perhaps most troublesome has been the change of US foreign policy toward Europe under the Trump administration. From the beginning of its term, the new administration has abandoned 60 years of bipartisan foreign policy by routinely attacking the EU as merely a protectionist vehicle of German power whose main purpose is to beat the United States in trade. It has been a cheerleader of Brexit and urged other member states to follow the UK out the door. It has undermined two of the EU's most prized foreign policy achievements—the Paris Agreement on climate change and the agreement with Iran to limit its nuclear program in return for an easing of sanctions. President Trump has even declared the EU a "foe" of the United States, while repeatedly refusing to criticize Russia or Vladimir Putin. His support for NATO, and its Article 5 guarantee of collective defense, has been inconsistent and grudging. His attacks on Germany, and even Chancellor Merkel, for Germany's trade surplus with the United States and its inadequate defense spending have been sharp. And the Trump administration has justified import duties on steel and aluminum, and potentially on cars, by stating that imports of these goods represent a national security threat, even at a time of peace and when purchased from allies (including the EU).

No wonder that the European Council President listed the United States as one of the main risks facing Europe in a letter to EU heads of government soon after the Trump administration took office.[5] Juncker concluded that the United States is "no longer interested in guaranteeing Europe's security in our place." By mid-2018, Tusk asked: "With friends like that, who needs enemies?" Trump has been an important wake-up call to Europe, he concluded; it cannot assume that the United States would be a steadfast ally in times of need. "He has made us realise that if you need a helping hand, you will find one at the end of your arm."[6] Chancellor Merkel, not known for exaggeration or sense of drama, noted that "the era in which we could fully rely on others is over to some extent… we Europeans truly have to take our fate into our own hands."[7]

The darkening geopolitical landscape led the EU to conclude in its Reflection Paper on the Future of European Defence, published in 2017, that "peace and security at home can no longer be taken for granted…the European Union and its member states have a duty and responsibility to protect citizens and promote European interests and values."[8] The problem, as the Reflection Paper recognized, is that Europe had failed to invest in its capacity to do so. Since 2005, military expenditures among the EU 28 had fallen by 12% in inflation-adjusted terms, while expenditures among many other powers, including Russia and China, had increased significantly. Europe had for many years been spending half of what the United States spends on defense, in terms of both gross expenditures and

---

[5] Letter by President Donald Tusk to the 27 EU heads of state or government on the future of the EU before the Malta summit, January 31, 2017. http://www.consilium.europa.eu/en/press/press-releases/2017/01/31/tusk-letter-future-europe/.

[6] Remarks by President Donald Tusk ahead of the EU-Western Balkans summit and the Leaders' agenda dinner, May 16, 2018. https://www.consilium.europa.eu/en/press/press-releases/2018/05/16/remarks-by-president-donald-tusk-ahead-of-the-eu-western-balkans-summit-and-the-leaders-agenda-dinner/.

[7] "Wir Europäer müssen unser Schicksal in unsere eigene Hand nehmen," *Süddeutsche Zeitung*, May 28, 2017. https://www.sueddeutsche.de/politik/g-7-krise-wir-europaeer-muessen-unser-schicksal-in-unsere-eigene-hand-nehmen-1.3524718.

[8] Reflection Paper on the Future of European Defence, June 7, 2017. https://ec.europa.eu/commission/sites/beta-political/files/reflection-paper-defence_en.pdf.

as a percentage of GDP. Most EU members of NATO were spending well below the agreed 2% GDP goal. Two EU members, France and the UK, have represented nearly half of total EU military spending; following Brexit, the figures for the EU 27 look even worse.

Inadequate spending inevitably has had dire consequences on military readiness. In my many meetings at the EEAS, senior officials pointed out that readiness levels for many key defense equipment, such as fighter jets and attack and transport helicopters, stood at less than 50% in several member states. Studies have claimed that less than 3% of European troops (40,000 men) are deployable due to shortages of equipment. That compares to the 200,000 troops that the United States deploys overseas. But the problem has been even worse than a lack of resources; just as serious, the EU 28 have been wasting vast resources by failing to achieve economies of scale through common weapons procurement and research and development, as well as failing to achieve interoperability of existing weapons systems. Around 80% of defense procurement in Europe is on a national basis, leading to duplication and capability gaps. Europe has not only been underspending, it has been spending wastefully.

The result is predictable. According to the European Commission, there are 178 different weapons systems in the EU, compared to 30 in the United States; there are 29 types of destroyers/frigates in the EU, compared to four in the US; there are 20 types of fighters planes in the EU, compared to six in the US; there are 42 tanker aircraft (of twelve different types) for air-to-air refuelling in the EU, compared to 55 units of four types in the United States; there are 37 types of armored personnel carriers in the EU, compared to nine types in the United States; there are 17 types of main battle tanks in the EU, compared to four in the United States; and there are more helicopter producers in the EU than there are governments able to buy them.[9] This is plainly absurd. But fixing the problem has been hard as many European governments are intent on protecting their national defense "champions" who often have significant political clout.

Perhaps the most egregious problem has been that many member states spend a small percentage of their defense budgets on equipment. Although NATO agrees that members should spend 20% of their defense

---

[9] European Commission Factsheet on Defending Europe. https://ec.europa.eu/commission/sites/beta-political/files/defending-europe-factsheet_en.pdf.

expenditures on equipment, few actually do so. Belgium has been, perhaps, the most striking example. My jaw dropped when I noted that it was not only spending a paltry 0.9% of its €500 billion GDP (roughly €4.5 billion) on defense, and that 90% of that amount was earmarked for personnel (salaries and pensions, for example). If it were to meet the twin NATO guidelines above, Belgium would be spending considerably more on equipment. The failure of many European countries to shoulder their burden is clearly unacceptable, as US presidents of both parties have pointed out over several decades.

In response to the challenge of spending scarce euros to maximum effect, the EU has focused on creating the conditions for more defense cooperation, maximizing output and efficiency of defense spending, including by promoting collaborative armaments projects, pooling of resources, encouraging role specialization, and reducing redundancies in weapons programs. Some progress has been made over the past decade. The European Defence Agency serves as a central hub for European defense cooperation by promoting collaboration among its 27 EU members (Denmark opted out) in many areas, including procurement policies and research and development efforts. The Organisation for Joint Armament Cooperation, among Belgium, France, Germany, Italy, Spain, and the UK, serves as a central procurement body for important armament programs. Some countries have joined together in the European Air Transport Command to pool and share assets in military air transport, air-to-air refuelling, and aeromedical evacuation. There are examples of EU member states working together closely, such as the Belgian and Dutch navies. Since 2010, the UK and France have agreed to share equipment, conduct exchanges among their armed forces, provide access to each other's defense markets, and set up a Combined Joint Expeditionary Force. European defense cooperation remains largely a patchwork of bilateral or multilateral arrangements.

The EU recognizes that it needs to do more. Shortly after the start of the Juncker Commission's five-year mandate in 2015, President Juncker declared:

> I believe that we need to work on a stronger Europe when it comes to security and defence matters. Yes, Europe is chiefly a 'soft power.' But even the strongest soft powers cannot make do in the long run without at least some integrated defence capacities.

The EU's Common Defense

The Lisbon Treaty provides that CSDP shall include the development of a common Union defense policy that will lead to a common defense, when the member states decide unanimously. Over the past few years, there has been some rhetoric (albeit rare) by a few EU officials, including by President Juncker, about the need for an EU "army."[10] It was ill-advised because it complicated the debate in the UK regarding Brexit. The UK tabloid press pounced on these statements as confirmation that the EU is seeking to create a "super state" when there is no evidence to suggest that this is indeed the direction of travel.

Despite the occasional rhetoric about a European army, the reality is that there has been very little traction for such an idea ever since 1954 when the French Parliament ended discussions about a European Defence Community that would have included a European army, a European Minister of Defence, and a common defense budget. A European Corps (Eurocorps), consisting of troops from five EU member states, became operational in 1995 and remains outside of both EU and NATO structures. But it remains a relatively modest affair: A Franco-German Brigade, established in 1987 and consisting of about 5000 troops, is the only military formation permanently under the command of the Eurocorps.

At a 1998 summit meeting between French President Jacques Chirac and UK Prime Minister Tony Blair at St. Malo, France, the two countries agreed that the EU should "have the capacity for autonomous action, backed up by credible military forces, the means to decide to use them, and a readiness to do so, in order to respond to international crises." The concept of what "autonomy" is and from whom Europe should be autonomous was left unclear. The meeting at St. Malo gave birth to CSDP, new institutions such as the EU Military Staff and the Intelligence Centre, and the headline goal of deploying 60,000 troops for up to 60 days and 6000 kilometers from Brussels.

The crisis in transatlantic relations in the aftermath of the US decision to invade Iraq prompted French President Chirac to propose a

---

[10] Andrew Sparrow, "Jean-Claude Juncker Calls for EU Army," *The Guardian*, March 8, 2015. https://www.theguardian.com/world/2015/mar/08/jean-claude-juncker-calls-for-eu-army-european-commission-miltary.

fully fledged defense union among France, Germany, Belgium, and Luxembourg—described by *The New York Post* as the "Axis of Weasel."[11] Although that didn't lead anywhere, there has been slow but consistent progress toward a far more modest objective of creating an autonomous European military capability.

Between 2000 and 2006, the EU worked on developing a rapid reaction force capable of being deployed on the ground within 5–10 days of EU approval and capable of being sustained for several months in a variety of "limited intensity" CSDP operations, such as conflict prevention, evacuation, brief support of existing troops, delivery of aid, and post-conflict stabilization (prior to the deployment of larger forces). In 2007, the EU announced that the rapid reaction force was fully operational, meaning that the EU could deploy simultaneously two battalion-sized forces ("Battlegroups") of 1500 troops each, plus command and support services. The Battlegroups are drawn from every EU member state (except Denmark and Malta), as well as five non-EU countries. Larger member states have generally contributed their own Battlegroups, while smaller ones collaborate to create common groups. Each group has a "lead nation" that takes operational command. While the rapid-reaction force looks good on paper, none has ever been deployed, largely due to slow decision-making and uncertainties about how missions would be financed. Participating member states must cover their own costs, a burden that is especially troublesome for smaller states.

The deterioration of Europe's security environment during 2013–2017 led 25 EU member states (all EU members minus the UK, Denmark, and Malta) to activate in September 2017 a hitherto unused provision of the Lisbon Treaty. This provision, called the "sleeping beauty" of the Treaty by President Juncker, is related to the ability of certain EU member states to enter into "permanent structured cooperation" (PESCO) with one another to jointly develop defense capabilities and make them available for EU military operations. Like the Battlegroups, one of the purposes of this cooperation is to rapidly deploy and sustain combat missions for the purposes of joint disarmament operations, humanitarian and rescue tasks, conflict prevention and post-conflict stabilization, peacekeeping, and peacemaking. But the aim appears broader than the Battlegroups in that it seeks to promote cooperation on very specific projects. Among

---

[11] Deborah Orin, "Axis of Weasel – Germany and France Wimp Out on Iraq: Colin Raps French, German Wimps," *The New York Post*, January 24, 2003. https://nypost.com/2003/01/24/axis-of-weasel-germany-and-france-wimp-out-on-iraq-colin-raps-french-german-wimps/.

the first projects to be approved were the development of a prototype for a European Armoured Infantry Fighting Vehicle, the creation of a European Medical Command to provide collective EU medical capabilities to support military operations, a Cyber Rapid Response Team, and a project to standardize and simplify European cross-border military transport.

PESCO has been trumpeted by its supporters as a step-change in EU military cooperation and operational readiness. One of the reasons is that the commitments of PESCO members—including the pledge to regularly increase defense budgets in real terms and to pursue national investments in defense with due consideration for the EU's collective needs—are intended to be binding. These commitments will be subject to regular review by the European Defence Agency and the European Union External Action Service. A member state that underperforms can, in theory, be removed from PESCO by a qualified majority vote by the other members (although that seems quite unlikely).

Nonetheless, there is reason to be skeptical about PESCO. The relevant provision of the Lisbon Treaty envisages that PESCO would be suitable only for member states "whose military capabilities fulfill higher criteria" for the purpose of entering into "the most demanding missions." Although specific PESCO projects are exclusive to a subset of EU member states, PESCO itself applies to nearly every EU member state, including minnows with extremely modest military capabilities, but not the UK (one of the two most effective military powers in the EU) after Brexit. That suggests that it may not serve as a truly effective vanguard.

PESCO has reawakened old concerns in the Trump administration about the "three D's" that Secretary of State Madeline Albright had warned about in 1998: That an enhanced European defense identity would *duplicate* NATO force planning, command structure, and procurement decisions; *de-couple* European decision-making from broader alliance decision-making; and *discriminate* against NATO members who are not EU members (including the US, Canada, Turkey and Norway).

Importantly, the point about non-duplication was neither defined nor intended to mean that the EU should not develop certain capabilities that already exist in NATO. Indeed, the Clinton administration sought to prod European allies into developing precisely such capabilities. PESCO does not seem to pose a risk to NATO. Capabilities developed under PESCO remain the property of the member states, rather than becoming collective EU assets, and therefore remain available to NATO, as well as the EU. Moreover, one of the criteria taken into account in the selection of PESCO projects is whether they respond to NATO priorities. With 22 countries belonging to both the EU and NATO, strengthened EU capabilities are destined to benefit NATO. The PESCO projects that have been launched so far appear to bear this out; for example, NATO's heavy military forces will be the greatest beneficiary of the PESCO project to improve cross-European military mobility. While NATO officials have occasionally expressed fears about duplication, especially if the EU moves to build a fully functioning operational headquarters, they have usually concluded that it should be welcomed if PESCO improves Europe's ability to contribute to the common defense.

With regard to the fear of de-coupling, the Lisbon Treaty recognizes the pre-eminence of NATO in terms of European security and does not interfere with the choices of member states regarding their security and defense policies. President Trump's grudging reaffirmation of the NATO Article 5 mutual defense guarantee has done more to promote de-linking than any European defense initiative by giving rise to questions about the dependability of US military support in the hour of need.

With regard to the third "D," the Trump administration appears to be concerned about a different form of discrimination, namely against US defense contractors. This fear may be legitimate, but it has nothing to do with PESCO. EU member states have often given preference to national or European suppliers, over US competitors, even when the former provide less cost-effective or technologically advanced solutions. Washington has raised the alarm about alleged "poison pills" that would prevent companies based outside the EU, including the US, from participating in military projects.[12] Given the critical importance of stretching limited defense budgets and enhancing military capabilities, US-headquartered companies should not be excluded from defense procurement or research in Europe, especially when those companies have shown long-term commitment to investing and creating jobs and skills in Europe. Fortunately, European

---

[12] Guy Chazan and Michael Pell, "US Warns Against European Joint Military Project," *Financial Times*, May 14, 2019. https://www.ft.com/content/ad16ce08-763b-11e9-bbad-7c18c0ea0201.

Commission President Ursula von der Leyen has stated her commitment to "an open and competitive European defense equipment market."[13]

US charges of discrimination ring pretty hollow. The Defense Department is required to "Buy American" first as a general rule. "Buy American" laws, tightened under the Trump administration, require foreign firms competing for federal defense contracts to show that more than half of their products' contents are US-made. There are other laws, especially the so-called Berry Amendment that requires certain items purchased by the Defense Department to be entirely domestic in origin.

It also needs to be acknowledged that a true transatlantic partnership in defense requires a European partner that has an economically healthy and technologically advanced defense industry. That can't be the case if the US aggressively lobbies European governments to purchase US military equipment. I remember attending a meeting between National Security Adviser Tony Lake and Italian Foreign Minister Susanna Agnelli when I was a young staffer at the National Security Council. The briefing paper I had written contained many economic and political issues of importance to US–Italian relations, but Lake chose to raise the last and arguably least important talking point about Italy's pending purchase of air-to-air missiles. Agnelli's response was tart: "The relationship between our two countries is not just about Italy buying your military equipment." Similarly, French Foreign Defense Secretary Florence Parly has recently observed that the mutual defense clause of the NATO treaty does not require European allies to buy American fighter aircraft: "It's called Article 5, not Article F-35."[14]

If PESCO contributes to higher European military expenditures, it should be welcomed. The United States has called for precisely that during many decades. The real concern in the United States should be whether PESCO will do anything at all, not whether it will do too much. It appears to bear the hallmarks of yet another political statement, short on substance; indeed, Berlin favored an all-inclusive club in order to send the message of European unity at a time of increasing European fragmentation.

---

[13] Mission letter to Thierry Breton, commissioner-designate for the internal market. https://ec.europa.eu/commission/sites/beta-political/files/president-elect_von_der_leyens_mission_letter_to_thierry_breton.pdf.

[14] Paul McLeary, "French Defense Chief: 'It's Called Article 5, Not Article F-35,'" *Breaking Defense*, March 18, 2019. https://breakingdefense.com/2019/03/french-defense-chief-its-called-article-5-not-article-f-35/.

Concerns about the Battlegroup concept and the limitations of PESCO led French President Emmanuel Macron to propose creating another EU military force, called the European Intervention Initiative (EI2), in a major foreign policy speech at the Sorbonne University in September 2017. Launched in July 2018 with nine EU members, EI2 is intended (like the Battlegroup concept) to be a force that can be rapidly deployable in times of crisis. But it is different in that it lies outside of EU structures and is not tied to CSDP, includes a smaller group of European countries, and has a common budget and doctrine. EI2 also ultimately aims to create a shared vision regarding security concerns and the means to address them. It is intended to operate with streamlined decision-making and enhance the ability of its members to act together on missions as part of NATO, EU, UN, or other ad hoc coalitions.

One of the reasons EI2 is significant is that it is political, rather than military. Despite France's commitment to the EU, it has lost faith in the EU's ability to deliver an effective military solution and it was, furthermore, willing to break with Germany on this significant issue. Germany has joined the initiative, but unwillingly. As a rare example of a split between Paris and Berlin, it risks causing another fracture line in the European project.

While it remains too early to assess whether the objectives of PESCO or EI2 will be achieved, several things are already clear. The concepts fall well short of an ambition to create a European army. Their purpose is to complement NATO, not to undermine it, as NATO's Secretary General Jens Stoltenberg has himself observed. There is no reason to think many Europeans are trying or will ever try to undermine or replace NATO. Even the UK, traditionally opposed to any effort at creating a European defense alliance, joined EI2 because it believed that the initiative is compatible, rather than competitive, with NATO. (It also joined to ensure a seat at the table in order to prevent the project from ever evolving in that direction.)

No one seriously believes that Europe can defend itself against a major threat, such as a Russian invasion of the Baltic Republics, without NATO's support. Increased European defense integration may well complement NATO by generating military efficiencies to the benefit of both NATO and the EU. As a series of collaborative projects, PESCO does not risk diverting limited resources away from NATO. EI2 might hypothetically do so in the event of concurrent EI2 and NATO missions that drew on the same military assets. The risk does not appear significant, especially as the French seem focused on using EI2 to relieve their own operations in Africa. Moreover, the small risk would be worth the price if Europe's military asset base grows.

The ambition of EI2 to develop a common "strategic culture" in the EU is laudable but challenging. I witnessed repeatedly during my mandate how different groups of EU member states have radically different perceptions of external threats. The UK and France have been the only EU member states that have frequently assumed responsibilities for major military engagements in the region (including in Africa and the Middle East). Member states in Scandinavia, the Baltics, and Eastern Europe understand very well the dangers from an aggressive Russia. Those in the South, on the other hand, consider migration as a far bigger threat; in the years following Russia's invasion of Crimea and Southeast Ukraine, Italy and Greece (joined by many others) consistently tried to water down sanctions on Russia and pleaded that sanctions were having a disproportionately negative effect on their economies. Germany has been extremely reluctant to deploy its soldiers in military operations (most notably refusing to support the EU-led NATO mission to prevent Gaddafi's crimes against humanity in Libya). Four of the six non-NATO EU countries decided not to get involved.[15]

Adding to the challenge of developing a common "strategic culture" is the fact that the European public appears unwilling to fight, even for NATO allies. As noted in Chapter 7, a 2015 opinion poll by the Pew Research Center indicated that if Russia were to attack one of its neighboring countries that is a NATO member, nearly half of those Europeans polled would oppose using military force to defend it. Of those Germans polled, 58% said that they would not be willing to fight, as opposed to 38% who said they would. The figures were similar for the French and the Italians. With attitudes like that, it will be politically very challenging to justify increased military spending and to ensure that the Article 5 mutual defense guarantee appears rock solid to those who might be tempted to challenge it.

While the EU continues to speak about "strategic autonomy," the idea remains ill-defined. If it is about acting independently on major international issues, including security challenges, the EU will continue to fall short for some time. If it is about setting objectives, making decisions, and

---

[15] Katie Simmons, Bruce Stokes, and Jacob Poushter, "NATO Publics Blame Russia for Ukrainian Crisis, but Reluctant to Provide Military Aid," *Pew Research Center*, June 10, 2015. http://www.pewglobal.org/2015/06/10/nato-publics-blame-russia-for-ukrainian-crisis-but-reluctant-to-provide-military-aid/.

mobilizing resources in less challenging areas without having to depend on the decisions and assets of others (including the United States), the progress is more promising.

The EU has enhanced its ability to manage modest operations autonomously (without relying on bases belonging to NATO or post-Brexit Britain). As a step in that direction, the EU opened a permanent headquarters for military operations in March 2017. Its immediate objective has been to assume the management of the three existing EU training missions in Mali, Somalia, and the Central African Republic. By the end of 2020 it aims to have the ability to assume command of military operations of roughly 2000 troops deployed as part of the CSDP.

In the past few years, there has been important progress toward the goal of improving defense cooperation on weapons systems. Launched in 2016, for example, a European Defence Fund has focused on maximizing the output of military expenditures by coordinating and supplementing national investments in defense research. From 2020 onward, the Fund expects to provide €500 million in grants, fully and directly funded from the EU budget, for collaborative research in critical areas of innovation to be agreed by the member states. The Fund has also focused on creating incentives for member states to cooperate on the joint development and acquisition of defense equipment and technology. The Fund expects to provide €1 billion per year in co-financing for collaborative projects, involving at least three EU member states, in areas of defense equipment and technology such as drone technology and satellite communications. Every euro in EU funding is expected to generate an additional four euros from the private sector, for a total investment of €5 billion per year.

In sum, there is reason to believe that despite past failures and the present hype, the EU is both investing more in defense and improving the operational capabilities of its armed forces. The EU has realized that it cannot continue to be the only vegetarian in a world of carnivores. Many recent developments underpin the renewed focus on defense. These include external threats from Russia, more widespread violence in the Middle East, the continued attacks of Islamic terrorist groups and a new US administration that is unpredictable and eager to break up the EU. At the same time, an economic recovery has made it easier to spend taxpayers' money on security. On the negative side of the ledger, the exit of the UK from the EU results in the loss of significant operational military capabilities in the EU. The EU's short-sighted decision to exclude the UK from the more military sensitive parts of its Galileo Navigation System has pushed the UK to build its own system, requiring substantial investment that could be better deployed elsewhere. Nonetheless, Brexit also removes one of the biggest obstacles to greater European military integration.

Most important, the European Union and NATO are working more closely than ever before. This is only natural as the two institutions are based on common values, resources and challenges. The "Berlin Plus" arrangements described earlier show that the US and NATO are willing to facilitate European efforts to assume greater burdens of European security without having to rely on the United States. Admittedly these arrangements have only been used twice by the EU, in 2003 when it replaced a NATO mission in the Former Yugoslav Republic of Macedonia and in 2004 in Bosnia and Herzegovina.

EU-NATO relations are evolving. Until 2016, closer EU-NATO ties were blocked due to the tense relationship between Cyprus, a non-NATO EU member, and Turkey, a non-EU NATO member. In February 2016, however, NATO responded favorably to a joint request by Germany, Greece, and Turkey to assist in efforts to deal with the refugee crisis in the eastern Mediterranean. The maritime mission provided the EU's border management agency Frontex and the Greek and Turkish navies valuable reconnaissance about human trafficking, as well as ensured that the navies did not encroach on each other's territorial waters (that abutted each other in the narrow passage between the Greek island of Lesbos, the main destination of Syrian refugees, and the Turkish coast).

Efforts that US Ambassador to NATO Doug Lute and I undertook to deepen EU-NATO ties bore fruit in a joint declaration by the two organizations at the NATO summit in Warsaw in July 2016. The declaration identified 42 concrete proposals to work more closely together in seven different areas, including countering "hybrid threats,"[16] cyber security, and operational cooperation at sea and on migration.

An EU-NATO declaration in July 2018, two years after the Warsaw summit, noted that the organizations now exchange real-time warnings on cyber attacks, participate in each other's exercises, and work together in responding to the refugee and migrant crisis. And the declaration urged

---

[16] The EU defines "hybrid threats" as the combination of "conventional and unconventional, military and non-military activities that can be used in a coordinated manner by state or non-state actors to achieve specific political objectives." They can be "multidimensional, combining coercive and subversive measures, using both conventional and unconventional tools and tactics."

strengthened cooperation in a number of areas, including military mobility, counterterrorism, and the ability to cope with chemical, biological, radiological, and nuclear-related risks. A European Centre of Excellence for Countering Hybrid Threats has been established in Helsinki to provide EU member states and NATO allies with analysis, training, and exercises. There has been increased cooperation between the two organizations' strategic communication teams about how to combat disinformation, including through social media.

The time may finally have arrived when the EU can take serious steps toward greater military integration. The European public wants this, as does NATO. The geopolitical environment demands it. Most important, there are signs that, unlike previous proposals that focused on facilitating information exchange and building bureaucratic institutions, such as command structures, current proposals quite rightly focus on building additional capabilities. While higher defense spending has never been popular in most European countries, justifying it as an EU project may well make it more palatable than doing so because NATO, dominated by Uncle Sam, demands it. There are many threats of a not purely military nature that can more appropriately be met by the EU because of its unique mixture of coercive military power and "soft power" tools—including diplomacy, trade, foreign aid, and the promise of entry into the EU club. The fact that President Macron invoked article 42.7 of the EU Treaty, consisting of a mutual defense obligation among member states, rather than NATO's Article 5 guarantee of collective defense, is just one illustration.

Greater EU military integration is something that should be embraced in Washington as it is squarely in line with the justified demand, made by US administrations over many decades, that Europe should assume greater responsibility for its own defense. As long as NATO's centrality continues to be recognized and the focus remains on building capabilities, improving efficiency, and ensuring interoperability of weapons systems, EU military integration can only benefit European and transatlantic security.

As this book was going to press, the new Commission was outlining its priorities for its five-year term. It is already clear that President von der Leyen, formerly Germany's minister of defense, believes that the new Commission should more forcefully use the powerful tools at its disposal, including with regard to other global powers. She has stated that the EU "needs to be more strategic, more assertive, and more united in its approach to external relations." This focus is clearly prompted by concerns that the EU is facing a more threatening and uncertain global context than ever before.

She has instructed Josep Borrell, the High Representative of the Union for Foreign Policy and Security Policy, to strengthen the EU's capacity to act "autonomously" and to promote its values and interests around the world. When putting forward proposals, Borrell is instructed to use EU treaty clauses that allow certain decisions on CFSP to be adopted by qualified majority voting (rather than unanimity). He will also seek to promote a genuine "European Defence Union" during the next five years. As long as the UK was a member of the EU, such proposals were unimaginable.

It is also significant that von der Leyen has instructed Thierry Breton, commissioner for the internal market, to lead a new focused portfolio on defense industry and space, backed by a newly created directorate-general responsible for that area. The fact that Breton is French and close to French President Emmanuel Macron, who has repeatedly stressed the need for greater EU ambition in defense, suggests that the EU may finally place defense higher on its list of priorities.[17]

Acknowledgements The contribution of Caroline Wefer is gratefully acknowledged.

[17] Mission Letter from Ursula von der Leyen to Thierry Breton, November 7, 2019. https://ec.europa.eu/commission/sites/beta-political/files/president-elect_von_der_leyens_mission_letter_to_thierry_breton.pdf.

Part III

Saving the Planet Together

CHAPTER 11

Climate Change and the Environment

Cooperation on the environment, especially relating to the combat against climate change, has been one of the most successful and noble aspects of the US-EU partnership. The US Mission to the EU played a subsidiary role in this partnership during my diplomatic mission because the experience and negotiating power on the US side resided with the State Department and with several specialized government agencies in Washington. But during my regular interactions with the technical experts on the environment and climate who formed part of the US Mission staff, I witnessed the breadth and depth of the US-EU partnership to save the planet. As a result of various EU treaty changes in the 1990s that gave the EU increasing authority to take domestic and international actions in these areas, the key EU players have been the European Commission's directorate-generals for the environment (created in 1981) and for "climate action" (created in 2010).

I have had a specific interest in environmental issues, resulting from my father's long involvement in them. One of my early memories is as a nine-year-old sitting with my sister in the public gallery of the United Nations Conference on the Human Environment in Stockholm in June 1972. My father was a delegate to the conference and apparently thought this would be a great way to start the family's summer holidays. (Two decades later he was a delegate to the UN Earth Summit in Rio de Janeiro.) Bringing the family to an environmental conference was in keeping with my father's regular habits of enlivening dinner table conversations at home with topics

© The Author(s) 2020
A. L. Gardner, *Stars with Stripes*,
https://doi.org/10.1007/978-3-030-29966-8_11

Fig. 11.1 Ambassador Gardner, his father Richard Gardner, and Vice President Gore in the Vice President's office, spring of 1995 (*Source* From author's own collection)

such as the Antarctica Treaty, air and maritime pollution, deforestation, wildlife protection, and ownership of the world's oceans.

In the mid-1980s, my father introduced the family to a young senator from Tennessee—Al Gore—whose passion for the environment was infectious and who soon became a close family friend. When I regularly met with him as Vice President one decade later during my service in the White House, I would marvel at an enormous picture on the wall of the earth taken from outer space. Seen from afar, the earth seemed such a small, brittle, and beautiful creation (Fig. 11.1).

The challenge of rising temperatures, largely the result of fossil fuels burned by human activity, is obviously an existential issue for all of us. There is no "Planet B." The challenge is also horribly complex for many reasons. Nearly every human activity emits greenhouse gases that contribute to an atmospheric "greenhouse effect" trapping infrared radiation that warms the earth's surface and its oceans. Addressing the challenge therefore implicates most aspects of daily personal life and economic activity, requiring individuals to change their habits and corporations to take expensive actions. At the same time, the threat to our planet remains clouded by some uncertainty and is rather distant, at least beyond the planning horizons of governments and individuals. To many governments, taking tough choices now seems less appetizing than kicking the can down the road for future generations to deal with. Since emissions everywhere contribute equally to the problem, unprecedented international cooperation is required, even among countries that have radically different levels of development and views about who is responsible for implementing solutions.

Perhaps the thorniest aspect of the climate change problem is that it involves a conflict between what is required and what is fair. Developed and developing countries have clashed about this topic for decades. Developing countries insist that there is a "carbon debt" that must be paid. According to this view, developed countries put most of the greenhouse gases in the atmosphere during their process of carbon-powered industrialization that made them rich and therefore must shoulder the burden of saving the planet from global warming. Developing countries have grudgingly accepted to take actions to address global warming only if they are consistent with poverty reduction and economic growth. While conceding the point that they bear a special responsibility, developed countries argue that the planet cannot be saved if developing countries, now responsible for well over half of global emissions (and growing fast), don't share in the pain of emissions reductions. The most significant example is China: Its emissions were about one-third the size of the United States' in 1992 but are now about twice the size. The emotional depth of this divide is particularly strong between the United States and the developing world:

> A billion Chinese and a billion Indians want to live like middle class Americans, and they see no reason why they should put their dreams on hold when the Americans are unwilling to give up their SUVs and shopping malls.[1]

Complicating these resentments and geographical divides, the rules governing climate action in the key international forum, the UN Framework

---

[1] Yuval Noah Harari, *Homo Deus* (London: Penguin, 2017), p. 250.

Convention on Climate Change (UNFCCC), remain based on consensus with every country having veto power. That makes decision-making devilishly complicated when over 190 countries are represented and each, no matter how small, carries the same weight as all the others. The body overseeing the work of the UNFCCC, the United Nations, is often criticized for being bureaucratic, unwieldy, and ideologically laden—not the ideal traits required to take quick, complex, and bold decisions. In short, rapidly decarbonizing the world economy while ensuring global growth to fuel rising standards of living for a growing population is perhaps the most difficult task humanity has ever faced.

The US and the EU have not been the only key actors in shaping policies to address this task: Others, especially China but also Brazil, South Africa, and India (known as the BASIC countries), have emerged as important players in the past decade because of their traditional opposition to ambitious binding cuts in global emissions. The influence of developing countries has been growing, reflecting not only their growing share of global emissions (around two-thirds), but also their growing economic and political clout. The US and EU shares of world population, GDP, and emissions have been steadily declining at the same time. A host of sub-federal governments (such as cities and regions) as well as national and international non-state actors, including corporations, grassroots movements, and NGOs, have increasingly shaped the climate policy debate and implemented important measures to reduce emissions.

Notwithstanding the growing universe of actors addressing climate change over the past three decades, the willingness and ability of the US and the EU to adopt leadership roles domestically and internationally have proved crucial. As the world's leading economic and political power, the nursery of high-tech innovation, the largest source of emissions per capita and the only country capable of influencing Chinese policy, the United States has arguably been the indispensable actor on climate change.

But the EU has also been instrumental because it has stood virtually alone (since the 1990s) among industrialized nations in its persistent commitment to aggressive global action to address climate change. Moreover, measures within the EU (such as an emission trading system and promotion of renewable energies) have provided an important policy laboratory for the world. The EU has provided "leadership by example" by undertaking deep emissions reductions (often unilaterally) and providing significant funding to developing countries to assist their transition to lower carbon intensity economies. As the world's largest internal market and one of the top destinations for foreign direct investment, the EU has exercised significant influence over global regulations relating to environmental policy. Its historic and cultural links with many developing countries, especially in Africa and island states that are especially vulnerable to the effects of global warming, have been instrumental in achieving global consensus on the way forward.

Differences in Transatlantic Views on the Environment

The US-EU partnership on environmental issues has been complicated by transatlantic divergences in attitudes toward the environment. Generalizations contrasting a more enlightened Europe caring about the fate of the world with a selfish, individualist United States oblivious to the environmental consequences of its current consumption are obviously simplistic. Nonetheless, there are some valid contrasts that may be drawn. While there certainly are many environmentally conscious voters in the United States (and not just on the coasts and in urban areas), it is generally true that concerns about the environment rank more highly in Europe than in the United States in polls about voter priorities. The open spaces and abundant natural resources in the US breed a view that natural resources are inexhaustible. In a recent poll conducted by the Pew Research Center, only two in ten Republicans believe that climate change should be a top priority (two-third of Democrats think so).[2] Europe's higher population density and relative resource scarcity encourage greater concern about the environment.

It is also generally true that Europeans are more trusting of government intervention, as well as the opinions of experts and bureaucrats, than their American cousins. Moreover, Europeans are generally less confident in technological or market-based solutions. They have largely seen climate change as a moral issue involving responsibility for planetary stewardship and fairness to future generations and developing countries rather than primarily as an economic issue focused on short-term costs and benefits (even though these have had to be taken into account in extensive impact assessments). According to the EU, technological innovations and

---

[2] Brian Kennedy and Meg Hefferon, Pew Research Center, August 28, 2019. https://www.pewresearch.org/fact-tank/2019/08/28/u-s-concern-about-climate-change-is-rising-but-mainly-among-democrats/.

flexible solutions promoted by the United States, such as "carbon sinks" (reservoirs that store carbon extracted from the atmosphere), setting a price on carbon emissions through the trading of permits, or paying third countries to make emissions reductions, should not detract from the primary goal of reducing emissions and changing lifestyles at home.

There is also some merit in the view that Europeans are more risk averse, at least regarding the climate, than Americans. According to the precautionary principle, enshrined in EU treaties, the lack of full scientific certainty, including with regard to environmental risk, should not stand in the way of action to avoid the risk when there is reason to believe that it is serious and/or irreversible. US regulations typically depart from a reverse burden of proof: A policy or action should be permitted unless it is proven to be unsafe. Unlike the US, Europe has never been willing after the early 1990s to postpone regulations limiting emissions on account of incomplete scientific consensus about climate change or require that these regulations be cost-effective as long as there is a threat of serious and potentially irreversible environmental damage.

While the US has been the champion of several international environmental treaties, especially in the 1970s and 1980s, the history, size, and geography of the United States have often led many Americans to be skeptical about international law and multilateral efforts that impinge on US sovereignty. With the federal government sometimes unwilling or unable to negotiate international measures on the environment, subfederal actors such as states and cities have filled the void by showing leadership on issues such as automotive fuel standards and building codes.

In addition to its genuine concern about the planet, the EU has had many other motivations to be a leader on climate change. As the world's biggest importer of hydrocarbons and because of its high degree of import dependency (90% for oil and 60% for gas), the EU has naturally sought to promote energy efficiency and renewable energies within the bloc. At the same time, European industry has been eager for the EU to level the playing field globally to ensure that it is not at a competitive disadvantage with industries from countries not subject to rigorous environmental standards. Some EU companies may have seen a competitive advantage in adopting tighter standards within the bloc (at least for a while) in order to achieve leading market positions in certain environmental goods and services for export.

While there have been important differences between the EU and the US approach toward climate change, these differences pale in comparison with the areas of agreement and the gulf between the positions of developed and developing countries. It is certainly not true, as some critics have suggested, that the EU has always been a flag bearer of progressive climate policies while the US has always been a reluctant and even obstructionist laggard. Each has exercised leadership, albeit at different times and in different ways. During the 1970s and 1980s, the US was clearly more active in implementing tough domestic environmental regulations and in pushing for international treaties. During the period from the early 1990s until the election of President Obama in 2008, the US withdrew from its leadership role (albeit continuing to shape the climate change debate) and the EU became the most vocal player pushing for aggressive action. During Obama's two terms, the US and the EU jointly exercised leadership in the climate change debate, before the US once again withdrew under the presidency of Donald Trump.

In order to appreciate just how unusual and impactful it was for the US and EU to exercise joint leadership during President Obama's two terms in office, it is worth reviewing how they alternated leadership on the atmosphere and climate change during the prior three decades.

US Leadership in Protecting the Ozone Layer

During the 1970s, environmental pressure groups wielded considerable political power in the United States. The Environmental Protection Agency (EPA), founded in 1970, started responding to widespread concerns about the environment by proposing tough regulations in many areas, including relating to air and water quality, controls on lead-based paint and gasoline, and the phase-out of ozone-depleting chemicals such as chlorofluorocarbons (CFCs) that were being used as aerosol propellants. The regulatory activity on the environment, begun in the first half of the 1970s under the Republican administrations of Richard Nixon and Gerald Ford, sped up under the Democratic administration of President Jimmy Carter and continued right through the 1980s, despite President Ronald Reagan's relatively laissez-faire approach to business and skepticism about environmental issues.

With the US adopting environmental standards that were more restrictive than in any other industrial nation, businesses and government sought to promote these standards internationally in order to avoid a loss of competitiveness. The United States played key roles in shaping the 1972

Stockholm Conference, that I observed as a boy, as well as many international environmental conventions. The most dramatic example of US leadership on international climate issues is the 1987 Montreal Protocol on Substances that Deplete the Ozone Layer.

The ozone layer in the atmosphere shields the earth from the sun's harmful ultraviolet radiation. Evidence that CFCs contributed to the depletion of the ozone layer emerged in 1974, with subsequent research demonstrating that CFCs used in common consumer products such as aerosols, refrigerants, foam blowing agents, solvents, fire extinguishers, and pesticides are major culprits. The problem of ozone depletion received significant media and public attention in the United States thanks to the vivid image of a thinning planetary protective shield and warnings about skin cancer.

Consumers responded by rapidly decreasing their consumption of products containing CFCs, partly because these products were not central to daily life and switching to products with similar but safer characteristics did not impose large costs. Chemical manufacturers in the United States, most notably DuPont, softened their opposition to regulation because they considered it inevitable and because they had identified environmentally friendly alternatives to CFCs that were not costly to adopt and even offered export opportunities. As a result of the EPA's order in 1978 to ban the use of fluorocarbon gases in "non-essential" aerosol propellants, US production of aerosol quickly dropped by nearly 95%.

US pressure on European governments to pass equivalent legislation was not successful at first. EU member states accounted for 40% of global CFC production and about 30% of global CFC consumption, generating a significant surplus for export. European chemical manufacturers, such as the UK's Imperial Chemical Industries, generated significant profits from the sale of CFCs worldwide and had not moved as quickly as their US competitors to identify alternatives. Until the mid-1980s, European public opinion remained relatively indifferent to the fate of the ozone layer. In a foreshadowing of similar arguments that the United States would make about efforts to address climate change one decade later, European governments largely adopted the view of their chemical industry that concerns about CFCs were not based on "sound science," that it was best to "wait and learn" rather than be rushed into action by "scaremongering," and that restrictions on CFCs would impose high costs and job losses in return for speculative benefits. But with new evidence in the mid-1980s that the ozone layer over Antarctica had declined by 40% over the past three decades and that the resulting "hole" had grown to the size of the United States, European public opinion, governments, and industry began to shift toward accepting the need for domestic and international regulation.

Although the Reagan administration had harbored reservations about further restrictions on CFCs, a groundbreaking study by the President's Council of Economic Advisers in 1987 concluded that the depletion of the ozone layer would cause millions of cancer deaths in the United States and helped establish definitively that the costs of non-action dwarfed the costs of action. The US Senate voted, by an overwhelming majority, that same year to ask the president to take aggressive measures against all ozone-depleting substances (ODS). While the analysis of domestic costs and benefits suggested that even unilateral action to reduce CFCs would have been worthwhile, the United States considered an international agreement to be preferable in order to level the international regulatory playing field and because the health benefits would be substantially higher. The fact that only about thirty nations participated in the negotiations (compared to more than six times as many in the subsequent climate change negotiations) certainly facilitated a rapid and successful outcome.

As a result of US leadership, twenty nations, including most of the major CFC producers, reached a binding agreement in Montreal in 1987 to protect the ozone layer. The Montreal Protocol, which entered into force two years later, required immediate and substantial reductions in numerous ODS, with phase-out schedules shortened and further restrictions introduced on an expanding list of substances during eight subsequent treaty revisions.

One of the incidental effects of the Montreal Protocol was that CFCs were rapidly being substituted by hydrofluorocarbons (HFCs), ozone-friendly chemicals that are up to 4000 times more powerful than carbon dioxide in promoting climate change. In response to this development, the signatories to the protocol agreed on an amendment in Kigali in 2016 that requires the reduction of HFC use by 80–85% by the late 2040s and that will therefore help the planet avoid a half-degree centigrade of warming by the end of the century. The amendment came about in large part thanks to US diplomacy with China and India and to EU diplomacy with other developing countries, especially in Africa.

The Montreal Protocol is one of the most remarkable examples of international cooperation for several reasons. The treaty has been ratified by 197 parties (196 states and the European Union), making it the first universal treaty in United Nations history. Moreover, only 14 years elapsed between the scientific evidence of the risk of ozone depletion and decisive action to address it. By contrast, the world community is still struggling after three decades to implement a durable and ambitious climate change regime to address global warming.

The protocol came about because all the large emitters of ODS undertook to take strong action. Most of the ODS reductions occurred in Western industrialized countries that have on average complied with, and sometimes even exceeded, their international commitments. Once a reluctant follower of the United States on ozone protection, the EU joined the US in pushing for the total elimination of CFC use by 2000; both achieved the goal several years early, partly because the costs of doing so were smaller than anticipated due to rapid technological innovation.

Developed countries overcame objections among developing countries, especially China and India, by guaranteeing them financial assistance to pay for the costs of implementation and by giving them a ten-year grace period before assuming any obligations to reduce their production and consumption of CFCs (both were low but were projected to increase substantially).

Finally, as a result of the treaty, global emissions of nearly one hundred ozone-depleting chemicals have been reduced by 95% and atmospheric concentrations of such chemicals have been declining since 1994. Climate projections indicate that the ozone layer will return to 1980 levels between 2050 and 2070. Global savings from the agreement's public health benefits have been estimated to be over one trillion dollars. In the US alone, approximately 280 million cases of skin cancer (including 1.6 million skin cancer deaths) and more than 45 million eye cataracts have been avoided.[3]

THE EU EMERGES AS THE LEADING GLOBAL ACTOR ON CLIMATE CHANGE

With international efforts to curb ozone depletion well on their way, attention turned to how human activity was contributing to the threat of global warming. In 1988, the United Nations established, with the active

---

[3] Judy Garber, Assistant Secretary of State for Oceans, *Diplomatic Note: Saving the Ozone Layer*. https://medium.com/statedept/saving-the-ozone-layer-e4764f686cef.

support of the United States and the European Union, the Intergovernmental Panel on Climate Change (IPCC) to provide periodic scientific assessments about climate change. Its regular publications, based on ever greater and more detailed data, have served as an important catalyst for action. A few years later, the European Union and small island states that fear being inundated by rising seas joined together to call for mandatory reductions of carbon dioxide and other greenhouse gases responsible for global warming. The international debate about climate change has focused ever since on whether national emissions targets are necessary and, if so, whether they should be voluntary or binding and how they should be implemented.[4]

In the negotiations leading to the adoption of the UNFCCC at the Rio Summit in June 1992, the EU called on all industrialized countries to take binding measures to stabilize their greenhouse gas emissions at 1990 levels by the year 2000. But the United States and other developed economies resisted. President George Bush, who was up for re-election in November, had promised: "The American way of life is not up for negotiations. Period." As a result, the convention only refers to the stabilization of greenhouse gases in the atmosphere at levels that would prevent "dangerous" climate change as a voluntary goal, without specifying any measures or timetables necessary to achieve it. Moreover, the convention merely states (in rather fuzzy prose) that the goal should be achieved "within a time frame sufficient to allow ecosystems to adapt naturally to climate change." Having succeeded in diluting climate change goals and bowing to international pressure, President Bush signed the convention and the United States was the first industrialized country to ratify it.

The UNFCCC set the stage for all subsequent international negotiations to address climate change. Despite its purely voluntary nature, the convention has grown in significance because its membership is universal and because it has established some guiding principles for future discussions. It drew a firewall between developed countries, named in an annex to the convention, and developing countries, with the former expected to assume the lead in combating climate change under the principle of "common but differentiated responsibilities and respective capabilities" (CBDRRC).

---

[4] Daniel Bodansky, "Bonn Voyage: Kyoto's Uncertain Revival," *The National Interest*, September 1, 2001. https://nationalinterest.org/article/bonn-voyage-kyotos-uncertain-revival-372.

According to that principle, all states have a shared obligation to protect the environment and developed countries assume special responsibilities because of their greater historical role in generating pollution and their greater economic and technological capacities. Not only should developed countries take the lead on emissions reductions, for example, they should assume responsibility for assisting developing countries to adapt to climate change and to respond to natural climate-induced disasters.

While the US and the EU have endorsed the concept, they have consistently opposed suggestions that current generations of US and EU citizens should accept potentially unlimited liability for the actions of their ancestors, that developing countries are exempt from any legally binding commitments to take action, or that there should be a static division between countries based on historical responsibilities rather than evolving economic circumstances and contributions to global pollution.

This CBDRRC firewall almost immediately became a source of enormous controversy because it did not reflect the reality that many countries classified as "developing" (such as Singapore, South Korea, and Qatar) were in fact among the richest in the world and did not need special assistance. As the emissions of developing countries surged ahead (with China becoming the world's biggest emitter representing one-quarter of global emissions in 2012), many countries (especially the United States) felt that the firewall needed to be modified.

The convention set science-based procedures for determining what constitutes a dangerous accumulation of greenhouse gases in the atmosphere. Over time the parties to the convention have determined that this means limiting global average temperature increases to less than 2 degrees centigrade compared to "pre-industrial" levels (an undefined term but one some experts understand as referring to levels existing just before the industrial revolution). The convention was also significant because it allowed, in line with US preferences, individual countries to adopt and implement their own measures to reduce greenhouse gas emissions. At the same time, the UNFCCC establishes a collective procedural obligation to report publicly on these measures so that they can be reviewed by other nations. The purpose of the system is to exert peer pressure and to enable parties to the convention to take "appropriate action," including tougher measures in subsequent protocols if commitments are insufficient.

Around the time of the negotiations relating to the UNFCCC, the United States and the EU started swapping positions as leader and follower, respectively, on climate change. Several environmental issues in the 1980s, such as the death of forests due to acid rain, radioactivity due to the Chernobyl nuclear disaster and the thinning ozone layer over Antarctica contributed to the European public's awareness of humans' negative impact on the planet. Environmental issues regularly topped the list of voters' concerns in numerous opinion polls. The Green political movement, that had started in 1983 as a fringe phenomenon in Germany, quickly grew and spread to the rest of the continent, not just Scandinavia but also Belgium, Netherlands, Luxembourg and elsewhere, where they became part of the mainstream by the early 1990s. Green parties were not only represented in national parliaments and in the European Parliament, but were also winning cabinet posts (typically the ministry for environmental affairs).

Several EU member states, especially Germany, the Netherlands, and Denmark, moved quickly to adopt strict environmental standards. Seeking to avoid exposing their businesses to a competitive disadvantage compared to firms in other less regulated EU states, they looked for allies in the European Commission and the European Parliament to export their higher standards throughout the EU. The European Commission acted to harmonize environmental standards when more stringent national standards threatened to create non-tariff barriers that would fracture the common market. At the same time, revisions to the EU treaties shifted decision-making from unanimity to qualified majority. The accession of Sweden, Austria, and Finland (three fervently Green countries) in 1995 helped tip the balance in the Council, representing the ministers of the member states, toward strict EU-wide policies on the environment.

In the United States, however, concerns about the environment had dropped far down the list of voter concerns. The Clinton–Gore administration that took office in 1992 was unable to pass much federal pro-environmental legislation, especially after both houses of Congress flipped from Democratic to Republican majorities in the 1994 mid-term elections. And although it shared the EU's support for an international agreement that would contain legally binding emissions targets for developed countries, while exempting developing countries, the administration repeatedly failed to persuade Congress. Faced with no domestic pressure to reduce its carbon emissions, US industry was also opposed to having obligations imposed by treaty.

Transatlantic Frictions Over the Kyoto Protocol

Negotiations to establish such a treaty began in Berlin in 1995 and were concluded two years later in Kyoto. The United States, and Vice President Gore in particular, shaped many of the aspects of the 1997 Kyoto Protocol, including several "flexibility mechanisms." One of these mechanisms was the establishment of five-year commitment periods, the first scheduled for 2008–2012, to meet targets for the reduction of greenhouse gas emissions. The five-year period allowed countries to average their yearly reductions to smooth out fluctuations due to unusual weather or economic conditions. Market-based mechanisms included the ability of developed countries to achieve their emissions reduction targets by buying emissions allowances from countries emitting less carbon than they were entitled to and by investing in emission reduction projects in the developing world where they were cheaper to achieve than at home. Moreover, developed countries could offset carbon emissions with the extraction of carbon from the atmosphere and its subsequent sequestration in forests and underground reservoirs.

The EU provided the leadership in seeking bold and binding targets for the reduction of greenhouse gas emissions. It initially proposed a 15% reduction of such emissions by 2010 compared to 1990 levels on condition that others would follow. The United States argued in favor of stabilization of emissions at current levels; even such a modest commitment required a significant reduction below projected increases in emissions according to forecasts of business as usual. In the end, the EU did win the argument for a more ambitious target but settled for an average reduction by developed countries of 5% during a five-year commitment period ending in 2012. The EU and the US assumed commitments to reduce their emissions by 8 and 7%, respectively.

The reluctance of the United States to embrace the EU's aggressive emissions reduction proposals may be explained by their different economic circumstances. EU emissions had declined after 1990 in large part due to the UK's switch from coal to gas and Germany's closure of inefficient East German plants after unification; neither of these decisions had anything to do with climate change. Moreover, the US had experienced faster economic growth than the EU in the 1990s. As a result, the Kyoto targets arguably required the United States to make a much greater effort than the EU to reduce emissions. A major reason why the EU wanted the US to accept deep binding emissions reductions, and why it opposed US efforts to introduce market-based "flexibility mechanisms," was that the EU wanted to reduce the competitive advantage the US enjoyed in energy prices.

It was clear on both sides of the Atlantic from early in the negotiations that the Kyoto Protocol was going to have a very tough time in the US Senate, where it needed to be approved. Even though the United States had succeeded in achieving many of its goals, the negotiating process had an air of unreality because the US could not join the Protocol as drafted. In 1997, the Senate adopted a unanimous non-binding resolution asking President Clinton not to agree to any agreement limiting greenhouse gas emissions if it would harm the economic interests of the United States. The resolution found that exempting developing countries from obligations to reduce emissions was "inconsistent with the need for global action on climate change" and "environmentally flawed." As it was highly unlikely that developing countries would agree to any burden-sharing, the resolution essentially demanded that the United States should reject any commitments at all. Bowing to intense international pressure, the Clinton administration signed the Protocol in September 1998 but sought to mollify the Senate with a promise that it would not take any steps to implement the Protocol before ratification and that it would not seek ratification unless it had obtained "meaningful participation" from developing countries.

The arrival of the George W. Bush administration in 2000 turned the United States from a reluctant architect of the Kyoto Protocol to an open antagonist. While the fate of the Protocol in the United States had been in limbo, it was now declared effectively dead. According to the United States and other critics, the Kyoto Protocol was fatally flawed even when it was signed because it left over 50% of the world' emissions unregulated. By the time the protocol entered into force in 2005, developing country emissions, especially in China, India, and Brazil, accounted for over 60% of global emissions and were rising every year. The firewall between developed and developing countries, in which only the former assumed obligations, and the artificial division of the world into one of the two groups appeared increasingly archaic.

The Bush administration disengaged the United States from climate change negotiations and promoted a different vision from the one of the Clinton administration. It advocated a "wait and see" approach, similar to the one Europe adopted before the Montreal Protocol, and invoked scientific uncertainties about global warming as an excuse to reject meaningful action. The US would only undertake voluntary measures to reduce its "greenhouse gas intensity" (measuring greenhouse gas emissions per dollar of economic output). Those measures would simply confirm what was already occurring in the US economy and would result in emissions increases.

Despite its flaws, the Kyoto Protocol has provided several important contributions. While the promise by developing countries to reduce their emissions by an average of 5% below 1990 levels was rather modest, the protocol is the first time that developed countries have agreed to reduce emissions from a wide range of greenhouse gases generated by numerous economic activities. Whatever its flaws, the protocol represents a first step in a serious effort to address a serious problem and as such was no small achievement. 192 countries signed *and* ratified the protocol; only the United States, Afghanistan, and Sudan failed to do so. Moreover, the protocol reflects the reasonable view held by most countries (except the United States) that developed industrial countries should take the lead in combating climate change given their contribution to the problem and their ability to fix it.

The protocol also enshrines market-based "flexibility mechanisms," most notably providing a framework for a global market in emissions trading for the first time. While the EU was initially wary of such an emissions market, it launched the world's first (and biggest) international emissions trading system in 2005. The system operates in 31 countries, limiting emissions from roughly 11,000 heavy energy-using installations and airlines operating among these countries, and covers more than 40% of the EU's greenhouse gas emissions. Initial teething problems due to an oversupply of carbon emissions allowances, resulting in a carbon price too low to incentivize reductions in emissions, were fixed in 2014–2016.

Negotiations leading to the Kyoto Protocol also provided some valuable lessons that ultimately shaped the future evolution of climate change negotiations. They showed that legally binding emissions reductions targets are not always worth much in practice, especially without a credible enforcement mechanism. Such targets might also scare away some countries, such as the United States, that regard them seriously as obligations that they must fulfill, rather than as commitments that they should achieve.

US failure to ratify the protocol not only undermined the effectiveness and durability of the agreement in and of itself, it also made it highly unlikely that China, India, and other significant emitters in developing countries would ever sign up to any commitments. The United States was not alone: Canada simply walked away from the treaty in 2012 once it became clear it would never meet its obligations; Russia, Australia, New Zealand, and Japan didn't sign up to a second commitment period lasting between 2013 and 2020. Only the EU, Norway, Iceland, and Switzerland delivered on their obligations in the first period between 2008 and 2012 and assumed new ones in the second.

The flaws of the Protocol suggested that a more promising avenue to build a durable and ambitious climate change regime in the future would be built incrementally and modestly from the ground upon the foundation of public support. Domestic policy had to lead international policy, rather than the other way around, especially in the United States.[5] In the late 1990s and throughout much of the following decade, many politicians and voters in the United States continued to question the scientific certainty that human activity contributes to climate change. Polls during the period showed that climate change ranked far below the economy and health care as priorities. The Kyoto Protocol seemed to present the reverse situation from the Montreal Protocol ten years earlier: In the latter case, the benefits of action (even unilateral action) by the United States to reduce ozone-depleting emissions clearly outweighed the costs; in the former case, it seemed that the United States would have to shoulder disproportionate costs compared to other countries, disrupting its citizens' way of life, while it had less to fear than many other countries from climate change.

US opposition to accepting carbon emissions reductions caused outrage around the world about perceived US selfish exceptionalism. But it also galvanized the EU to embrace its new role as the leading climate change evangelist on the world stage. Representing half of non-US industrialized country emissions, the EU was destined to have an important voice. Notwithstanding the US formal withdrawal from the Kyoto Protocol in March 2001, the EU kept fighting for it, spearheading an international agreement in Marrakesh to implement the Protocol and ratifying

---

[5] Daniel Bodansky, "U.S. Climate Policy After Kyoto: Elements for Success," Carnegie Endowment Policy Brief, April 2002. https://carnegieendowment.org/2002/03/25/u.s.-climate-policy-after-kyoto-elements-for-success-pub-937.

the Protocol itself in 2002. The EU also convinced Russia to do so in 2004, in return for supporting Russian entry to the World Trade Organization. Since Russia represented 11% of global emissions, this was an important milestone toward reaching the threshold necessary for entry into force in 2005—ratification by parties representing 55% of total 1990 CO_2 emissions from industrialized countries. Moreover, the EU launched an emissions trading system in 2005 and rapidly expanded its climate legislation that promoted, for example, electricity produced from renewables, the improved energy performance of buildings, the use of biofuels in transport, and combined heat and power production. By the end of the Kyoto Protocol's first commitment period in 2012, the EU had overachieved its target of reducing its emissions compared to 1990.

A report by the IPCC in 2007 injected a sense of urgency about climate change, even in the United States. The report pointed to increases in global average air and ocean temperatures, widespread melting of snow and ice, and rising average sea levels as further evidence of global warming due to an unprecedented concentration of greenhouse gases in the atmosphere from human activities. In order to prevent catastrophic consequences from global warming, the IPCC concluded that global greenhouse gas emissions would have to peak in the following ten to fifteen years and by 2050 would have to be reduced to less than half of the level of emissions in 2000. The United States continued to refuse any binding emission reduction targets and to insist that any future emission reduction commitments would have to be accompanied by similar commitments from the developing world. But it now appeared willing to contemplate long-term action on climate change under the auspices of the UNFCCC.

The EU continued to take the lead. In 2007, the European Commission stated that the EU should adopt the necessary measures and spearhead an international effort to ensure that global average temperatures do not exceed 2 centigrade compared to "pre-industrial" levels. That target became the foundation for subsequent global climate change negotiations. EU heads of state acted on that recommendation the following year by committing to reduce greenhouse gas emissions by 20% compared to 1990 levels, irrespective of what other countries might choose to do. Moreover, they committed to increase the percentage of renewables in the energy mix to 20% and endorsed a target to improve energy efficiency by 20%, both by 2020 compared to 1990 levels. The legislative package was formally adopted in 2009, several months before negotiations in Copenhagen to find a way forward on climate change that would command greater support than the Kyoto Protocol.

Barack Obama's victory in the US presidential election of 2008 heralded a new beginning (at last) for US support of environmental protection, and measures to curb global warming, both at home and internationally. Abandoning his predecessor's conviction that any measure to protect the environment would necessarily undermine the economy, Obama believed that reduced reliance on imported fossil fuels would contribute to national security and that significant further global warming represented not only a direct threat to the homeland because of flooding of coastal areas but also a series of indirect threats such as the increased fragility of developing countries, radicalization, and mass migration that could destabilize US allies and interests. As early as 2009, the Department of Defense started identifying climate change as a key factor affecting national security challenges.

President Obama did not believe that a healthy environment comes at the expense of a healthy economy. As I repeatedly noted in my own speeches around Europe, landmark environmental legislation in the 1970s and 1980s did not prevent the US from doubling the size of its economy, improving technological innovation, creating numerous well-paying middle-class jobs, and generating many billions of dollars in economic productivity. As the president liked to argue:

> The old rules may say we can't protect our environment and promote economic growth at the same time, but in America, we've always used new technologies – we've used science; we've used research and development and discovery to make the old rules obsolete.[6]

Achieving technological leadership in renewable energies offered enormous scope to dominate important export markets. New environmental legislation could be justified, not because it was necessary *despite* damage to the economy, but because it would generate significant benefits in health, energy savings, and avoided damages.

In the face of national polls indicating that few Americans considered climate change to be a national priority, the president moved quickly to

---

[6] Address at Georgetown University, June 25, 2013. http://ens-newswire.com/2013/06/25/president-obamas-climate-change-speech-full-text/.

take action. In 2009, the EPA ruled that greenhouse gases pose a danger to human health, thereby creating its authority to regulate them. The president issued executive orders, thereby bypassing Congress, that required federal agencies to reduce their greenhouse gas emissions and enhance their use of renewable energies. He also unveiled new national standards for automobile fuel economy and the first-ever federal greenhouse gas emissions standards for cars and trucks. US emissions were already declining as demand shifted from coal to natural gas. That shift was due in part to the surging supply and declining prices for natural gas resulting from a boom in fracking.

The Copenhagen Conference

Within months of his inauguration, President Obama launched a Major Economies Forum on Energy and Climate to facilitate a candid dialogue among major developed and developing economies and to drive a convergence of views before a major international climate change conference in Copenhagen at the end of 2009. On the eve of the conference, the president made a pledge to reduce US greenhouse gas emissions by 17% by 2020, with the ultimate goal of an 80% reduction by 2050, compared to 2005 levels. The pledge pushed drastic action further into the future than the EU's pledge, but the promise of a significant shift in US climate change policy invested the United States with renewed authority.

President Obama's actions meant that the United States had finally returned as a key player in the international climate change debate after one decade's absence. During that decade, the EU had been the preeminent player even though it lacked the economic or political power to force major emitters like the US, China, India, and Brazil to take action and despite its declining share of global emissions. It exercised influence as an exemplary standard setter undertaking deep unilateral emissions reductions and as a thought leader regarding strategies for climate change action. The new engagement of the US and the fact that climate change action clearly required active participation of the most significant developing countries (over whom the United States had far greater influence than the EU) meant that the EU lost its preeminent role.

Several factors further undermined the EU's influence on the eve of the Copenhagen summit. Internal divisions among EU states became far more marked after the entry of ten new members in 2004. While Scandinavia, the UK, and the Netherlands continued to push for aggressive action, including unilaterally by the EU, Poland and the Czech Republic were far more skeptical. The Czech Republic, holding the six-month rotating presidency of the EU during the first half of 2009 on the eve of the Copenhagen summit, wanted the EU to focus on energy security rather than climate change, described by President Vaclav Klaus as a "dangerous myth." Poland and the Czech Republic vetoed an effort to increase the EU's unilateral commitment to reduce greenhouse gas emissions to 30% by 2030 compared to 1990 levels. They also help block an EU proposal to make a significant financial commitment to climate mitigation efforts on the ground that the manner of allocating the contribution among member states should be based primarily on their ability to pay, rather than their responsibility for greenhouse gas emissions.

EU efforts to project a coherent position during the Copenhagen negotiations were also undermined by its institutional framework. Under the EU treaty rules then in effect, the EU was represented at Copenhagen by a "troika"—the European Commission, the EU member state currently holding the EU presidency, and the EU member state scheduled to hold the EU presidency for the following six-month period. This troika negotiated on the basis of a mandate adopted unanimously by heads of state. This meant that coordination meetings had to be held at every major stage of the negotiations, substantially reducing the EU's ability to respond quickly and flexibly to events. The decision of several member states to participate and negotiate independently also fostered confusion among other countries about the EU's position.

The EU's difficulties to project a single voice on the international stage were addressed in part in early 2010 when the European Commission tasked a single Commissioner, the well-connected former Danish Minister for Climate and Energy Connie Hedegaard, to represent the EU on climate change. The influence of the EU increased further when European Commission President Juncker combined the role with the energy portfolio and tasked the highly capable former Spanish Minister of Agriculture, Miguel Arias Cañete, to take charge.

There were two other actors, in addition to the United States and the European Union, that made their presence felt. The first was a grouping consisting of an Alliance of Small Island States, as well as African and least developed countries. This grouping possessed little economic or political power, but nonetheless wielded significant moral authority, in part because of a very vocal contingent from civil society. The second actor was a powerful BASIC bloc of countries, consisting of Brazil, South Africa, India, and China. The bloc's influence was not only a reflection of its economic power and percentage of global emissions, but also a result of its ability to speak with a single voice. The most important issue uniting the bloc's members was the view that developed countries should bear the burden of addressing climate change and any efforts by developing countries should not be an obstacle to their economic development.

China emerged at the Copenhagen conference as the new "indispensable nation," along with the United States, without whom a comprehensive deal would be impossible. On the day following the US announcement of its new offer to reduce greenhouse gas emissions, China stated that it would take voluntary measures to cut its own emissions relative to economic growth by 40–45% by 2020 compared to 2005 levels. Although this meant that its emissions would continue to climb steeply, they would do so at a slower rate. The measures were voluntary, not binding, but were the first indication that China was prepared to take any action to address climate change.

Expectations leading up to the Copenhagen conference were high. The conference had been called to settle the thorny issue of what the international climate change regime would look like after the expiry of the Kyoto Protocol's first commitment period in 2012. The unofficial slogan of "Hopenhagen," as many Danes called it, was "seal the deal." With a record 115 heads of state or government present and more than 40,000 people registered as delegates, the conference was one of the largest environmental meetings in history. Despite the high expectations, the conditions for a global consensus were simply not present. Senator John Kerry observed soon after his arrival in Copenhagen that "The negotiations were even more constipated than I expected."[7] This "constipation" was due to the rigid division of developed and developing countries into opposite blocs. As Commissioner Miguel Arias Cañete, EU's chief climate change negotiator during 2014–2019, has put it: "the story was about countries against countries, developed versus developing, them and us."[8]

---

[7] John F. Kerry, *Every Day Is Extra* (New York: Simon & Schuster), p. 560.

[8] Speech by Commissioner Miguel Arias Cañete, December 14, 2015. http://europa.eu/rapid/press-release_SPEECH-15-6320_en.htm.

The two sides continued to have radically different understandings of their "common but differentiated responsibilities and respective capabilities," the formula first formalized at the Earth Summit in Rio in 1992. This structural divide was deepened by the effects of the 2009 economic crisis, hardening the unwillingness of countries to undertake economically painful decisions. President Obama's eagerly anticipated address to a packed room of delegates, restating pledges to reduce US greenhouse gas emissions by 17% by 2020 compared to 2005 levels and to help mobilize $100 billion of climate finance by 2020 for developing nations to cope with the effects of climate change, failed to break the conference's deadlock.

Disaster was averted on the final formal day of proceedings due to a whirlwind of bilateral and multilateral meetings among the heads of state and government of 25 countries, including all of the world's major economies. The critical moment occurred when President Obama walked unannounced into a private meeting among the leaders of the BASIC bloc. After less than an hour, they emerged with a three-page document that left many details to be filled in later but offered a way forward. Due to the opposition from a handful of countries, the closing plenary session merely took note of the Copenhagen Accord without endorsing it. As such, it remains a political document only without any recognized legal status (unlike the Kyoto Protocol).

For the EU the failure of the Copenhagen conference to produce a legally binding agreement with specific targets and timetables, coupled with the fact that the US and the BASIC bloc had brokered a deal without its involvement, represented bitter disappointments. Not surprisingly, the US had a different view. Not only had the president's diplomacy proved pivotal, but the agreement incorporated many of the key ideas that the US had been promoting. Most importantly, the agreement represented the first time in history that all major economies had accepted their responsibility to confront the threat of climate change. Whereas the countries willing to accept the emissions targets under Kyoto represented only a quarter of global emissions in the first commitment period, and 15% in the second commitment period, countries representing more than 85% of global emissions put forward emissions pledges under the Copenhagen Accord.

While the Copenhagen Accord did fall short of expectations, it laid the foundation for a significant re-engineering of the architecture for a future international agreement on climate change.[9] It represented a more flexible approach than in the past: one that was voluntary and bottom-up as it relied on nationally determined pledges, rather than top down as a result of internationally mandated targets. It assumed that making such pledges transparent and subject to regular international review would be an effective catalyst for action. It weakened the firewall between developed and developing countries, while maintaining some aspects of differentiation, by calling upon all countries to report on their emissions and mitigation actions. In a major step forward, even developing countries agreed on the principle that their actions, not just those of developed countries, would be subject to international review. China, in particular, had resisted this notion until the last day of the conference.[10]

Developed countries committed to mobilize significant financial resources to assist developing countries to cope with climate change: roughly $30 billion during 2010–2012, with a goal of $100 billion per year by 2020 conditional upon "meaningful mitigation actions and transparency on implementation" by the aid recipients. Emissions reductions and developed countries' financing pledges would be subject to rigorous measurement, reporting, and verification according to future guidelines.

The Copenhagen Accord was vague and required significant detail to be worked out. But had the EU been pushing for a more aggressive agenda in the room with the US and the BASIC bloc, it is possible that the Copenhagen Conference would have ended with no agreement at all.

In the wake of its frustration at Copenhagen, the EU "only had one option: wipe the tears, get its act together and keep pushing…creatively, strategically."[11] The entry into force of the Lisbon Treaty in December 2009 and the creation of a new directorate-general for "climate action" within the European Commission a few months later facilitated the EU's ability to represent the EU with a single voice in international climate negotiations and to ensure a coherent policy within the bloc.

---

[9] UNFCC Framework Convention on Climate Change Draft decision -/CP.15, December 18, 2009. https://unfccc.int/resource/docs/2009/cop15/eng/l07.pdf.

[10] Todd Stern, "The Future of the Paris Climate Regime," Yale Law School, April 10, 2018. https://www.brookings.edu/on-the-record/the-future-of-the-paris-climate-regime/.

[11] Speech by Commissioner Miguel Arias Cañete, December 14, 2015. http://europa.eu/rapid/press-release_SPEECH-15-6320_en.htm.

It continued to push for a global binding deal with legal force to supplement or replace the Kyoto Protocol. As a result, a conference of the UNFCCC parties agreed in 2011 to seek to negotiate "a protocol, another legal instrument, or an agreed outcome with legal force"— a deliberately vague formula that bridged the gap between those countries (including the EU) that wanted a new international treaty, and other countries (especially India) that wanted to leave the issue of legal form open. The formula was acceptable to the United States because the outcome of the negotiation was to apply to all UNFCCC parties, without differentiating between developed and developing countries. While the formula did not require a fully binding legal instrument, it clearly intended to create an agreement with more binding force than the Copenhagen Accord.[12]

The European Union and the United States continued to disagree on some important points regarding the architecture of a future global accord on climate change, but they were both aligned in seeking an ambitious outcome. For the first time in the history of international climate change agreements dating back to the Montreal Accord, they were effectively acting as co-leaders that were united far more than they were divided on points of substance. That made all the difference in ensuring a successful outcome in the Paris climate change conference in 2015.

THE PARIS CONFERENCE

The Obama administration's pro-environmental domestic agenda made the United States a far more congenial partner of the EU than in the past, even if legislative reform proved difficult. Although a bill envisioning emissions trading barely failed in Congress in 2010 due to mid-term elections that put both the House and the Senate under Republican control, the administration moved quickly, especially in its second term, to act under the president's executive authority to significantly reduce emissions from power plants, the transportation sector (including cars, heavy-duty trucks, and aircraft engines), the oil and gas industry, agriculture, landfills, and coal mines. Rapid job growth in the clean energy economy reinforced the president's mandate for taking such actions. By 2015, four times as

---

[12] Sue Biniaz, "Climate Change Negotiations: Legal and Other Issues on the Road to Paris," *Case Western Reserve Journal of International Law* (2016). https://scholarlycommons.law.case.edu/cgi/viewcontent.cgi?article=2238&context=jil.

many Americans were employed by renewable energy companies than by the fossil fuel industry. Thanks to rapid price declines due to technological advances, renewable energy had become the dominant trend in new power installations.

Moreover, the United States made several key contributions in the years leading up to the Paris conference that helped ensure its success. One was its $3 billion pledge to the Green Climate Fund established at the Copenhagen Conference to assist developing countries to address climate change. (By the time President Obama left office in 2017, only $1 billion had actually been transferred). Another key contribution was its role in shifting the position of China. The decision by the US Embassy in Beijing in 2010 to publish air pollution statistics online that contradicted Chinese government numbers helped raise the salience of smog as a major domestic health issue in the subsequent years, especially among urban middle classes in large cities.

Secretary Kerry's tireless secret shuttle diplomacy with China on climate change paved the way for the announcement by Vice Premier Zhang Gaoli at a UN Climate Change Summit in September 2014 that China would soon announce post-2020 actions on climate change that would include "marked progress in reducing carbon intensity" and "the peaking of total carbon dioxide emissions as early as possible." Two months later in Beijing, one year before the start of the Paris conference, President Obama and President Xi Jinping declared their bilateral intention to reduce emissions: While the United States pledged to reduce emissions by 26–28% by 2025 compared to 2005 levels, China pledged to "achieve the peaking of CO2 emissions around 2030" or earlier if possible as well as to "increase the share of non-fossil fuels in primary energy consumption to around 20% by 2030."[13]

That declaration, in turn, paved the way to a US-China Joint Presidential Statement on Climate Change in late September 2015 that set forth a joint vision for the Paris conference and reiterated each side's domestic actions to address climate change. In that statement, China provided more detail than it had previously on its efforts to reduce the "intensity" of its emissions measured in terms of carbon dioxide emissions per unit of GDP, as well as on its plans to introduce an emissions trading system, to promote low-carbon buildings and transportation, and to introduce

---

[13] "U.S.-China Joint Announcement on Climate Change," The White House Office of the Press Secretary, November 12, 2004. https://obamawhitehouse.archives.gov/the-press-office/2014/11/11/us-china-joint-announcement-climate-change.

tougher fuel efficiency standards. The United States cooperated closely with France, the host of the conference, in a similar France-China Joint Presidential Statement on Climate Change in November.[14]

The EU also made important contributions in the period leading up to Paris. Its efforts to address climate change were even more ambitious than those of the United States: In October 2014, it announced a legally binding target to reduce greenhouse gas emissions by at least 40% by 2030 compared to 1990 levels, a legally binding target to increase the share of renewables to at least 27% of EU energy consumption by 2030, and an indicative target of improving energy efficiency by at least 27% by 2030. And in 2014, the EU and its member states pledged €14.5 billion to the Green Climate Fund. Equally important was its co-sponsorship of a coalition of small island states, enlarged to countries of Africa, the Caribbean, and the Pacific, that contributed significantly to the 2015 climate change conference in Paris.

The Paris conference was the culmination of 23 years of international efforts under United Nations auspices since the Rio Earth Summit to forge collective action to combat climate change. For about 20 years, since the negotiations around the Kyoto Protocol, those efforts had been locked in stalemate. Although the conference was formally the result of four years of preparatory work, it in fact began with the arrival of the Obama administration (and new US climate change policy) seven years earlier. Had the Paris conference failed, the world would have been left without any effective global plan to prevent an increase in global warming. In that event, global warming was predicted to reach as much as 5 degrees centigrade over current temperatures, a level that would render uninhabitable large areas of the globe. As EU Commissioner Arias Cañete noted: "This was the last chance. And we took it."

Expectations for a successful outcome in Paris were extremely high, especially after the disappointment in Copenhagen. There were more than 50,000 participants, including 19,000 government delegates and 150 heads of state or government from 196 countries, 6000 representatives from non-governmental organizations and business, and 2800 members of the press. As the conference opened in December 2015, just several

---

[14] "U.S.-China Joint Presidential Statement on Climate Change," The White House Office of the Press Secretary, September 25, 2015. https://obamawhitehouse.archives.gov/the-press-office/2015/09/25/us-china-joint-presidential-statement-climate-change.

weeks after terrorist attacks had killed 130 people in Paris, it was unclear whether a compromise could be reached. The successful outcome was due to many factors, including US diplomatic outreach to China and India, EU diplomatic outreach to a broad coalition of largely developing countries, and the careful preparation and skillful diplomacy of the French hosts.

The US and the EU agreed on several key objectives for the Paris conference. Both wanted it to be ambitious, in the sense that it had to present a serious path forward to curbing global warming such that the earth's climate would avoid catastrophic and irreversible changes. They both wanted it to be durable, in the sense of having an indefinite duration unlike the Copenhagen Accord that involved one-shot pledges covering the period up to 2020. Both wanted it to be inclusive, in the sense that it had to include efforts by all countries and that it had to gain universal acceptance, unlike the Kyoto Protocol that bound countries representing only a minority of global emissions. Both agreed that while the responsibilities of rich and poor countries had to be different, especially regarding emissions reductions and financial contributions, the old static divide between developed and developing countries needed to be more flexible to reflect the latter's increasing wealth and role in climate change. Both wanted a mechanism for regular reviews of national commitments to reduce emissions to enable increasing levels of ambition to reflect public pressure and technological advances. And they agreed that countries' emissions reductions commitments must be transparent and that countries must be accountable to deliver and update these commitments, as well as subjecting them to international verification. Such an agreement would send a powerful signal to the markets and to citizens of all countries that the decarbonization of the world economy is irreversible.

But there remained important points of division between the US and the EU even as the conference began. The EU urged, in the face of US resistance, that the agreement be in the form of a legally binding international treaty. Whereas the EU had long resisted the view of the United States (as well as other major emitters like China and India) that only voluntary action would be compatible with national sovereignty, it had come to accept in the years leading up to the Paris Agreement that bottom-up nationally determined emissions reductions could be as effective as a top-down set of rules. Nonetheless, the EU pushed for the strictest binding rules in as many areas as possible. And the EU pushed for the deepest cuts possible in national emissions while the United States remained concerned about undertaking unrealistic objectives damaging to its economy.

The US and the EU were instrumental in bringing about the final compromise. The EU backed down from its insistence that nationally determined emissions cuts needed to be legally binding. The US agreed to text, especially important to South Africa, regarding "loss and damage" that accepted the principle that developing countries are entitled to special aid to mitigate the impact of climate change and to respond to climate-related disasters, without conceding that developed countries bear the historical liability to compensate developing countries for the former's role in climate change. Other countries compromised as well. China and India agreed to language that expressed an aspiration to limit the increase in global warming to 1.5 degrees centigrade.

The agreement had to be carefully constructed. As US chief negotiator Todd Stern has observed, the Paris Agreement successfully found the sweet spot between what was possible and what was necessary:

> It is easy to demand what seems necessary without regard to whether it's politically impossible, and also easy to do the politically expedient without much regard for what's necessary. Finding the sweet spot is hard.[15]

Building on some of the ideas contained in the Copenhagen Accord, the Paris Agreement represents a paradigm shift compared to prior approaches to addressing climate change: It blended elements of a top-down and a bottom-up approach; rejecting the strict division of countries that had characterized climate change regimes, it found a middle ground on the issue of differentiation by charting a middle course between those obligations that applied universally and those that applied principally to some nations; it blended obligations that were legally binding with those that were not; and, perhaps most importantly, it relied on peer pressure and the evolution of norms to drive more ambitious action when rigid rules wouldn't work.

Did the Paris Agreement achieve its objectives? It certainly meets the objective of inclusiveness because roughly 190 countries, representing

---

[15] Todd Stern, "The Future of the Paris Climate Regime," Yale Law School, April 10, 2018; Daniel Bodansky, "The Paris Climate Change Agreement: A New Hope?" *The American Journal of International Law* 11 (2016): 269.

more than 95% of global emissions, are signatories. It may not be as ambitious as many would have liked, but it nonetheless represents a serious and potentially durable way forward. Whereas the Rio Earth Summit had nebulously called for the stabilization of greenhouse gas concentrations in the atmosphere that would prevent dangerous human interference with the earth's climate, the Paris Agreement was the first time that the international community agreed that this would mean limiting a temperature increase to no more than 2 degrees centigrade above pre-industrial levels. The agreement also includes an aspirational goal, reflecting the strong lobbying of islands and other vulnerable states, to limit the temperature increase to 1.5 degrees centigrade and to achieve greenhouse gas "neutrality"—net zero emissions resulting from balancing carbon emissions into the atmosphere with the permanent removal of carbon from the atmosphere—by the second half of this century.

The US and the EU were among the first countries to submit their "independent nationally determined contributions" to reduce emissions in March 2015. While the former pledged to reduce its emissions by 26–28% by 2025 compared to 2005 levels, the latter pledged to reduce them by 40% by 2030 compared to 1990 levels. By the time the Paris conference had started, more than 180 had submitted contributions and today nearly every country on the globe has done so. The total of the contributions still falls short of what is required to deal with global warming as they are unlikely to impede a rise in global temperatures of 2.7–3 degrees above pre-industrial levels. But they represent a massive improvement over the 4–5 degree centigrade of global warming that would have resulted from business as usual. As one observer noted: "The deal alone won't dig us out of the hole that we're in, but it makes the sides less steep."[16]

The negotiators were aware that the voluntary contributions filed at the start of the negotiations and even by the time of the agreement's ratification would be insufficient, but they believed that the contributions would be a useful foundation. The voluntary contributions can take many forms, general or specific, conditional or unconditional. But the accompanying system requiring nations to be transparent about their contributions and to report on their progress in implementing them, as well as to submit to international monitoring and review, incentivizes countries to

---

[16] Fiona Harvey, "Paris Climate Change Agreement: The World's Greatest Diplomatic Success," *The Guardian*, December 14, 2015.

put their best foot forward. Most countries are prepared to go to great lengths to avoid being "named and shamed."

Every five years, starting in 2023, the parties to the agreement would meet to conduct a "global stock take" based on the best available science to assess their individual and collective progress in meeting the agreement's long-term goals. Based on these assessments, the parties must file subsequent voluntary contributions every five years that are increasingly ambitious. Rather than being punitive, the compliance system seeks to assist laggards in meeting their goals. The Paris Agreement provides support to developing countries, including money to invest in green infrastructure and technology, as well as to adapt to the consequences of climate change that they are already facing. Moreover, the agreement provides an important signal to public and private actors that they should prepare for the end of the fossil fuel era.

Critical to the achievement in Paris was the negotiation by the United States and the European Union of a hybrid agreement that combined binding and voluntary elements in a legal instrument that could satisfy the formal requirements of a treaty while at the same time enabling the Obama administration to sign it under its executive powers that did not require legislative approval. The issue of the legal form of climate change agreements had bedeviled every prior negotiation: While the United States had been willing to accept a legal instrument applicable to all parties, China, India, and other large developing states had only been willing to accept a legal agreement if it contained emission reduction obligations that bound only developed states. The fact that the Kyoto Protocol contained such asymmetrical and binding obligations was the key reason why the United States stayed out. The Copenhagen Accord applied to all countries but was a non-binding agreement.

The EU had for many years pushed energetically for the Paris Agreement to be an international treaty with binding nationally determined contributions. Such an instrument would require formal ratification, normally with legislative approval. The EU reasoned that such an instrument would express at the highest levels of government an intent by signatories to be bound by its terms. It would provide a higher assurance of implementation and compliance. Unlike a political agreement signed by the executive branch of government acting alone, a treaty would be more likely to survive changes in administration and would entail more reputational costs if breached. It would mobilize participation by civil society, business, and the media. It would engage legislatures and strengthen domestic laws that could be relied on before national courts.[17]

The US had persistently objected to the EU's focus on the binding legal form of the nationally determined contributions for several reasons. It pointed out many examples of non-compliance with legally binding commitments, as well as of compliance with non-legally binding ones. Moreover, the US had argued that insisting on legally binding commitments might lead to a lower level of ambition, especially with regard to emissions reductions. Focusing on making national commitments transparent and subject to public reporting and review might lead to greater ambition and better practical results.

The US objection was also grounded in a fundamental legal problem. The US Constitution requires "treaties" to be approved by two-thirds of the US Senate, an outcome that was highly unlikely in the case of the Paris Agreement. Many international agreements of the United States, however, are adopted as "executive agreements," in most cases with the approval of Congress, but in some cases by the President acting alone. The US negotiating team wanted to ensure that the Paris Agreement, while formally meeting the requirements of a treaty, could fall within this latter category. In order to do so, the provisions of the agreement had to fall within authorities already delegated by Congress to the president under existing legislation and his general foreign policy powers. Moreover, the agreement could not commit the United States to international obligations, such as binding emissions reductions targets or financial commitments, beyond those necessary to implement the UNFCCC that the Senate had already ratified.

The US and the EU struggled to find a solution that would satisfy each other's basic requirements. The solution was a hybrid between "obligations of result," such as the Kyoto-style targets that the US couldn't accept, and "obligations of conduct," which the EU found to be too soft. Some obligations in the agreement would be of the former variety, some of the latter. Some "obligations of conduct" were expressed in precise

---

[17] Jacob Werksman, "The International Legal Character of the Paris Agreement," Brodies Lecture, February 9, 2016. http://www.law.ed.ac.uk/other_areas_of_interest/events/event_documents/BrodiesLectureontheLegalCharacteroftheParisAgreementFinalBICCLEdinburgh.pdf.

terms and tied to specific objectives (including to reduce emissions), so that they amounted to meaningful obligations. The result of this hybrid approach was an agreement that was more binding than the UNFCCC but less binding than the Kyoto Protocol.

Even though the Paris Agreement does not carry the title of a treaty in the United States, there is little dispute that the agreement's legal form makes it a treaty under international law. Many international treaties contain provisions that do not create legal obligations. With regard to the key issue of emissions reductions, the operative text of the agreement amounts to an obligation of conduct, not result. Each party is legally bound to prepare, communicate, and maintain successive "nationally determined" voluntary "contributions" to reduce emissions. Moreover, each party is legally bound to pursue domestic mitigation measures with the aim of achieving the objectives of these contributions. But while each party must take these identifiable steps, their contributions do not amount to Kyoto-style obligations of result. Moreover, while the parties reaffirmed a collective target (already expressed in the Copenhagen Accord) of mobilizing $100 billion per year by 2020 to assist poor countries to address climate change, the agreement does not contain quantified financial obligations for individual countries.

While this struggle over legal form may sound rather technical and perhaps even unimportant, it could be argued that the fate of the planet depended on its outcome. The final text of the Paris Agreement, circulated by the French hosts shortly before the closing plenary, replaced the word "should" with "shall" in a key provision, converting the form of "nationally determined contributions" into a binding legal requirement that would have required Senate approval and therefore the withdrawal of the US from the deal. The substitution was quickly corrected as a clerical error and the plenary voted on the amended version. That was fortunate as there would have been no deal without the United States.

In addition to finding the "sweet spot" on the issue of the legally binding nature of the agreement, the US and the EU were instrumental in negotiating a new and more flexible interpretation of the long-standing principle of "common but differentiated responsibilities and respective capabilities" that better reflected contemporary realities. The issue cut across all the elements of the agreement: mitigation, adaptation, finance, and transparency.

The agreement upholds two basic ideas: First, that countries' responsibilities for addressing global climate change should be differentiated according to past contributions to the problem and their present capacity to respond; and second, that developing countries shall not be obliged to take actions that exceed their capacities or that are inconsistent with their priorities for growth and development. However, the Paris Agreement eliminates the firewall establishing separate rules for developing and developed countries. All countries must deliver nationally determined contributions to mitigate climate change, but all countries can self-differentiate by deciding what they want to do. Furthermore, developed countries must adopt strict, absolute emission reduction targets while developing countries are "encouraged to move over time towards economy-wide emission reduction or limitation targets in light of different national circumstances." While the agreement reaffirms the financial commitments of developed countries, it enlarges the donor pool by encouraging other countries to provide financial support. Although all countries must be transparent in the way they report on their contributions, the rules provide flexibility in implementation to those countries that "need it in light of their capacities."

In summary, the Paris Agreement stands as a monument to what the US and EU can do to advance important global priorities when they work together. Not only did they manage to overcome substantial differences in approach between them, but they also were critical actors in getting global participation. Especially important in this regard were the EU's steady efforts prior to Paris to build a coalition of developing countries seeking an ambitious deal. The coalition included progressive Latin American and Caribbean countries, small island states, and least developed countries. The decisive moment in the Paris negotiations came when the United States unexpectedly joined this coalition. That decision, in turn, led Brazil (one of the core members of the BASIC coalition) to join and further isolated China and India in the homestretch of the talks. As EU Commissioner Arias Cañete put it: "all of a sudden the debate was not about developed versus developing. It was about the willing versus the unwilling. And no one wanted to be seen as the unwilling."[18] Nonetheless, Nicaragua resisted until Pope Francis convinced its president to sign the deal.

Thanks to their efforts, the agreement entered into force in November 2016, far faster than anyone would have dared to predict. Despite its flaws, it establishes for the first time an ambitious, durable climate regime

---

[18] "Historic climate deal in Paris: speech by Commissioner Miguel Arias Cañete at the press conference on the results of COP21 climate conference in Paris," The European Commission, December 14, 2015. https://ec.europa.eu/commission/presscorner/detail/en/SPEECH_15_6320.

that applies to all countries, provides strong accountability and transparency measures to ensure that countries do what they say, and focuses not only on reducing greenhouse gas emissions, but also on delivering financial and technical assistance to countries that need it to adapt to climate change. The agreement is a finely tuned balance that is the result of multilateral innovation in the face of gridlock. It is also a bet that nations will drive each other into a spiral of upward ambition to combat global warming. As Todd Stern, the US negotiator, has observed:

> A bet on the rising norms and expectations is at the heart of the Paris Agreement. If [it] is to succeed, this bet, above all, has to pay off.[19]

It may be too early to tell whether countries will fulfill the expectations of the agreement in this regard. But already the agreement has mobilized numerous sub-federal and non-state actors, including regions, cities, companies, and non-governmental organizations to take action. The emissions reduction pledges of these actors may well have as big an impact, or perhaps even a greater impact, than the national pledges.

Most importantly, the agreement is a departure from business as usual. It sends a clear signal to the market that the world is progressing inexorably toward a low-carbon future. John Kerry argues that the real success of the Paris Agreement is that it mobilized the private sector:

> It was an invitation to the marketplace to get the job done and make money doing it....Paris was inviting the private sector to save us from ourselves.[20]

The Paris Agreement may help to accelerate investments in the new climate economy, driving faster technological advances and rapidly reducing costs of producing renewable energy. Even in China, the world's largest emitter, renewable energy has become the dominant technology for new power installations. A virtuous cycle of technology and investment resulting in more efficient green power should strengthen social norms about climate change and the political will to make increasingly more ambitious voluntary emissions contributions. That virtuous cycle will be necessary to

---

[19] Todd Stern, *The Paris Agreement and Its Future* (Washington, DC: The Brookings Institution, October 2018).

[20] Kerry, *Every Day Is Extra*, p. 572.

enable the US and the EU to meet their mid-century strategies of cutting greenhouse emissions by 80% below 2005 and 1990 levels, respectively.

Achieving "net zero" emissions—balancing the introduction of new greenhouse gases in the atmosphere with the extraction of an equivalent amount from the atmosphere—in the second half of this century will require a massive shift in our energy mix. In a detailed report issued in 2016, Shell Oil estimates that it would entail changing the mix from the current 80% reliance on hydrocarbons to 40% reliance on wind and solar, 20% on nuclear and hydro, 15% on biofuels, with the remaining 25% on fossil fuels (mostly natural gas) balanced by carbon sequestration.[21] It is also clear that emissions from international aviation and shipping, major contributors of greenhouse gases, will have to be included more comprehensively than they are today. The international aviation and shipping sectors would be one of the top dozen greenhouse gas emitters in the world if they were treated as a country.

Achieving these goals will require continued US-EU co-leadership. Alas, the Trump administration announced within several days of assuming power that it would withdraw from the Paris Agreement (Fig. 11.2). While the administration has respected the legal provision in the agreement establishing a four-year withdrawal period, the US has rejected its voluntary emissions reduction contribution and has refused to participate in any of the important follow-up action items after Paris to define the technical rules, guidelines, and procedures necessary to implement the agreement. The US withdrawal from its leadership role risks undermining the delicate balance underpinning the deal. As Todd Stern, US lead negotiator at Paris under President Obama, has pointed out:

> many countries swallowed hard in Paris to accept paradigm-shifting provisions that they saw as necessary to get the United States on board. Having taken those sometimes difficult steps, urged on by the United States, they

---

[21] For more, see the "A Better Life with a Healthy Planet" page of Shell's website: https://www.shell.com/energy-and-innovation/the-energy-future/scenarios/a-better-life-with-a-healthy-planet.html.

then turned around to discover that, less than 18 months later, the United States had jumped ship.[22]

The EU and even China have stepped up to fill the vacuum left by the United States. A broad coalition of sub-federal actors in the United States, including states, cities, civil society, and business, have also taken important measures to ensure that the United States respects its commitments. California has been a trendsetter for many years on climate change, including on fuel standards (although President Trump is seeking to revoke its authority to set its own standards). The EU has been active in exploring ways of collaborating with key actors like California and nine Eastern states that operate CO_2 cap-and-trade emissions systems. It has worked with the largest US cities that are members of the Global Covenant of Mayors for Climate & Energy to support voluntary action to combat climate change and with leading business leaders, such as with Michael Bloomberg, in an effort to manage the global transition away from coal.

It is highly unlikely that the Paris Agreement can succeed unless the United States re-engages soon. At a conference in Katowice, Poland, in mid-December 2018, the signatories to the accord agreed on a 250-page rule book that details, for example, how countries should monitor and report their greenhouse gas emissions and the efforts they're taking to reduce them. But the United States partnered with Russia, Saudi Arabia, and Kuwait to water down approval of a landmark report on the need to keep global warming below 1.5 degrees centigrade. The Trump administration has ensured that meetings of the G-20 no longer refer to "global warming" or "decarbonization." It has sought to roll back US environmental regulations in many areas, including relating to coal-fired power plants and methane emissions by the oil and gas industry.

Perhaps worst of all, the Trump administration has given legitimacy to Americans who are in denial about climate change. A poll conducted in September 2019 showed that 15% of Americans believe that climate

---

[22] Todd Stern, "The Paris Agreement and Its Future," Brookings, Paper 5, October 2018. https://www.brookings.edu/wp-content/uploads/2018/10/The-Paris-Agreement-and-Its-Future-Todd-Stern-October-2018.pdf.

Fig. 11.2 Cover of *Der Spiegel*, Issue 23 (2017) after President Trump's Decision to Withdraw the US From the Paris Agreement (© Edel Rodriguez. Reprinted with Permission from *Der Spiegel*)

change is not occurring or that it is not due to human causes. That figure is the highest in the world, nearly three times the global average.[23]

Even if the United States re-engages under a new administration, it will be a challenge to regain the leverage and credibility the United States enjoyed in climate negotiations under the Obama administration. US re-engagement will be crucial to ensure that current pressures on the Paris Agreement are resisted. Developing country signatories, some motivated by ideological reasons and others by concerns about meeting rigorous obligations with regards to accounting and reporting, have been using the negotiations on implementation to reinstate the old firewall between developing and developed countries. These signatories are also concerned that pledges by developed countries to provide financial assistance to developing countries will fail to meet the targets under the Paris Agreement, especially since the Trump administration has refused to disburse the remaining $2 billion owing out of its total $3 billion commitment to the Green Climate Fund.

One of the European Commission's legislative priorities for its 2019–2024 mandate may complicate transatlantic cooperation on climate change. It has promised a (WTO-compliant) tax to be imposed at EU borders on the carbon content of goods imported from countries that do not put an equivalent price on carbon (as would be the case of the United States). The idea behind this tax is that EU economic growth and the effectiveness of EU climate policy are undermined by the relocation of carbon-intensive production by EU firms to non-EU countries that are shirking their responsibilities to save the planet.

It would be a tragedy if the US and the EU remain at loggerheads on the environment. There is literally no time to waste. Together they can make an enormous difference, as proven by the efforts at Montreal, Kigali, and Paris. Among the hugely promising areas for collaboration is promoting the improvement in the energy efficiency of air conditioners, refrigerators and other products that will need to switch out of HFCs because of the Kigali amendment to the Montreal Protocol. According to two experts, just a 30% increase in the efficiency of India's air conditioning units would save enough electricity to avoid having to build 140

---

[23] John Burn-Murdoch and Leslie Hook, "Survey Underscores High Levels of US Scepticism on Climate Change," *Financial Times*, September 15, 2019. https://www.ft.com/content/e5374b6c-d628-11e9-8367-807ebd53ab77.

medium-size power plants to meet peak demand by 2030.[24] Emissions reductions will have to be accompanied by significant carbon sequestration (amounting to hundreds of billions of tons of CO_2) if the goals of the Paris Agreement are to be reached. The US and the EU are leaders and natural partners in this goal.

US-EU Cooperation on Environmental Protection

There are many other areas of environmental protection on which the US and the EU work closely together in addition to climate change. Fortunately, the cooperation has remained robust in many areas throughout the Trump administration regardless of the US withdrawal from the Paris Agreement and wider US-EU tensions. These areas include the combat against illegal logging, the protection of endangered fish and wildlife, and the protection of the Arctic and the world's oceans, especially the Atlantic. The main actors in this cooperation have been the European Commission, on the side of the EU, and the US Fish and Wildlife Service (part of the Department of the Interior), the National Oceanic and Atmospheric Association (part of the Department of Commerce), and the State Department's Bureau of Oceans and International Environmental and Scientific Affairs.

The US and the EU have long cooperated in the work of the Convention on International Trade in Endangered Species of Wild Fauna and Flora (CITES) established in the mid-1970s as a response to growing concerns that over-exploitation of wildlife through international trade is contributing to the rapid decline and potential extinction of many species of plants and animals around the world. An intergovernmental agreement among 183 parties, CITES operates a system of permits and certificates that are required before listed specimens may be imported or exported. Global efforts such as CITES reflect a consensus that wildlife trafficking is not only destructive of the world's ecosystem, but also feeds a significant international criminal network, the fourth largest after those trafficking in drugs, people, and arms.

One of CITES' signature achievements has been to crack down on illegal logging, one of the most destructive acts against wildlife as it threatens entire habitats rather than a single species of animal. Much of the

---

[24] Mario Molina and Durwood Zaelke. https://www.unenvironment.org/es/news-and-stories/reportajes/el-protocolo-de-montreal-el-triunfo-de-un-tratado.

illegal logging targets rare tropical species prized by the luxury hardwood furniture industry, especially in China. Since 2013, the US and the EU have spearheaded measures in CITES to prevent the international sale of rosewood logs illegally cut in Madagascar's northeastern rainforests until Madagascar makes further progress in its plan to identify and take control of undeclared, hidden stocks of rosewood.

As a result of combined US and EU pressure, CITES threatened in 2014 to impose trade sanctions on Thailand, including a ban on the highly remunerative export of reptile skins and orchids, if Thailand failed to act against ivory trafficking. In response, Thailand took comprehensive new legislative and enforcement measures to halt the import, export, trade, and sale of ivory from African elephants. Today it is no longer considered a main hotspot for ivory trafficking.

Since 2013, the US and the EU have also spearheaded measures in CITES to protect five species of shark from overfishing due to the demand for shark-fin soup, considered a delicacy in Asia. These measures were historic because many previous efforts had failed, largely because of opposition from China and Japan. Before they were put in place, humans were killing sharks at a clearly unsustainable rate—100 million per year, equivalent to 6–8% of the global population. As sharks are slow to mature and have few offspring, overfishing has led to dramatic reductions in shark populations (as high as 90% for some species in some regions) with knock-on effects throughout the downstream food chain. The elimination of the sharks as top marine predators, for example, has led to increased populations of rays that have decimated the scallop industry in some areas.

The US and the EU have also been active partners on a wide range of issues relating to the world's oceans. The link between oceans and the climate is strong: For many years, the oceans have prevented even faster global warming from occurring by absorbing 25% of carbon dioxide emissions and 90% of the world's heat. Marine and coastal ecosystems serve as a life support system by preserving biodiversity and trapping carbon. But the oceans are coming under increasing strain. Even if global warming is limited to 2 degrees, many ocean species risk extinction and virtually all coral reefs will disappear. On a trip to the Great Barrier Reef in December 2017, I was shocked to see large stretches of dead coral.

Secretary Kerry had a particular interest in the topic and played a critical role, with active EU support, in launching a series of conferences on Our Oceans. The conferences attracted global representation to address such issues as sustainable fisheries, marine pollution, and climate-related impacts on the ocean. The ones hosted by the United States in 2014 and 2016 resulted in the protection of millions of square kilometers of ocean and multi-billion-dollar pledges to protect the ocean from dangerous activities such as pollution and overfishing. The yearly conferences continue to this day and make an important contribution to raising international attention to the world's oceans.

The US and the EU naturally pay particularly close attention to the Atlantic Ocean. Together with Canada, they have launched an Atlantic Ocean research alliance to deepen cooperation in areas including sustainable management of ocean resources, seabed mapping, the sharing of data, and the mobility of oceanic researchers.[25] But the US and the EU are also active partners on a broad set of global issues relating to the oceans.

The US and the EU, two of the world's largest harvesters and importers of seafood in the world, for example, have been leaders in combating illegal, unreported, and unregulated (IUU) fishing, one of the most serious threats to sustainable fishing and to marine biodiversity in the world's oceans. IUU fishing has devastating environmental and socioeconomic consequences, especially for coastal communities in developing countries who rely on fisheries for their livelihood and protein. In an agreement signed just before I arrived in Brussels, the US and the EU agreed to take a range of measures, cooperating closely in regional and international organizations designed to combat IUU fishing.[26] In 2018, the EU and the eight Arctic states (Canada, Denmark, Finland, Iceland, Norway, Russia, Sweden, and the US) signed an agreement not to engage in unregulated commercial fishing in the central Arctic Ocean for an initial period of 16 years. Although commercial fishing is not occurring now and is unlikely to occur soon in this area because of ice cover, that could change in the medium to long term because the Arctic region is warming at three times the global average rate. The parties to the agreement

---

[25] Galway Statement on Atlantic Ocean Cooperation, May 23–24, 2013. https://ec.europa.eu/research/iscp/pdf/galway_statement_atlantic_ocean_cooperation.pdf.

[26] "Fisheries: European Union and United States agree to strengthen cooperation to combat illegal fishing," The European Commission, September 7, 2011. https://ec.europa.eu/commission/presscorner/detail/en/IP_11_1007.

wished to act as a precaution to ensure the conservation and sustainable management of fish stocks in this delicate ecosystem.[27]

Without continued close collaboration of the US and the EU on climate change and a wide range of environmental issues, the future of the planet is, simply put, in doubt. They are essential partners in ensuring the continued habitability of that small sphere, suspended in space, that I used to look at in Vice President Al Gore's office so many years ago.

---

[27] The text of the agreement may be found at: https://eur-lex.europa.eu/resource.html?uri=cellar:2554f475-6e25-11e8-9483-01aa75ed71a1.0001.02/DOC_2&format=PDF.

CHAPTER 12

Foreign Aid and Humanitarian Assistance

The US and the EU together provide two-thirds of global humanitarian assistance for the alleviation of emergencies arising from natural and manmade disasters and 80% of global foreign aid for longer-term development assistance programs. There is no other foreign policy area in which the US and the EU enjoy such a dominant global role.

The entire post-war transatlantic relationship is arguably rooted in humanitarian assistance and foreign aid. The reconstruction of Western Europe was due in large part to the 1948 Marshall plan in which the United States provided over $12 billion (nearly $100 billion in 2016 US dollars) in economic assistance over a four-year period. The motivations were mixed, of course: partly humanitarian in order to provide relief to people lacking food, shelter, and basic services, but also to promote prosperity, democracy, and stability in Europe and therefore create both a bulwark against Communism and future customers of US exports. The massive reconstruction effort, in which my maternal grandfather was involved, served as an inspiration for a growing system of grants and low-interest loans provided by the United States and later Europe to poor, newly independent countries in Africa and Asia.

Humanitarian assistance and foreign aid address different challenges. Moreover, the former is delivered according to need and the principles of impartiality and humanity, whereas the latter often reflects strategic political and economic interests of the donors. And yet the two are intimately related. If immediate relief is not coupled with long-term policies to promote structural changes, history will simply repeat itself and require the

US and the EU to undertake repeatedly costly emergency measures to respond to disaster. Indeed, some short-term solutions can be counter-productive: The dumping of food aid in local markets to address urgent food needs, for example, can undermine the ability of poor countries to develop sustainable farms and functioning markets.

During my diplomatic post, I witnessed first-hand how the US and the EU work together in several areas of both humanitarian assistance and foreign aid. There are notable differences in how they pursue their agenda, including their degree of willingness to partner with the private sector and the military, but these have not prevented frequent and deep collaboration.

THE STRUGGLE TO CONTAIN THE EBOLA OUTBREAK IN WESTERN AFRICA

In the fall of 2014, my wife and I found ourselves in a large, abandoned field in downtown Brussels to visit the training site of Médecins Sans Frontières (MSF), also known as Doctors Without Borders, a non-profit and non-governmental international medical organization of French origin best known for its projects in conflict zones and in countries affected by endemic diseases. We were impressed by the explanations about how the modular kits in the large containers lying in a storeroom could be rapidly shipped to humanitarian disaster zones around the world and assembled on site within hours to provide functioning power generators, water purification, lodging for aid workers, medical treatment, and waste disposal. The logistical know-how and deep experience of MSF made it the first, and sometimes most significant, responder to major medical emergencies.

Although the logistics were interesting, what really grabbed our attention was the sight of several of the organization's instructors training staff on how to put on and take off protective clothing to avoid contamination. The eight-piece clothing, entirely covering the human body, looked like a space suit but was more ominous because it was being worn on land to respond to the outbreak of the Ebola virus in West Africa in March 2014. The scene reminded me of *Outbreak*, a film released in 1995 starring many Hollywood icons, including Dustin Hoffman, Kevin Spacey and Morgan Freeman. The film was about the public panic and response by military and civilian agencies in the wake of a fictional outbreak of an

Ebola-like virus in Zaire, and later in a small town in California. A real-life outbreak of the Ebola virus was ongoing in Zaire when the film was released. The film contained exaggerations to enhance its shock value but wasn't too far from fact.

We were transfixed by the demonstration. Our guide told us that medical staff could only wear the space suit for several hours in real-world conditions on the ground because temperatures inside the suits can easily reach up to 46 degrees centigrade (nearly 115 degrees Fahrenheit). The suit takes a long time to put on in order to ensure that the body is entirely protected from contamination. Taking off soiled suits requires even longer (up to twenty minutes) because of a meticulous and rigorous twelve-step process that healthcare workers must repeat three or more times per day. It was clear that there is no margin for error. We were also shown disinfection routines, sample containment wards for infected patients, and the incineration units for soiled clothing and used equipment.

During the first months following the detection of an Ebola outbreak in March, MSF was the most effective response of the developed world. MSF remained on the ground throughout the crisis, even when 28 staff members contracted the virus and 14 died. On top of this risk of infection, MSF workers also faced angry opposition from villagers suspecting that the treatment facilities were spreading the disease. MSF had to close one facility in southern Guinea after being attacked in April 2014 by a stone-throwing mob. Villagers later killed eight African members of an MSF team trying to raise awareness of Ebola in the region. Despite these risks, MSF had nearly 300 international workers and 2900 local employees fighting the outbreak by the time my wife and I were touring the facility in Brussels.

By contrast, the EU and its member states struggled to come up with a coherent and decisive response in the early months of the crisis. This was disappointing in light of the EU's deep partnership with Africa, Europe's proximity to the continent and greater vulnerability to a spread of Ebola, and the history of France and Britain as former colonial powers in Guinea and Sierra Leone. Similarly, the initial US response was slow and focused on domestic preparations. It took until the fall of 2014 for the US and the EU to respond in a coordinated fashion.

Our joint response should have been more effective. As I toured the MSF facility I recalled how, as a young Director for European Affairs in the White House in 1994–1995, I had played a role in the US-EU New Transatlantic Agenda that had specifically flagged the importance of transatlantic cooperation on infectious diseases:

We are committed to develop and implement an effective global early warning system and response network for new and re-emerging communicable diseases such as AIDS and the Ebola virus, and to increase training and professional exchanges in this area. Together, we call on other nations to join us in more effectively combating such diseases.[1]

We did not make as much progress on this key challenge as we would have liked in the subsequent twenty years.

Our MSF guide explained that an Ebola outbreak starts when a human has direct contact with the blood, body fluids, or organs of infected animals, such as bats, chimpanzees, monkeys, or gorillas. The transmission of the virus from that human to other humans occurs through personal direct contact either with the patient's blood or other body fluids (including sweat and saliva) or through contact with objects, such as needles and syringes, that contain these fluids. Transmission of the virus often occurs through caregivers such as family members or medical personnel in homes or healthcare environments where infection-control practices are weak. Ebola crises, such as the one in Zaire that occurred when *Outbreak* was playing in movie theaters, can be amplified by the transmission of the virus in overcrowded hospitals and burial practices in which highly infectious corpses are washed or touched by family and members of the community in a sign of love for the deceased.

Ebola is a disease from one of the deeper circles of Dante's Hell. Fortunately, it is not transmitted through the air, like influenza or tuberculosis, or transmitted before symptoms appear, like measles or HIV. Nonetheless, it can result in terrible consequences for its victims and can spread quickly if not brought under control. In its early phase, victims of Ebola can be misdiagnosed because it is relatively rare and because some of the symptoms, including fever, fatigue, muscle pain, and headache, are difficult to distinguish from those of other infectious diseases, such as malaria and typhoid fever. Victims often subsequently experience vomiting, diarrhea, rashes, and hemorrhages resulting in internal and/or external bleeding. The dysfunction or collapse of multiple body organs leads to severe injury and often death. The fatality rate varies from 25 to 90%, depending on the strain.

---

[1] The document was signed in Madrid at a US-EU Summit on December 3, 1995. http://www.europarl.europa.eu/cmsdata/124321/new_transatlantic_agenda_en.pdf.

The Ebola outbreak in West Africa in 2014 was first reported by the World Health Organization on March 23 in a remote, forested region of south-eastern Guinea bordering Liberia and Sierra Leone. Multiple chains of transmission of the virus had gone unrecognized for months. By the end of the year, the virus had claimed 6000 lives and had infected 17,000 persons; by March 2015, the numbers were 9200 dead and 22,900 sick; and by the time the crisis had been brought under control in March 2016, the dead numbered 11,325. The number of infections and deaths far exceeded those in approximately twenty previous outbreaks since the 1970s in central and eastern Africa; in each of those outbreaks, the number of reported cases never exceeded 500.

There were many reasons for the severity of the crisis. Like the remote areas of central and eastern Africa where prior outbreaks occurred, the virus appeared in a remote area of Guinea. Normally, this might have helped contain the disease, but in an unfortunate twist of geographic fate the region lay at the junction of Guinea with Sierra Leone and Liberia where people regularly move across borders. The region's lack of rudimentary public health infrastructure, partly because of its recent history of civil war and violence, and its lack of experience with a previous outbreak of the virus compounded the problem.

As the virus spread to urban areas and expanded into an epidemic, the number of cases quickly overwhelmed the capacity of diagnostic and other healthcare facilities. At the onset of the outbreak, there was a very small number of experienced healthcare workers to deal with it, including in Europe and the United States. Even at MSF, involved in most of the prior outbreaks, there were only 40 "veterans." Medical teams were simply not prepared to deal with a disease that kills at least 50% of its patients and for which no treatments existed. Had Ebola been a First World disease, there would have been a vaccine. But there wasn't because, in the eyes of the major pharmaceutical companies, the numbers of patients are small, and nearly exclusively in the Third World. The business case for the recovery of significant upfront research and production costs had simply not been present.

Some Ebola Treatment Units (ETUs) were filled beyond capacity, requiring the facilities to turn away people suspected of having the disease, thereby fostering new chains of transmission. One of the critical factors in bringing an Ebola outbreak under control—an exhaustive tracing of contacts between victims and others with whom they had been in contact—was absent. Moreover, poor infection control in hospitals led to many infections and deaths among healthcare workers and a rapid collapse of the region's healthcare system. The control of other devastating viruses, such as malaria, and even the provision of routine medical services declined. I had seen reports from our embassies that people who collapsed from heart attacks were sometimes left to die because no one wanted to touch them for fear that they had contracted Ebola. Children started missing out on education because of school closures.

Generalized fear and even panic threatened to devastate the region's economies, especially by reducing agricultural output and trade, while driving up prices. My friend and former colleague Samantha Power, US ambassador to the United Nations during President Obama's second term, visited Brussels several times to brief and coordinate with EU officials on the Ebola crisis after her trips to the infected region. On one of those trips, she relayed reports that farming communities were "eating their seeds," indicating not only that current harvests were poor but warning that future harvests and even food security were in danger. A total collapse of civil society was imminent as governments lost control of the situation.

In the early days of the crisis, the EU allocated extra emergency funding to MSF and other humanitarian organizations, such as the Red Cross and Red Crescent, the International Medical Corps, Save the Children and the International Rescue Committee. The aid contributed to the faster deployment of doctors and nurses and the purchase of diagnostic equipment and medical supplies. Disaster Assistance Response Teams of the US Agency for International Development (USAID) and teams from the Atlanta-based Centers for Disease Control and Protection (CDC) were deployed to the region to carry out an assessment of what needed to be done. The US airlifted significant amounts of personal protective gear, generators, and medical equipment. By early summer, it seemed that wiring funds and providing assistance from a distance would be enough as the number of reported cases leveled off and then dropped, suggesting the outbreak could be contained as in the 23 previously reported outbreaks in Africa since 1976.

Instead, the virus spread. By late July it reached, for the first time in history, densely populated metropolitan areas, not only in the three countries of origin but further afield. A traveler with Ebola had flown from Monrovia, Liberia, to Lagos, Nigeria, Africa's most populous city (with 21 million inhabitants) where he had contact with multiple people who later contracted the illness. A massive effort by the Nigerian government, assisted by the CDC, managed to contain the outbreak to just 19 cases in two cities. By early August, the World Health Organization categorized the outbreak as a "public health emergency of international concern," a declaration that caught media headlines and unlocked significant new funding. Claus Sorensen, an old friend and the director-general of European Civil Protection and Humanitarian Aid Operations (ECHO), conceded that in an Ebola crisis "speed is of the essence, and there is a feeling that all of us have been behind the curve."[2]

The decisive factor in galvanizing action in the EU and the US was a series of shocking announcements regarding the Ebola infections outside Africa. In late July and early August, two US citizens, including a doctor with Samaritan's Purse, were repatriated to Atlanta, where they (successfully) underwent treatment for Ebola in a specialized isolation ward in Emory University Hospital. They were the first two patients ever to receive such treatment in the United States. In early October, two Spanish priests died in Madrid after contracting the virus in Sierra Leone; a nurse who had treated them also tested positive (but later recovered), the first person to have been infected outside of West Africa. Shortly thereafter a Liberian national who had recently returned from Liberia to the United States died of Ebola in a Dallas hospital. The nurses who had cared for him contracted the virus but recovered.

On top of the shock of Ebola infections appearing in Europe and the United States, public health authorities on both sides of the Atlantic conducted modeling about the potential spread of the virus. The results were sobering: In September, the CDC estimated that approximately 555,000 Ebola cases (1.4 million cases when corrected for under-reporting) could occur in West Africa by January 20, 2015, if approximately 70% of all persons with new cases were not effectively isolated. The World Health Organization projected that new Ebola cases could reach 10,000 per week by December. When respondents to a telephone poll were asked in October whether they were concerned that there would be a large outbreak of Ebola in the United States within the next 12 months, 50% reported that they were "very" or "somewhat" concerned.

The initial US response (before October) was largely domestic because the country was not prepared for an epidemic of this magnitude. When

---

[2] Andrew Higgins, "European Leaders Scramble to Upgrade Response to Ebola Crisis," *The New York Times*, October 8, 2014. https://www.nytimes.com/2014/10/09/world/european-leaders-scramble-to-upgrade-response-to-ebola-crisis.html.

the crisis broke out, only one facility in the United States (the CDC laboratory in Atlanta) was qualified to test for Ebola and there were only three facilities that could treat Ebola patients; by January 2015 there were 55 laboratories in 43 states that could do so and by October there were 51 treatment centers in 16 states. During that period, 150,000 healthcare workers received instruction on how to identify, isolate, diagnose, and care for patients under investigation for Ebola.

The CDC and Customs and Border Protection implemented intensive screening of air passengers arriving from West Africa. There was significant public support for cutting off all air links with West Africa and quarantining anyone who had recently been in the region. While generalized measures of this kind were avoided, the Defense Department did impose a 21-day quarantine for all personnel returning from Ebola-affected areas, regardless of risk, because of political rather than scientific considerations. The presidential commission established to review the government's response to the Ebola crisis was scathing in its final report. It criticized federal, state, and local unpreparedness to cope with the threat of an epidemic and the government's focus on the political implications of public reactions rather than on the underlying health concerns.[3]

By the end of the year, the US government's response started shifting decisively toward attacking Ebola at its source. President Obama was clear about the stakes:

> this is an epidemic that is not just a threat to regional security – it's a potential threat to global security if these countries break down, if their economies break down, if people panic. That has profound effects on all of us, even if we are not directly contracting the disease.[4]

The United States and the EU (as well as its member states), together and in parallel, supported by the African Union and several African countries, finally undertook a major and highly successful effort to bring the crisis

---

[3] "Ethics and Ebola: Public Health Planning and Response," Presidential Commission for the Study of Bioethical Issues, February 2015. https://bioethicsarchive.georgetown.edu/pcsbi/sites/default/files/Ethics-and-Ebola_PCSBI_508.pdf.

[4] Remarks by the President on the Ebola Outbreak, September 16, 2014. https://obamawhitehouse.archives.gov/the-press-office/2014/09/16/remarks-president-ebola-outbreak.

under control. Washington focused on Liberia, while Paris focused on Guinea and London on Sierra Leone.

Speaking at the CDC in mid-September, President Obama announced that the US military had recently dispatched 3000 personnel to Monrovia to establish a base under the control of US Africa Command. Its main objectives were to build 15 ETUs, including new isolation spaces and more than 1000 beds, and to recruit and train more than 1500 medical personnel to staff them. The Department of Defense built seven mobile laboratories in West Africa that cut turn-around times for testing blood samples from five to seven days to between three and five hours, thereby freeing up bed space in overcrowded clinics and hospitals. The UK and France quickly followed the US example with similar military missions of their own to Sierra Leone and Guinea to build hospitals and diagnostic centers; our experts often singled out the UK effort as being rapid and effective in bringing down new infection rates.

In addition to these efforts, thousands of CDC employees and government-supported civilians were deployed in all of West Africa, partnering with national governments to train healthcare workers, treat patients, staff field laboratories, trace contacts of patients to identify chains of transmission, develop border and airport-screening programs, promote safe burials, and educate communities. The United States was to airlift more than 400 metric tons of personal protective equipment and other medical and relief supplies during the subsequent months. In the fall of 2014, the White House announced major efforts to accelerate the development of vaccines (to prevent new infections) and therapeutics (to treat those already infected). And in December the US Congress overwhelmingly supported legislation providing $5.4 billion in emergency funding for the CDC and other health services, the State Department, and USAID; much of this funding was earmarked for the prevention, detection, and response to the Ebola crisis in West Africa, as well for efforts to assist in the region's recovery.[5]

The EU made an important contribution as a coordinator and donor. The European Centre for Disease Prevention and Control, headquartered in Sweden, coordinates the work of health experts in different countries but does not have its own emergency-response teams. Similarly, EU member states, rather than the European Commission, dispose of their own

---

[5] "FACT SHEET: Progress in Our Ebola Response at Home and Abroad," The White House Office of the Press Secretary, February 11, 2015. https://obamawhitehouse.archives.gov/the-press-office/2015/02/11/fact-sheet-progress-our-ebola-response-home-and-abroad.

medical personnel, hospitals, labs, and stock of specialized equipment. But as the only European body with a global picture of the fast-moving epidemic, the European Commission successfully played the role of "traffic cop" to ensure that Europe's response was consistent and effective. That role included the identification of the type and destination of emergency supplies for West Africa, providing a clearinghouse of information about the crisis and the disease, and the creation of a list of available member state assets relevant for the treatment of Ebola in Europe.

The European Commission also played a key role in identifying European assets and trained personnel that could be deployed for the medical evacuation of patients back to Europe and in negotiating a US-EU agreement about when US and European patients could call on their respective emergency medivac "air bridges." Ensuring that international healthcare workers could be airlifted to equipped facilities in Europe within 48 hours was critical to the ability of the US and EU to recruit such workers.

In October, the EU appointed Christos Stylianides, Commissioner for Humanitarian Aid and Crisis Management, as EU Ebola Coordinator to ensure that the EU institutions and member states acted in a coordinated manner with each other and with international partners. In addition to the directorate-general for humanitarian aid, other Commission departments were involved in the response to the Ebola crisis: These were principally the Directorate-General for International Cooperation and Development (DEVCO), the counterpart to USAID and responsible for foreign aid, and the European External Action Service (the EU's diplomatic service with delegations in most countries around the world). The role of other departments also had to be coordinated: The directorate-general for health identified facilities in member states that were willing and able to accept Ebola patients; the directorate-general for internal affairs (including justice and law enforcement) coordinated entry and exit procedures at airports in case of travelers suspected of having Ebola; and the directorate-general for research worked to promote vaccines and therapies.

The EU was also an important donor to help combat Ebola in West Africa. The European Commission and EU member states contributed almost €2 billion (without counting the value of in-kind contributions from many member states such as personal protective equipment, vehicles, and field hospitals). Of this total, the European Commission contributed €870 million out of the EU budget for emergency measures, financial support for the African Union's own medical mission to the region, and long-term relief (such as budgetary support for the restoration of vital public services and the strengthening of food security). Moreover, the European Commission announced substantial funding from the EU budget to promote projects on Ebola research, including immediate large-scale clinical trials of potential vaccines and tests of existing and novel compounds to treat Ebola. The European Commission also partnered with the European pharmaceutical industry in launching a €280 million longer-term research program involving clinical trials of new Ebola vaccines, the development of fast diagnostic tests, and new approaches to manufacture, store and transport vaccines.

In summary, while the US and EU were both slow in responding to the Ebola crisis, by the fall of 2014 they had significantly scaled up their efforts and were working very closely together to provide an effective series of measures that brought the crisis under control by the summer of 2015. The lessons learned from that dramatic experience—including European Commission coordination of EU member state activities and intensive US-EU coordination to combat epidemics—are important for coping with future humanitarian disasters. The lessons enabled the US and EU to respond to an outbreak of Ebola in the Democratic Republic of Congo (DRC) in May 2018, the second worst in history and the longest and deadliest of the nation's nine previous outbreaks. US-EU cooperation will be equally important in dealing with the outbreak of coronavirus.

Working Together on Other Humanitarian Challenges

While Ebola and other epidemics are just one area where the US and EU have worked well in humanitarian assistance, they are emblematic of the many other examples of how they are indispensable partners in alleviating suffering around the globe. One example is their delivery of aid to those suffering from the Syrian civil war that has displaced over 6 million people and killed 400,000. The war has been catastrophic, but it would have been far worse without US and EU efforts.

Under the EU's 2014–2020 multi-annual financial plan, the European Commission's annual humanitarian assistance budget averaged €1 billion per year and is projected to rise under the 2021–2027 budget cycle. In addition to the formal budget, the EU has drawn from other sources to spend hundreds of millions of euros annually to respond to unforeseen events and major crises, including the humanitarian disaster caused by the Syrian civil war and the refugee crisis in 2015–2016. Several EU member states—especially the UK, Germany, and Sweden—are generous donors of humanitarian assistance as well. Together with the EU, they provide roughly the same amount of funding as the United States ($7 billion per year as of 2018). US funding, largely administered through a specific bureau within USAID (the Office of US Foreign Disaster Assistance), has responded to the same emergencies as the EU—not only the Ebola outbreak, but also the Syrian civil war and many other crises concentrated in the Middle East and Africa. Both the US and the EU contribute significant amounts through United Nations agencies such as the UN High Commission for Refugees, UNICEF, and other non-governmental organizations such as the World Food Program and the International Red Cross.

The predominance of the US and the EU as humanitarian assistance actors means that their practices shape those of other donors, including states, NGOs, and multilateral organizations. When we join forces to minimize overlaps or inconsistent approaches, we ensure that our dollars and euros have maximum impact, leading to real improvements in the lives of millions of people affected by humanitarian assistance. As one study rightly pointed out:

> Failure by these two parties to enhance their cooperation…would result in additional, yet avoidable, human death and suffering…and could lead to increased insecurity and instability across the globe., threatening US and EU strategic interests.[6]

US administrations of both political parties have recognized the importance of this partnership and for good reason. The George H. W. Bush administration launched an annual strategic dialogue on humanitarian assistance with the EU at senior levels in USAID, the State Department and ECHO, supplemented with regular contacts on the ground among field officers. In the New Transatlantic Agenda concluded in 1995 under the Clinton administration, the US and the EU set forth an extensive list

---

[6] Julia Steets and Daniel Hamilton, eds. "Humanitarian Cooperation: Improving US-EU Cooperation," Report by the Global Public Policy Institute and the Center for Transatlantic Relations, 2009. https://www.urd.org/IMG/pdf/Humanitarian_Assistance_GPPI_complet.pdf.

of areas where they should work closely, including improving the effectiveness of international humanitarian relief agencies, and urged the creation of joint missions whenever possible, greater operational coordination, staff exchanges, and information sharing. Close dialogue has continued since then, despite the turbulence of US-EU relations during the presidency of Donald Trump.

Working Together on Foreign Aid and Development

The US and the EU provide an even larger share of total foreign aid than they provide of total humanitarian assistance. The United States is the largest single provider of foreign aid, accounting for one-quarter of the $150 billion disbursed worldwide every year. But the EU, together with its member states (especially Germany, the United Kingdom, and France), provides over half the total foreign aid disbursed. While the US contribution appears generous, it represents only slightly more than 1% of the US federal budget and about 0.18% of US GDP, far below the equivalent percentages of many EU member states.[7]

The US-EU partnership on foreign aid has worked well, in part because the two are the biggest players globally. An even bigger reason for the successful partnership is that they share values and objectives such as the promotion of human rights, democracy, good governance, gender equality, and open markets. Nonetheless, their policies occasionally reflect different outlooks and priorities.

US foreign aid policy is often shaped by national security concerns, especially during major wars, and devotes significant resources to military and non-military security assistance (concentrated in Afghanistan, Israel, Egypt, and Iraq). Moreover, US foreign aid is sometimes used as a tool to open global markets to US exports and is often tied to the purchase of US

---

[7] The United Nations has urged countries to spend at least 0.7% of their GDP on foreign aid, a target met by Sweden, Luxembourg, Norway, Denmark, the Netherlands, and the United Kingdom. According to an opinion poll conducted in the United States in 2014, Americans on average think that 26% of the federal budget is spent on foreign aid; given this misconception, many believe that the US should reduce its spending (unlike their European counterparts who support giving generously). *See* Bianca DiJulio, Jamie Firth, and Mollyann Brodie, "Data Note: Americans' Views On The U.S. Role In Global Health," Kaiser Family Foundation, January 23, 2015. https://www.kff.org/global-health-policy/poll-finding/data-note-americans-views-on-the-u-s-role-in-global-health/.

goods and services (especially food). Some US aid is explicitly made conditional on the recipients' agreement to take certain actions. For example, the Millennium Challenge Corporation, a foreign aid agency established by but independent from the US government, provides large five-year grants to countries that meet certain political and economic criteria and sign up to "compacts" detailing the domestic policies they will pursue.

By contrast, the EU's commitment to development assistance is grounded in a widely shared feeling among the European public that the eradication of extreme poverty is a moral obligation and an investment in Europe's long-term security. Unlike the United States, that has the luxury of large oceans on either side, Europe is far more exposed to instability on its borders. Without development assistance, significant migration flows into Europe from Northern Africa and the eastern Mediterranean are certain. While the EU's development assistance is not shaped by military considerations or the desire to promote exports, the EU has recently moved closer to the US view that aid should be subject to strict conditions about the behavior of recipients, especially their willingness to undertake economic reforms.

Most US presidents have considered foreign aid as an investment in global and US security and prosperity, and a significant pillar of US foreign policy, rather than a gift to undeserving foreign countries. President Trump has departed from that consensus by considering foreign aid wasteful and ineffective unless given to allies. In his 2018 speech before the UN General Assembly, President Trump made the latter point in stark terms: "Moving forward, we are only going to give foreign aid to those who respect us and, frankly, are our friends."[8] His White House now appears to see Africa largely as a playground of big-power rivalry, where Chinese and Russian influence is on the rise. Other than as a destination for growing US exports and investment, Africa appears to be of little inherent interest.

The president's budgets have regularly proposed massive cuts in foreign aid. His 2020 budget has called for 20% cuts in the foreign aid budget—a target that is not only immoral but geo-politically nonsensical in light of the growing influence of China and Russia in Africa and other parts of the developing world. Fortunately, Congress has maintained most of the programs, partly in sympathy with the argument that deploying diplomats and development experts today is cheaper than deploying

---

[8] Remarks by President Trump to the 73rd Session of the United Nations General Assembly, September 25, 2018. https://www.whitehouse.gov/briefings-statements/remarks-president-trump-73rd-session-united-nations-general-assembly-new-york-ny/.

troops tomorrow. In an open letter to Congress in 2017, more than 120 retired admirals and generals argued cogently:

> We know from our service in uniform that many of the crises our nation faces do not have military solutions alone...[the] State Department, USAID...and other development agencies are critical to preventing conflict and reducing the need to put our men and women in uniform in harm's way...The military will lead the fight against terrorism on the battlefield, but it needs strong civilian partners in the battle against the drivers of extremism – lack of opportunity, insecurity, injustice and hopelessness.[9]

As with humanitarian assistance, the 1995 New Transatlantic Agenda also tried to introduce greater structure around US-EU cooperation on foreign aid, especially in their joint efforts to "help developing countries by all appropriate means in their efforts towards political and economic reforms." But efforts at a structured dialogue suffered from disagreements in other areas and were only revived when the US and EU launched a Development Dialogue in 2009.[10] Although the annual meetings at ministerial level have not always occurred as envisioned by the Dialogue, regular meetings at senior levels and continuous technical exchanges between staff, at headquarters and especially in the field, have enabled the parties to exchange information on policies and programs, as well as to promote greater policy consensus and coordination.

The US-EU annual summit in 2014 that I attended several weeks after I arrived in Brussels issued an ambitious set of targets for the parties' development agenda.[11] Some of the objectives were aspirational, such as delivering on the "unfinished business" of the Millennium Development Goals, a set of eight extremely ambitious international development goals for 2015 (including the eradication of extreme poverty and hunger) that had been established by the United Nations in 2000. These goals have been replaced by the UN's 17 Global Goals for Sustainable Development, an agenda of social and economic development objectives for 2030 that the US and the EU support.

---

[9] The full text of the open letter can be found here: http://www.usglc.org/downloads/2017/02/FY18_International_Affairs_Budget_House_Senate.pdf.

[10] 2009 US-EU Summit Declation, November 3, 2009. http://www.europarl.europa.eu/cmsdata/122880/Joint%20Statement%202009%20EU-US%20Summit.pdf.

[11] EU-US Joint Statement, March 26, 2014. https://www.consilium.europa.eu/media/23902/141920.pdf.

US-EU cooperation on foreign aid is not always easy because each party has different budgetary cycles, implementation systems, and measures to ensure accountability. Much of the "real" day-to-day work occurs in the field in dozens of countries, making coordination from headquarters in Washington and Brussels rather complex. Even when coordination is successful, moreover, it can be overtaken by fast-moving events. Representatives of USAID often observed to me that they preferred to deal with EU member states—such as the UK, the Netherlands, Sweden, and Denmark—because they were less bureaucratic and nimbler than the EU.

Nonetheless, the constant dialogue between the US and the EU has enhanced their mutual trust and the effectiveness of their foreign aid programs. One example is how each party has increasingly relied on the other's geographic expertise: USAID relies on France and the EU in francophone Africa where the US has a relatively more modest presence; the EU relies on the United States in the Horn of Africa where the former lacks the latter's resources and expertise. During my diplomatic mission, USAID and DEVCO evidenced their mutual trust and intent to specialize by signing an agreement enabling each to fund the other's projects.

An important by-product of the US-EU dialogue on development is that it has forced each side to coordinate better among its own government departments. In the case of the EU, that means DEVCO, the European External Action Service and also the Directorate-General for Neighbourhood and Enlargement Negotiations (that implements assistance programs in the Western Balkans, Turkey, the former Soviet Union, and the Maghreb). In the case of the United States, that means not only USAID, but also includes the State Department and even the Defense Department, the Department of Health and Human Services, the US Treasury, and the Department of Agriculture. This internal coordination can sometimes be more challenging than transatlantic coordination, as I witnessed many times.

The US and the EU development dialogue has covered a wide range of topics. One of the areas of focus has been the challenge of how to improve the "resilience" of developing countries. In the development context "resilience" means the ability of people, households, communities, countries, and systems to mitigate, adapt to and recover from shocks and stresses in a manner that reduces chronic vulnerability and facilitates economic growth that is fairly distributed across society. Resilience can be strengthened in many ways: for example, with cash transfer programs to provide a safety net to the poorest households in drought-prone areas; by vaccinating livestock and planting crops that are more resistant to pests and drought; through early warning systems and insurance against extreme weather, plagues, and earthquakes; and with budget support for countries to maintain vital state functions, including policing and health care services.[12]

The dialogue has also covered topics such as the effectiveness of aid in achieving economic or human development, adaptation to climate change (especially developing countries' implementation of low-carbon growth strategies and adaptation to harsher weather), improving the availability and accessibility of food ("food security"), the interplay between security and development, electrification (with a focus on rural areas in sub-Saharan Africa), and health. The last four areas merit further elaboration.

At the 2009 G-8 summit in L'Aquila, Italy, members of the G-8 and other donors, including the EU, pledged $22 billion to support food security over a three-year period. That initiative led to the launch at the G-8 summit at Camp David in May 2012 of a New Alliance for Food Security and Nutrition between the donors and ten African countries suffering chronic food shortages. The purpose of the initiative is to attract private investment in agriculture, to complement public investment and create the right conditions for the recipient countries to increase agricultural productivity, adopt improved production technologies (including improved seed varieties), and improve their post-harvest management practices to reduce their dependency on food imports and food aid. Under the "cooperation frameworks" signed with the donor countries, the recipients agree to implement reforms in a wide variety of areas, including infrastructure improvements, regulatory and tax reforms, and easier conditions for the marketing and trade in farm products.[13] Another important example of US-EU cooperation to promote food security in the developing world was the agreement by the Bill and Melinda Gates Foundation and the European Commission to provide $300 million each to fund agricultural and climate-change research during 2018–2020 to assist farmers with crop improvement, protection, and management.

---

[12] The signature of a cooperation agreement between the US and the EU in 2015 on the sharing of data received from the EU's Copernicus constellation of earth observation satellites will assist joint efforts to manage and mitigate natural disasters. https://landsat.gsfc.nasa.gov/united-states-and-european-union-sign-cooperation-arrangement-on-copernicus-earth-observation-data/.

[13] European Parliament, "The New Alliance for Food Security and Nutrition in Africa," November 2015. http://www.europarl.europa.eu/RegData/etudes/STUD/2015/535010/EXPO_STU(2015)535010_EN.pdf.

The US and the EU have both focused on the importance of providing security as a precondition for effective long-term development. Their common views have translated into practical consequences on the ground. For example, the EU and the US ambassadors to South Sudan, working with the United Nations, averted a military confrontation between two tribes a few years after the country achieved its independence in 2011. The *Lou Nuer* and *Murle* tribes had been fighting each other for decades over cattle, with revenge killings occurring frequently. The ambassadors traveled together by helicopter to remote and dangerous areas to negotiate with the tribe's leadership and local elders to mediate an end to the impending conflict. As major providers of aid, the EU and especially the US were successful because they insisted that peace was a precondition for continued aid.

Electrification is another focus of US-EU cooperation on development. Two-thirds of the population of sub-Saharan Africa, around 590 million people, lacks access to power. That number is growing as rapid population growth creates demand that outstrips increased supply from investments in electrification. The remaining one-third cannot consume as much power as it would like because of blackouts and brownouts. In rural areas, the average electrification rate is only 16%. The main reasons for this situation include droughts that affect hydropower capacity, aging infrastructure and poor maintenance, unreliable fuel supply and inadequate transmission and distribution capacity.[14]

Lack of electricity has numerous dramatic effects: For example, it stunts industrial growth and agricultural yields, hurts healthcare services (such as hospital care and the delivery of drugs requiring refrigeration), impedes digital connectivity that is increasingly essential to participate in the knowledge economy, and increases the number of premature deaths, especially among women and children, because of household air pollution caused by the use of solid biomass for cooking and of candles and kerosene lamps for indoor lighting. Electrifying Africa, especially sub-Saharan Africa, is therefore crucial to progress; at the same time, electrification using cleaner fuel sources, such as natural gas and renewable energies, will be key to avoid major harm to the environment from

---

[14] Simone Tagliapietra, "Electrifying Africa: How to Make Europe's Contribution Count," Bruegel, June 2017. http://bruegel.org/wp-content/uploads/2017/06/PC-17-2017_1.pdf.

meeting the energy needs of a rapidly growing population with dirty coal or oil.

Ensuring that all people in sub-Saharan Africa have access to electricity by 2030, one of the UN's Sustainable Development Goals, will require a major effort by the region's governments and the international community, above all the United States and the European Union. According to various estimates, the region will need to increase its electrical capacity by about 400 gigawatts and invest at least $40 billion per year to achieve this goal.[15] Attracting that investment from the private sector is a huge challenge because almost none of sub-Saharan electric utilities are currently financially sustainable due to artificially low tariffs, low operational efficiency due to losses during transmission and distribution, and poor bill collection. Wasteful subsidies incentivize inefficient forms of energy, disincentivize maintenance and investment, and overwhelmingly benefit higher income groups. Political patronage, corruption, and a poor regulatory environment present further challenges.

Investments in the electricity sector are overwhelmingly in the traditional fossil fuel sector generating power on the grid rather than in the renewables sector generating power off the grid. The latter, especially in the form of solar photovoltaic, small hydropower and small wind turbines, are especially relevant for the three-fifths of the population that lives in rural areas. Even despite ongoing technological improvements that increase efficiency, renewable energy projects require significant upfront capital commitments and high transaction costs relative to the amount of power produced and the return on investment. Sub-Saharan Africa will only be able to substantially increase electrification rates, especially with renewable energy projects in rural areas, through energy sector reform and international public–private partnerships that mobilize private capital.

There are dozens of international initiatives originating in Asia, the Middle East, Europe, and the Americas to improve access to power in Africa. China is increasingly active, including in sub-Saharan Africa where Chinese contractors (the vast majority of them state-owned) were responsible for 30% of new electrical capacity between 2010 and 2015. The US

---

[15] 2017 Estimates from Enerdata and the International Energy Agency, cited in Simone Tagliapietra, "Electrifying Africa: How to Make Europe's Contribution Count," Bruegel, June 2017. http://bruegel.org/wp-content/uploads/2017/06/PC-17-2017_1.pdf.

and the EU are working closely to align their initiatives to promote electrification in sub-Saharan Africa. In 2014, they signed a memorandum of understanding that outlined their cooperation to reduce energy poverty and increase energy access in sub-Saharan Africa.[16] Although the MOU is non-binding and does not require either party to make financial commitments, it establishes a structure for cooperation in several areas, including joint financial support, stimulating private sector investment, and the alignment of technical assistance and reform efforts.

As of 2017, there were 26 separate initiatives originating from the member states and the EU institutions. While it is understandable that various member states wish to have separate initiatives to promote national political and commercial interests, it appears rather inefficient for the EU institutions (the European Commission and the European Investment Bank) to have numerous ones as well. Nonetheless, during the five years ending in 2020, the EU budget alone allocated more than €2.5 billion in grants to support sustainable energy in sub-Saharan Africa; those grants enabled the private sector to commit several times that amount in equity and debt capital as well. Together with the member states, the EU has supported projects that have brought electricity to more than 100 million people in the region.

One of the key projects is the European Commission's Electrification Financing Initiative (ElectriFI) to support the adoption of renewable energy, with an emphasis on decentralized energy solutions in rural areas around the developing world, principally in sub-Saharan Africa. USAID not only assisted the European Commission to structure the program but also approved a US investment of €10 million in ElectriFi. That investment represented a crucial "seal of approval" that enabled the European Commission to access a far larger pool of capital than would otherwise have been possible. ElectriFI provides financing and technical support, even at an early stage and in partnership with other funders, to enable projects to overcome gaps in available market financing and achieve maturity in order to attract private long-term capital.

The United States has also been active in promoting the electrification of sub-Saharan Africa. Power Africa, announced by President Obama in 2013, is the largest public–private partnership in history, involving many agencies of the US government, African governments, more than 100

---

[16] Memorandum of Understanding between the United States and the European Union for Reducing Energy Poverty and Increasing Energy Access in Sub-Saharan Africa, signed July 14, 2015. https://www.usaid.gov/sites/default/files/documents/1860/EU%20Signed%20MOU%20from%20July%2014%202015.pdf.

private sector partners and international organizations like the African Development Bank and the World Bank. Power Africa was underpinned by the US Electrify Africa Act of 2015, passed with overwhelming bipartisan support to promote African developments, as well as to assist US exports and counter Chinese influence. Power Africa was one of the few Obama-era executive decisions that President Trump did not cancel upon entering office; indeed, his administration supported it as a model for how governments can leverage private capital to build infrastructure.

The aim of the initiative has been to finance by 2020 30 gigawatts of electricity capacity and 60 million new domestic electricity connections, especially from renewable projects in rural areas, by unlocking sub-Saharan Africa's substantial wind, solar, hydropower, natural gas, and geothermal resources. By the end of 2018, Power Africa had attracted over $54 billion in commitments and had catalyzed about $18 billion in investment into 120 power projects and over 10 gigawatts of capacity. These projects connected about 12 million homes and 53 million people. Most of these connections are from solar lanterns that power a single light and enable the charging of a mobile phone. As basic as that may sound, even such connections can result in dramatic improvements in livelihood. Power Africa is moving beyond these connections to include larger, more on-grid power projects using non-renewable sources.

In addition to the power sector, both the US and the EU are actively engaged in the promotion of global health. For example, they are the main contributors to the Global Fund to Fight HIV/AIDS, Tuberculosis and Malaria and to the Global Alliance for Vaccines and Immunisation (GAVI). They sit on the governing boards and closely align their policies.

Founded in 2002 as a partnership among governments, non-governmental organizations, and the private sector, the Global Fund raises and invests the world's money—about $4 billion per year—to support programs in more than 100 countries that combat the three deadliest infectious diseases. The EU (the European Commission and EU member states combined) and the United States provide roughly 46 and 36%

of the Global Fund's financing, respectively.[17] The health programs supported with this money have reduced the number of deaths caused by HIV/AIDS, TB, and malaria by one-third since 2002 and have saved 27 million lives, the majority of these in sub-Saharan Africa, as of the end of 2017.

The Global Fund has enabled millions to be on antiretroviral therapy and therefore to be spared the death sentence that HIV/AIDS used to represent. Of the 37 million people living with HIV, 22 million are on antiretroviral therapy (17.5 million of these thanks to the Global Fund). Improved access to HIV treatment has cut the number of AIDS-related deaths in half since the peak in 2005, from 1.8 million to under 1 million in 2017. However, HIV infections remain very high and especially among adolescent girls and young women who are up to eight times more likely to be HIV positive than young men in some African countries. On the current trajectory, the Global Fund is unlikely to meet its goal of reducing new infections to 500,000 globally by 2020. In addition to the terrible human cost of the disease, the economic impact of HIV/AIDS is estimated to be over $7 billion in lost earnings in 2020.

The Global Fund provides more than 65% of all international financing to combat TB. The Global Fund has disbursed about $6 billion in the fight against TB by the end of 2017. Much of this has focused on expanding molecular diagnostic technology which delivers faster and more accurate results, supporting programs that identify those living with the disease without treatment, and enabling millions to be treated. Progress is being made: The mortality rate for TB fell by 42% between 2000 and 2017. But TB remains a serious threat to global health security because it is highly contagious, airborne and increasingly drug resistant. It remains the leading cause of death from infectious disease, with 1.3 million deaths per year, not including HIV co-infections. Deaths from drug-resistant TB are responsible for about one-third of all deaths due to

---

[17] The United States also commits billions of dollars to combat HIV/AIDS through the President's Emergency Plan for AIDS Relief, launched by the Bush administration in 2004. Moreover, the Bill and Melinda Gates Foundation has also given €62.5 million in grants and guarantees to co-finance a European Commission program that mobilizes private investment in laboratory facilities that provide diagnostic services for HIV/AIDs, TB and malaria.

antimicrobial resistance worldwide; if trends continue, 2.6 million people will die of drug-resistant TB by 2050, costing the global economy trillions of dollars in lost output.

The Global Fund is also the leading provider of funding to combat malaria, a disease transmitted to humans by mosquitoes. Malaria is a major killer: In 2017, there were 220 million infections and 435,000 deaths from malaria (most of them children under age 5). In Africa alone the economic impact of malaria is estimated to be $12 billion per year, including the costs of healthcare, absenteeism, days lost in education, decreased productivity, and loss of investment. But thanks to the support of the Global Fund, hundreds of millions of insecticide-treated mosquito nets have been distributed and over 100 million cases of malaria have been treated by 2017. As a result, global malaria deaths have dropped by 60% since 2000. Unfortunately, progress has stalled in the past few years due to drug and insecticide resistance. Some countries are even losing ground to the disease.

Launched in 2000 with the help of a $750 million five-year pledge from the Bill and Melinda Gates Foundation, GAVI is an international organization that brings together the public and private sectors in the shared goal of creating access to new and underused vaccines for children living in the world's poorest countries. The US and the EU are among GAVI's six original donor countries; as with the Global Fund, they are the largest donors, providing roughly $270 million each per year. GAVI estimates that it has helped treat over 690 million children and has prevented more than 10 million future deaths in the first 17 years of its existence.

Looking to the Future

Demands on foreign aid and humanitarian assistance are certain to grow in the future, principally because of population growth and climate change, causing extreme weather patterns (including heat and drought), pests, disease, and rising oceans. Some studies predict that of the 2.4 billion increase in world population between 2015 and 2050 1.3 billion will be in Africa. The OECD estimates that by 2030 half a billion people may be living in "fragile states," defined as countries that are incapable of exercising basic functions, because of climate change and conflict.

Every year hundreds of millions of people require humanitarian assistance, largely because of natural disasters and conflicts. Hunger is one of the main urgent challenges: The Food and Agriculture Organization estimates that over 800 million people suffer from food insecurity, of which over 100 million (roughly half of them children) face acute hunger, even starvation. Only one-fifth of children affected by severely acute malnutrition receive adequate care, with the result that many become ill and suffer impaired growth and cognitive development.

There are nearly 70 million people around the globe—principally in Syria, Turkey, Lebanon, Palestine, Yemen, Afghanistan, South Sudan, Somalia, and Myanmar—requiring protection, shelter, food, and other basic services due to forced displacement, often lasting a decade or more. Very often these people lack access to water, sanitation, and hygiene, resulting in heightened risk of epidemic outbreaks.

The World Bank estimates that 38% of land area worldwide, home to approximately 70% of the world's population, is exposed to drought. At the same time, rapid population growth and urbanization are contributing to a steady increase in the demand for water. As a result, the number of people without access to safe drinking water is expected to double by 2025 to 2 billion.

In light of increasing demand for urgent humanitarian assistance and longer-term development aid, the US and the EU, including its member states, need to build on their cooperation as the world's leading donors to coordinate more frequently and deeply than ever before. This coordination is not only necessary to make the dollars and euros stretch further, but also to ensure that their common values shape the global development agenda despite the rapid rise of new state donors (especially China) that are focused almost exclusively on the expansion of political power and economic ties, rather than the promotion of democracy, human rights, and good governance.[18]

The US and the EU also need to work together to ensure that their activities in foreign aid and humanitarian assistance are consistent with the growing role of private development assistance coming from NGOs, foundations, and corporations in the OECD. It will be more challenging, but important, for the US and EU to reconsider some of their policies that undermine their joint objectives to promote more stable economic and political conditions in the poorest countries. In the case of the US,

---

[18] European Parliamentary Research Service, "Addressing Global Poverty and Insecurity Through Better Transatlantic Cooperation," September 2016. http://www.europarl.europa.eu/RegData/etudes/BRIE/2016/586646/EPRS_BRI(2016)586646_EN.pdf.

that means its practice of tying aid to the purchase of US agricultural commodities. In the case of the EU, that means its practice of dumping into African markets the cheap surplus food that results from generous European production subsidies; and it also means its opposition to genetically modified food and feed that prevents African countries from accepting some food aid and planting more resilient crops.[19]

Acknowledgements The invaluable assistance of Dr. Emmanuel De Groof in the preparation of this chapter is gratefully acknowledged.

---

[19] "Better Dead Than GM-Fed," *The Economist*, September 19, 2002. Emmet Livingstone, "How EU Milk Is Sinking Africa's Farmers," *Politico*, April 8, 2018.

CHAPTER 13

Conclusions

When I reflect on the direction of US-EU relations, my thoughts frequently return to a tale of two speeches delivered in the same city by two US secretaries of state: the first by John Kerry in early October 2016 and the second by Michael Pompeo in early December 2018.[1] The speeches were both held at the Concert Noble, a historic building in the center of Brussels. Although both speeches dealt with the transatlantic relationship, they could not have been more different in style or substance.

I was in the front row for the first speech and had contributed to it. Secretary Kerry, in his last few months on the job, was passionate and humorous. During his speech and the question period, he impressed the audience of senior political and business leaders with his command of the subject matter. He demonstrated that he had been born to be Secretary of State and, thanks to his many years as chairman of the Senate Foreign Relations Committee and strong family connections to France, that he knows Europe intimately. I was not present at the second speech, but I saw the video and spoke to many who were. Secretary Pompeo delivered the speech in a rather brusque manner and did not stay for

---

[1] Remarks on the Transatlantic Relationship by John Kerry, October 4, 2016. https://2009-2017.state.gov/secretary/remarks/2016/10/262750.htm; Remarks by Secretary Pompeo at the German Marshall Fund, December 4, 2018. https://ua.usembassy.gov/remarks-by-secretary-pompeo-at-the-german-marshall-fund/.

© The Author(s) 2020
A. L. Gardner, *Stars with Stripes*,
https://doi.org/10.1007/978-3-030-29966-8_13

questions. According to the *Financial Times*, Pompeo left his audience "open-mouthed."[2]

At my suggestion, Kerry referred to Belgium's motto "*L'Union fait la force*" (unity makes strength) and to the US equivalent, "*E Pluribus Unum*" (out of many, one). He made a strong endorsement, as had so many of his predecessors from both political parties, of the EU and a strong US-EU partnership:

> I cannot emphasize too strongly the twin propositions that unity within Europe, and partnership between the United States and Europe, remain absolutely indispensable to global security and prosperity...We should never take for granted the good that has been achieved by the unity of Europe.

In an oblique reference to the very different views of Donald Trump, Kerry argued that the United States acting alone simply cannot address all the world's challenges without allies, including Europe, and the multilateral institutions that were shaped by the transatlantic community after World War II:

> You can't just sit here in Europe and we can't just sit across the pond in the United States and somehow believe you can wall yourself off from the world. Not in today's economy, not in today's world, not in today's marketplace, and not with today's security challenges....

Kerry catalogued many of the achievements of the US-EU partnership, including the Paris climate change accords, the Iran nuclear deal, the implementation of biting sanctions on Russia and Iran, the cooperation in dealing with the Ebola outbreak in West Africa, and the coordination of foreign aid and humanitarian assistance. This book has described these and several other important areas of cooperation in some detail (Fig. 13.1).

Pompeo's speech presented the opposite view of multilateralism and the European Union:

> Multilateralism has too often become viewed as an end unto itself. The more treaties we sign, the safer we supposedly are. The more bureaucrats

---

[2] Editorial Board, "Mike Pompeo's Threadbare Defence of US Leadership," *Financial Times*, December 2, 2018. https://www.ft.com/content/93946f66-f964-11e8-8b7c-6fa24bd5409c.

Fig. 13.1 Ambassador Gardner and Secretary Kerry at Brussels airport in the Summer of 2016 (*Source* From author's own collection)

we have, the better the job gets done…Is the EU ensuring that the interests of countries and their citizens are placed before those of bureaucrats here in Brussels?…We aspire to make the international order serve our citizens – not to control them.

My successor, Gordon Sondland, thought that the speech was "very subtle." I thought it contained grotesque cartoon-strip caricatures, including the suggestion that EU bureaucrats are placing their interests above those of EU citizens. Anyone with even a rudimentary understanding of the EU knows that its bureaucracy is hardly excessive, even compared to a single US government department (the Department of Veterans Affairs employs ten times the number of bureaucrats), that the EU is controlled by the member states and has increasingly become more intergovernmental, and that regulation comes about because the member states propose much of it and agree to all of it.

Sondland repeated similar caricatures of the EU. According to him, bureaucrats of the European Commission "are off in a cloud, regulating to their hearts' content…" They are utterly obstructionist: "…if I ask someone at the EU what time it is, the answer is 'no.'"[3] His EU expertise stems from being the founder of an Oregon-based hotel group who contributed $1 million to President Trump's inauguration through several limited liability companies.[4]

No US administration, Democratic or Republican, and no European country, has considered multilateralism as an end unto itself. None has ever believed that we become safer simply by signing treaties. None has ever wanted an international order to subjugate its citizens. Membership in international organizations and participation in an international rules-based order do not usually subtract from sovereignty. To the contrary, they often enhance it. In his speech, Pompeo paid fulsome tribute to George H. W. Bush, who had died a few days before, but I doubt very much that Bush would have agreed with a single word as he was a fervent believer in multilateralism. Before the Trump administration, US presidents and secretaries of state would have agreed with the closing statement of Secretary of the Treasury Henry Morgenthau at the Bretton Woods conference in 1944:

> We have come to recognize that the wisest and most effective way to protect our national interests is through international co-operation — that is to say, through united effort for the attainment of common goals.[5]

The entire postwar system and its defining institutions—including the World Bank, the International Monetary Fund, and the World Trade Organization—are based on this foundation.

The contradictions in Pompeo's speech were manifest. He exhorted every country to put its national interests first, just as in the United States, but suggested that every country would do best to simply follow the US lead. There was no explanation of why some rule-breaking by a few countries and occasional overreach by some organizations justified

---

[3] David Herszenhorn, "Trump's Man in Brussels Slams 'Out of Touch' EU," *Politico*, December 10, 2018. https://www.politico.eu/article/trumps-man-in-brussels-slams-out-of-touch-eu/.

[4] Emily R. Siegel, Andrew W. Lehren, Brandy Zadrozny, Dan De Luce and Vanessa Swales, "Donors to the Trump inaugural committee got ambassador nominations. But are they qualified?" *NBC News*, April 3, 2019. https://www.nbcnews.com/politics/donald-trump/donors-trump-inaugural-committee-got-ambassador-nominations-are-they-qualified-n990116.

[5] Martin Wolf, "Bretton Woods at 75: Global Co-operation Under Threat," *Financial Times*, July 10, 2019. https://www.ft.com/content/e82a1f48-a185-11e9-a282-2df48f366f7d.

tearing down a multilateral rules-based system that has served the post-war world so well. He did not explain how a might-makes-right world in which every country fights according to the laws of the jungle will make anyone better off, including the United States. The suggestion that the Trump administration was breaking new ground by putting US interests first was insulting to prior administrations of both parties that clearly sought to do the same. The reality is that "America First" policies under this administration have usually meant "America Alone."

Pompeo's speech revealed the deep disdain for the European Union that has characterized the Trump administration at the highest level. This disdain may be based on the view that the EU is a minor player in the realm of military and security policy. That view reminds me of Stalin's foolish question that underestimated the Vatican's power: "How many divisions does the Pope have?" That was obviously the wrong question and it is obviously the wrong metric to judge the EU. The EU is not a superpower in the traditional sense, but in trade and in the regulation of certain sectors, especially data privacy and the digital economy, it is a world leader that sets global standards.

This "Brussels effect" will be a major phenomenon for many years to come. One recent study has found that nearly half of roughly 450 active legislative proposals across the world relating to antitrust, digital taxation, content regulation, access to data, and the breakup of technology firms originated with the EU or individual member states.[6] The "Brussels effect" has recently been accentuated by a far more active regulatory approach in the EU than in the US toward competition law and merger control. Antitrust prosecutions, for example, have dropped significantly under the Trump administration. Scrutiny of the digital economy is also tougher in the EU.

Some officials in the White House appear to think that the EU is worse than a distraction: It is based on the illusion that countries can pool their sovereignty for the greater good. The EU, according to this view, is a nuisance because it magnifies the EU's influence on the world's stage, complicating the ability of the US to get its way. President Trump has said as much when he repeatedly describes the EU as a "consortium" set up by Germany to get its way in trade. Astonishingly, Trump has even described the EU as a "foe" and has said that it is "worse than China,

---

[6] Madhumita Murgia, "Europe a 'Global Trendsetter on Tech Regulation,'" *Financial Times*, October 30, 2019.

just smaller."[7] This is the view of a property developer focused entirely on maximizing short-term advantage. This book has described how absurd that view is, even in the contentious area of trade.

The Trump administration's disdain for the EU reflects a shocking degree of aggressive ignorance about the EU. In a lengthy article about the president's "Trump doctrine" on foreign policy, former Deputy National Security Adviser for Strategic Communications and Speechwriting Michael Anton states:

> Washington has encouraged its friends and allies to cede their sovereign decision-making, often to anti-American transnational bodies such as the EU…[8]

Anti-American? I doubt he has spoken to a fraction of the high-level EU executives that I have over many decades. Many have waxed emotional to me about how much the US has meant to them. Commissioner Andrus Ansip of Estonia, for example, would relate how he would eagerly listen to Radio Liberty and Voice of America when growing up under Soviet tyranny. Commissioner Vytenis Andriukaitis of Lithuania showed me mementos in his office relating to his involvement in the anti-Soviet underground. Like many others, the United States has been their North Star. I could point out dozens of other examples. Even Commissioner Margrethe Vestager, whom Trump has described as that "tax lady who really hates us," is certainly not anti-American. There isn't a shred of evidence to support the criticism.

In a line of argument that probably reflects the Trump administration's view about the EU, Anton argued that the EU:

> was a fraud from the beginning…it was sold to the European public on false pretenses: it was supposed to make travel easier and lower trade barriers and other costs of doing business across borders while allowing states to maintain their sovereignty and citizens their individuality. But if anyone had forthrightly told European voters that "Brussels is going to henceforth

---

[7] Doina Chiacu and Roberta Rampton, "Trump says EU treats U.S. worse than China does on trade," *Reuters*, May 17, 2019. https://uk.reuters.com/article/us-usa-trade-eu/trump-says-eu-treats-u-s-worse-than-china-does-on-trade-idUKKCN1SN2FJ.

[8] Michael Anton, "The Trump Doctrine," *Foreign Policy*, April 20, 2019. https://foreignpolicy.com/2019/04/20/the-trump-doctrine-big-think-america-first-nationalism/.

regulate the size and shape of your vegetables and dictate your immigration and border policies," most would have instantly replied, "No, thanks."[9]

These Alternative Facts would be accepted in some of the tabloid rags of the United Kingdom. Even a cursory reading of the Wikipedia entry for the EU, however, would reveal that this is just plain wrong. European integration was conceived in the aftermath of war, by the survivors of war to prevent further war. The EU has indeed made travel easier, lowered trade barriers and other costs of business. But not only: It has enabled generations to travel and study freely within the EU and it has made the EU more prosperous and secure in all the ways described in this book. That is why so many European countries have wanted to join (and why so many more are lining up to enter). Regulating the size and shape of vegetables is a tiny and absurd example that amuses more than it informs. Member states retain control of their borders, although the EU has been increasing its role (with member states' support) in order to ensure that the EU has common policies to deal with migration flows.

In the weeks following the 2016 presidential election, I worried that the new president simply didn't understand the EU. I worried that he was getting twisted advice about the desirability of Brexit from Nigel Farage, a demagogue whom I had frequently seen perform in the European Parliament. I was struck that in Trump's first call with a senior EU official, European Council President Donald Tusk, Trump asked pointedly which country would follow the UK out of the EU and refused to believe Tusk when he said that none would. My worries were confirmed over time. The president appears to believe that Brexit was merely a manifestation of the desire to "take back control," similar to his own campaign rhetoric about blaming foreign forces and unaccountable bureaucrats for all evils. Quite to the contrary, Brexit will prove bad news for the EU, the UK, and the United States itself for all the reasons stated in this book.

It rapidly became apparent that Trump didn't only believe Brexit is great but that a rapid hard Brexit was *desirable* despite the mountain of evidence to the contrary. Robert "Woody" Johnson, co-owner of the New York Jets football team before being appointed as the US ambassador to the Court of St. James, has been an avid cheerleader for Brexit despite the fact that roughly half of the British public opposes it. Moreover, Trump has clearly sought to *promote* further exits in order to undermine the European Union. He has avidly courted the most euro-skeptic leaders in

---

[9] Michael Anton, "The Trump Doctrine," *Foreign Policy*, April 20, 2019.

the EU member states, especially in Hungary, Poland, and Italy, while repeatedly insulting German Chancellor Angela Merkel and humiliating British Prime Minister Theresa May. No wonder that President Tusk took the historically unprecedented step of listing the United States as one of the key geostrategic risks facing the EU. Tusk told fellow EU leaders that thanks to Trump "we have got rid of all illusions. He has made us realise that if you need a helping hand, you will find one at the end of your arm."[10]

The extraordinary anti-EU aggression from the Trump administration is one of the reasons why the EU is seriously concerned about a global context that is becoming more threatening and uncertain. As a result, European Commission president von der Leyen has described her Commission as "geopolitical." She has noted that the EU "needs to be more strategic, more assertive, and more united in its approach to external relations."[11] The concrete manifestations of this new approach, as set forth in the European Commission's policy program and instructions to the new commissioners, include the objective that the EU should strengthen its ability to act "autonomously" and promote its values and interests around the world. Moreover, the program of the European Commission is focused on enhancing Europe's "technological sovereignty" and promoting investment in key industries through an industrial strategy. The creation of a new directorate-general for the defense industry and space is potentially significant. So is the intent to use whenever possible EU treaty clauses that allow certain decisions on common foreign and security policy to be adopted by qualified majority voting (rather than unanimity).

The words "sovereignty" and "autonomy" have rarely been uttered before in the hallways of the Brussels bureaucracy. Time will tell whether the European Commission can deliver on its promise of being more assertive in promoting its interests in a more challenging world. But if it does, Donald Trump can certainly take some of the credit. The European Coal and Steel Community, the precursor to the EU, was in part the legacy of Joseph Stalin. Could a more "geopolitical" EU be the legacy of Donald Trump?

---

[10] Press Release of the European Council, May 16, 2018. https://www.consilium.europa.eu/en/press/press-releases/2018/05/16/remarks-by-president-donald-tusk-ahead-of-the-eu-western-balkans-summit-and-the-leaders-agenda-dinner/.

[11] Mission Letter from Ursula von der Leyen to Josep Borrell, September 10, 2019. https://ec.europa.eu/commission/sites/beta-political/files/mission-letter-josep-borrell-2019_en.pdf.

That would not be the only irony. Despite his best efforts, Trump will fail to promote more Brexits. Indeed, Brexit and Trump himself have served as a mighty vaccine against euro-skepticism. Much of Europe is aghast at the dysfunction of the UK political system over the past few years, the decline in sterling and foreign direct investment, the possibility of Scottish secession, and the certainty that the UK will play a far diminished role outside the EU. Recent Eurobarometer polls show that support for the EU has gone up since the Brexit referendum as citizens fear the consequences of losing the advantages of membership. No EU member state is following the UK out the door. Even Brussels-bashing populists want to stay within the club. Although some populist movements, especially in Italy, strengthened their position in the much-feared 2019 European elections, the four leading centrist parties in the European Parliament largely retained their aggregate position of decisive influence.

The Trump administration's policy of actively seeking the breakup of the European Union reminds me of the famous statement, often ascribed to Napoleon's chief of police Fouché after the execution of Louis Antoine de Bourbon, Duke of Enghien: "*C'est pire qu'un crime; c'est une faute*" (it's worse than a crime, it is a blunder). It is a blunder of historic proportions for all the reasons set out in this book.

The United States and the European Union have cooperated intensively, and should continue to do so, especially in the three areas that I have identified: commercial policy; security; and saving the planet. The nine specific policy chapters describe the important work we have done in trade policy, digital policy, and data privacy (commercial policy); military security, sanctions, energy security, and law enforcement (security); and climate change, foreign aid, and humanitarian assistance (saving the planet). My focus has been on the Obama administration because that is what I personally witnessed. But that work built on the achievements of prior administrations. Why on earth destroy this essential partnership?

There is no doubt that the exit of the United Kingdom will weaken the EU. Nearly every piece of analysis about the impact of Brexit on the EU and the US-EU relationship that the Obama administration prepared, and in which I was closely involved, has proven to be accurate. Shorn of the UK, the EU may be a less effective partner on sanctions policy, law enforcement, and military security cooperation because the UK has been such an important contributor to the EU in these areas, in both financial and intellectual terms. It will be harder for the United States to ensure alignment of interests with the EU on trade, digital policy, and data privacy without the UK remaining on the inside to promote an open, free-market approach that balances security with privacy. The United States will no longer be able to rely, as it has in the past, on the UK as a source of information and ally on the inside of the EU club. While it is true that the EU is getting rid of an ever-present pebble in its shoe and can now proceed faster in certain policy areas, the EU 27 will have lost a capable member that has provided leadership in key areas. Nonetheless, the partnership between EU and the US will remain critical to address many issues of regional and global concern.

My successor has defended the Trump administration's new approach to the EU by claiming that it is a long-overdue focus on cutting deals rather than useless diplomacy:

> We're interested in substance and then resetting certain relationships between us that have gone completely out of balance, instead of coming here and taking nice photos and attending lovely soirées and allowing the underlying issues to fester.[12]

Perhaps my highly qualified predecessors and I failed to realize that we were waltzing from one cocktail reception and photo op to another, rather than doing any real work to promote US and shared transatlantic interests. History will judge what is real work that leads to results and what is empty sloganeering that is needlessly destructive.

In the area of trade, where I devoted a substantial portion of my time, the US and the EU have made significant progress liberalizing world markets through multilateral and plurilateral agreements. We failed to get TTIP over the line, to my great regret, but we did make progress and we prepared the ground for an ambitious agreement (or series of agreements) in the future.

President Trump likes to claim that the EU is highly unfair with the US in transatlantic trade. While there are indeed areas where the EU imposes significant barriers, especially in agricultural trade where the imbalance contributes to the overall trade deficit, it is of course absurd to suggest that the US doesn't impose significant barriers of its own. Trump keeps

---

[12] Demetri Sevastopulo and Guy Chazan, "US Rift with Europe Widens Ahead of Orban Visit," *Financial Times*, May 12, 2019. https://www.ft.com/content/c17089f0-748f-11e9-be7d-6d846537acab.

repeating that the EU imposes a 10% tariff on imported cars, higher than the US 2.5% tariff on EU car exports. What he doesn't mention is that the US imposes a 25% tariff on imported pickup trucks, whereas EU tariffs are far lower.

Trump's obsession with the $168 billion merchandise trade deficit with the EU (in 2018) is also misplaced. As Dan Hamilton, one of the most experienced experts on the EU and transatlantic trade, has pointed out, "trade in goods, as even trade itself, is a misleading benchmark of international commerce."[13] The US surplus in services trade (especially digitally deliverable services) and US so-called primary income from foreign affiliate earnings as well as investment income earned in Europe more than offset the merchandise trade deficit.

When the Trump administration withdrew from the Trans-Pacific Partnership (TPP) and essentially abandoned TTIP, the net result was a setback for US farmers, ranchers, and manufacturing exporters who want to sell in global markets. Asian countries, including Japan and Vietnam, rushed to the EU to conclude free trade agreements because they felt abandoned by the United States and did not want to be left alone with China. Canada and the EU proceeded to conclude a deep and comprehensive free trade agreement as well. As a result, the members of TPP appear to have better access to Asian markets, including Japan,[14] than their US counterparts and Canadian exporters have better access to the EU market than their US counterparts. Now how exactly does any of that advance US commercial objectives?

The EU's power to negotiate trade agreements on behalf of its members naturally enhances its negotiating leverage, something that irritates the Trump administration. The president would much rather deal with each EU member state on its own to exert maximum pressure. When the president met German Chancellor Angela Merkel in the Oval Office in April 2017, he asked her ten times if he could negotiate a trade deal with Germany. Each time she replied that the US could only negotiate a deal

---

[13] Dan Hamilton, "Transatlantic Policy Impacts of the U.S.-EU Trade Conflict," Testimony to the Subcommittee on Europe, Eurasia, Energy and the Environment of the Committee on Foreign Affairs, U.S. House of Representatives, June 26, 2019. https://transatlanticrelations.org/wp-content/uploads/2019/06/HFAC-US-EU-testimony-June-26-2019-dh-final.pdf.

[14] As this book was going to press, the US and Japan were in the process of finalizing a partial trade deal that appears to open up Japan's agricultural market to US goods in exchange for some cuts to US industrial tariffs.

with the EU. On the eleventh refusal, Trump finally got the message and replied: "Oh, we'll do a deal with Europe then."[15] In a separate exchange with European Commission President Jean-Claude Juncker, Trump said he wanted to do a deal with him, not with the European Union. Juncker politely replied that a deal with him was a deal with the EU as the European Commission has sole responsibility for trade matters.[16]

The US and the EU should restart their transatlantic free trade discussions but based on the lessons outlined in this book's chapter on trade. Seeking the fragmentation of the EU and repeatedly threatening it with tariffs on spurious national security grounds are misguided policies. They should also restart their work on sponsoring plurilateral trade liberalization, including the Trade in Services Agreement and the Environmental Goods Agreement discussed in chapter 4.

A US-UK free trade deal is desirable, but it will not be quick or easy and it should not come at the expense of a far more meaningful US-EU deal. A US-UK agreement will be burdened by many of the same obstacles as in the latter. Even if one is signed, it is highly likely that the UK will not get as favorable terms as the EU would get in a US-EU deal because of the UK's diminished leverage. And it may have to "pay" for the agreement by aligning itself with the United States on a host of issues unrelated to trade. The UK may be desperate to show it has an alternative to the EU, but it should also be realistic about the chances of a real estate developer being sentimental about the special relationship. The Trump administration's threats to impose arbitrary import tariffs on UK exports if the UK implements a digital services tax is just one sign of how the relationship could become turbulent.

The Trump administration has quite rightly increased the focus on unfair Chinese trade practices. But it makes no sense that the United States has failed to engage with the European Union on reforming the WTO and jointly pressuring Beijing to play by the rules. Although the United States probably agrees with the vast majority of the EU's very specific proposals for WTO reform, it has preferred to deal with China alone outside the WTO. The administration does not appreciate that together

---

[15] James Dean and Bruno Waterfield, "Trump Puts EU Ahead of Britain in Trade Queue: Merkel Lands Brexit Victory for Brussels," *The Times*, April 22, 2017.

[16] Markus Becker, Susanne Beyer and Peter Müller, "'I Kissed Putin ... It Certainly Didn't Hurt Europe,'" *Der Spiegel*, November 1, 2019. https://www.spiegel.de/international/europe/interview-with-eu-commission-president-jean-claude-juncker-a-1294486.html.

we would be far more effective in dealing with China and that changes in trade rules promoted by both would have far greater legitimacy.

I have greater sympathy for the view, exploited brilliantly by the Trump administration, that world trade rules have failed to work for the middle class. Global trade liberalization has generated enormous prosperity and is often unfairly blamed more than technology and automation for causing job losses (especially in the manufacturing sector) and wage stagnation. Nonetheless, global elites, including on both sides of the Atlantic, have failed to plan for the trauma that has accompanied the benefits of trade. The anger felt by middle-class voters about free trade is real and needs to be addressed. I was reminded of this by some fan mail I received several minutes after appearing on CNBC in April 2019 in which I criticized Trump's threatened tariffs on the EU:

> Your traitorous support of asshole Europeans has come at the expense of (me) poor and middle class Americans (there are very few middle class Americans left due to traitors like you)...f you. The great US has been supporting the turds in Europe for decades...Europeans have been eating our lunch for decades...unfair and illegal trade practices (on their part)..and their refusal to contribute to their OWN EUROPEAN DEFENSE...fuck Europe and fuck people like your traitorous ass that like to contribute to their unfair shit...

My fan was shooting at the wrong target, of course. Trade and Europe are not the enemy. As many Presidents (even before Trump) have stated, Europe has indeed been a free rider of the US security guarantee for far too long and many successfully nudged some European states to do more. The point remains valid even in light of the fact that Europe has shouldered more burdens than the United States in other areas, such as climate change and immigration.

A major focus for US-EU cooperation in the future should be on ensuring that the spoils of trade are shared more equitably. The case for free trade will continue to be challenged if the lion's share of benefits accrues to the already prosperous and well educated, while blue-collar workers continue to fall behind and suffer from economic anxiety. In the mid-1960s, male high-school graduates in the United States were about as likely to be in the workforce as college-educated men and were earning slightly less than the latter; half a century later, high-school graduates had fallen substantially further behind.[17] While social welfare systems in Europe have prevented income inequalities from rising as fast as in the United States, the European middle class has experienced, like the American middle class, far more serious wage stagnation in the decade ending 2014 than in the prior decade. President Obama eloquently captured the challenge in an Address to the People of Europe in April, 2016:

> ...the economic anxieties many feel today on both sides of the Atlantic are real. The disruptive changes brought about by the global economy, unfortunately, sometimes are hitting certain groups, especially working-class communities, more heavily. And if neither the burdens, nor the benefits of our global economy are being fairly distributed, it's no wonder that people rise up and reject globalization. If there are too few winners and too many losers as the global economy integrates, people are going to push back.[18]

It is no good preaching the gospel of trade's wealth creation when job losses are visible and concentrated. It may be unfair to point to Chinese imports as the scapegoat, but they have unquestionably played a major role. According to one study, they eliminated nearly one million American manufacturing jobs from 1999 to 2011 (the figure rises to 2.4 million if suppliers and other related industries are taken into account).

The rich world has neither dedicated the resources nor the effort to cushion the blow from globalization and free trade. Members of the OECD set aside an average of only 0.6% of GDP per year on "active labor-market policies" such as job centers, retraining schemes, and employment subsidies to ease transition to new types of work. The United States spends just 0.1% of its GDP on such policies.[19] Its Trade Adjustment Assistance Program, dating back to 1962, is underfunded, complex, and ineffective. With a modest budget of about $1 billion per year, it pays

---

[17] By 2014, 83% of male high-school graduates were in the workforce, against 94% of those who finished college; they were also earning 60% of what college-educated males were earning. "Coming and Going: Truth and Myth About the Effects of Openness to Trade," *The Economist*, October 1, 2016. Statistics from a report of the Council on Economic Advisers.

[18] Remarks by President Obama in Address to the People of Europe, The White House Office of the Press Secretary, April 25, 2016. https://obamawhitehouse.archives.gov/the-press-office/2016/04/25/remarks-president-obama-address-people-europe.

[19] "Coming and Going," *The Economist*, October 1, 2016.

for retraining of workers who lose their jobs because of foreign competition. But that retraining is too often ineffective as it does not translate into marketable skills: Workers remain jobless or with lower incomes than those who signed up for unemployment benefits and looked for other work.[20]

Every other major economy spends at least twice as much on national trade adjustment assistance programs as the United States. France and Germany spend five times as much, while Denmark spends 20 times as much. Although Britain's economy is about twice as exposed to foreign trade as that of the US, it provides almost no assistance to those displaced by globalization and trade.[21] Its "rapid response service," with the princely budget of several million pounds per year, can't provide much training and support in the case of mass redundancies. This insouciance has real-world effects, as made patently clear in the Brexit referendum. For example, those regions most exposed to Chinese competition had the highest percentage of voters seeking to leave the European Union.

The EU's Globalisation Adjustment Fund has a budget of just €150 million for the period 2014–2020 and is rather limited in scope, especially as it can only be applied in circumstances where over 500 workers are made redundant by a single company or if a large number of workers are laid off in a specific industry or region. EU member states can't continue to expect the European Commission to promote trade liberalization without also giving it a proper budget to provide a safety net on a pan-European basis.

The US and the EU should cooperate, preferably on a multilateral basis, to crack down on multinationals' tax avoidance; negotiate with China agreements to correct significant Chinese overcapacity in key products such as steel; and cooperate at the WTO to attack unfair trading practices, especially by China, including the theft of intellectual property and continuing restrictions on Chinese market access. Both the US and

---

[20] Peter S. Goodman, "More Wealth, More Jobs, But Not for Everyone: What Fuels the Backlash on Trade," *The New York Times*, September 28, 2016. https://www.nytimes.com/2016/09/29/business/economy/more-wealth-more-jobs-but-not-for-everyone-what-fuels-the-backlash-on-trade.html.

[21] Edward Alden, "How to Help Workers Laid Low By Trade – And Why We Haven't," PBS, November 16, 2016. "How to Help Workers Laid Low by Trade," "Collateral Damage," *The Economist*, July 30, 2016. The budget of Britain's trade adjustment assistance program in 2012 was a pitiful £6 million. Only 15% of those on unemployment benefit receive any sort of training.

the EU have an interest to ensure that their systems for screening foreign investments prevent the acquisition of strategic technologies that can lead to the loss of security or long-term competitiveness. Governments need to convince the public that protection is legitimate, while protectionism is self-defeating and the first is possible without the second.

While trade is a hugely significant feature of US-EU relations, this book's section on commercial issues also addresses two other important aspects: data privacy and the digital economy. The Trump administration has fortunately protected the achievement of the Privacy Shield Agreement. But numerous legal challenges before EU courts to various means of transferring personal data from the EU to the US may mean that further intensive work will be necessary to ensure data flows may continue without endangering the important work US intelligence services do to protect citizens on both sides of the Atlantic. The US and the EU will need to continue collaborating intensively to ensure that their high standards of data privacy are as similar as possible and that they become de facto global standards. While pursuing the necessary goal of data protection, both sides must avoid data protectionism. The latter would stunt innovation and global growth, as well as give authoritarian regimes all over the world further excuses to build national data fortresses.

Similarly, as a vibrant economic area with many of the world's most innovative companies and over 800 million sophisticated consumers, the US and the EU have a joint interest in continuing their collaboration on the digital economy. We don't know what new technologies will develop in the coming years. We do know, however, that how we coordinate now on these issues will determine whether we end up building incompatible regulatory frameworks that stunt growth or instead are able to harness the promise of new technologies for the good of Americans and Europeans alike.

The US should join with the EU, as it has proposed, to counter Chinese attempts to define the technologies of the future. Such an alliance would focus on pooling research in such areas as robotics, 5G technology, the Internet of Things, artificial intelligence, nanotechnology, 3D printing, and self-driving cars—all critical to maintain transatlantic economic competitiveness. Together the US and the EU can set global standards in these and other areas; if each goes its separate way, the Chinese will do so. That is clearly China's intent, as evidenced by their growing influence in bodies such as the International Telecommunication Union and the

International Organisation for Standardisation that set technical criteria for new products and technologies.

As we harness the opportunities of digital disruption, the US and the EU will also need to focus on addressing the challenges, including to our labor markets, our tax base, and our middle class. The consequences of each side pursuing different, and perhaps incompatible, approaches in its competition policy and taxation rules respecting the digital economy would be extremely negative. While the US has legitimate concerns about discriminatory digital services tax regimes being introduced in the EU, it should continue to work within the OECD to achieve a global compromise or, failing that, it should bring a complaint to the WTO rather than impose unilateral sanctions.

This book's section on security covered areas where the US and the EU work together to improve their mutual security. In addition to cooperating with many EU member states on law enforcement issues, the United States should continue to reinforce its cooperation with Europol in the many areas detailed in this book, including online child sexual exploitation, human smuggling, drug and weapons trafficking, and terrorism. Fortunately, the Trump administration has seen the value of this cooperation, despite its disdain for the European Union. A key next step will be for the US and the EU to negotiate an agreement enabling law enforcement authorities on either side of the Atlantic to request internet service providers on the other side to provide electronic evidence necessary in criminal investigations (subject to due process safeguards and data protection requirements).

Moreover, military security cooperation should continue as long as the EU's military missions are complementary to, not competitive with, NATO's role. That has certainly been the case, especially in Africa, as this book has argued. There is almost no indication that the EU's future ambitions in this area will be any different. With Britain's departure from the EU, the US concern should be that the EU will have insufficient means to provide security in its neighborhood, not that it will be too autonomous.

The US and the EU should continue to work together on promoting European energy security for the good of Europe and the United States. Washington should not allow the short-term goal of promoting exports of LNG to dominate the far more important objective of minimizing European over-reliance on Russian gas. Gazprom's plans, including the completion of the Nord Stream II pipeline, represent a continued threat in this regard, notwithstanding the important achievements in recent years to diversify energy sources and import routes. New sources of gas, especially in the Mediterranean, need to be brought to European markets as quickly as possible. By providing appropriate political and economic conditions, the US and the EU can ensure that this happens.

Future crises will require that the US and the EU continue to impose and implement tough sanctions programs, just as they have done so successfully in the cases of Russia and Iran. While there is no doubt that the US can inflict pain even when acting unilaterally, as is clearly the case currently in its sanctions program against Iran, past history suggests strongly that sanctions are only effective in the long run if implemented in coordination with allies and when they enjoy widespread international legitimacy. Short-term efforts by the United States to exploit the role of the dollar and its predominant role in the international financial system yield tactical advantages, but at the risk of undermining US leverage in the long term as non-dollar payment systems and alternatives to the SWIFT secure financial message service evolve.

Finally, the US and the EU are natural partners in their ultimate goal of saving the planet. As the largest providers of humanitarian assistance and foreign aid, it is imperative that they continue to coordinate their policies to relieve suffering and promote sustainable development in the developing world. If they do not, they will waste money and perhaps even pursue incompatible goals. Cooperation in these areas is crucial to address the risks that poverty and climate change will unleash even more terrorism and mass migration that will strain our democratic societies. The ability of the US and the EU to come together to achieve an ambitious outcome at the Paris climate change accords, and their continuing collaboration in many areas of environmental protection, including the protection of endangered species and the oceans, demonstrate what they can achieve.

It is doubtful whether the EU and progressive forces in the United States, including some states, cities, and businesses, can ensure the implementation of the goals in the Paris climate change accords if the US federal government remains unengaged and Chinese emissions rise (as they are projected to do by 2.6% in 2020). The Von der Leyen Commission has committed to a Green Deal for Europe that will include a 2030 goal of cutting emissions by 55% and enshrining carbon neutrality by 2050 into EU law. But these measures are not enough by themselves. In light of the alarming signals that the earth's atmosphere is warming at an increasingly rapid pace, with potentially irreversible and catastrophic consequences for the human race, it is essential for the US and the EU to collaborate once again to combat climate change, as they did so effectively under the Obama administration.

There is so much more the US and the EU could be doing beyond the areas described in this book. For example, both sides are engaged in ambitious programs to improve our knowledge of the human brain. Researchers on both sides of the Atlantic are seeking to map and simulate the human brain in order to improve the diagnosis and prevention of brain disorders. Although they are regularly keeping each other informed of their objectives and progress, there is ample scope for them to be working together under a common program to avoid duplication and ensure faster progress. Similarly, both the US and the EU are engaged in ambitious programs to combat the growing global threat of antimicrobial resistance. Current trends suggest that drug-resistant infections will spread widely over the coming decades if we do not curb the use of antibiotics and accelerate the pipeline of new antimicrobial drugs.

Less concretely, but just as importantly, the US and the EU need to work together to preserve open, liberal societies that respect human rights and democracy. In order to do that, we need to work on preserving "the topsoil of trust," in the words of Tom Friedman. Without trust in institutions, nothing can grow. Vladimir Putin has predicted that liberal values have become "obsolete" and have "outlived their purpose."[22] We must prove him wrong.

Populist demagogy on both sides of the Atlantic is promising attractive sound bites but no solutions to our common challenges. Democracy risks dying in darkness as politicians brazenly feed the voters "alternative facts." The United States and the United Kingdom, two of the world's oldest parliamentary democracies, are in serious crisis. Like the third generation in Thomas Mann's novel *Buddenbrooks*, the US and the EU are at risk of forgetting the virtues of their ancestors and gambling away their precious inheritance. If we do that, autocratic regimes around the world, including China and Russia, will increasingly shape the values and set the rules for the future. As Benjamin Franklin was reported to have said at the signing of the Declaration of Independence: "We must, indeed, all hang together or, more assuredly, we shall all hang separately."

---

[22] Lionel Barber, Henry Foy, and Alex Barker, "Vladimir Putin Says Liberalism Has Become 'Obsolete,'" *Financial Times*, June 28, 2019. https://www.ft.com/content/670039ec-98f3-11e9-9573-ee5cbb98ed36.

In this age of social media and politics as entertainment, it seems fitting to end with some tweetable summaries of this book's arguments: The postwar multilateral system deserves protection; as 60 years of bipartisan US foreign policy have shown, the US and the EU are essential partners; if they want to go far, not just fast, they must go together; they have an opportunity to continue setting global rules for trade, privacy, the digital economy, protection of the environment, and so much else; our destinies are intertwined. A song by Joni Mitchell puts it succinctly: "Don't it always seem to go / That you don't know what you've got till it's gone?"[23]

[23] Big Yellow Taxi. Lyrics @Sony/ATV Music Publishing LLC, Crazy Crow Music/Siquomb Music Publishing.

Stars with Stripes